Chasing the Lizard's Tail

Jens Finke

i

impact books

First published in Great Britain in 1996 by
Impact Books, Axe and Bottle Court,
70 Newcomen Street, London SE1 1YT

ISBN 1 874687 36 6

Made and printed in Great Britain by
The Guernsey Press Co. Ltd., Guernsey, Channel Islands.

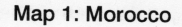

Map 1: Morocco

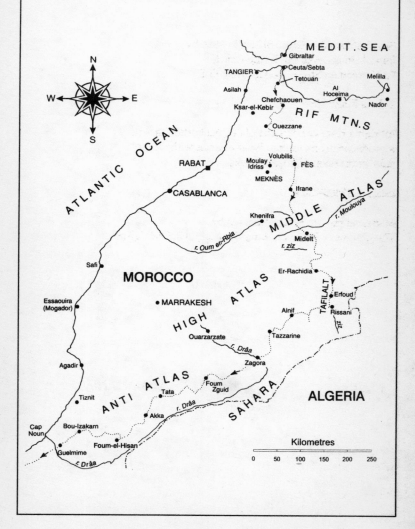

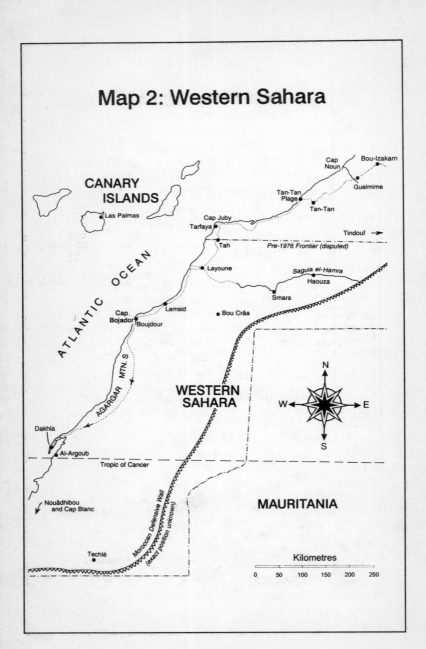

Map 2: Western Sahara

CANARY ISLANDS

Las Palmas

ATLANTIC OCEAN

Cap Noun

Bou-Izakarn

Tan-Tan Plage

Guelmime

Tan-Tan

Cap Juby

Tarfaya

Tah

Tindouf →

Pre-1976 Frontier (disputed)

Layoune

Saguia el-Hamra

Haouza

Smara

Lemsid

Cap Bojador

Boujdour

Bou Crâa

AGARGAR MTN. S

WESTERN SAHARA

N

W   E

S

Dakhla

Al-Argoub

Tropic of Cancer

Nouâdhibou and Cap Blanc

Morocan Defensive Wall (exact position unknown)

MAURITANIA

Techlé

Kilometres

0   50   100   150   200   250

Map 3: Mauritania

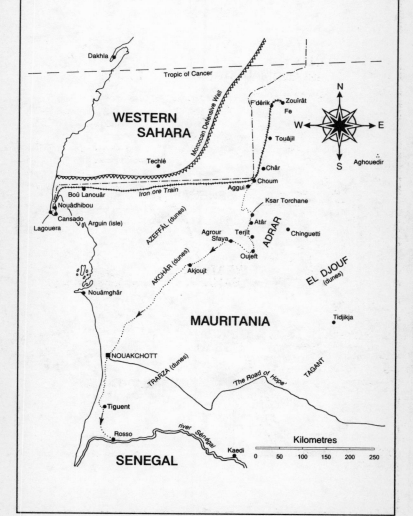

Map 4: Senegal and Gambia

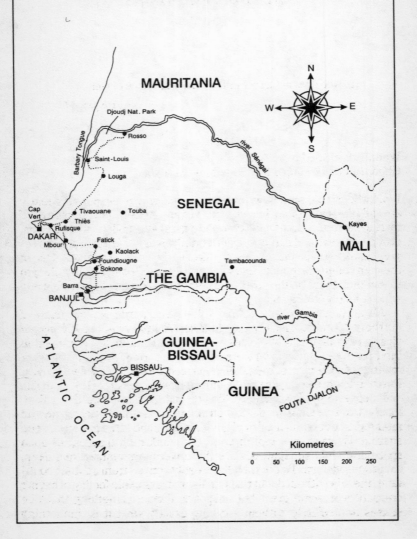

CHAPTER ONE

THE RIF MOUNTAINS

He who does not travel will not know the value of men.

Moorish proverb[1]

Wednesday, 30 March 1988.
Chefchaouen, Western Rif Mountains, Morocco.

Four wheezy old men in wrinkled grey and brown jellabas sit silently around the cafe table beside me, sipping coffee and smoking kif marijuana from carved cherry-wood pipes. Big hollow saucer eyes, drooping brown and narcotic, glance briefly over at me as wisps of olive-grey smoke escape into golden shafts of early morning sunlight. One of the men coughs raspingly, sneezes, and then lets loose a glob of phlegm to join the others on the cobbles. Another clasps a hand to his chin and winces loudly, rolling his eyes in pain.

All around Chefchaouen, and rolling eastwards across much of northern Morocco, rise the craggy limestone peaks of the Rif, jagged shards of orange and black that pierce a bright blue sky. Wrapped in their lee, like a thick shawl worn against the springtime chill, are thick mantles of sweetly scented sanobar firs, cedar forests, and olive groves. Further down, the slopes bristle with small terraces of barley, cannabis and peppermint. Everywhere, donkey paths crisscross the hills – lonely trails leading to distant farmhouses perched way up in the mountains, over which pairs of golden eagles and kites are often seen soaring. Everywhere, too, there is the comforting freedom of open space and vivid sunlight, despite the towering mountains and deep, cavernous valleys. To the traveller freshly arrived from another continent, there is without doubt that familiar but intangible feeling of having crossed over some great but unspoken divide, something that one senses immediately without knowing exactly what it is. Something

1

romantic perhaps, the romance of the new and the unknown. Or else the comforting impression of somehow returning to a land dreamt of long ago... Whatever, for the first few days it sufficed simply to inhale the sweet new air for me to feel almost childishly happy, full of a facile joy and even the hackneyed but wonderous bewilderment of innocence.

The Rif is a rugged land, unspoilt, a land of dreamy interlocking valleys, gorse-filled gullies, and rippling streams delineated by pink ribbons of blossoming oleander, or else whispering reed veils. Wherever one looks, the land is flecked with the vibrant yellow of madder bloom and marigolds. There are fig trees, prickly pear cacti and darker looming shadows. In the ravines the mountains have tumbled in perilous cascades of ochre and clay, almost bloody in parts. It is a land reminscent of the Taurus mountains, or of southern Spain, only seventy miles away across the Straits of Gibraltar.

To most first-time travellers from Christian lands, like myself, the first comparison to be drawn is invariably one with Biblical times. The Berbers, who form the majority in the Rif, still travel on foot or by mule or donkey trap, at a gently lolloping pace of life that only adds to this initial impression. Picturesque limewashed hamlets of maybe half a dozen squat houses lie half-hidden behind secretive woods of aspen and fir, and in places, low forested hills caress surreal lakes painted an opaque turquoise blue, beside which a handful of copper-coloured shepherd's tents might be pitched. In the stone-walled fields and orchards, small bands of farm labourers – male and female together – can be seen tilling and sowing, clearing the land with scythes. Elsewhere, peasants too poor to afford cattle drag their ploughs through the unyielding soil.

The Berbers are an intensely proud people, distinct both culturally and racially from the city-dwelling Arabs. In the main, they are a short but hardy race, with richly bronzed faces, many deeply lined seemingly through years of laughter. Their features are a strange and unique blend of European and Arab, and with their shining wide-open eyes and high cheekbones, there is at times even a hint of the Oriental. Their origins, however, are very much obscure, and continue to elude the classifying grasps of even the most learned anthropologists. What *is* certain is that the Berbers are Africa's only white-skinned *indigènes*, an enigma in a continent full of riddles. The women, especially, have handsome, almost chiselled features which, if not elegant, are most certainly dignified. Most of them still wear the traditional and highly coloured garb, consisting of towel-like *foutas*, aprons, shawls and headcloths, topped with wide-brimmed Mexican-style sombreros adorned with ribbons and pompoms. Their delight in colour extends even to their socks. Currently favoured is bright green or scarlet, often one of each worn on the same pair of feet. The men, in contrast, dress mainly in earthy shades, mostly grey and brown. Their jellabas – thickly woven ankle-length cloaks – differ from their cousins the Turkish kaftan and Egyptian *galabeya*, in that they sport unusually long and pointed hoods, sometimes a full two feet in length, that are often used as impromptu shopping bags! In cold weather, when the hood is worn folded right-up over the eyes, tapering to a point at the top, their wearers resemble the Dark Age sorcerers and wizards of European legend.

The atmosphere is one of change, from the cold isolation of the harsh mountain winter to the warmth and bustle of an African summer. The spring breeze is crisp and fresh as it whispers gently through the leafy branches of the tree-lined square.

Opposite the Cafe Djibli at which I am sat is the old orange kasbah, an imposing sandstone citadel that was built by Portuguese captives following their army's annihilation in 1578. The unfortunate prisoners were also obliged to construct the dungeons in which they were then incarcerated until their deaths. The story still brings smirks to many a face. Propped up at the kasbah's wooden gate, an old man sleeps bolt upright. He seems unconcerned by the clatter of chairs and tables being dragged outside from the cafes. A narrow cobbled alleyway winds between the kasbah and the Grand Mosque, a beautiful building limewashed all over save for its peculiar octagonal minaret, decorated in blood-red brick and stuccoed orange plaster. The rest of the Place Uta el-Hammam consists of several more cafes, dingy eat-houses, a handful of stores, and the police station, outside which a couple of fat officers sit for most of the day, cigarettes or fat oily joints hanging limply from their fat oily lips.

The first pigeons and turtledoves have arrived, and swoop restlessly between the kasbah ramparts and the silken boughs of a mulberry tree. The first small-time merchants and traders arrive, some pushing home-made barrows and carts, others barely able to walk under the burden of their wares. A trio of peddlars unveil great strings of household implements shipped in from China, everything that the modern Moroccan housewife might wish for. Others simply upturn plastic buckets, upon which they then place their hopes. In time, both the square's fountain and the entire length of the kasbah's eastern battlements become cluttered with a myriad items for sale. There are cracked wooden doors leaning against stained mattresses, these in turn

3

draped with brightly coloured feminine kaftans. Odd shoes lie scattered beside an rusty Spanish typewriter, and a couple of sparrows sit squabbling on absolutely the most repulsive sofa I have ever seen – purple-brown nylon decorated with a liberal sprinkling of yellow, shocking pink and fluorescent green flowers.

A few other traders – tough old Berber ladies from the mountains – sell sprigs of fresh mint, onions and garlic. Some carry their grandchildren in the style of American Indian papoose, swaddled and strapped onto the women's chests or backs. Almost all the Berber ladies are small, but quick and expressive in their movements, deceptively strong, wiry, and often arrive in town bent at right-angles under the weight of their bales. Their palms and soles are decorated like tattoos with the amber-brown dye of henna, a herb much prized among Berbers for its property of toughening the skin and so preventing blisters, sores or stings. On Mondays and Thursdays – souk days – entire families descend from all over the Rif to sell cheese, butter, fruit, vegetables, straw, herbs and other natural produce, and return wearily home in the evening with their sturdy mules laden with gas cannisters, oil-filled jerry cans and dead weight sacks of flour.

Behind the cafe is the *medina* [literally 'old city', from the Prophet Muhammad's Arabian refuge]. Rising over six hundred feet within half a mile, the *medina* is Chefchaouen's oldest quarter, and is situated on the uppermost reaches of the Djibála range of the Rif mountains, beyond which the slopes become too acute and prone to landslides to be habitable.

The town was founded in the year 1471 by Moulay Ali ben Rachid, a descendant of the illustrious Moulay Idriss, 8th century founder and father of Muslim Morocco. As an outpost from which to repel the Portuguese, and later Spanish, incursions, ben Rachid could not have chosen better. To the east, the town is protected by the impenetrable mountains, whilst to the west, the site commands a broad sweep over the valley of the river Laou, which meant that potential assailants would have been obliged to climb for over two miles in full view of the tenacious defenders. The twin crescentic peaks that both defend and tower over the town have lent their name to Chefchaouen. In Djibála dialect, it means the View of the Horns.

Almost completely encircled by its 16th century battlements, Chefchaouen really does give the impression that time has stood still. Secluded, and for centuries inaccessible even to the sultans of Fès (200km to the south), it is as though the town has felt no need at all to progress into the 20th century. It is as though its walls have guarded for so many years not only against the aggressions of men and their armies, but against Time itself. Everywhere, one is reminded of the past. Backing on to the Cafe Djibli is an old *fondouq* courtyard – a large caravanserai where the rich spice and slave caravans of old found accomodation, and where blacksmiths and the town's last Jewish saddlesmith practised their trade, the latter eventually to emigrate after the Six-Day War. Although the camels have long since gone, there are still mules and asses aplenty, slipping and sliding on the steep burnished cobbles of the *medina*.

The atmosphere of the place, needless to say, is overwhelmingly medieval. Its labyrinthine maze of narrow cobbled streets, blind alleyways and hidden squares remain as vibrant and animated as, I imagine, they always have been. Crooked steps wind steeply between two and three storey dwellings, rising and falling, twisting and turning as in strange, unsettling dreams. Heavy, bolt-studded doors seem to spin secretive whispers for, as is common throughout Morocco, houses tend to look inwards onto private tiled courtyards and gardens, rather than out onto the streets where children scramble and play in stagnant trickles of water and sewage. In places, it is well advised to walk only in the centre of these streets, to minimise the risk of airborne garbage, bathwater, and much worse besides, as I once found out to the cost of a shirt!

Whilst the atmosphere is medieval, the architecture is Andalusian, a legacy of seventeen Muslim and Jewish families who arrived here in the 16th century having fled the systematic persecution of the Catholic Reconquista. On almost every street corner, invariably festooned with ivy or grape vines, ceramic-tiled fountains gush forth the cold waters of the mountain springs. Above, beyond the limewash of the walls, there are brown tiled eaves and ornamental archways, iron-grilled balconies, carefully carved wooden blinds and astonishingly intricate trelliswork. Simple but imposing lintels and gables of red terra cotta crown small dark doorways secured with wrought-iron latches and handles, doorways so low that even I had to stoop to enter. Bronze door knockers form lions or the downward pointing Hand of Fatima. The latter, named after the daughter of the Prophet, is a charm that is found throughout North Africa and the Middle East. It is a symbol that is commonly believed, like henna, to ward off Evil Eye, a curse that has been around since the Carthaginians, and perhaps earlier still.

From afar, the town looks like a great wasps' nest, its dwellings constructed one on top of the other to form an amorphous mass of mortar, wood and paint. Chefchaouen is an admittedly beautiful blot on an otherwise unblemished landscape, and comparisons with other

5

towns spring readily to mind. So very much like images of the steep cobbled inclines of Quito, or one of the *pueblos blancos* of the Sierra de Cadiz, or the abandoned Basilicatan cave-town of old Matera in which Pasolini filmed *The Gospel according to St Matthew*. The resemblance to the latter is all the keener at night, when the sickly-sweet aroma of mint tea finally drifts away, and the rising facades light up like fireflies in eerie glows of yellow and green. It is at night, too, that the town takes on all the disquieting charm of Baghdad's *Arabian Nights*, for it is then that one is plunged into a twilit world of clawing shadows and mysterious, shrouded figures that scurry noiselessly past to unknown destinations. At night, it is all too easy to imagine the town swarming with gangs of Moorish cut-throats and blood-thirsty brigands, and it is hard to walk about without feeling one's heart pounding squarely in one's mouth. And it was not just me who felt both excited and scared – many Chefchaouenis themselves go to astonishing lengths to avoid having to venture out alone after sunset. Night-time is the preserve of ghosts and ghouls alone.

But in daylight, the *medina* is without doubt one of North Africa's prettiest. Certainly, its inhabitants think so, for they have painted their town in the celestial colours of white and sky-blue, with the result that even under the dreariest of skies, the *medina* retains a light-hearted gaiety, a place where it is almost impossible to feel under the weather. In some quarters, even the pavement has been whitewashed, and it was only with a certain deference that I dared tread along them, lest I defile their virginal beauty with ugly scuff marks.

In the early mornings, before the sun has had time to heave itself above the encircling mountains, traders set up makeshift stalls to sell fresh goats' milk, roundels of tangy goat cheese, and necklaces of sticky ring doughnuts that resemble bagels – a reminder of Morocco's once numerous Jewry. Then, when the first of the sun's rays begins to sweep through the sleepy streets, tiny box-like shops hidden down darker alleyways open to business, selling freshly ground coffee, bouquets of jasmine, and great pyramids of round, unleavened bread that are displayed alongside fat French-style baguettes. Later, on flat terraced rooves festooned with washing and Berber rugs out for an airing, women can be seen scrubbing clothes, or chattering and laughing as they shell peas and peel vegetables in preparation for lunchtime's *tajines* and couscous.

Skinny flea-bitten cats, scabrous and dirty, limp across the square from the kasbah, only to be chased away by impish gangs of stone-toting children. Later, an equally scabrous beggar is chased away by the waiter, who then for a moment grins at me as though to elicit some kind of approval. The day's first hustlers have appeared, ready to pounce on busloads of day-tripping Spaniards from Tangier. Preying upon the least confident-seeming members of the group, the *faux-guide* offers through double talk, breathtakingly audacious guile, and finely-honed doublethink, various introductions to touristic bazaars, invariably the ones that pay a hefty commission on sales to the gullible. In Chaouen, clouds of tennis-shoed, short-clad, knuckle-kneed tourists pile out of air-conditioned coaches every day, 'doing' Morocco via 4-star hotels and the automatic camera. But because they bring money, it is too easy to forget the irony that many parts of Morocco – especially the imperial cities of Fès, Meknès and Marrakesh – are rapidly losing that very same 'authentic' feel that the tourists adore so much.

In the Place el-Makhzen, around the corner from the cafe and near the chain-run Parador hotel, is a small but predictable collection of bazaars. They are predictable in that they will feed the unwary visitor (including myself, on one occasion) all sorts of lies and tall stories to get them to buy something they don't really want and in any case can buy much more cheaply elsewhere. If one were only to take the time to find the right places, the quality doubles and the prices halve again. The specialities include hand-crafted silver teapots and trays, a bewildering array of unfired clay pottery, terra-cotta braziers, *sibsi* pipes for smoking kif, and, of course, leatherware. It is said that when the Spanish colonists first set foot in the town in 1920, they were as astounded to hear ringing but anxious praise for the 15th century Queen Isabella of the Catholics, as they were to see Berber craftsmen still tanning leather in the manner of 12th century Córdoba, an art that had long been lost to the Iberian peninsula.

The other craft for which the Berbers are justifiably renowned is weaving. Woollen rugs and carpets are still painstakingly woven to age-old patterns on rickety wooden contraptions; abstracts that are uncannily similar to ancient Aztec designs. Indeed, there are many (as yet unexplained) similarities between the Berbers of Northwest Africa and the Indians of Mexico and South America. Not only the designs of their textiles, but their traditional dress (the wide-brimmed hats, especially, are identical in every respect to those worn by the Huichol peyote-Indians of Mexico's Zacatecas plateau), the drug culture, the at times shamanic mysticism (of which more later), and even physical similarities, point to a link that rises above mere coincidence (or Spanish influence). Both peoples, of course, have the Atlantic in common. Is it possible that the ancestors of the Aztecs are the very same as that of the Berbers, and that years before Columbus, some of them had ventured across the ocean to reach the New World?

To return to the bazaars of Chefchaouen: the rapid growth in tourism is having the unfortunate side-effect of reducing quality and corrupting designs to make them more pleasing to the Western eye. Another recent loss was the departure of Chefchaouen's last Jewish family, which deprived the town of its traditionally high-standard silver jewellery (Arab Jews were famed for their decorative damascene inlaying, perhaps because Muslims feared Evil Eye lest they dared mix metals). Another loss is the wonderfully chaotic souk enclosure, which has been earmarked to give way to a coach park. Still, I suppose one has to admit that tourism has given the town a new lease of life, for better or worse, and not least for its children. On countless occasions I received shouted demands for dirhams and pens, and much more besides. I once saw a French couple surrounded by a group of screaming children, one of whom brandished a tiny terrapin, its carapace cracked, under the man's nose. 'Five dirham, or I kill it!' taunted the little monster, and so the man paid up. A few minutes later, the children returned, only this time with a frightened chick, and again the foreigners succumbed to the demands of the aspiring extortionists!

As morning gathers momentum, so the square becomes busier. There is a constant stream of people, rushing, dawdling, bored, animated, anxious, tired... It is a pleasure for me, having spent an exhausting month cycling here from England, to do nothing more strenuous than sip coffee and watch the world roll on without me. A man walks about peddling wire bird cages. Another winds his way around the cafe tables selling sweet pastries from a tray – honey and fig rolls, coconut buns scented with almonds, and vanilla or cumin shortbreads. A youth rushes by on a motorbike, another on a squeaky bicycle without a saddle. All the time, children too young or lazy to go to school, dash about madly, shouting and screaming. Play fights are common, although many end in tears and howls of retribution, or else a volley of stones. At one point, the old men beside me grew tired of all the fracas, and themselves resorted to throwing gravel at the children.

A tipper-lorry arrives from the valley to deposit its load of firewood beside the cafe, and soon, members of the local porters guild lumber up to carry the wood into the *medina's* 400-year-old Moorish baths, the *hammam*. It is a task that can take all of two days. Unfortunately, at the time of my visit infidels were forbidden to enter the *hammam* since, like the mosques, it is a place of purification which must not be despoiled by dirt of the impure.

Presently, a grubby kid brandishing a stick screams past the cafe in hot pursuit of a hoop, as an old Arab woman, her dark eyes flashing, hobbles the other way. She is veiled entirely from head to toe in a white silken haik. Elsewhere, a gaggle of Berber grandmothers, perhaps great-grandmothers, lean over each other's shoulders, whispering secrets and giggling like little girls. A wheelbarrow rushes past, the young boy inside it squealing and screaming as his brother careers out of control towards a knot of policemen. The kids are hounded away, and the scabrous beggar reappears, this time hopping and skipping in barefoot circles around the square.

A group of elderly shopkeepers, usually either greatly respected or envied, huddle in the shade of a nearby olive tree. Beside them stand two men wearing burgundy-red fezzes [*tarboushes*], the brimless felten hats said to have originated in the erstwhile capital of Morocco. The hats became all the rage a few decades ago, as a symbol of nationalist pride both during and after the Franco-Spanish protectorate, but they are now an increasingly rare sight in a country where woolly hats and Western clothes have found greater favour. Among the young, especially, it is 'cool' to be seen to be Western. Schoolchildren with outsize notebooks and folders saunter by in a colourful display of brand names: Levi's, Reebok, Blue Mag, Patrol, Zico... One guy, with assiduously trimmed designer stubble and brilliantined hair, struts about aimlessly in cowboy boots and Spanish jeans, expecting, I suppose, the young Spanish *señoritas* to fall for his rather dubious charms.

The European influence sometimes makes for comical sights. I once saw an elderly and rather portly Berber woman stride purposefully past the cafe, her breasts heaving like an ocean swell. She wore a baby boy tied to her back, and a T-shirt with fluorescent green and orange lettering that blared: 'Big Rock Candy Mountain'!

* * *

The tempting smell of *harira* and *baisa* drifts across from the restaurant next door. *Harira* is a cheap and simple soup made from chick peas, noodles, tomatoes and almost anything else at hand. Countless variations of it are to be found throughout Morocco, and there is much disagreement over which recipe is best. *Baisa*, on the other hand, is generally considered to be a speciality of Chefchaouen, and is popular among Berbers as the day's first repast. It is a thick, pea-green soup made from dried *foul* [fava, or lima beans], garlic and pepper, garnished with olive oil and sun-dried red chillis, and served with a generous hunk of bread. I order one to go with my coffee, very sweet and milky. As elsewhere in the world, coffee is drunk only in the morning. Thereafter,

9

it is interminable glasses of the ubiquitous mint tea, served in tumblers full of fresh spearmint and seasonal orange blossom. Later, towards midday, comes the lingering aroma of woodsmoke and of the day's first *tajines*: a thousand different ways of combining vegetables with meat or fish in an earthernware pot of the same name. A particularly exquisite local variant contains red mullet, onions, garlic, butter, lashings of olive oil, *foul*, raisins, saffron and lavender, roasted for an hour in a baker's pinewood oven.

By mid morning, both the pulse and the heat have increased considerably, and so I move inside. The interior of the Cafe Djibli [the 'Mountain Man'] is a charmingly decrepit kind of place, seemingly always only one step away from anarchy. Yet, somehow, it manages to exude a remarkable atmosphere of calm and cordiality, despite the sometimes evil stench from the toilet. At the top of a steep flight of stairs I found myself in the passageway between the bar on the right and the saloon on the left. Its rickety chairs and tables were bent and shattered from past debâcles, and had a painful tendancy to collapse when used. From the ceiling hung spinning columns of flies, to which no one except myself ever paid the slightest attention. The straw-coloured paint was flaking off the walls, in parts revealing cooler shades of turquoise and blue, and at the far end of the room, under the obligatory (if crooked) portrait of King Hassan II (mid-1970s version in military uniform, severe sideburns and square-rimmed shades) was the television. It was covered, like a parrot cage, with an orange tea-towel – the football was not until tomorrow. The bar itself was cluttered with empty glasses and trays. There were three bottles of fruit syrup, two large tins of Nescafe, and one of Lipton Yellow Label tea, as well as the usual bottles of fizz. No alcohol, of course: 'an abomination of Satan's handiwork', although this did not seem to bother the large number of Berbers I met who were more or less constantly pissed on cheap wine and duty-free whisky cadged from tourists. Perhaps this seemingly irreligious behaviour owes something to the Qur'an's delightful descriptions of the gardens of Paradise, where the thirst of Allah's true servants 'shall be slaked with Pure Wine sealed [with] musk' that will neither dull the senses nor befuddle them. It seems as though many of Chefchaouen's inhabitants simply cannot wait patiently enough for death and the promised Elysium!

The mottled orange-tiled balcony betrays better than anything else the not-so-secret vices of the cafe and its regulars: rotting tarot cards, shattered bottles of vodka and whisky, dozens of crumpled cigarette cartons, and torn pieces of blue and yellow cellophane in which kif and hashish is kept.

About two dozen men were sat around, variously engrossed in games of dominoes, cards, and a complicated version of pachisi. Above their heads, and mingled with the flies, hung a blue cloud of kif smoke. The cafe is popular, and by midday, every day, it was packed to the rafters. Constant animation – voices overlapping like syrup, laughing, shouting, gesticulating. 'Hey!' exclaimed the young cook from the eat-house downstairs. 'De hiss hiss de happee hippee house, yess?'

I greeted my new acquaintances – Abdsalam, Saïd, Abdul Latiff and Mohamed – and joined them in a game of cards. The cheating was incredible, and we enjoyed ourselves like children ('Please, it is not cheating,' explained Abdsalam, 'but a show of great skill!') Abdsalam was 38. He was a disarmingly polite and gentlemanly hashish dealer with six teeth and a penchant for Aristotle and Shakespeare. He wanted his remaining teeth pulled out because presently he was unable to eat his beloved sweets for all the pain they caused. Abdsalam was tall, lanky, and wore a red and black woollen cap over his rapidly disappearing hair, which he shaved off every six months regardless. Once married to an Englishwoman named Diana, or so he said, he had spent the best part of the 1970s working as a translator for the Moroccan embassy in Somalia, and in consequence had acquired the grandiose nickname of The Professor. He now divided his time between Chefchaouen and a small Mediterranean fishing village at the mouth of the river Laou, dabbling in big-time hash smuggling and the small-time importation of blue movies.

Over often intense games of dominoes, Abdsalam liked to regale us with improbable stories. He was also an incurable snob. Said he with astonishment of a group of German tourists the year before last: 'And they did not even have the money for fifty kilos!' He quickly added, in case I doubted: 'It was *good* quality too, ah yes, you know me Jens.'

I never quite managed to understand Abdsalam, for, in spite of a rigid streak of rationality, he was also, like many Berbers, a bit of dreamer. This year, as every other, he was hoping for the Big One, about half a ton or thereabouts, so that he could rebuild his family's mountain cottage and retire in style. At heart, I think, Abdsalam was soft and quite unabashedly romantic. He enjoyed long, rambling walks in the flower-strewn countryside; he talked fondly of love's mysterious wiles in the manner that a twelve year old might; and he had much fun poked at him because he fed the wiry stray cats that dwelt in the kasbah, something for which, Abdsalam knew very well, Sufi saints were renowned.

Saïd was the oldest of the group, a small Djibli in his mid-forties, although his burnished, leathery face added at least another twenty years to his appearance. Saïd was the undisputed joker of the pack, a

11

born clown, and never did I see him with anything other than a cheerful grin stretched wide across his face. With his jug-ears, lop-sided nose, bristly tufts of hair and gold-capped teeth, he made everyone smile regardless of what he did. He lived up in the mountains with his second wife and their three children, and was employed in the manufacture of septic tanks on behalf of the government. Saïd was simple in the best way – uncomplicated, unfailingly friendly, and unswervingly pious. For instance, when not working he dressed in jeans and trainers, but still attended the prescribed five daily prayers at the Grand Mosque. For me, Saïd's most endearing feature was his laugh, the most infectious I had ever heard, and one that burst out at even the very slightest provocation. Starting with a tremulous and braying *eeee-eeeee*, within seconds he was off on an unstoppable sequence of high-pitched wheezes and drawn-out neighs that only ended a good few minutes later with Saïd quite literally rolling around on the floor in fits and convulsions, his face sodden with tears.

Abdul Latiff was the chief offender as regarded starting Saïd on his roller-coaster rides. He was a heavily bearded Flemish-looking man, broad-faced and quite possibly of Hispanic origin, who with his spectacles could easily have fitted the parts of either a scholarly headmaster or a wind-hardened North Sea trawlerman. In fact, he ran a French-style restaurant near the Parador hotel, and prided himself on shark trophies that he caught himself and then sold to tourists. He was fluent in seven languages, all self-taught. The other three – Mandarin Chinese, Slovak and Czech – were, he admitted with disarming modesty, a little rusty. Like the others, he was a lifelong and incessant smoker of kif.

The youngest of the four – a Djibli in his early twenties, and in a sense the protégé of the group – called himself 'Mohamed Cinque' after the widely revered 'father' of modern-day Morocco (and one-time enemy of the Riffian Berbers), the 23rd Alaouite Sultan, King Muhammad V. Mohamed Cinque had brown eyes that were soft and sleepless, and like Saïd, wore a lugubrious grin that seemed never to leave his face. His hair was a tangle that sprayed out wildly from his scalp, as though each and every strand were trying to find a direction unique to itself. Mohamed's habit was to walk, sometimes for days on end, in aimless agitation across and around the peaks and rivers and gullies of this rebellious land. It is perhaps no irony that, given the persecution which the Sultan inflicted on the Berbers, Mohamed Cinque was mad. He talked incessantly both to furniture and himself, in a mixture of French and Djibála dialect, and even had official documents to certify his insanity. These were in effect a governmental waiver anticipating any petty crimes he might commit in his madness, were he that way inclined (which he wasn't. He was merely mildly schizophrenic). I admired Mohamed in the way that any other 19-year-old admires a gentle, smiling lunatic.

During a lull in the game – the conversation momentarily paused – Abdsalam let loose a sudden volley of violent and exaggerated gestures, amounting to a convoluted insult along the lines of Saïd's family having once bred monkeys for a living. The punchline was: 'And now look at him since they planted kif!' Everyone roared with laughter. Humour is notoriously difficult to translate, but for what it's worth, I shall try anyway. The implication of the jibe was two-fold. Firstly, the fact that many Djibála did indeed once breed monkeys for a living has given rise to interminable insinuations about buggery, ape-like wives, baboons of ancestors, and the like. The second implication, from the Holy Qur'an, plays on the first: 'Be ye apes,' it says of infidels, 'Despised and rejected.' The joke was old, but no matter – the Djibála, whose Arabic is cursed with a strong accent, have always been the butt of the townspeople's jokes, who consider mountain Berbers both ingenuous and stupid, rather like the English consider the proverbial Irishman.

Although the humour is barbed, and certainly childish, there is ample room for revenge. After some thought, Saïd retaliated by accusing the townspeople and Abdsalam himself of not even being able to differentiate hashish from henna (a common enough ruse for the hippies), nor, for that matter, between runner beans and pea pods. Again, there was laughter, before Abdsalam interjected by recalling that the gates of Chefchaouen were until recently closed at sunset in order to keep the Berber 'apes' out of town. But the hilarity was again cut short when Saïd pointed out that Abdsalam himself was half Djibli, and so the tables were turned. The ribaldry, no matter how offensive, was nearly always taken in good humour, because sooner or later everybody got humiliated and so the scores remained *kif-kif*, level.

Saïd eventually left us for the third prayer of the day, *al-Asr*. It was four o'clock, and a few minutes later, el-Haloof arrived, a bulky Teuton attired in an off-white jellaba and yellow leather slippers. Wolfgang Schwein first arrived in Morocco three and a half years ago, then learnt to speak Arabic and was given the nickname *halouf*, the wild pig [*schwein* being German for swine]. He moved to Chaouen last autumn after having been kicked out of the small mountain village that he'd adopted. Some problem with the local drugs mafia, or so everyone else said. He made his living by ripping-off, and occasionally threatening, German tourists in need of the odd kilo of dope. Because of his name, he suffered much the same kind of taunts as the Djibála, for in Islam, as in Judaism, swine along with apes are considered unclean: 'Those who incurred the curse of God and His wrath... He transformed into apes and swine'. Yet el-Haloof himself was indisputably bigoted, and oddly enough, not only against Jews but Arabs as well (and as he was rather large of frame, few cared to argue). Myself he disliked intensely on account of my Semitic nose. His racism, I guess, was his idea of fitting-in with his own cartoon-stereotype of Arab behaviour. It reflects well on the open-mindedness of the Riffian Berbers that el-Haloof was the only man in this region I was ever to hear publicly mouthing-off anti-Semitic sentiments.

Every so often, a young *garro* would make the rounds of the cafe with a box of duty-free Marlboro or Winston cigarettes, selling them as singles together with rolling papers at a dirham each to make joints. The extent to which the use of marijuana (hemp) is an accepted feature of Riffian life was, to me at least, astounding. Until, that is, I learned that, by one theory, the Rif has lent its name to one of America's more popular terms for a joint, a reefer. Like alcohol in the West, the uses of marijuana are many and varied, and in my experience I guess that over half Chefchaouen's inhabitants use dope regularly, women included. Cannabis is a drug that cuts right across the social spectrum: cultivators, labourers and students, soldiers, policemen and even town governors. The only distinction is that of age. Older people tend to smoke kif [Arabic *kayf*, meaning pleasure, hence the expression *kif-kif* pleasures balanced]. Kif is finely chopped sun-dried marijuana mixed with a little black tobacco, which has a pleasantly sweet taste and an effect aptly described by its name. The younger generations, on the other hand, prefer hashish, the stronger resin of cannabis [and hence the Arabic term *hacheichi* dope-fiend, which gives us the word 'assassin'].

Although the possession of dope is theoretically illegal, in practice it is a very different matter. Along with caffeine, marijuana is one of the few stimulants not expressly forbidden by the Qur'an. Coffee, it is argued, is anti-soporific and therefore helpful to nocturnal devotions, while the mind-expanding effects of cannabis are ideal for the mystical brand of Islamic Sufism preferred by the Berbers (especially when given the interdiction on alcohol). The Riffians themselves claim the right to cultivate and use cannabis from the 14th century Black Sultan and *hacheichi*, Abu'l-Hasan, and until recently, a Spanish fiat of 1921 authorising the cultivation of *Cannabis sativa* could be seen on a roadside plaque near Ketama – a town one hundred kilometres east of Chaouen and notorious for its mafiosi.

Unfortunately, the well-documented state of paranoia that cannabis intoxication induces in some people remains nonetheless, lurking just beneath the superficies of carefree hedonism. An example: one evening, whilst playing dominoes with Abdsalam, a gendarme strode briskly into the cafe, evidently from his haste and po-faced expression still on duty. Abdsalam, who for some reason found himself in the possession of half a kilo of prime resin, became nervously distracted and turned a noticably pale shade of grey. I looked around, to see that a lot of other people too had whitened somewhat, and several smouldering joints were held trembling under the tables. After a few anxious moments, there was a short scuffle, and then a few shouts, before the suspected thief was bundled out into the night. The relief that followed was almost tangible, as a dozen *sibsis* were hurriedly filled to calm the nerves.

* * *

I was staying at the Pension Kasbah, a short stone's throw from the cafe, and what travel guides might refer to as 'cheap and cheerful'. Beside the *de rigueur* population of fleas and cockroaches, its guests were, with very few exceptions, Berber farmers or Arab merchants from afar, which made for much more entertaining encounters than those in the more usual establishments. As the only European resident at the Kasbah, I was subjected to the greatest curiosity, which on two occasions spawned no-nonsense requests to see whether my penis really had been left as nature intended...

In the 1930s, the hotel was used both as an illegal gambling joint and as an artists' hang-out, a place where singers, poets, musicians and other degenerates could meet to drink, smoke, and of course dance, alongside two resident whores who doubled as belly dancers. Chefchaouen has long been known for its hedonism. At wedding celebrations in the town's heyday in the 16th and 17th centuries, not only topless belly dancers but equally lascivious male *zefen* dancers would entertain the guests to the joyful strains of Andalusian string orchestras, in addition to a copious supply of wine (not that much has changed in this respect). In more recent times, the town has cultivated musicians in addition to kif, most notably Fatah, a slave's son whose music reflects the pounding rhythms of West Africa, and Rouicha Mohamed, whose traditional whirling trance music, much liked by teenage girls, I was to hear along the length and breadth of the kingdom.

Hakim, the rather effeminate concierge, was himself a singer (falsetto) and dreamed of learning flamenco in the famous old school of Córdoba. A slight figure, with pale waxy skin and wavy hennaed hair, he

15

appeared to be not a day over fifteen, despite sharing his age with Abdsalam. He sank an astonishing amount of whisky, or *matarata* as he preferred to call it, averaging one 75cl bottle every other day. In between, presumably to blot out any gaps of horrifying sobriety, he indulged a penchant for boiled opium poppy heads. *Papaver somniferum* brings nausea, oblivion, and perverse nightmares, and, astonishingly, is still used by mothers to sedate their too-mischievous children!

More astounding still was that Hakim *never* went out in public without wearing full make-up: Clinique foundation and cherryade lipstick given him by an English guest, authentic mascara from Algeria, kohl, blusher and nail varnish. And just in case one still doubted his sexuality, he would openly flaunt it by wearing bicoloured *baboush* slippers in yellow *and* red, since men traditionally wear the former, and women the latter. On one particularly hungover morning, Hakim confided that what he really wanted to do in Spain was to have a sex-change ('a critical operation' he said). When I asked why, he sighed and confessed: 'Because it hurts so much.'

I couldn't help feeling sorry for Hakim, and yet, although he was certainly not a braggart, when I pressed him he claimed to have bedded precisely 238 male lovers (a statement that followed his reeling back in horror when I suggested that women might not be so bad after all!) It was a claim which Hakim proudly substantiated by producing an immaculately-kept list, going back over twenty years, detailing names, dates, places, nationalities, and marks out of forty! Unsurprisingly, Hakim was rather well known in Chefchaouen, and was called Mimi by the not-so-kind, a taunt to which he responded with hideous displays of tittering, meowing and otherwise coquettish mincing. Sometimes, he would wake me up in the middle of the night with a gentle tap-tapping on my door and then, incredibly, a verse from some god-awful Arabic serenade complete with drunken nasal whines, gob-stopping inflexions and ear-piercing yowls. 'Yensh, you shtill awek?' he would slur solicitously through the keyhole…

Unfortunately for Hakim, even were I that way inclined, I doubt that I'd consider the prospect of becoming number 239 as that much of a compliment. William S. Burroughs would have had no such qualms in the crazy International Zone of pre-independence Tangier, the 'Interzone' where 'The days glide by strung on a syringe with a long thread of blood.' The self-appointed father of the Beatnik generation, Burroughs, too, was homosexual and hooked – 'a grey, junk-bound ghost'. To pay for his 'little chickens' as he called his Moroccan lovers, Burroughs had $200 wired to him every month from the States. In 1959, the year he completed *Naked Lunch*, a gay junkie spelt money, and so it seems that he was tolerated. Hakim, for his part, believed that his sexuality *had* to be tolerated because his late father had been town governor and Hakim, therefore, had access to all the official papers and documents relating to the more sordid secrets of Chefchaouen's otherwise respectful inhabitants.

The Pension Kasbah has two floors. The upper is a gloomy balcony opening onto a dozen cell-like rooms. Its tiles were strewn with blackened roaches and small pellets of ash from kif pipes, and rancid smoke lingered on the ceiling. I had room number eight, far enough from the toilet to avoid the worst of its stench. Measuring precisely 6½ by 6½ feet, there was only just enough room for the mouldy bed and the empty carcass of a three-legged imitation Louis XVI dressing table. The window – barely wider than my forearm – had fallen off its hinges and was kept under the bed for fleas and cockroaches to congregate under. The door, equipped with a doll's house padlock and two nail coathangers, had, like the walls, been painted a shade of turquoise so shocking that I could only bear to live in the room at night.

Yet, after a few days, I was surprised to find myself actually beginning to *like* the room, despite the cockroaches, mosquitos and innumerable bed-bugs. The room began to take on an odd kind of charm, a little, I suppose, like that which oozes from flab-wrinkled old faces smeared hopefully with cheap make-up and even cheaper perfume. As a lady, the Pension Kasbah would, in her time, have been the greatest slut around. The stern-faced gentleman who had reluctantly shown me to the hotel (I had asked for somewhere cheap) had clicked his tongue and shaken his head in disapproval, and had then warned me to always be on my guard.

At times, I found it easy to picture scenes from room number eight in times gone by. Let us imagine the gloomy flickering of a shaded oil lamp placed on a low square table, over which a couple of shadowy figures crouch, fingers bristling, furtive stickleback card sharps turning eager tricks in the lingering soupy-sweet smoke of exhausted pipes and fumes. There is silence, of course, but for the cards and die striking the wooden skirt of the green baize table, on which someone has placed a half-drunk bottle of rotgut wine... Or perhaps one should add another lamp, take away the table, and fill the room with sumptious velvet wallhangings, cushions, pillows and rugs. There are a dozen grimebesmeared bottles, some on their sides, that earlier contained *ashashin*, the evil black juice of which Hakim was so fond. There are perhaps six or seven people in all – including one of the belly dancers – all reclined, all in various inebriated states of undress and incoherent vapidity...

17

Another possibility was inadvertently suggested by Hakim, who re-counted that the hotel – so unassuming from the outside – had for a long time played host to the mysterious and ill-reputed *toq-toqa*, a dance intended exclusively for complaisant young boys. They were often waifs, orphans, or even slaves, whose primary function was first to tease and then to accept all offers (for a fee). The Djibála, indeed, have a particular and peculiarly open tradition of homosexuality, which was once so unashamedly public as to permit the holding of weekly auctions of boys in the Place Uta el-Hammam. This seditious event survived until 1937, when it was banned by the Spanish authorities. As to why the Spanish took twelve years to do so is anyone's guess. But the thought of the *toq-toqa*, and therefore of what my bed must once have been used for, quickly put an end to my train of imaginings.

Glancing briefly around the hotel, it was obvious to anyone that fate had caught up with the Pension Kasbah. Downstairs, the only reminder of days gone by were the few remaining panels of Turkish wall-hangings, threadbare, but beautiful all the same. Apart from these, there was a broken and dusty television, some odd pieces of furniture, and a couple of glazed pottery fish nailed to pillars. Time, too, had caught up with the proprietor, a Mr. Salah M'baz, who at somewhere between eighty and ninety years old suffered from blindness and an uncontrollable gangrene that disfigured much of his legs. Hakim informed me that he also had a brain tumor, and that he was slowly becoming senile as a result. To illustrate: one day, I was surprised to see Mr. M'baz at the post office in the town's Spanish-built quarter, sat against a wall with his hand twisted into a cup. As far as I knew, he had no need to beg at all.

Mr. M'baz slept downstairs on an old green sofa, and had taken to shouting out verses from the Qur'an in his slumber.

* * *

The moon was a fat grinning almond that shone brightly through the latticework screen of room number eight, starkly silhouetting its bronze spiral motifs against the sulphurous yellow of the bed.

I was woken just before four o'clock by a most incredible sound. A painful, almost mournful sound. A song full of heavy-hearted sorrows, yet full of deliciously unexpected turns of phrase.

The muezzin's lone call to prayer from the minaret of the Grand Mosque slices the silence with a force so controlled, so resonant, and yet with such growling insistence, that one cannot fail to be startled on hearing it. The first line of the call is followed by a fragile silence, still whispering the last echoes of the phrase. Then the silence is suspended once more, this time by the muezzin of another mosque, following on the lead of the first, repeating the phrase in a higher, more distant voice, adding a surreal depth and sense of the timeless to the atmosphere. But before he has had time to complete the sentence, the first muezzin begins his second phrase, and the voices harmonise briefly, wrapped and intermingled, before separating to continue once more along their solo paths. Thus the song progresses: first a phrase, then momentary silence, then an answer, harmony, and siamese phrases, then silence again, and all the time the words echo just once in the mountains above. Slowly, imperceptibly, the tempo increases and the silences grow shorter as other muezzins join in the dawn chorus, and within minutes I am always captured by the singular beauty of this crepuscular song.

It was Friday, the Muslim sabbath, and black prayer flags were fluttering from the minarets. Apparently, the flags are a tradition that dates back to the rowdier days of the Andalusian return, a time when people would be so drunk from the week's revelry that they needed reminding of this, their holy day. In effect, the first few phrases of the Friday morning call to prayer finish with a pleading: 'Come to prayer, come to security … Prayer is better than sleep.' Friday is a day of piety and reflection, a boon for the beggars, and a day on which people will often visit the graves of their dead. Friday is also the occasion for wearing one's best clothes: pristine cream or white jellabas for the men, and the brightest and most joyful of kaftans for the women. Friday is the day when one can see old men with sticks and loosely tied turbans, their fluffy white beards brushed straight like cotton flax, shuffling up the steps that lead into the mosque.

Morning passed by quickly over tea and coffee with Abdsalam, who was eagerly recounting his numerous and invariably fruitless amorous escapades, as well as his equally fraught dope-running adventures. There was that starlit trek in the Rif a few years back, dogged by that idiotic Dutch hippy who'd persisted in using flashlights in range of army checkpoints, and then the supposedly reliable contact who disappeared with the whole caboodle. Then there was the story of the dinghies, one of which was at the bottom of the Straits of Gibraltar, and the other that had floated aimlessly after an drunken diversion had used up all the gas! I was also told the tale of the one hundred thousand peseta bribe that a Spanish customs official had accepted on the beach at Ceuta, after having discovered a suitcase full of…

Abdsalam talked candidly, if not always convincingly, of how easy and lucrative it was to smuggle cannabis into Europe, and I sensed that he was keeping half a weather eye (and ear) trained firmly on me. But

I had other plans – I had decided, for a reason that I have still fully to comprehend, to try and cycle into the Sahara.

We often spent our mornings in the serene calm of the kasbah gardens, along with a painter called Mohamed. Married, with nine children (number ten on the way), and particularly fond of gin and Cuban cigars, Mohamed kept a mistress that everyone (including his wife) knew all about. At present he was busy painting a long cloth banner for the local council. It read: 'Pay attention! Be careful when you drive!' Mohamed then spent the next ten minutes running around the gardens shouting 'Toot-toot! Vroom-vroom!' much to the consternation of the tourists that were being taken on a guided tour of the kasbah.

Mohamed's latest *œuvres d'art* were out to dry: rather average watercolours that were nonetheless popular with the tourists, as well as the resident one-eyed ginger tom, who always made a point of urinating on them! What Mohamed didn't realise was that the greatest work of all was his petal-dusted pallet, awash with so many colours that it looked as though a rainforest had melted over it. At this time of year, the kasbah gardens too were a riot of colour: sunburst marguerites, marigolds, tea and damask roses, weeping willows, a couple of ivy-wreathed date palms, orange and cherry trees, olives and figs... There were buttercups and lilies, nettles, pansies, primroses, violets, and gaudy clusters of geraniums. There was also a large datura tree with long fluted red and yellow flowers. The Arabs call it *rhaïta*, from its flowers which resemble a droning oboe of the same name. If eaten, it is said that the flowers can kill a donkey or else drive a man mad. Indeed, the slipping of *rhaïta* flowers into the food or drink of one's 'friends' is a not-uncommon practical joke, and has the effect of reducing the victim to a semi-vegetative state of temporary paralysis. Some joke.

The gardener in charge of the kasbah, like so many others in Chefchaouen, was also slightly mad. In the gardens, he grew poppies which he jealously guarded for their opium, and sometimes, when pushed, liked to prove his machismo by munching *rhaïta* petals. Last year, however, his machismo was somewhat dented by an unforeseen infestation of rats in his palm trees – even in the very highest fronds – and people still reminisced with much mirth about the invasion. So, in order to pre-empt this year's strike, the gardener had borrowed his son's catapult, which he used in the meantime to bag braces of pigeons for making *b'stilla*, a pie with a millefeuille pastry crust (or, to be pedantic, cent-quatre-feuille).

This Friday, a small group of us spent a hilarious morning with a cheerful and completely toothless old man called Mustafa Aziat, who was seventy-one years young. He wore a magenta fez and drank litre-bottles of Gin Clipper. On this occasion, he was pissed as a newt, and had just returned from an early morning visit to the hillside tomb of the saint Sidi Abdallah Habti. In the hand not carrying his bottle he held a large, battered and extremely out of tune *'aoud*, an eleven-stringed lute, with which he proceeded to howl the more scurrilous verses of the Qur'an whilst gleefully rolling his eyes and licking his lips. Another half bottle later, Mustafa was happily defiling and blaspheming otherwise solemn funerary dirges, yelling as loudly as his voice would allow as he thumped mercilessly and equally tunelessly on his instrument.

Contrary to appearances, I do not think that Mustafa had intended any disrespect with his gin-besotted visit to the holy mausoleum of the saint, nor by the ribaldry in the kasbah that followed. In fact, his physical and mental state was, if anything, admirably suited to the brand of Islamic Sufism that is prevalent among Maghrebi Berbers. To explain this, one must go back to the centuries immediately following the Prophet Muhammad's death, a time of great religious and military expansion. It was in the wake of the first Arab invasions of Northwest Africa, in the 7th and 8th centuries, that Islam was first brought to Morocco. The Berbers, who had populated this region possibly several millennia before the Arabs got here, had every reason to reject the doctrine of these unwanted visitors. Nonetheless, they embraced the new religion with open arms, for they found in it many elements that were common to their own thinking (the belief in a single god, for example). But rather than adapt themselves to the new religion, the Berbers in typical fashion adapted the religion to suit their existing needs. As a result, to this day Islam among the Berbers retains a significant element of pre-Islamic beliefs and traditions, combining strands of paganism, animism, and even black magic with the more orthodox teachings of the Qur'an. There is white magic too, in the form of soothsaying witches called *chouafa*, remarkable old women who can be found at the gates of cemeteries, and who may, on request, mix strange brews and potions with which to exorcise demons or else embellish one's unhappy love life!

The tradition of both black and white magic is so common as to be tacitly acknowledged by the state, for the national flag depicts a pentagram, a symbol that has been used since the very earliest times as an emblem of magic and mystical spirituality. The three things which the Sufis hold in the highest regard are ecstasy (*jadhba*), travel [along the Path] (*soluk*), and gnostic ascent (*'oruj*). The element that all three qualities have in common is the piety of the individual, and his or her ability to determine what is and what is not to be done. Sufism is much more of a personal creed than the rigid and sometimes alienating populism that orthodox Islam can be, and therein lies another clue as to how the Berbers were able to accept the new religion. It is one's personal belief in Allah, much more than the rituals associated with established religion, that reigns paramount for Sufis. So, for example, there are many Berbers I met who, despite professing to be deeply religious, failed even to undergo the prescribed five daily supplications. Even Abdsalam – who used to drink, who smokes pot, commits adultery, does not comply with the daily prayers, and eats pork – was able, quite sincerely, to consider himself a good Muslim.

To the foreign traveller like me, Sufism is most visible in the cult of saintly *marabouts*, the tombs of which (numbering hundreds, if not thousands) are found throughout the kingdom. The *marabouts* were mendicant preachers in times now past; religious ascetics who, like St Francis of Assisi, won the respect and veneration of the people through their uncommon piety, or an even scarcer ability to perform miracles. Many *marabouts* founded religious orders or brotherhoods, and in time came to be revered as saints. Even nowadays, many of their tombs remain the focus for annual *moussem* fairs, as well as being places of pilgrimage where, despite grumbling disapproval from the more traditional urban mosques, the intercession of the dead saint, or his *baraka* (divine blessing), may be obtained to solve personal problems.

It was odd for me, coming from a continent where magic and spirits now reside only in cinema and fairy tales, to realise that throughout Morocco, indeed Africa, the existence of otherworldly spirits is widely believed in, and even in the more sceptical of minds, disbelief is tempered by a residual baggage of wary superstition. The spirits are called *djinn*, normally invisible presences that can, on occasion, assume human or animal forms, or appear as voices to influence men with their supernatural powers. *Djinn* [hence the English words 'genie' and 'genius'] are to be found everywhere: in rushing cascades, gloomy copses, caves, mountains, plains, deserts... If needed, they can be prayed to, or else kept at bay with talismans and charms like the Hand of Fatima.

One of the more colourful and avidly followed creeds of Sufism is *jadhba*, or ecstasy, involving the renunciation of the material world and the embracing of the purely spiritual. In a temporary form, this involves the extinction of the individual consciousness, and hence the ecstatic union with Allah. This exhalted state of transcendency is called *Fana* ['the end of the world', hence the word 'fanatic']. It is not difficult to see how alcohol, marijuana, and other drugs can aid one in this quest. Other, rather less orthodox, stimulants once used to attain *Fana* include flagellation, hyperventilation, and even eating live scorpions or the vomit of holy men! Severe dizziness and self-hypnosis have much the same effect, the most famous example being the Mevlana of Persia, Jalal al-Din al-Rumi's order of 'whirling dervishes' who attain communion with Allah through their frenzied dancing. Similarly do the 'howling dervishes' attain fleeting nirvana through the pain of gashing themselves with knives. The fakirs that one sometimes sees in European cities, owe their art and their roots to these Sufic traditions. Walter Harris, a correspondent for *The Times* who visited Morocco around the turn of the century, mentioned seeing a snake charmer who, on having first skaken and grunted himself into a religious frenzy, proceeded to allow the serpent to sink its fangs into his tongue, so that he would then parade around with the beast suspended from his mouth, the fakir seemingly feeling no pain.

One of the most remarkable manifestations of this kind of mystical Sufism takes place in Marrakesh's celebrated Djemâa el-Fna square. It is a chaotic and much loved stage for musicians, dancers, acrobats, jugglers, snake charmers, quack doctors, dentists, beggars, peddlars, hustlers, hash vendors, and other peripherals. In the scant shade afforded by the few palm trees that line the northern edge of the square, and in view of the ice-capped High Atlas, sits an old man who spends his days beside a Persian *narghili* water pipe. He is a *bouhelli*, a long-haired drinker or smoker. Throughout the day, from dawn to dusk, friends and customers alike come to sit with him to partake of the cool blue smoke of the pipe, and the cool blue rhythms of the *ganga* drums and *haejuj* bass lute belonging to a band of folkloric musicians installed in the cafe next door. The musicians are members of the Gnawa, a clan of Negro *griots* originally from Guinea [*griots* are itinerant singers; guardians of tradition, family histories, fables and genealogies]. The Gnawa are a remnant of a Sufi tradition which revered saints capable of inducing trances. Claiming spiritual descent from Bilal, the Prophet Muhammad's first muezzin, they are also known as the Demon Dancers. For an hour or so, the *bouhelli's* visitors sit, stare, listen and dream, intoxicated by the entrancing beauty of the duet between the drums of the earth and the lutes of the sky...

This, announced Abdsalam, was the nearest he'd ever got to attaining *Fana*.

* * *

I left Mustafa, Abdsalam and the others early in the afternoon, in order to climb up to the hilltop ruins of a nearby mosque, passing en route the rushing cascades of Ras el-Ma, the Head of Water. Standing on top of the crumbling minaret, it was easy to see how Chefchaouen had for so long withstood military attack and attempts at occupation. Indeed, it took the Spanish a full seven years to subdue the paltry forty miles between the town of Tetouan and Chefchaouen, and even then they were expelled in 1924, to the cost of over ten thousand dead and wounded. The leader of the rebels was Abd el-Krim, the 'Wolf of the Rif' and now a national hero, whose force of irregulars succeeded for over a year in keeping the might of the Spanish army at bay.

This fierce determination to remain independent was nothing new. For over four thousand years, or at least since recorded times began, the Berbers have carried from one generation to the next their ancestors' fearsome reputations for rebellion, for freedom of thought and expression, for stubbornness, and (less commendably, perhaps) their xenophobia. A reflection of their staunch pride was that, until only recently, the Berbers liked to call themselves *Imazighen*, the noble or free ones, and the lands that they occupied in the Rif, Atlas and Sahara, were known to Moroccans and Europeans alike as the Bled es-Siba, the Lands of Dissidence. Even the Romans, whose military might crushed all resistance in Europe and elsewhere in North Africa, were unable to exert even nominal control over the Rif. Rome's only lasting legacy in these parts was the name that it gave to its unruly inhabitants: Barbarians, whence Berbers. According to some lexicographers, the Romans borrowed the word from the Arabic 'barbara', meaning to talk noisily and confusedly, and, quite possibly therefore, impertinently.

In Chefchaouen itself, the rude Berber pride finds expression in even the youngest of children who, when barely able to walk, will already have acquired the habit of hurling rocks and stones at the white-faced Europeans, to taunts of '*N'srani! N'srani!*' – Nazarene! Nazarene! The Berbers' hatred of Christians is a relic of a time, not so long ago, when we Europeans considered it our duty and mission to 'civilise' the world. In Chefchaouen, the effects of this arrogance were such that, until 1920, only three Christians had dared visit the town. The celebrated French explorer and missionary, Vicomte Charles Eugene de Foucauld, became the first in 1883, but spent only an hour in the town dressed as a rabbi (a perfect example, incidentally, of the tolerance shown by Moroccan Muslims towards their Jewish counterparts, perhaps because both groups had suffered equally at the hands of Iberian Catholic intolerance). The second Christian to set foot in Chefchaouen was Walter Harris who, in 1888, narrowly escaped discovery by entering the town disguised as a Moorish merchant, and by leaving it as a vagabond. In *The Land of an African Sultan*, Harris described his impulse for visiting the town thus:

24

I do not know whether it was merely from love of adventure, or from curiosity to see a place that, as far as is known, has been only once before looked upon by Christian eyes, that I made up my mind to attempt to reach Sheshouan, a fanatical Berber city... the very fact that there existed within thirty hours' ride of Tangier a city into which it was considered an utter impossibility for a Christian to enter.

The dangers of not going disguised were well illustrated by the third *N'srani* to visit the city, an unfortunate American named William Summers, who was poisoned here in 1892 and died a few years later from the lingering effects.

As I stood atop the ruined mosque – my face blistered from the wind and my eyes feasting on the sheer beauty of the panorama – it struck me that it would be reason enough to fight merely for the awesome beauty of these mountains. Although this may sound a little odd to us Europeans more used to living in towns and cities, the Berbers have little difficulty in understanding love for land itself (as opposed to land as a symbol, whether of race or religion). It seems to me that the soul of the Berber, like that of the black African, is inextricably entwined with the soul of the soil. It is a symbiosis that we Europeans have all but lost. I think it is also fair to say that the fierce pride of the Berbers is quite simply a *natural* pride. So, when the Berbers, and especially the Djibála, seem to appear cowed, indifferent or ingenuous, the simple fact is that they do not care so long as the matter in hand does not impinge upon their pride. Even physical occupation by a foreign army (for instance, the Spanish) can reasonably be tolerated, so long as it does not threaten the sanctity of the individual. It is through the independence of mind of every man and every woman that the Berbers have survived, for the essence of the Berber 'race' is individuality, and is thus indestructible. So, when the Arab townsman jokes unkindly about the Djibála hillbilly, it is not without a certain wary respect, the same respect shown by one taunting a vicious but caged wild animal, a beast that may yet one day break free to wreak revenge on its former tormentors.

Indeed, whenever the Berbers have felt too much pressure coming from outside, they have invariably rebelled, and have invariably kept intact their all-important identity and pride. Even the Spanish, who succeeded for a few decades in establishing a nominal protectorate over the Rif, were faced with constant harassment. The only difference between the Spanish and the Portuguese was that the former showed themselves more tolerant of local mores and sensibilities, to the extent that they even constructed the very mosque that I was standing on; but even this has become a subject of Berber pride. According to the guides, it was ruined by a divine bolt of lightning because it had been built by infidels.

The attitude of the Berbers to their rulers, whoever they are, is succinctly captured in a stern warning engraved on one of the ornamental archways leading into Chefchaouen's *medina*: If you do not work well for the people, your demise shall be slow and painful.

* * *

One o'clock heralds a chorus of muezzins, calling the faithful to the second prayer of the day, *Addohr*. From the mountains, one can hear at least six distinct voices, over which the bird song continues regardless. Compared to the twilight call of morning, the four songs that follow are much less meditative and more urgent, and the brief sensation of silence that follows is more impatiently awaited.

Except for the few hours of absolute silence between midnight and the dawn call, there is always music in Chaouen. It might be Fayrouz or Farid el-Atrache on a cassette player, or else the insistent yodelling of a lunatic. Whatever, it is rare indeed to hear nothing at all. A couple of youths – regulars in the cafe – have a green 1970s transistor radio that they spend much of their time hunched over, listening intently to discordant snatches of Bob Marley and Hendrix beamed over from Spain. To the foreign ear, music might also simply mean the sound of spoken Arabic itself, which is one of the world's richest and most melodic of languages. It possesses an emotional power that I have not heard equalled, power to such an extent that even a single word can reduce a naughty child to tears. Arabic has everything: coarseness, power, beauty, and the ability to imbue meaning over and above the words themselves with the most delicate (and often imperceptible) turns of inflection or fractional changes in tone. And as a written language, there is nothing to surpass its beauty.

One evening, in the cafe with the usual crowd, we became aware of a distant and unusual commotion. First, a series of indistinct chants accompanied by slow but unremitting clapping. Then, the nasal drone of *rhaïtas* and thumping drums, and finally the lighter, snaking strains of pipes and violins – a wedding. As the music grew louder, the Place Uta el-Hammam began to fill with people, chattering excitedly. A sudden chorus of welcoming (but ear-splittingly shrill) ululations from the female retinue announced the arrival of the procession. At its head marched the musicians, three rows of three men, dressed in pale cream jellabas and plum-red *tarboushes*. The drummers looked cheerfully around, signalling to friends in the crowd, but the flautists stared dead ahead, oblivious to the hordes of inquisitive onlookers that the spectacle was attracting. The faces of all the families concerned expressed great animation and joy, and there was much shaking of hands and proud smiles. Behind the musicians came the bride herself, carried aloft by four men in a green *'ameria*, a kind of sedan chair gaily decorated with garlands and candles. Tradition dictates that the bride be carried from her natal home to that of her new husband, to symbolise a gift given from one family to the other. But her expression, on this happy occasion, would remain forever a mystery, because the *'ameria* is designed to shield her from the prying gaze of the crowds. The full pleasure of her supposed virginal beauty is reserved for her husband alone. Others joke bawdily that the sole purpose of the *'ameria* is really to disguise the bride's hideousness. At any rate, the once vitally important public display of soiled bed sheets after the consummation is now more likely than not faked with the aid of a liberal sprinkling of chicken or goat's blood.

Later that evening – the sky studded with stars and the moon encircled with two rings of ochre – Mohamed Cinque began drumming quietly on a table. At first, few paid even scant attention. Then a little faster he drummed, faster and a little louder, then faster and louder still, until soon everyone had stopped their contests of dominoes and pachisi, and instead listened intently to the drumming. It was a very lonely performance, but full of crazy ideas and rhythms, crazily shuddering rhythms, rhythms of the earth pounding louder and louder above the chatter in the square below. Faster and faster Mohamed drummed until, under the influence of kif and hash, his audience had become totally mesmerised. When, of a sudden, he stopped, one could sense the disappointment hanging thickly in the air, the expectation for more, and the electric mood that had surrounded us all. This was pure jazz, as pure as I'd ever heard. For sure, his tabletop drumming didn't exactly have the range of a saxophone, but it was on a par with Bird's flightiest notions, with all the cool serenity of Coleman Hawkins or Ben Webster, and the sudden and unexpected improvisions of Monk's piano. Mohamed, of course, didn't know, or even less, care.

I was stood at the balcony of the cafe terrace, staring with mad Mohamed at the gemstone stars and the green slice of the moon. 'It's a beautiful night.' I said, feeling a little self-conscious. He nodded. It *was* a beautiful night. And from a distance came joyous shrieks, summoned by the faked evidence of a newly consummated marriage.

* * *

27

I woke late, feeling dreadful. My face had, for some unknown reason, swollen so much that I looked as though I'd gone ten rounds in a fist fight. I also discovered that I could swallow with only the greatest difficulty. By midday my tonsils and uvula had ballooned quite visibly, as had the lymph glands under my chin. I decided that a swim would be as good a cure as any for whatever it was that I had, and certainly the walk down the mountain across flower-strewn paths and gushing rivulets was tonic enough. Better still were the cold waters of the river Laou, a milky blue ribbon that snakes its way through a tangle of trees and shrubs, rock screes and fields of spring wheat. But still my throat hurt, and by the time I'd walked the three miles back to Chaouen, I was feeling faint and nauseous. A visit to the hospital resulted in a double shot of penicillin and a prescription for various antibiotics. These, I swallowed with much pain.

By evening, however, my head was spinning and swimming. I bought some cheese and placated an ugly-looking guide who was frustrated almost to the brink of violence because I still hadn't sought his services. I drank a bowl of *harira* in a restaurant but my head felt even worse. Then I confused *harira* with *tajine* when paying, and stumbled out with a one-eyed weirdo who didn't speak anything but the local Arabic dialect. He was drugged to his eyeballs, and forced into my hand an unwanted pellet of *sputnik* hashish, repeating the word over and over again.

Sputnik...

Sputnik...

Sputnik...

By now my head was too pained to think straight, let alone argue, and so foolishly I followed him into the unlit attic of another cafe, where we ordered tea and cakes.

Much as I tried, I couldn't communicate with him at all, not even in sign language. Slowly, the attic filled up with eight other youths, none of whom I could understand. A couple of them, though, had learned bits of other languages, and although the accents were precise, the phrases were total nonsense: 'Hey sor! I have you wunderbar schon nit grit ober die stab? ... Ja ja! Arabisch betrabisch, you want ex-ski zoom zoom only carpatout, Lon Don yes? ... Aha! Mansches Unit, hey, hey, vous alles tres camp, oui?'

I survived two hours of this, eventually resorting to total gibberish myself. My head was spinning more than ever. I said: *'Warum ist die Banane krumm?'* (a stupid German rhyme), only *krumm* means cabbage in Arabic and so someone said 'Good banana cabbage *kif-kif*, ja ja!' and nobody understood anything at all.

I ordered a freshly squeezed orange juice, but suddenly felt sick again and so cancelled the order and stumbled downstairs to get to the hotel. I recall as I left being told, in perfect French, that my weirdo 'friend' was a psychopathic junkie and that I'd better watch out. Oh yes, they said, I'd better watch out... I turned round to see my 'friend' leaning so close that he was almost breathing down my neck. He said something about *zero-zero* and so I turned again and in a panic ran back to the hotel, my vision blurring and darkening as I climbed the stairs. The TV sounded distorted and electronic and irregular, although it was only later that I realised that it didn't even work. As I fumbled with the padlock of the bedroom door my vision blacked out completely and the last thing I remember was hearing the tinkling of the key as it fell to the floor.

I came to a few seconds or minutes later, my head throbbing and my ears ringing. I tried to stand up but fell over again, and caught a glimpse as I did so of two strange faces staring at me from another room. Once inside (after a struggle), I threw-up violently, and then found that couldn't even fall asleep for the pain I was having in swallowing my saliva. I was worried and I felt the cold sweat on my back and on my forehead. Next morning I woke to find that my ears were still ringing and my head was still throbbing. I sat up, and was even more shocked to see that the skin all over my body had puffed up and had turned blue and scarlet. It was impossible to eat, even to swallow the pills that I'd been prescribed. I stumbled back down to the hospital where, slumped beside old Salah M'baz of all people, I waited for the eleven o'clock shift to start.

'Ah, you're allergic to penicillin,' the Chinese doctor informed me, though I'd already guessed that. 'Please, Sir, there is no cause for worriment,' he said, as another prescription was filled to cure the effects of the first, but by this time I'd had enough of the bloody things and threw the form away.

Three days later I began to feel much better, thanks to a diet of locally-pressed virgin olive oil, marjoram honey, lemons, half a dozen heads of garlic, and a few raw chillis. 'How's your throat?' people would ask. '*M'zien, alhamdulillah,*' I would reply, touching my heart with my right hand: 'Better, Allah be praised.' And they would smile and say, '*Alhamdulillah, alhamdulillah.*'

* * *

Dawn – the time of day when even an overcast sky appears pregnant with colour and promise. It was raining. Water was trickling from the window sill onto my bed. I could not sleep.

There was a translucent green house gecko stuck on the wall as I turned towards the window. Shiny and fat, it croaked oddly, like a female cuckoo. As I moved to look closer, my flickering shadow crossed the lizard, and it disappeared.

The sky outside hung like a tapestry, a cool majestic ultramarine that set-off strangely with the two shades of turquoise paint on the lattices. The mosques were slowly ending their serpentine calls. There was the howl of a cat. Or a baby, it was hard to tell.

There seemed to be a fight downstairs. The shattering of glass and splintering of wood invaded the twilight silence. The cocks began to crow. My candle flickered as people shouted and moved about. Someone opened a door, which squealed loudly. Then footsteps to the toilet and the click of a light switch. I thought that I heard someone shout a phrase in English, but the voice was drunk. Another crash, then silence. Then more footsteps and closing doors. The tension seemed to ease.

Just before eight o'clock the shouting took off once more. It was still raining, and the sky looked miserable now. My candle was finished. It was time to go.

CHAPTER TWO

FÈS

Man in the presence of man is as solitary as in the face of a wide winter sky...

Antoine de Saint-Exupéry, Wind, Sand and Stars, *1939*

The two hundred kilometres between Chefchaouen and Fès juxtapose with awesome beauty the rugged grandeur of the Rif with the calm serenity of the Sebou river basin. Coming from the north, jagged black cliffs and misty snow-capped peaks give way to gently rolling hills and great fields of all-shade green, peppered with poppy, wild iris, and the prickly Barbary fig. Thousands of tiny rivulets, swollen from the fresh rainfall, splashed and gurgled down the mountains. High above, I could see eagles soaring on warm Mediterranean thermals, and I could smell the delicate perfume of red-wooded fir in the dew, mingled with the intoxicating sweetness of manure. White egret and swift darted about clean, fish-fed waters, and muddy clay tracks dotted with miniature blooms of lilac and royal blue, wound like dreamlines across orchards of olive and almond. Bees burdened with bursting pollen sacks hopped from flower to flower: glistening buttercups and dandelions, silvery green pikes of purple thistles, and the surreal paper-like blooms of cacti. Columns of worker ants struggled to create some order out of the kaleidoscope of petals strewn over the steaming soil. A solitary dung beetle scuttled from under a leaf to a rock, and then stopped as though it had sensed that my gaze rested upon it. Two butterflies fluttered past my head as I cycled, and I swore that I could hear the beating of their wings.

Always there is music in the mountains, a hypnotic weave of Nature's rhythm and song: distant rushing cascades; the eternal whisper of a gentle breeze; the rattle-pulse of grasshoppers; the fine embroidery of birdsong. Wild ducks honked and hooted, imitating the claxons of the few buses and trucks that passed me by. Under their loads of leafy branches and hay, the latter looked like giant furry caterpillars as they ground up the winding roads. Now and then there were bursts like firecrackers from swallows, the cooing of pigeons and turtledoves, and the plaintive calls of cuckoos from ruined farmhouses. And between the songs of the heavens and the rhythms of the earth, the spooky heehawing of donkeys, the bleating of goats, and the howls and barks of the dogs that guarded them. Delacroix and Tennessee Williams, Truman Capote, the Millers, and Paul and Jane Bowles... I could easily see what had so enchanted them about Morocco, and it was similarly easy to sense the aura of simplicity and purity that had helped forge the hippy trails of the 1960s. The existentialists, the freaks, the beatniks and the bad poets, all were here, in addition to an inter-war community of pigsticking expats. *Chacun pour soi et à son goût.* For my part, I was both happy and relieved to be back on the road, if only for a couple of days until Fès. Surprise was probably my strongest emotion – surprise that I'd cycled from Manchester to get here, and surprise at my desire to travel on further south.

From Chefchaouen, the narrow mountain road wends its way past the tiny crossroads hamlet of Derdara to El-Had, through which the border of the Spanish and French protectorates used to run. The dilapidated ruins of the old frontier post still stand, in the form of dozens of crumbling and boarded-up *guichets*, their paint yellowed and flaking. Nearby houses lie half-buried under landslides. Nothing stirred.

Out of El-Had, the road snakes its way along the steep-sided valley of the river Lekkous. Sixty kilometres downstream is Ksar-el-Kebir – 'the Great Fortress' – where, in 1578, the twenty-six-thousand strong army of the young Dom Sebastião of Portugal was annihilated by the Moors. The Battle of the Three Kings, as it became known, rung the knell for imperial Portugal, which within two years had fallen under the rule of Spain's Philip the Prudent, the man who in spite of his name was to sail the Armada against England.

Further along the Lekkous, some seventy kilometres from Chefchaouen, is the mountain stronghold of Ouezzane, poised like a fat spider in the centre of a web of winding lanes, donkey tracks, and forbidding hedges of aloe, prickly pear, and bamboo. Ouezzane marks the ancient boundary between the Bled es-Siba and the Bled el-Makhzen: the 'Lands of the Treasury' over which the Fassi [pertaining to Fès] sultans and their armies held sway. Founded early in the 18th century by local sherifs, within a hundred years Ouezzane had acquired a fearsome reputation as one of the most lawless towns in Morocco. Its inhabitants, a broad mixture of Arabs and Berbers typical of Maghrebi frontier towns, had the proud saying: we have no need of the sultan, but the sultan needs us. Like Chefchaouen, the town has a distinctly Andalusian flavour, but little of Chaouen's charm or beauty. Half-built buildings shrouded in crazy wooden scaffolding mingle with ugly colonial-period villas, flapping yellow and blue tarpaulin hoardings, corrugated metal rooves and unpainted walls.

It started raining again and, despite the physical effort of cycling, I grew cold. In addition, the rain shrank my shorts so much that even pedalling downhill became difficult. The wind, too, picked up, at times gusting so strongly that I was obliged to stop cycling merely to prevent my being blown over.

In spite of the weather, I saw children everywhere. Or perhaps it was because of the weather – the all-enveloping mist and rain – that whenever I did see people or things that might be considered unusual, I remarked all the more keenly on them, for they appeared out of the downpour like ghosts materialising on a haunted schooner's deck. All along the road, if they were not busy playing chicken with buses or trucks, the children would sprint up beside me, and still find the breath to shout: *'Bonjour monsieur, ça va bien?'* or *'Hola, señor! Amigo!'* coupled with demands for dirhams, cigarettes, pens and sweets. There was also the occasional offer of 'Hash? Smoke? *Very* good quality!' whilst they stood puffing in the mist on imaginary cigarettes. Other people dropped their work just to stare and gaze for a moment at the passing cyclist. Some of them waved or shouted encouragement. All replied to a friendly greeting or smile. A blue Ford pick-up loaded with a dozen colourful Berber ladies zoomed by, its unusual cargo shouting jovial insults at the bedraggled Nazarene.

Here and there, often where I would least expect it, were tiny hamlets – a dozen dwellings at most – constructed of irregular rocks and stones, with overhanging thatches of soil, weeds and straw. Some had peculiarly English-style gardens and gated archways made of brambles, sweetbrier roses and twigs, that should have been adorned with wooden signs reading 'Home, Sweet Home'. I was continually surprised by the number of people out on the mountains on this dreary day, most of them working among terraced crops guarded by tin-rooved huts not unlike those in the Indian foothills of the Himalayas. At the village of Kharrouba, I had to make way for a funeral procession. The coffin was draped in a muslin shroud of tranquil green, the colour of Islam. In the falling rain, the solemn little procession moved slowly, and with little sound, to an olive tree, which it circled just once, before marching off and up into the hillside beyond, and back into the mist. Further on, where a flock of sheep obstructed the road, bored drivers chatted amiably with the shepherd as his livelihood waddled across and over the bridge.

In places, the mouldering remains of last year's haystacks steamed. Donkeys browsed on gently swooping hills scabbed with exposed rock and fleshy red soil. On the crests of the hills were beautiful little villages with modest minarets, low walls, and window frames plastered with limewash. Passing Aïn-Dorij, Mjara, and then a few citrus orchards and vegetable plots, the road wound its way down to the river Ouerrha. Its banks were flanked with soldierly ranks of silver-flecked black birches, and in its waters swam three cattle and a goat tended by a little boy. He was hardly older than six or seven, and laughed and giggled as he waved. Upstream, a solitary white heron stood stock still, greedily eyeing the waters. The river marks the southern boundary of the Rif and the beginning of a series of rolling pastures and flat, windblown spaces. Here, the spring mornings hang heavy with dew, wet and sweet, caressing the soil of Africa's dreaming. Here, too, there are broken-backed trees that look as though they have been standing forever. In a riverside cherry tree, a kingfisher sat waiting, while in the reeds and jungly broad bean plantations, prehistoric locusts hummed or snarled.

The first sign that I was getting close to Fès was the cherry trees that lined the road, their trunks whitewashed French-style. Then, several settlements containing unfinished concrete buildings. Nearer still, I passed the comical sight of a field that had sprouted hundreds of lampposts, and was merely awaiting the construction of the allocated roads and buildings!

'Hey, Frenchman! What are you doing?' It was a youth on a moped.

'Not French, English. What does it look like I'm doing?'

'Heh? Engleesh? Hey, meester, Fès no good! Too much a-hustle-la-bustle!' I carried on cycling.

'Hey, my friend! You wanna good time? I show you a good time. Listen, you want hash? You want chocolate? [slang for resin] I have contacts. I can get anything. You want smack?' I tried to ignore him.

'Aah, I know you, my friend. You were here last year. Come, follow me, I have a good time good place!'

I'd had the same reception on cycling into Tetouan, only then I'd ended up buying a carpet that I only got rid of in Chaouen. I wasn't falling for that old trick again, and eventually managed to lose my self-appointed 'guide' in the jumbled outskirts of Fès.

* * *

There is no city in the world quite like Fès. On approaching, it is a sprawl of ashen walls and green rooves that fills an entire valley like a river in flood, perennially shrouded in clouds of benzine grey. It is the most ancient, and indeed the greatest, of Morocco's imperial cities. With a population of over half a million, Fès is a crazy place: frenetic and frantic, teeming and claustrophobic, decrepit and majestic, rotten or even psychotic, but always vibrant, Fès attracts superlatives like wasps to a honey pot.

Narrow streets and dim filthy alleyways wind endlessly up and down, around and around, crammed with a heaving mass of people, of music, noise and smells, and braying donkeys that pull rickety carts laden with great piles of oranges or stinking hides. Fès is the last great medieval city on earth, frozen in a time when nomads from the Sahara and its southern fringes, and travelling merchants from as far away as Tunisia and Libya, Andalusia and Galicia, mingled with mountain Berbers and Arabs alike at the greatest cultural and commercial crossroads of Northwest Africa, confluence of the varied influences of Islam, desert, mountains and sea. The medieval comparison is irresistable. In almost every backstreet and alley, there are old men who look every bit like the gods and saints of a Dürer or Blake, complete with long white beards and furrowed brows. There are cringing beggars with no legs or arms, who will murmur disturbing curses lest one pass them by unnoticed. In the corner of one's eye, there are also mysterious shadows and hooded figures that seem to float behind screens of smoke spiralling up from charcoal-fired braziers. The air drips with the misty odours of musk and cinnamon, incense, urine and flesh.

Fès is at once both everything wonderful and loathsome about the human condition. One could compare it to an amethyst geode, filled with thousands of sparkling gemstones, or else the bloated and maggot-ridden underbelly of a society that has long since outgrown itself. Fès is also a city filled with the hauntings of past civilisations, a repository for the ravenous egos of sultans and conquerors of long ago, who have left their mark in rock and stone hewn of the blood of countless legions of slaves. The city has all the charm of Paris, Barcelona, New York or Berlin, successively conquered and deflowered, only without the deceitful facade of progress. It is a city stripped of all decoration and pretence, a naked throng of humanity, and unashamed at that. Fès is a sinister world of dark forgotten corners, cheap hotels and dank awakening dawns, a world of flick knives, blood-spattered needles and dangerous sex...

Though it is only too true to say that chaos thrives within its walls, within this chaos there is a bedrock of order too, for otherwise the city would long ago have blown away into the dust.

It was in the year 786 – one hundred and fifty years after the death of the Prophet Muhammad – that one of his descendants laid foot in Morocco. The man was Idriss ibn Abdallah, who was destined to become Moulay Idriss, patron saint of Morocco and founder of Fès. Implicated in a failed rebellion against the Arabian Abbasids, he had fled Baghdad and come to the 'Land of the Setting Sun', beyond which one could travel no further.

Idriss settled near the Roman ruins of Volubilis, the former capital of Mauretania-Tingitania and of King Juba II, descendant of Hannibal and husband of Cleopatra Silene. Moulay Idriss was quick to find acceptance among the Berbers as their imam and, before long, had established Morocco's very first independent Islamic kingdom. Near Volubilis, Moulay Idriss built his capital (which was later to be named in his honour), but more importantly for us, he was to lay the foundations of Fès el-Bali (literally 'Old Fès'), in a shallow river basin some sixty kilometres to the east, a site that was strategically situated at the convergence of major routes to all corners of the compass.

Unfortunately for Moulay Idriss, he did not live to see his plans come to fruition, for, despite having taken refuge at the very edge of the then known world, he was poisoned in the year 791 by an Abbasid agent under orders from Harun al-Rachid, anti-hero of *The Thousand and One Nights*. His son – Idriss II – however, resolved to continue his father's work, and began the construction of the town in earnest. By all accounts, the young Idriss was a remarkable man, and in time, like his father, was to accrue a reputation verging on the fabulous. At the age of four, it is said, the infant Idriss could read to perfection. At five he was able to write better than his mentors, and at the age of eight, he had memorised all 114 suras of the Qur'an. He became sovereign five years later, and began the construction of Fès at the age of 16, three years younger than I was. Walter Harris wrote: 'The history of Fez is composed of wars and murders, triumph of arts and sciences, and a good deal of imagination.' To this might be added that it is only through a *child's* imagination that a city such as Fès could even have been envisioned.

The growth of Fès was rapid, boosted early in the 9th century by two Arab migrations. The first were refugees fleeing civil war in Córdoba, who were to settle on the eastern bank of the river Fès in an area that became known as Adwat al-Andalus, 'the Andalusian Quarter'. The second great influx heralded from the holy Tunisian city of Kairouan, an exodus that followed in the illustrious footsteps of Sidi Uqba ibn Nafi, the Umayyad founder and governor of Kairouan whose crusading Islamic army had swept westwards a century earlier to convert the pagan Berbers. Together, these two migrations ensured that for centuries to come, Fès was to be a centre of unrivalled intellectual and artistic splendour, combining the traditions of ancient Rome and Greece with aspects of Judaism, Christianity and, of course, Islam. The Arab poet al-Maqqari, in whose opinion the Muslim city of Córdoba surpassed all others, noted that of its many virtues, the greatest of all was knowledge. To this might be added commercial acumen, and the skilled crafts of artists and artisans. The Kairouanese, for their part, brought with them all the spiritual glory of Islam. It was the Kairouanese who founded Fès' famed Qarawiyin mosque and theological college, which survives to this day as the oldest university in the world.

The city continued to blossom in the 11th century, with the coming of the Berber Almoravids [*al-Murabitun*]. They were crusading Islamic reformers from the Western Sahara, under whose rule, Islam was finally and firmly established throughout Morocco (*al-Murabit*, the singular of *al-Murabitun*, is the same as *marabout*). Yet the most astonishing millenarian legacy of the Almoravids is not Islam, but Fès' subterranean water and sewage system, an incredible feat of hydro-engineering that survives to this day in full working order. That the sewers have outlived every other Almoravid construction in Fès is an irony of the first magnitude. Faith and Sewerage, two of the most basic requirments of successful civilisation!

The Almoravids were in turn supplanted by the Almohads, Berbers this time from the High Atlas, who had despaired at laxening moral standards (the eternal corruption of power). The reign of the Almohads saw the establishment of the greatest and most durable Islamic empire that North Africa was ever to see, ruling at its zenith from the Atlantic to Cyrenaica, and from Castile to Timbuctoo. Their's was a time of burgeoning military power, of great civilisation, and a flourishing of the arts which combined the delicate artistry of Andalusia with the strength and pride of the Berbers (the Almohads built Seville's Giralda tower). Although Fès itself was largely ignored by the Almohads (the capital had been moved to Marrakesh by the Almoravids), their rule gave the Fassis their first real taste of trade and commerce through the expansion of the Saharan trade routes that were to become so important in the centuries to come (and along which, I was partly to travel).

The city's immediate fortunes changed for the better in the mid thirteenth century with the ascension of the Merinids, the last of the Berber dynasties, who moved the seat of power back to Fès. Their most visible work was the construction of an entirely new city – Fès Jdid

('New Fès') – on the southwestern edge of the old town. Fès Jdid's still largely intact system of double-walled battlements betray the fact that it was constructed as much to guard against the rebellious Fassis themselves as to repel the Iberian Catholics. Regardless, the following three centuries proved to be quite literally a golden age for Fès, for they saw a still greater expansion of the trans-Saharan trade with West Africa, a region famed since ancient times for its gold. Gold, of course, was money, which in itself prompted a cultural and intellectual renaissance. The *qa'ida*, for instance – the proper conduct of gentlemen – reached its final formulation, encompassing values such as courtesy, formality, politeness and hospitality, values for which Morocco is still well known. Architecture, too, attained a finesse never to be surpassed. Granada's Alhambra palace, the most beautiful Moorish construction that I have ever seen, is but one example.

After the Rise comes always the Fall.

1492 was a year of great fate. Not only did Christopher Columbus sail the ocean blue to discover America, but the Moorish kingdom of Granada – the last bastion of Iberian Islam – finally succumbed to the combined forces of Isabella and Ferdinand, Catholic queen and king of Castile and Aragon. In March of that year, the notorious 'Purity of Blood' laws were passed, which effectively offered Spanish Moors and Jews the options of conversion or expulsion, or worse… Over the next century, hundreds of thousands of refugees fled to North Africa, many settling in Fès Jdid, and in this chaotic atmosphere of war and flight, the Catholics pushed on and into the African continent, establishing control over a number of coastal positions (of which the enclaves of Ceuta and Melilla are retained to this day). From then on, Fès was to figure little in Moroccan history. That is, until 1912, when it became the unwilling stage for the signing of a treaty that partitioned Morocco between France and Spain: the infamous Treaty of Fès. Two weeks after the signing, open rebellion broke out in Fès el-Bali, in which eighty Europeans were lynched. The next day, the French bombarded the city and promptly compounded Fès' humiliation by moving the seat of power to Rabat, where it remains to this day.

Yet, what may appear at first sight to have been a disastrous episode for the city, in a sense helped to preserve its status as Morocco's most dearly loved symbol of nationalist pride, for it was never to be tainted by the stigma of having hosted the government of the infidels. We see in Fès today a personification of life, for she now gazes out at the twentieth century through tired and bloodshot eyes, perhaps half-blind or short-sighted, her former beauty shrivelled and scarred in old age.

Her heart still beats to the medieval rhythms of a time when the city was the greatest of all Islamic cities, perhaps even of the world. Even today, she commands very much the same respect and admiration that Athens and Rome must have attracted in days gone by. But Fès is more than just a crumbling monument to a millennia of government and the vicissitudes of war. Fès is a palpably living monument, as was sometimes depressingly obvious. Fès, like Morocco, like my grandmother, is a stubborn old woman who simply refuses to die.

* * *

After a confusing hour spent negotiating my way through the modern, French-built part of town, I found myself in a small, dark and old-fashioned coffee shop beside Bab Boujeloud – the main gateway into the thousand year old city of Fès el-Bali. Bab Boujeloud serves as a modern-day equivalent of the old camel caravanserais, for it is the terminus for buses and travellers from all over the kingdom.

Five old men were sat around, all with furrowed brows. All of them, too, had spectacles perched on their noses, and only loosely buttoned shirts. A couple of them distinguished themselves by poring over the morning papers, black coffee and packets of filterless cigarettes at hand. The only other customer in the cafe was about thirty years old, and wore blue denim jeans, a blue denim jacket, and a blue denim flop-hat. He also had blue eyes – unusual in Morocco – blue eyes that stared straight into mine with a icy coldness that was distinctly unnerving, icy blue eyes that only melted when the man's coffee was served.

The square and bus-station were buzzing. Morocco is a nation of people forever on the move. The hustlers and *faux-guides* were out in force, easily identifiable in their flashy zoot suits and Milanese brogues. They awaited the arrival of fresh-faced tourists with the eagerness of vultures scavenging for carrion. Young men in baseball hats and trainers glanced anxiously around, hawking digital watches and sunglasses. There were women veiled from head to toe in white linen, dragging complaining children behind them with thick, muscly arms. There were middle-aged men in the usual stripy jellabas and yellow *baboush* slippers, and others, more pious, in white robes, white turbans or skull caps, kneeling in prayer on the damp pavement. There were many dark faces, too, some with faintly Negroid features: a lasting reminder of the Maghreb's slave-trading days.

At the gaping entrances to the garages, some enterprising people had set up stalls, supplying almost anything that one might require on a long bus journey. There was freshly squeezed orange juice cooled on slabs of ice, bread and hard-boiled eggs, sweetcakes, yoghurts and cigarettes. Nearby, a glum teenager sat behind a barrow bedecked with pyramids of chocolate bars, chewing gum and boiled sweets. Hopeful olive oil vendors from the groves around Fès mingled with shoeblacks and boys peddling slices of chickpea flan from large metal platters. Other kids strutted about shouting '*el-ma!*' [water] which they dispensed in plastic tumblers.

A group of anxious and baby-faced soldiers remonstrated with a man who appeared to be in charge of the buses. One of the soldiers was quite flushed, and gesticulated fiercely at his watch. The other passengers – mainly old women wrapped in haiks – looked up only briefly, and then continued their conversations whilst chewing cashew nuts. A couple of Canadian back-packers with maple leaf flags stuck on their rucksacks descended from the Tangier bus, only to be mobbed by a crowd of hustlers. Other buses, also recently arrived, bore great netted cargoes of old bicycles, gigantic torn suitcases and vast garlands of straw hats destined for the bazaars.

One man, his face an etching of indefatigability, paced up and down between the knots of stranded travellers, reciting at breakneck speed paragraphs from some of the greatest works of Arabic literature: Qur'ans with gold-embossed moroccan binding, various collections of *Hadiths* (sayings of the Prophet, also available on cassette), paperback extracts from Ibn Khaldûn's monumental history of the world, the novels of the Egyptian Naguib Mahfouz, and cheap editions of love poetry.

The mournful clanging of a brass bell turned several heads. A wizened and mustashioed*garabe* water-seller had appeared. He looked morose, perhaps because the bulk of his business had recently been taken over by the children. He wore the *garabe's* traditional dress, consisting of a pompomed sombrero, a multicoloured sequined tunic, and a leather apron emblazoned with hundreds of old coins and copper trimmings. Over this was slung a goatskin bag, from which several brass tubes and taps protruded, altogether not unlike a pair of bagpipes. Hooked on to all this were ten highly polished brass bowls and cups. At first glance, one could be forgiven for mistaking him for an ironmonger!

Presently, the man who seemed to be in charge of the buses announced the imminent departure of the Rif service. 'Tetouan, Ouezzane, hash-hash, chocolaate!' he bawled, much to everyone's amusement. The soldiers, ladies, and a few wrinkled old men in ill-fitting shoes, stood up and prepared to do battle. In the cafe, the denim man took the announcement as a cue. He sidled up to me and unclasped his hands, to reveal two dozen cellophane-wrapped pieces of hashish.

Beside the bus station is Bab Boujeloud itself, a bulky triple-arched gateway that spans one of the city's busiest thoroughfares. The gate, in Mauro-Andalusian style (despite being built by the French in 1913) is one of over a dozen *babs* that ring the peripheries of Fès el-Bali and Fès Jdid. Its horseshoe arches are decorated with turquoise enamel tiles on one side, and deep blue on the other, patterned in the form of stars and curlicues. The pillars in-between bore the tattered remains of posters, which flapped in the breeze, whilst thousands of pigeons sat crooning in the pockmarked battlements. From the hills around Fès, these walls give the city an aura of having always been under siege. Not only the Iberians needed protecting against, but bands of anarchic Berber marauders. To the Fassi, the land outside the city walls must have seemed as hostile and inhospitable as a limitless ocean must appear to a shipwrecked mariner. The walls are most definitely a frontier: to pass under the arches of Bab Boujeloud is to enter a world at once both open and closed to strangers.

The actual quarter of Boujeloud lies just inside the battlements. Much of it consists of cramped dwellings and cheap hotels, decrepit, though not without a certain charm. A labyrinth of covered passages and metre-wide side-alleys opens onto half-hidden underground work-shops, timber houses with collapsing wrought-iron balconies, and strange, forbidding doors. For much of the day, the cobbled artery that slices through Boujeloud is a swirling mass of people, donkeys, mopeds and motorised carts, a torrent of sweat and shouts and elbows, and dislocated hands with nicotine-stained fingers that trail smoking fag butts in their wake. There are so many people that walking into the midst of them all is like learning to swim all over again. You have the choice of either standing aside and of being pushed in, or of leaping in yourself and hoping for the best. Fumes, fezzes, *hijab* veils, turbans, shawls, shorn scalps, skull caps, mysterious cloth-wrapped bundles, and sometimes even a television balanced on somebody's head, was usually all that I could see. That is, unless I looked down at the cobbles, where I once stumbled over a burst bag of offal, and another time a dead cat.

Above the mass of rippling heads, two minarets escape the chaos to greet the sky. The one on the right belongs to the battered 11th century mosque of Sidi Lazzaz, crumbling away in shades of mud-brown and a strange fawny-lilac, on top of which are the remains of a stork's nest. The other minaret, surmounted by two golden orbs, is part of the 14th century Bou Inania *madrasa*, Fès' largest and most ornate religious college, whose rectangular marble-paved courtyard is decorated in the most lavish fashion. There are inconceivably intricate swirling arabesques that have weathered to a rich olive-green (Baudelaire considered them the most spiritual and ideal of all designs), onyx columns and pillars, mosaics of amber, jade and blue, Moorish arches bridged with cedarwood panels bearing framed quotations from the Qur'an in flowery Kufic script, and, most incredible of all, fantastic cascades of vaulted stuccowork stalactites that look as though they were built by opium-crazed termites. Like the Moorish palace of the Alhambra, it is easy to become entrapped in the spiritual web of the *madrasa's* beauty, easy to sense the awe it inspires in the devout, easy to wonder at the divine perfection of His Creation. It is doubly incredible, since every inch of the building relies on abstraction alone for its power: the Qur'an forbids the depiction of any of Allah's creations on the grounds that such reproductions would inevitably deform His divinely wrought Perfection.

With its two hundred mosques and holy shrines, Fès contains more places of worship than any other Moroccan city. At its peak, early in the 13th century, Fès el-Bali alone boasted almost eight hundred mosques and mausolea for its 125,000 inhabitants. By the 17th century, however, the Scottish traveller William Lithgow reported (in his wonderfully eccentric *Totall Discourse of The Rare Adventures & Painefull Peregrinations of...*) that the places of worship were by far outstripped by some twelve thousand licensed brothels! As the Victorian traveller Budgett Meakin remarked:

> Fez is at once the most religious and the most wicked city of Morocco... the saints and sinners being for the most part identical.

Not even a hundred yards beyond the *bab*, the street dives sharply to the right and then again to the left. Here is a small collection of cafés and cheap eateries, displaying spicy *brochettes* on open grills, steaming vats of *harira*, pickled peppers, roasted sardines, oily aubergine fritters, *merguez* sausages and *kefta* meatballs. Around the corner is the Boujeloud picture palace, its walls plastered with lascivious posters advertising ambiguously-titled soft porn. The one that particularly sticks in mind was called *Les Aventures de Miss Jones*. This is the western end of the Talâa Kebira, a narrow cobbled street flanked with ancient timber houses that snakes its way along the length of Fès el-Bali to the Qarawiyin mosque, encompassing along its journey many of Fès' most atmospheric souks and markets. There are frequent traffic jams, caused more often than not by asses laden with huge coiled skeins of wool destined for the dyers' quarter at the far end of the *medina*.

The array of shops and boutiques, sights, smells and sounds, was bewildering, a strange and eclectic mixture of the old and new, the bizarre and the mundane. Music cassettes were stacked up beside grotesque boiled sheep heads, alongside embroidered sashes and braids, black tobacco, French aftershave, crystallised fruit and candied flowers, and unfortunate squawking chickens that hung upside down from the rafters. One little stall devoted itself exclusively to fizzy drinks. Another specialised in freshly pressed juices and milkshakes. Another sold only oils, including that of the argan tree which is believed to be an efficient panacea and preservative, and which the more fastidious *garabes* add to their water to leave a curious bitter-sweet aftertaste of almonds. Crowds of visiting Berbers milled around a hawker of coarse woollen clothes, while knots of fat Arab ladies imagined themselves dressed in semi-transparent *mansouria* robes and skimpy lace negligees. Elsewhere, younger women admired the latest in Bermuda shorts and T-shirts. All along there were tiny booths crammed with goods: joss sticks, brass trays and tumblers, knives, lutes, tam-tams, and pointed velvet slippers embroidered with scrolling golden filigree. Other traders specialised in ornamental daggers and swords encrusted with semi-precious stones, weapons that until the turn of the century were bought for use rather than mere decoration. In the wider parts of the street, beefy cooks served up snails, cooked in peppery brews flavoured with cumin and rock salt, which were eaten using bent safety pins pricked into grapefruits and lemons to keep them sterile.

Sometimes, through heavy wooden doors stood half ajar, I caught glimpses of private tiled courtyards and ablution fonts, but within seconds, someone would bump into me and once more I would be caught in the irresistable flow of people. It was an experience akin to being swept into the ever decreasing spirals of a whirlpool, inexorably drawn on to its centre. *La boîte à merveilles* (the box of wonders) – the title of Ahmed Sefrioui's fairy-tale novel about a child growing up in Fès – could just as easily be used to describe the city itself.

It is at dusk that the medieval presence of Fès really imposes itself. Evenings in the Talâa Kebira were a magical experience, when I stumbled around as in a dream, oblivious to the taunts of the hustlers and offers shouted from the first-floor balconies of bazaars. It was as though the enveloping blackness reduced the world to only a few feet around me, a blur of images, movement and colour, with maybe the odd ghostly face that swam in and out of momentary focus. Cosy glows from orange bulbs, the flickering of candles, shouts and disembodied voices, the smell of sweat, and the aroma of incense and charcoal. Walking, floating, being pulled along by the crowds. At times I was conscious of only a great whirl of images, as though I were sat on a painted horse of some fairground carousel. But in place of the melancholic steaming of psychotic organs there was the steady thumping of drums, providing the only form and continuity to all this madness, powering ever onwards into the night... But even at night, there were a few reminders of the twentieth century – the Talâa Kebira is the stage for voyeurs and youth alike, the latter showing off their expensive Western clothes. Add to this the youthful craze of displaying scooters and motorbikes, whether there is enough room or not, and the mayhem often became unbearable.

Only at around the time of the last prayer, *al-Ichae*, did the streets finally begin to clear and the sticky gloom of night seep in through the gaps between the buildings. Thereafter, there were only a few kids left out in the streets, playing football under the sparse fluorescent lights.

The Souk el-Attarine is the perfume and spice market, festooned with ornamental incense burners, and draped in a grey miasma of odours and sweat. Nearby is the *zaouïa* sanctuary of Moulay Idriss II, rebuilt in the 15th century, and a place where hundreds of pilgrims come each day to pay their respects, and hopefully to receive a portion of the good man's *baraka* in return. The plastic awning that covers parts of the souk (the rest is shaded under wicker matting), swells and falls in the wind. Under this shelter is to be found every spice, herb, magical charm and traditional remedy imaginable, a full listing and description of which could easily occupy a book in itself. A dwarfish Berber lady waddled about balancing an enormous slab of grey rock salt on her head, a luxury still mined in the desert, and one that is reputed to be good for the soul. A little girl played peekaboo around her mother's legs, who glared accusingly at me as she caught my gaze. Other girls stood giggling in the darker corners of the souk, while their brothers shouted and screamed insults at me. I must have presented a welcome change from taunting weary asses.

A short distance further on is the henna souk, a pleasant shaded square where great hessian sacks of the stuff are haggled over. Nearby shops and stalls sell waxy blocks of pungent amber-coloured deer musk, treacly black soap, medicinal barks, and large silvery slabs of toxic antimony, used for eyeliner. The celebrated Nejarine [Carpenters] fountain dominates a small triangular plaza at the head of the Souk el-Attarine, and has the calm and summery feel of a small town square on the French Riviera. The surrounding area contains the glittering jewellers' souk, not quite the same since the departure of the Jews. The fountain itself is decorated with turquoise *zellij* tiling – geometric mosaics made from chipped glazed tiles – a form of decoration that became popular under the Merinids. Like Moorish baths, fountains are a traditional gathering place for women, places where they can socialise without their menfolk, and without the more stringent restrictions of Islam, places where they can go to savour all the latest gossip as well as to purify themselves. When I first strayed into this part of town, in cycling shorts and shoes, my arrival warranted much muffled laughter and surreptitious finger pointing. I quickly got the hint, and slunk away.

In the midst of all this is Fès' most brilliant jewel, the Qarawiyin mosque and university. It was founded in the year 859 by Fatima el-Fihri, pious daughter of a wealthy Kairouan refugee. It is here, behind fourteen bronze-clad doors through which no Christian may enter, that much of Fès' intellectual and spiritual greatness was spawned. Capable of holding an astonishing twenty thousand worshippers, the Qarawiyin is not only Morocco's largest mosque, but the world's oldest surviving university, predating both Oxford and Cambridge by over three centuries. To many minds, it is rivalled in prestige only by the al-Azhar of Cairo. The knowledge that was developed and nurtured here was to play a vital role not only in Arab and Islamic history, but in that of Europe too. Even in its earliest days, the Qarawiyin had become the focal point not only for theology, at which it excelled, but for the disciplines of philosophy, medicine, poetry, history, astronomy, and mathematics. The last-named science especially owes a great deal to the learned men of the Qarawiyin. So strong was its reputation in this field that, barely a century after its foundation, the university attracted a certain Gerbert d'Auvergne – the future Pope Silvester II – who is believed to have brought back to Europe the system of Arabic numerals, the use of the decimal point, and the concept of the zero, all of which were developed in Fès for the use of mercantile cartography.

There are many other world-famous alumni from the Qarawiyin, of which the following I mention only because I have had recourse to them elsewhere in this book. Ibn Rushd (or Averroës), the 12th century philosopher and physician, was one of the earliest to influence European thought. His translations of Aristotle, and his attempts at reconciling Aristotelian thinking with Islam, was of seminal importance to European scholasticism, and as a result he was honoured by appearing in Dante's *Divine Comedy* as a 'distinguished heathen'. Ibn Khaldûn, the extraordinary 14th century Arab historian and geographer, author of an immense and exhaustive world history entitled *Muqaddimah*, is believed to have taught here. His contemporary, the historian Ibn Battuta, was unarguably the world's greatest traveller since Marco

Polo, and among many other things left us the earliest first-hand account of West Africa. Also taught at the Qarawiyin was Leo Africanus[2], to whom we are indebted for the foundations of much of our understanding of early North African and Sahelian history. In particular, his lavish description of the golden city of Timbuctoo [1526, *The history and description of Africa and of the notable things therein contained...*] was for centuries to inspire innumerable and ultimately futile European expeditions to Darkest Africa's best-kept secret.

Near the Qarawiyin is another triangular plaza, the Place es-Seffarine. It is dominated by an enormous fig tree, beside which, when I arrived, a couple of chestnut mules were nuzzling through the dirt. This is the heart of the ancient Adwat al-Andalus, where numerous braziers perform their anvil art to a loud and resonant rhythm of sorts, producing anything from candlesticks and censers to kettles and parts for *narghili* water pipes. The stores that line the place are painted a vulgar shade of lipstick mauve, but were thankfully hidden behind a clutter of brass tubs, some of them large enough to bathe in. In front of these were sat the proprietors, some in traditional *tarboushes*, *baboushes* and jellabas, others in tight nylon shirts and flared Terylene trousers straight out of the 1970s.

'Pssst... Hey, N'srani.' I turned my head. 'Pssst. You, yes you! I want to talk to you. Come here!' And so saying, whoever it was would usually place a fatherly arm around my shoulder, lead me to a less public spot, and then come out with the most incredible lies calculated to rid me of the burden of my wealth. On this occasion, the man wished to sell me a bath tub, or preferably five, with the promise that I was guaranteed to double my money on selling them in the Atlas mountains. Perhaps another time, I said, *Insha Allah* – if Allah be Willing.

An Image: as we were talking, an old man with a white beard, white turban and white jellaba rose by on a white ass. Behind him followed a blind man dressed all in black, who grinned broadly as he heard his stick strike the brass pots.

Around a few more corners and blind alleys, the one-thousand year-old tanning yards of Chouara suddenly imposed themselves on my senses, mostly in terms of smell. The stench of the noxious tanning lye was quite simply beyond description, and it is for this reason that the tanners' quarter is situated at the far north of the *medina*, beside the city walls where the river Fès flows out of town eventually to join the Oued Sebou. The busiest time of year for the tanners is after the religious festival of Aïd el-Kebir, fifty days after Ramadan, when

46

Abraham's willingness to sacrifice his beloved son Isaac for the love of God is celebrated by the ritual slaughter of a sheep or goat.

The actual process of turning rawhide into workable leather came, along with the crafts of metal- and woodwork, with the Córdoban refugees – in those days, absolute masters of their craft – and from whom come the terms cordovan leather, cordwainer, and the French *cordonnier*. To begin, the skins are stripped and cleaned at the Fondouq el-Laine, just off the Talâa Kebira, to which mules bring fresh skins from Boujeloud (which means 'Father of the Skins'). The next stage, at the tannery itself, involves a greenish concoction of either diluted pigeon excrement, water-logged wheat husks, or urine, any of which removes the hair and strengthens the leather. The tanners, understandably, are loathe to specify exactly which ingredients are used, perhaps to keep a trade secret, or more likely to avoid turning the stomachs of those who enquire. The penultimate stage is the tanning itself, which in the past involved a liquor made from tannin-containing bark, but which has now been superceded by chemicals.

The most picturesque element of the leather-working process is the dyeing, which takes place a short distance upriver in the Souk Sabbighin. The best view is afforded from a tiny bridge over the purple waters of a branch of the Oued Fès, where the souk resembles an enormous honeycomb, within which poppy and ox-blood coloured vats are arranged with geometric precision into units of four, eight or twelve. All around the souk, hung from ramshackle dwellings that look like some Victorian slum, were the finished products, assorted according to their colour. Bright blue seemed to be particularly popular at this time.

The scene below was utterly medieval. Perhaps a dozen workers were at work under a blazing midday sun. Semi-naked men and boys squatted over, or were actually stood in, the vats: stirring, scrubbing, rinsing or wringing. Throughout the day, asses arrived continuously, piled high with freshly tanned skins or great skeins of wool, which were then dumped in a corner of the souk beside similar heaps.

'Pssst!' said a voice behind me. I swivelled around, startled, to see a grinning boy, barely into his teens, who held out his right hand.

'Hello! I am Mohamed,' he said in faultless English, his left hand shielding the glare from his eyes.

We shook hands, after which little Mohamed screamed with laughter, and dashed away into a sidestreet. Somewhat confused, I glanced at my hand. Mysteriously, it had turned bright blue.

* * *

Fès is a city of a million secrets. At least, that's how it appears to the outsider.

The preceding pages have described only one street (the Talâa Kebira) and the small section of town concerned with leather-crafting, for which Fès and Morocco are justifiably famous. But all this is but a tiny sliver of Fès and of its daily life, and for the majority of Fassis, the area that I have described is equivalent to their town centre, a place where they do their shopping, but nothing much else besides. The real heart of Fès is rarely seen in the guidebooks, for it has few, if any, monuments or landmarks to be gawped at. The heart of Fès is its real secret, a haven of calm, sheltered from the hot sun, from the hustlers, and from the noisy bustle of too many people. The heart of Fès has tall anonymous walls and dark, shadowy buildings which, in the oldest parts, rise up skywards to block out the light. In places, the houses are cluttered so closely that they seem to climb all over each other, as though they had been forced to huddle up in order to make room for new arrivals. Many buildings have had to be supported with props and stays. Others have been left alone, and are half-ruined in consequence, shabbily patched up with rusty corrugated iron, wood from vegetable crates, and even plastic sheeting.

The streets are cobbled and narrow, dwarfed by the buildings, and seem to be mere intrusions, like deep gashes slit into a mass of mortar and wood. The most astonishing thing, however, is the realisation that gradually creeps up on the wandering intruder that these streets are almost eerily empty. It is startling to realise that one can actually *see* all the way down to the end of each passageway. One can actually stop to think, examine or stare, without immediately being shunted back into an endless flood of people. In these unhurried streets, I found it easier to note my surroundings: stone arches like those of Jerusalem, weathered limewash applied around small square windows, and overhanging grey-painted balconies festooned with laundry and the odd pot of geraniums. There are great doors and wooden gates made of sturdy thuja wood from the Atlas mountains, studded with row upon row of large, secure bolts.

There are no shops or stalls here, no souks or bazaars, just the wooden doors and shuttered windows, and the endlessly spiralling passageways that more often than not turn out to be dead ends. In many places, the streets are so narrow as to be impassable even to a moderately burdened mule, but whereas in the busier parts of town the streets can appear to wind as in paranoid dreams of lost hopes and dead ends, dreams with screams that no one can hear, and dreams of endless running with no escape, here, the streets have a calming, even serene feel to them (at least in daylight), somewhere where you feel no need to struggle free. There is without doubt an element of seduction here. One is at first enticed, then entrapped and enclosed, and finally blissfully lost. Old Fès is a haven of peace, a shaded oasis of calm that embraces its inhabitants and visitors as though they were its own children. There is no feeling of blind hostility, or of haste or oppression. Indeed, the silence is almost miraculous to someone having braved the crazy cacophony of the Talâa Kebira, the Talâa Seghira, or wherever, to get here. It is *so* quiet that on one occasion I gave a start when a large door opened suddenly and with a great creak to unleash a flood of children, the first human beings I'd seen in over half an hour.

Even the barred gates and imposing wooden doors have little that is personally antagonistic. On the contrary, these backwaters of Fès are perhaps the only place I have ever been to, where I have felt so strongly the feminine, motherly gender of a city, and the only place where I have ever understood the French delight in assigning sexes to inanimate things and objects. This motherly impression has an element of introverted privacy and secrecy, something perhaps inevitable among these anonymous walls and doors behind which whispers are traded. Fès is a city shrouded in a great veil of secrecy, a veil that I doubt even a lifetime would lift. It is this secrecy that makes Fès such a magical place.

* * *

It was during one of my aimless wanders around the old city that I met Abderrahim Ezzajli. Abderrahim had spent the last month in hospital, suffering from chronic bronchitis. He still found breathing difficult, despite which he continued to smoke. He had a sad face, red and round, with bushy eyebrows and milky brown eyes. He looked well over sixty, despite only being forty.

Abderrahim lived in the heart of 13th century Fès Jdid. In a dark, unlit corner of the *medina* (dark even in mid-afternoon), we were greeted by his 22-year-old son, who looked equally haggard and exhausted. He had finished his studies the year before and was now apprenticed to a carpenter, although he dreamed of studying choral music in Holland. His father explained that he felt guilty about his bronchitis, because it had forced his son to give up his dreams: the family needed to live somehow. Their home consisted of one all-purpose room, tattily painted in green and purple, that was lined with wooden benches that doubled as beds. The only other room was the toilet, the usual hole in the ground. That was all. No running water, no bathroom, and only a single gas burner on which to cook their meals.

49

The Ezzajli family's only luxuries were a silver tea service and electricity, which intermittently fed a couple of dim bulbs and the television.

Most of my three evenings with the Ezzajlis were spent in silence, staring sullenly at the television. Moroccan TV, like the Talâa Kebira, is an eclectic mixture of old and new, of Arab and Western influences. There were stiffly acted Egyptian melodramas, French wartime romances that few understood, and a fat bearded cook who wore a white turban and urged housewives to 'buy fish for the brain!' Ads for Royal Air Maroc publicised flights for this year's pilgrimage to Mecca: '*Bismillah* [In the Name of Allah]... our esteemed King and Leader... it is our pleasure... it is the duty of every good Muslim... the Hajj... you can fulfil your Hajj in luxury... apply now before it is too late.' But oddest of all, and to my lasting astonishment, was seeing both male *and* female body building, in addition to pro-wrestling, networked direct from the United States!

All this was interspersed with slick adverts for BMWs, washing machines, mosquito spray and ten-minute clips of political propaganda, consisting of carefully edited archive footage of dams, tanks, planes, harvests, wars, handshakes, visiting heads of state and cultural expositions. Since the 1970s, broadcasting and the printed media has been rigidly controlled by the government (ie King Hassan), and the newspapers habitually refer to the king with such epithets as 'the Unifier of the Country', 'His August Person', 'the Enlightened Guide and Liberator of the Nation', and 'the Reunificator and Sage of the People'. His Majesty occupies at least a couple of minutes air-time at the beginning of every TV and radio news bulletin, with interminable shots of dignitaries kissing his outstretched hands. Hassan II, like his father Muhammad V, in many ways epitomises the contradictions inherent in Moroccan life and politics. He treads a fine line (some say water) between outright dictatorship and benevolent patriarchy. He is all-powerful, yet presides over a semi-elected parliament. By many people – especially those of Arab descent – he is virtually worshipped, whilst among others – notably the Berbers – he is hated with an equal passion that is hard to understand.

Every public building, from humble cafés and bus stations, to mosques and government offices, has at least one portrait of the king, and in every major town there is without fail an avenue Hassan II or a boulevard Muhammad V. In spite of my abiding impression of this being a trifle Orwellian, it must be said that Hassan's rule has generally been for the better. Moroccans are, by and large, far better off than those of any other North African nation. There is stability, a strong economy, and only in times of natural disaster is there hunger. Indeed, it is no mean feat for King Hassan simply to have survived so long in an age and a continent that reacts with increasing violence towards its heads of state. Perhaps one contributing factor to Hassan's political longevity is his religious authority. During his thirty year rule, King Hassan has increasingly cultivated his claim to be a descendant of the Prophet Muhammad via Ali – the fourth Caliph of Islam – and holds the Almohad title of Amir al-Mouminine, the Commander of the Faithful. His role, therefore, as spiritual as well as temporal head of state, has served to undermine the urgency of the fundamentalist cause. Morocco, to her credit, shares few of the worries of other secular Arab states.

In the eyes of many simple Moroccans, Hassan's standing and *baraka* has also been greatly increased by his having escaped several coup and assassination attempts in the early 1970s, and most recently, in January 1988, a rumoured poisoning attempt. Abderrahim told me the oft-repeated story that in Fès Jdid's impressive royal palace – the Dar el-Makhzen – banquets are laid on each and every day, regardless of whether the king is or is not in residence. This, apparently, is a precaution against assassination, the logic being that hitmen will never know exactly where he is. For the same reason, whenever the king travels by rail, the entire network is closed down for the day, to the intense irritation of several youthful InterRailers I met on my travels.

Abderrahim did not like the king. The contrast between the Hassan's riches and his own poverty both shamed and disgusted him. When I tried to slip Abderrahim some money when I left, it was only with the greatest and most prolonged show of reluctance that he finally accepted.

* * *

Boulevard Hassan II, Fès Ville Nouvelle, 7.15am:

I managed, after considerable efforts, to acquire a visa for Mauritania, in addition to a warning from the Moroccan Minister for Youth and Sports, that I would be turned back as soon as I reached the frontier of the Western Sahara. The reason for this, he explained, was that there were certain 'difficulties' involving a small group of armed 'bandits'. This was a revelation to me. Further enquiries established the fact that the 'bandits' were in fact the Polisario Front, a guerilla movement dedicated to the overthrow of Moroccan government in the Western Sahara (formerly the Spanish Sahara), a territory that Morocco had occupied over a decade earlier. Apart from that, I knew that Mauritania had somehow played a part in this affair, but nobody (even the embassy) could tell me whether that country was still at war, and if so, with whom!

This, basically, was the limit of my knowledge regarding whatever lands lay between the southern fringes of the Atlas Mountains and the tropics of Senegal. According to the map in the Ministry of Youth and Sports, the latter lay some 2,200km south-southwest as the crow flies. What this meant in real road distances (assuming, of course, that there *were* any real roads) I had not the faintest idea.

As was usual, I found myself installed outside a cafe, awaiting the opening of the post office's poste restante counter.

In line with the commendable colonial policy of keeping intact Morocco's old *medinas* and 'native quarters' (unlike in Algeria), the French had ordered the construction of their administrative centre – the Ville Nouvelle – on wasteland to the south of the two ancient cities, where governmental offices, banks, plush hotels and the like, are now housed.

I would have liked here to have painted an impression of gradually decaying colonial grandeur, but the Ville Nouvelle isn't even that. It is lifeless, devoid of spirit, boring and grey. True, there is little of the squalor and claustrophobia of Fès el-Bali and Fès Jdid, but then there is little of their atmosphere either. Neither is there even a hint of improvisation, nor of inspiration – it all seems blandly anaesthetised by the tree-lined avenues and boulevards with their mock-Parisian street lights, and their solid but ugly tower blocks made of concrete and glass. Swanky French-style cafés complete the cultural transplant: shiny aluminium chairs are carefully arranged around coffee tables made of black marble and iron wrought into Art Nouveau. There are lampshades (also Art Nouveau), and stainless steel fans on the ceiling, which is plastered in gold and white. The walls are hung with various 1920s posters advertising French bicycles and Alsace beer. Between these are a handful of cracked mirrors and the obligatory black and white portraits of Kings Hassan II and Muhammad V, both ringed with damp. In one corner stands a giant cream-coloured fridge that commands us to drink Coca-Cola. Other placards advertise Sim Orange, and Hawaii pineapple pop.

My coffee is eventually served in a small china cup. Outside, a one-legged man with a piratic eye-patch hobbles between the tables, asking *les hommes d'affaires* for a few coins. He carries a dirty grey canvas sack over his shoulder, and looks as though he's been sleeping in the streets. The waiter, wearing a pink shirt and red velour waistcoat, politely, or pointedly, ignores him. The man beside me is vastly overweight, balding, and is reading the society page of the pro-government *Matin du Sahara*. Elsewhere, scribes sit on street corners with their typewriters, transcribing letters for the illiterate who number over half the population.

The boulevard is awhirl with vehicles and fumes. Red buses and anarchic taxis that honk their horns in ceaseless confusion, splutter by incessantly, gobbling up commuters as quickly as they spit them out. A fat-bottomed lady bounces along on an angrily complaining moped. There are snarling garbage trucks, slick Mercedes, a van advertising 'Shampooing TONIC', and comical Robin Reliants running errands for 'Sochepress'!

At half past seven, a policeman arrives to direct the traffic, and immediately causes a jam by chatting to the driver of a Coca-Cola lorry. A young girl with an ugly cratered face flits by wearing a painfully tight white miniskirt. Others wear gaudy nylon blouses and gold or silver shoes. An old tramp sits down behind the Sim Orange sign, and mutters incoherently. He might be talking to me for all I know. A middle-aged *garro* wearing mauve platform shoes tries to sell me a mauve packet of Marquise cigarettes. Another *garro*, much younger, walks by and grins amicably, which makes me realise that not that many other people are smiling around here. The Ville Nouvelle is awash with grim faces, largely minding their own business as they stomp blindly along the pavements, nervous hands clutching handbags or briefcases. A couple of soldiers with bulging guts strut arrogantly by, and people make way for them.

By a quarter to eight, another tramp has joined the first, and they're having a discussion about 'nothing':

'*Waelou, waelou.*'

'Waelou?'

'Waelou waelou! Waelou...'

'Waelou?'

'Wae! Loooo!'

A veiled lady wearing a pink kaftan walks past the tables with her right hand formed into a bowl. The waiter breaks out in a sweat. Then, a third beggar arrives. He is a hunchback with a stripy white and brown shirt.

The bus station of Bab Boujeloud is the best (or worst) place to observe beggars, where ten minutes before each coach leaves, it is invaded by all the unfortunates of old Fès, fishing around for an early morning share of the travellers' good cheer. Almost all the beggars are in some way professional, if only because they have no other option. My experience of them was first-hand, on a trip to Rabat to obtain the Mauritanian visa and the necessary permission-cum-disclaimer from my embassy to travel there. A blind old man with milky eyes thrust his right hand under my chin, and muttered a few words. At first, I tried to ignore him, but the old man simply waited, his hand cupped only inches from my mouth. In the end, my conscience turned guilty and flowed into my pocket. The same treatment, I observed with a wry sense of consolation, was meted out equally effectively to the other passengers. Often, I saw mother and child working the buses together. One woman actually clasped my shoulder, and then my shirt, to prevent my escaping. That time, my uneasy conscience was betrayed by the beads of sweat that appeared on my forehead.

The most bizarre (and therefore effective) beggars were those with grotesque injuries. The worse and more hideous the deformation, the more lucrative it was for begging. I saw people so monstrously deformed that even the most hardened Moroccan travellers winced and reached for the coins in their pockets.

My reaction to all this, as a European and therefore comparatively rich visitor, was a disconcerting clash of feelings. Pity mingled with outrage at their arrogance, disgust was coupled with guilt, and horror softened my sense of impotence at my inability to give to them all. In the end, however, all my feelings gave way to mere irritation and anger at their pushiness, which in my eyes reduced them to the status of hustlers.

Fès was doing strange things to my mind. After only a week, the city had succeeded in depressing me something rotten. Even in the Ville Nouvelle, with its European aspirations, I began to feel like an intruder, almost as much as I did when being hounded through the *medinas*. I had also developed a persistent headache that refused to go away. No matter how much I tried, I couldn't fit in. No matter how much I tried, I couldn't avoid the unwanted attentions of the hustlers. Chefchaouen had been small enough to allow me to get to know almost everyone and everyone to know me, whereas in Fès, I would always, no matter how long I stayed, be regarded only as a rich *N'srani*. I hated that. I hated the fact that I had always to be on my guard, that I was always to be a target, that I rarely had a moment to myself. I hated the glib patter that greeted my every move, the arrogance of my peers, their bigotry, and the ironical accusations of racism that were levelled at me whenever I refused to fall for whatever ruse had been laid. On one occasion, stolen car radios were thrust under my nose. When I refused to buy, the man hissed insults straight into my ear, and then spat at my shirt.

Rarely in Fès did I find a trace of Kerouac's 'fine Arabs who never even looked at me in the street but minded their eyes to themselves'.

Thirty years on, Fès has a reputation for hassle and hustlers rivalled only by Tetouan and Tangier. Fès is too large and too confined a place to avoid categorising and generalising. The individual becomes swamped by the collective force of so many people. The individual begins to feel claustrophobic and paranoid. There are too many people and too little time for thought or reflection. The amphetamine bustle of Fès contrasted painfully with the calm that the alluring desert afforded my imagination. I began to feel isolated and ostracised, perhaps perversely so given the attention that I invariably attracted. I was made to feel guilty about my foreignness.

Historically, I was not alone. Fès is a city that has invariably devoured foreigners, and therein lies one undoubted secret of its survival. Beware the fate accorded to the Portuguese prince Dom Ferdinand who, in 1437, was hung like a pig through his heels from Fès Jdid's Bab Dekakene for four days, and was then stuffed with straw and put on display for another 29 years as a warning to future unwanted visitors. Others were more lucky, and were incarcerated in the dungeons of Zibbálat en-Nasára – the Dunghill of the Nazarenes. Even Moroccan Jews (who had settled here centuries before the arrival of the Arabs) were treated as outsiders. René Caillié (arguably the first Christian to return alive from Timbuctoo, in 1828) remarked of Moroccan Jewry: 'they are in a pitiable condition, wandering about almost naked, and continually insulted by the Moors; these fanatics even beat them shamefully, and throw stones at them as at dogs...'[3]

In retrospect, I can understand why some writers have spoken with so much romance about Fès' 'Great Imperial Walls of Silence'. There are so many voices in Fès that one cannot hear anything but a great din of silence. Once, when I was walking down a little side street in search of a newspaper, I saw a hunchbacked beggar woman. I watched her for a long time, before I realised that she was sobbing, quietly, shamefully, and alone. Another time, I saw a one-legged man get knocked over by a ladder protruding from a mule. As he scrambled around the dirt for the remains of a parcel of monkey nuts, not one person stopped to help him back to his feet. When I approached him (out of guilt), he shouted at me to leave him be. His eyes were as blindly paranoid as my own were, on occasion, to become.

If there is only a single cloud in an otherwise clear sky, that cloud is conspicuous, but if there are many clouds, they all become unremarkable.

CHAPTER THREE

THE ATLAS MOUNTAINS

...the most fabulous mountains of all Affricke [that] shineth often many times with many flashes of fires, and his haunted with the wanton lascivious Aegipans [Goat-Pans] and Satyres whereof it is full, that it resoundeth with noise of hautboies, pipes, and fifes, and ringeth again with the sound of tabers, timbrels and cymbals.

Pliny the Elder, Natural History, 77 AD

I left Fès still pursued by hustlers, who ran alongside the bike, snapping with the steady persistence of starving dogs. One of them had the nerve – and the humour too – to insist on trying to sell me a ticket for a nonexistent train journey to Timbuctoo, and all with such flawless sincerity.

The first dozen kilometres along Route Principale N.24 cut across a sumptious agricultural land, the road itself lined with cypress. Lush irrigated fields of barley, maize and poppies flashed by, then small orchards of almond, citrus and strangely twisted olive trees. Then came richly verdant hills, laced and spotted with violent explosions of red and violet, white, orange, blue and yellow. As the road gradient rose, so did the temperature and the wind, and before long I was sweating and cursing as I struggled up the last twisting hairpins towards the village of Imouzzer-Kandar.

A small and calm settlement, four thousand feet up on the ledge of a limestone plateau overlooking the checkerboard fields and woods of the Saïss plain, Imouzzer-Kandar marks the beginning of the Berber-dominated Middle Atlas. It is a region, like the Rif, that was known until sixty years ago as the Bled es-Siba, and that the French military called the *'zone insecurité'*. The town is the domain of the Aït-Seghrouchen tribe (*aït* meaning 'children of' and hence 'tribe'), some of whom lived until the turn of the century in caves at the far end of the village. For much of the sixty-odd kilometres to Ifrane – 'the Caves' – the road skirts the beautiful *Route des Lacs*, a land thick with heavily scented cedar forests, sparkling waterfalls and mineral springs. It is a haven for wild flowers. Violets, primrose, lemon verbena, pink azalea and purple rosebay, are among the few that I could identify. It is a land very reminiscent of the little I recall of the Lebanon Mountains on the Beirut to Damascus highway, that I had visited aged five. At any rate, the region was tranquil enough for a homesick French governor to order the construction of Ifrane in 1929; a mountain sanctuary well away from the chores and headaches of colonial Morocco. The town reminded me of villages in the Massif Central and the Jura, with its leafy roads and avenues, alpine-style chalets and lovingly nurtured gardens of geranium and hibiscus hedged with bougainvillea. King Hassan reputedly ordered the evacuation of Ifrane a few years ago when he realised that his vacation palace on the outskirts of town – a kitsch Gothic chateau with mustard walls and a green roof – was open to voyeurs from the hills facing it!

Azrou, fifteen kilometres further on, is the first real town of the Middle Atlas, and stands at the conjunction of roads from the imperial cities of Fès and Meknès, and the Middle Atlas trading towns of Khenifra and Midelt. Its towering kasbah was built in 1684 by the Alaouite sultan, Moulay Ismaïl, to control the rich caravan routes from West Africa. As a result, Azrou grew quickly and become an important trading centre. The 55 year rule of Moulay Ismaïl [1672-1727], although fabulously cruel and brutal, brought Morocco one of her few interludes of calm and prosperity, the nation having fragmented into innumerable fiefdoms and sultanates after the fall of the Merinids. The legacy of Ismaïl's rule of iron survives in a magnificent collection of architecture, all on a monumental scale. So prolific was Moulay Ismaïl's building programme that it is easy to believe that virtually anything and everything of historic significance in Morocco was built by him. Beside a string of fortified kasbahs built to supress revolts and impose his will on the people (including Rabat's Oudaïa fortress, and the renovation of Chefchaouen's kasbah), his greatest and most astonishing construction was the city of Meknès itself, inspired, it is said, by Louis XIV's equally outlandish creation of Versailles.

The key to Ismaïl's power was his infamous Black Guard, an army of Negro manservants (*abidin*) which was bred up, using slave girls, from an initial 16,000 to create a force of over 150,000 troops, in its time one of the largest in the western hemisphere. Legend has it that when the *abidin* died, their bodies were used as building material in the rapidly rising battlements of imperial Meknès, slaves in death as in life. Like all megalomaniacs, Ismaïl was a man blessed with the power to remain always as a spoilt child. Apart from his megalomaniacal thirst and despotism (which was said so ferocious to turn white with fright the hair of babes in arms), Moulay Ismaïl was also renowned for his voracious sexual appetite. Contemporary accounts report that he kept a harem of over five hundred concubines and, as a result, fathered more than one and a half thousand children! The problem with this was that, when the sultan finally deigned to die, the bickering of his many sons caused Morocco to sink once more into a morass of anarchy and disunity from which, ironically, it was next rescued only earlier this century by the French.

Ill luck determined that I was not to make it to Azrou, for I mistakenly took a left turn on to a small secondary road leading eastwards, only discovering my error a good half hour later. Being too lazy to turn back (something I hate to do), I decided to take advantage of fate by trying out both myself and the bicycle over a rough unsurfaced *piste*, cutting twenty kilometres across the foothills of the Middle Atlas to rejoin the road proper to the south of Azrou. I reasoned that if either myself or my bike could not manage even this little bit of rough riding, then there was little point in attempting an excursion into the Sahara.

Past the aptly named Valley of the Boulders, the road started abruptly upwards through a dark and steep forest of purple juniper, oak trees and 120ft Blue Atlas cedars. This is the eastern periphery of the ancient Gouraud forest (of which some trees are over eight hundred years old), and in which wild Barbary apes are said still to roam. Further up, at a gradient where I had to push the bicycle, an old Berber goatherd sporting a woolly bobble hat, slid out noiselessly from the trees, and then stared nonchalantly as I stumbled past huffing and puffing. My breathless greeting prompted a cheerful cackle from his toothless mouth. '*M'zien, m'zien,*' he urged encouragingly. '*Makein mushkil!*' I shouted back. No problem.

A little further up, the trees began to thin. Eagle country. Up and over the mutton-clouded pass of Tizi-n-Tretten (2104m), the *piste* reverted unexpectedly to asphalt, before swooping down into a wide grassy plain, and then down again into the three-lift ski-resort of Mischliffen: a small collection of hotels and villas with a season lasting approximately five weeks. Now, in April, the place was completely deserted, marooned in a sea of rocks and volcanic craters. After Mischliffen, the road wound down still further through a short stretch of alpine firs, before the hills parted to give way to a wide and windblown plateau. To either side rose gently sloping escarpments, crowned with a few cedars and spruce, while from the shards and stones of the plateau itself sprouted grasses and a few down-bearded thistles. The air was cold and soothing.

At the southern edge of the plateau, the road joined Route Principale

N.21, built on an ancient caravan trail from the Algerian Sahara, three hundred miles southeast. A few yards after the conjunction of the roads, the land dropped away. In the very distance, the pastel-rose peaks of the main ridge of the Middle Atlas reared up into a lilac sky. The mountain sides – great interlocking hulks – were grey and black, scarred by ancient glaciers as well as by the sun. Straddling the foreground stretched layer upon layer of hills, lower peaks, and tree-topped hillocks, across which the lonely road unwound like a spool of cream-coloured ribbon. With the abundance of the intense but soft light, and from my still elevated vantage point (over 5000ft), cycling for the next hour was like floating high above the land, looking down upon and indeed over the extended horizon. The scenery was so dramatic and so rapidly changing – every few hundred yards the road would reveal yet another variation of the panorama – that even crossing it on a pushbike seemed to be too fast a mode of travel. Atlas is a land that begs for a little time from the traveller, a place whose atmosphere should be savoured like a good cognac, and not just gulped down in one go.

Richard Hakluyt, 'Preacher, and sometime Student of Christ-Church in Oxford', and Elizabethan England's greatest geographer, wrote of the Atlas:

> the aire in the night season is seene shining, with many strange fires and flames rising in maner as high as the Moone: and that in the element are sometime heard as it were the sound of pipes, trumpets and drummes: which noises may perhaps be caused by the vehement and sundry motions of such firie exhalations in the aire, as we see the like in many experiences wrought by fire, aire and winde.

Rising near the Atlantic coastline, and petering out as far east as Tunisia, the Atlas Mountains are at their highest and most impressive in Morocco. Here, they form three major ranges: the Middle Atlas, the High (or Great) Atlas, and the Anti (or Lesser) Atlas. All three lie diagonally from east-northeast to west-southwest, and on a map (or with an open imagination) resemble the pleats and rumples of a gigantic cloak of rock. Many of its plains and plateaus have been denuded by the elements, and consequently look bald and monochrome: green in spring, brown in summer and autumn, and (in some places) white in winter. Only rarely do the these mountains bear much resemblance to the lush beauty of the Alps, though the Atlas has a kind of rough, uncut beauty all of its own. The Atlas is very much a borderland – not so much politically as geographically – for immediately to the south lies the

Sahara, the greatest desert in the world. It is only Atlas that prevents northern Morocco from succumbing to its sands.

The Berbers call the Atlas *Idráren Dráren*, the Mountains of Mountains. Atlas is the fitting domain for a thousand fables and legends, a land of celebrated saints and fierce, rifle-brandishing Berber horsemen of old. The Atlas is a land of nightmarish trees twisted by evil forces, and cascades and streams infested with *djinn*. Particularly feared are black demons with burning hands and laughter like that of angry thunderstorms. Through the ages, these ancient mountains have drunk the blood of countless invasions and revolts. Hannibal came to these wild lands for the elephants with which he crossed over the Alps, creatures that roamed the region over two thousand years ago according to Hanno the Carthaginian, the first man to circumnavigate the African continent. The folded pillars of Atlas, with its high, windswept plateaus and dark, magical caves, are also part of a world once inhabited by 'the most cruel and devouring lions in all Africa' (Leo Africanus), as well as leopards, hyenas and a host of legendary beasts and other cerebral monsters. For thousands of years these mountains represented the very edge of the known world. It is a place well suited for one of the greatest and most famous legends of them all, that of the Titan Atlas:

This Atlas [wrote Ovid] surpassed all mortal men in size. He was the lord of earth's furthest shores, and of the sea which spreads its waters to receive the panting horses of the sun, and welcomes his weary wheels. No neighbouring kingdoms encroached upon Atlas' realm. In his meadows strayed a thousand flocks, all his, and as many herds of cattle; and he had a tree on which shining leaves of glittering gold covered golden boughs and golden fruit.

The giant was foolish enough to take part in the failed rebellion against Zeus, and so, in punishment, was sentenced to bear the burden of the heavens upon his shoulders for all eternity. In a variation of the legend, recounted by Ovid in his *Metamorphoses*, Atlas was visited by Perseus seeking the golden fruit, who turned the Titan into stone using the gaze of the Gorgon Medusa's severed head:

Atlas was changed into a mountain as huge as the giant he had been. His beard and hair were turned into trees, his hands and shoulders were mountain ridges, and what had been his head was now the mountain top. His bones became rock. Then, expanding in all directions, he increased to a tremendous size – such was the will of the gods – and the whole sky with its many stars rested upon him.

61

Herodotus, writing well before the advent of Islam, noted that the native 'Atlantes' knew the mountain as 'The Pillar of Heaven'. Curiously enough, the Arabic word for mountain – *jabal* (*djebel* in Moroccan dialect) – is used in the Qur'an also to mean 'Great Man' or 'Chieftan' (metaphorically speaking, a man as big as a mountain), especially one who has been subjugated or destroyed by Allah.

All the way to the village of Timahdit, I was scarcely able to catch my breath through sheer exhilaration at the beauty of these mountains. The setting sun caught the peaks and the mackerel sky in a blaze of colour, and I reached Timahdit, 110km from Fès, in a state of mind comparable to ecstasy, a state of mind above all of extreme ebullience. What a welcome contrast this all was to the claustrophobic squalor of Fès.

A small village of unpainted limestone buildings and dusty streets, Timahdit sits in all isolation half way up the bleak northern ridge of the main Middle Atlas spine, overseeing a realm of open pasture patterned with dry-stone walls, barren grey slopes, cliffs gouged with cascades and rock screes, and airy woods of fir and pine. Flanking the village are little terraces of ripening maize and barley, and a scattering of polka dot olive groves, watered by a crystalloid tributary of the river Sebou. In the pastures there are miniscule hamlets – usually a couple of thatched huts and a tent – the whole enclosed by fences of brittle thorn brush to exclude wild animals and other beasts.

The day was already old when I arrived. Laughing children could be seen and heard almost everywhere, leading their charges back towards outlying farmhouses. Night-time gaslights flickered into life as the sky deepened from a rosy-mauve to brush strokes of aqueous violets and sultry lilacs, then sparks of electric purple and finally a smooth, deep ultramarine. Older girls returned to the village alongside their mothers, with great bundles of firewood perched on their backs, and as the sun finally slipped beneath the craggy horizon, the muezzins began their ancient snaking calls, the refrain passing from mosque to mosque as though a gift. Traders closed shop and made their way to prayer, as tentative slivers of smoke rose up from the bakeries, only to linger over the hot alleyways and straining rooftops. My nose caught mingled whiffs of jasmine, roses and mint. I sensed an aura of anticipation, perhaps because there was but a day remaining until the beginning of Ramadan, or perhaps because I was so happy and so relieved to be on the road again.

Women of all ages milled around a pebble-strewn square beside a mosque, chattering and laughing. Some carried babies and toddlers on their backs. Others were old and wrinkled. All seemed to be laughing. Some of the oldest ladies reminded me of Omi, my grandmother: forever old in my memory, hunchbacked, with shrunken figure, tough, brawny, wiry, stubborn, and yet indefatigably cheerful. Many bore indigo tribal tattoos on their foreheads – simple symmetrical arrangements of lines and dots – and their hands and wrists were decorated with intricate patterns made from henna. The patterns, in addition to the herb itself, are protection against the Evil Eye. The tattoos and henna were the limit of their make-up. Jewellery, however, was displayed in abundance: thick silver bangles and bracelets, chunky rings, richly beaded earrings, strange amulets, and much prized amber-beaded necklaces. Of these, the amber resin can, in times of need, be scraped, then ground to dust, burnt and the smoke inhaled to relieve colds.

The clothing of these women was a riotous cacophony of colour. The majority were dressed Victorian-style in floral patterned dresses and pale work aprons, which suited them remarkably well. Except for the very young, their hair was tied back into scarves, worn loosely and for much more practical reasons than mere religious obligation. Like their Riffian cousins, the Atlas Berbers are fiercely proud of their independent spirit. Although Muslim, the women enjoy a level of freedom unprecedented among their Arab counterparts – a combination of Qur'anic teaching and surviving pre-Islamic tradition ensures a uniquely open-minded approach to life and to the world outside their particular corner of the mountains. In the High Atlas, for instance, the Aït-Haddidou tribe hold an annual three-day *moussem* where women are expected to *choose* their partners, a custom unheard of in the Arab world. The women's independence shows itself in other ways too. When I stopped in the village to buy bread and yoghurt, I was followed around by a group of four or five middle-aged women, one of whom (the smallest) amused herself and her friends by repeatedly pinching my bottom! What could I do but carry on as though nothing was happening? When I eventually reached a bakery, the women dashed in front of me to bar the entrance, showing only their backs. When, after a few minutes of acute embarrassment, they finally turned around to face me, the small woman handed me three loaves, pinched me once more for good measure, and to shrieks of laughter demanded to know which one of them I fancied for supper!

* * *

The morning air drifted cool and misty. As had been usual when cycling through Europe, the first thirty or so kilometres passed by easily enough on my empty stomach. Although the scenery was still stunning, a certain level of dessication became evident. Whereas a few kilometres to the north, the grass was lush and green, here it was sparse and yellowed, despite the fertile volcanic soil. Trees and shrubs, too, were less frequent, and much more isolated. Then, as the road continued up through the wide valleys, all remaining signs of cultivation and irrigation disappeared altogether, leaving only virgin pasture which, save for the tarmac road, was unblemished by any sign of humanity. Here, also, the mountains seemed improbably close, their peaks almost tangible, and so small, as though they had kept their form but had simply shrunk to a quarter or less of their original size. High above soared a trio of golden eagles, scouring for movement the chalky dazzle of the bones and skeletons that lay strewn across much of the land. Columns of ants filed across the shimmering road as the sun beat relentlessly down. In the yellow stubble grass impatient locusts itched, while by the roadside the odd lizard grinned mischievously. These hills and mountains had a definite frontier-feeling about them, even though I was still a good 250km from the Sahara. It was a distance, nevertheless, that I was avidly counting out as the asphalt whirled beneath my feet.

Just when I was beginning to wonder whether the Sahara had somehow managed to breach the mighty barrier of the Atlas, I came upon a welcome roadside fountain, one of the many sources of Morocco's largest river, Oum-er-Bia, the Mother of Spring. The effect of the cold waters on the land was immediate, spawning fresh green grass which in turn had attracted a handful of pastoral nomads and their dusty, rawhide tents. Beside these, a few goats and mules grazed contentedly. From April to October, these semi-nomads roam, and indeed rule, the plains, before the ice and snow closes in. Then, they spend their time in remote and often cut-off villages, sitting out the long, cold winter nights.

Past the fountain, the road veered to my left and due south, to begin a steep climb up and on through the now familiar evergreen oaks and cedars to the Col du Zad (2178m). Along the way, I passed the stranded 'Express-Relax' coach from Meknès, behind which half its passengers – mostly women – were trying to push it back into life! Near the neck of the pass, the tussocks of vegetation vanished once more, leaving only naked, ravaged peaks, fleshy in colour, arid and rock-strewn. But slipping over the brim of the Zad, another astounding sight met my eyes, sneaking into view as I imagined a hidden Tibetan kingdom might appear from behind a great sheet of Himalayan ice. In the space of only a few dozen yards, the horizon lengthened from two or three kilometres to seventy, perhaps even eighty, as though the earth had suddenly swallowed itself. The southern horizon, across a heat haze, was dominated by the eternally snow-capped eastern ridge of the High Atlas, breaking into a wispy sky of varying shades of azure and lilac. Straight ahead, in the centre of the range, was the highest of these peaks, the Djebel Ayachi (3747m). She is the 'Mother of the Waters' who misled early explorers into thinking that she was the highest mountain of all North Africa (that accolade belongs to Mount Toubkal, further west, which rises to an altitude of almost fourteen thousand feet, three times that of Ben Nevis). In the middle distance stretched a great desertic valley of beige and brown, the cause of the heat shimmer, and a daunting prospect to have to cycle over. A little closer was a short spine of ribbed and dotted hills, whilst in the foreground – all around me and framing the panorama like an Ansel Adams shot of Yosemite Valley – a few stunted and diseased cedars stood like skeletons to attention on the rusty soil.

As I descended, every corner turned saw the land grow richer and greener. Cycling was effortless, and I shot free-wheeling through the hamlet of Aït-Oufella and onto the plain. There, at its very edge, grew thousands of blood-red poppies and waist-high yellow broom, bursting from a rich myrtle-green meadow. It took me a while to pick out the three tents pitched on the near fringes of the desert scrub, for they lay low and almost invisible against their monochrome backdrop. A couple of mules and dromedaries stood idly nearby, saddled with red and black woollen rugs and metal hoops from which to attach tents and their poles. This was my first sighting of camels in their natural environment, and an event that brought a rush of adrenalin carousing through my veins. I felt tantalizingly close to the desert.

Further into the plain, the vegetation thinned out once more, in parts leaving only a few dishevelled clumps of bleached stipple-grass and brittle bushes, clinging desperately to otherwise bare rock. Boulojoul, the first settlement, turned out to be a lifeless semi-desert outpost: a motley collection of modern buildings and whitewashed tree trunks that for some reason are much admired by administrators and officials. The only other things of note in this dreary place were a few crumbling villas bounded by dessicated gardens, a dusty police jeep, and several official-looking signs. Zeïda, a small settlement situated beside an opencast lead mine, was much the same. Whatever its history, it now serves only as a faceless stopover for buses and other infrequent traffic, with a couple of neon-signed petrol stations and a few dust-blown cafes to cater for road-weary travellers. I saw no one when I passed through

Zeïda, and felt like some outlaw cowboy riding into a tumbledown ghost town after a shoot out. The buildings – grey or brown mud-brick and concrete – seemed to have curled up like tortoises inside their shells to shelter from the heat. Only the shimmer on the road gave any impression of movement. From here on – all the thirty kilometres to Midelt (the commercial and administrative centre of this forlorn region) – there are no more settlements (and I saw no vehicles either). The name given to this plain is singularly appropriate: the Arid Plateau. Its colours consist entirely of subdued tones of ochre and beige, grey and bleached-out red. For mile upon mile, the only company I had were the rickety telegraph posts that flanked the road. Some had had their conductors shot up. Others had simply been pulled down. The silence, though, was beautiful, as indeed was my exhaustion. It felt so good to be in total control of what I was doing, even if it was ever so slightly masochistic... The difference with Fès was that here, out on the open road, I was responsible for everything I did. I was able to decide, and decide in my own time, whereas in Fès, I was continuously being side-tracked, harangued, pulled-aside, and being urged to do things that I didn't really want to do. Sometimes, I like to think that obtaining freedom is only the easy part, and that using that freedom is when it gets difficult. But as I cycled on past those interminable busted telegraph poles, I felt sure that there was a lot to be said for freedom as an end in itself.

* * *

The Arid Plateau is actually not a plateau but rather a valley, polished smooth by the action of countless millennia of heat and abrasion. Through it flow the seasonal tributaries of the Oued Moulouya, ultimately to the shores of the Mediterranean. But as I crossed it, most of the watercourses had long since dried up, leaving only grotesquely contorted gorges of a sickly greeny-grey clay, that looked like an unravelled brain (if that were possible), or else a twisted mass of petrified snakes. Through sun-baked eyes they could even have been the bloody locks of Medusa's severed head:

> As the victorious hero [Perseus] hovered over Libya's desert sands, drops of blood fell from the [Gorgon's] head. The earth caught them as they fell, and changed them into snakes of different kinds. So it comes about that that land is full of deadly serpents.
>
> Ovid, *Metamorphoses*

The only serpents that I was to see in Morocco were dead – squashed by cars. The land itself, though, often seemed deadlier. Here, it was bare but for one or two stunted bushes, tussocks of fern-like weeds, ground-hugging thistles and a few withered and grey plants. The sky too was grey, but for a small patch of wispy cloud that hovered over the distant mountains. In parts, the little clumps of savannah grass were wholly swallowed up by the sand, only their wizened tips betraying their presence. The ancient hills to either side, too, had been scrubbed bare over the ages, and now rose only a couple of hundred feet above the Arid Plateau, whilst smaller hillocks nearby looked like sand dunes, and perhaps they were. It is hard to believe that a thousand years ago, the Arab geographer el-Bekri reported that the plain of the Moulouya boasted an abundance of cereals and richly watered pastures, upon which roamed great flocks of sheep and oxen. Now, the only things to roam this land was when the hot wind summoned enough courage to throw up tiny dust squalls – *ebliss*, the devil of carnal desires, a term used also to describe the charms of a young woman.

I reached Midelt at about three in the afternoon (I had no watch, but usually managed to tell the time from the sun). With a population of around sixteen thousand, Midelt is one of the Atlas' larger towns. It is a sleepy place though, encircled by water storage towers and vast slag heaps from nearby mines. To the south, the town is dominated by the towering iceberg peaks of the Djebel Ayachi, its foothills crisscrossed with mule and donkey tracks. Midelt has a relaxed enough feel to it, if only because of the oppressive heat and the dearth of things to do. Midelt is the site of the central souk of the Aït-Idzeg tribe, and has the usual handful of mosques, concrete-box shops, equally bland offices, a bank and, to my surprise, a ready supply of would-be guides clad in snakeskin shoes. Further exploration unearthed the Hotel El Ayachi, the Excelsior restaurant, and the Hotel Roi de la Biere, all showing that in Midelt, at least, tourism has already left its mark. More striking, however, was the fact that everything seemed to be coloured either orange or red, when what I longed for (to ease my sunburn and eyestrain) were cooling shades of white, green or blue. To elaborate: the road was covered with red dust, the dust devils that danced across it were red, the walls of the buildings were coated in red plaster, the chalets that the French built were roofed with red tiles, the bizarre crystallised 'desert roses' found in the market were red, my skin was red, the surrounding desert was red, and, if I stared too long at the sun, my vision turned red too. The red ink in the large thermometer nailed to the door of the general store hovered at around 40 Celsius, with the highest temperature recorded since January chalked up at 48.

The hottest time of year was still to come.

I was hounded out of Midelt by a hustler who, like the chap on the motorbike on the approach to Fès, had asked what I was doing with my bicycle. I fatuously told him that I was playing a grand piano, to which he understandably became a little irritated and called me a dog.

It was towards late afternoon that the road finally began twisting, at first painfully and slowly, up and onto the High Atlas and Tizi-n-Talrhemt, the Pass of the She-Camel. Until their demise a century or so ago, the pass had been used by gold- and spice-carrying caravans from West Africa, a trade that began in 9th century, and perhaps earlier still. The name of the pass comes from the Qur'anic parable of the apostle Salih, who attempted to demonstrate the truth of his Faith to the non-believers of Thamud by presenting them with God's she-camel: 'This she-camel of God is a sign unto you: So leave her to graze in God's earth, and let her come to no harm, or ye shall be seized with a grievous punishment.' Alas, the citizens of Thamud chose to ignore this threat, and instead hamstrung and slew the poor beast, whereupon the people and buildings of Thamud were destroyed by a dreadful earthquake. It is perhaps because of this that camels are rarely, if ever, slaughtered by nomads.

As I struggled up the mountain, passing twisted lotus trees and perilous rock slides, the sky clouded over to bring relief from the biting sun. Just before the summit, where the slope of the road mercifully slackened and the tarmac clung to one side of a wide and breezy valley, I was spotted by a group of goat-tending children further down to my right. I waved at them, and they waved back, before scrambling up the mountainside to greet me. It was with a twinge of fear that I realized that I had been duped, for they were brandishing rather big branches in their sweet little hands. I pushed and pulled harder on the pedals, hoping to outpace them, but to no avail, for they had already reached the road ahead of me, and were jumping around impatiently awaiting my arrival. The normally deflective 'Peace be on you' seemed only to further encourage their malevolent intentions. As I cycled on uneasily, one of the children – the one with both the biggest grin and the biggest stick – stepped out in front of me, whirling the branch above his head to encouraging jeers from the others. Quickening to a sprint, which was difficult enough after a wind-beset climb with thirty kilos of baggage and bike, I charged at him yelling, arms and legs flailing, and to my relief somehow managed to avoid the thrusted branch. A hail of other sticks and then rocks followed, but thankfully, they were all too late to meet their target.

It is this region of the High Atlas, lying between Midelt and the city of Er-Rachidia on the desert's edge, I found out later, that is the heartland of the Aït-Haddidou (they who hold the 'Moussem of the Bridegrooms'). In addition to being incurable romantics, they were, until recently, a tribe notorious for their raiding, and were only 'pacified' in the 1930s. Old habits obviously die hard. The Aït-Haddidou are a division of the Aït-Atta group of Berbers who populate much of the High Atlas and its Saharan fringes, of whom Walter Harris wrote: 'They are a fierce tribe... intent upon the annexation of everybody else's country and property'. In consequence, the hills hereabouts are dotted with old French Foreign Legion outposts, and there is a waterhole which someone in the past helpfully christened: 'Drink and then Flee!'

Down from Tizi-n-Talrhemt, I all but flew into an enthralling landscape of wide and spacious interlocking valleys, populated with stunted lotus trees, juniper and ash. The chill was unexpected after the fierce heat of the Arid Plateau, though it was a pleasant shock to see several steaming patches of half-melted snow and ice, which in places nourished small patches of pea-green grass. The first settlement – some fifteen kilometres from the pass – consisted of angular whitewashed rows of concrete and clay buildings, lounging one of the dry tributaries of the river Ziz (the Gazelle), that I was to chase until it eventually disappeared into the desert sands. The more recent buildings were constructed in mock Ouarzazate style: rectangular flat-topped structures, their rooves edged with triangular whitewashed battlements pricked up like ears. There was a blacksmith, a pharmacy, and a general store, outside which a tobacconist's sign swung noisily in the wind. I half expected tumbleweed to blow across the road and to hear the crack of gunfire or the whooping of Little Bighorn's Indians.

The settlement, it turns out, was built on the site of an ancient *n'zala*, a pitching ground erected for the sole purpose of lodging caravans overnight. This particular *n'zala* was usually reached after 5 days' travel from Fès (compared with two on my bicycle). The Tafilalt oasis, where I was heading, would have been another five or six days distant (120km). For me, this meant only another day of cycling.

Venus, as ever, was first out in the evening sky. Then, from over the encircling mountains, rose the new moon, a sliver-thin crescent that seemed to embrace the planet in its cusp. This is the traditional sign for the beginning of the month-long fast of Ramadan. The fourth Pillar of Islam, Ramadan falls in the ninth month of the Hejiran lunar calendar. It is *Ramz*, or the Hot Month (a throwback to the pre-Islamic, pre-lunar calendar). The fast commemorates the time, in the year 610, during which the Qur'an was revealed to the Prophet Muhammad in his mountain cave retreat. Throughout the month, Muslims are expected to abstain from food, drink, smoking and sex between sunrise and sunset. The reasons are various: to cultivate spiritual well being, compassion and charity; to purify both one's body and soul; but above all, to demonstrate one's subservience to Allah. The focal point of Ramadan is Mecca's Ka'bah, the most sacred pilgrim shrine of Islam, which occupies the site of Abraham's sacrificial altar (Abraham is seen as the founder of monotheism). The Ka'bah contains the venerable Black Stone which, by one theory, is a meteorite, the very same which was given to Abraham by the archangel Gabriel.

Man has always nurtured a great fascination for the sky. The birds that flew above showed, if ever he doubted, that there were limits to his abilities, that no matter how hard he tried, he could never properly emulate the feat of the birds. The sky is beyond reach. The sky is mysterious, and the sky is beautiful. The sky is the dwelling place of spirits and gods. The sky is Heaven. To reach out and touch the sky has been the dream of mankind since time immemorial. Since time immemorial, it is to great mountains that holy men and religious sages have gone to encounter the Divine. Atlas, after all, held the sky on his shoulders (and it is thought that the Greeks originally knew the name 'Atlas' from a primitive astronomer). In legend, the first man to climb the Pillar of Heaven that was Atlas was Hesperus, who wanted to come closer to heaven and to watch the stars. For his audacity, he was swept away in a sudden storm to became the Evening Star (Hesperus, or Venus). It is also in the High Atlas, that the 12th century theologian Ibn Tumert founded the Almohads – al-Muwahhidin, 'the Affirmers of God's Unity'. I found it easy to see whence they drew their spiritual and moral strength.

Mountains all over the world represent Utopia, the marriage of Heaven and Earth. Olympus – the Mountain of the Gods – was a place which in time and legend detached itself from earth to become the heavenly abode of the greater gods. In the Himalayas, mountains are often holy, forbidden places, where only the semi-divine may reside, and are sometimes themselves said to be gods. The Alps were first climbed by Neolithic shamens in search of spiritual guidance. Moses descended Mount Sinai with fresh wisdom for Mankind. Noah's ark is said to have come to rest atop Mount Ararat. Ancient Jewish Kabbalists equated mountains with temples, in whose innermost sancta resided the philosopher's stone. The word that the Arabs use for minaret is *sawma'a*, which means mountain top.

Perhaps because of my own impending success (after all, I had almost cycled all the way from Manchester to the Sahara), that night I too gazed at the moon and the stars with much more reverence than to which I was accustomed. I gazed up at something that I did not understand, at something that I found at once beautiful and reassuring. I felt, possibly for the first time in my life, as though I were living a most beautiful dream.

* * *

I awoke at dawn, only to fall asleep for another hour or so. When I did eventually manage to crawl out of my sleeping bag, I was accosted by a couple of young goatherds who, unusually for Moroccan women, walked straight up to me and in unison shouted *'Banjoo, messieu!'* I returned their greeting somewhat groggily, as they sniggered and moved closer still. One of the girls was dressed in a coarse cotton smock, and held one hand over her nose in a manner characteristic of many Berbers (and that at first I mistook for a comment on my personal hygiene). The other was barefoot, her legs grey, dusty and scabby. Both wore woollen headscarves adorned with silver sequins and brightly coloured strands of wool, and bore three vertical blue lines on their chins – the mark of the Aït-Haddidou. The first girl pushed her face so close to mine that I could smell her breath, but she just stared into my eyes – straight into the eyes of the Nazarene – her mouth frozen in a semi-quizzical grimace. She giggled, and then said a lot of things very quickly that I didn't understand. The girls hung around for about an hour, and only returned to their goats having conned me out of a bag of boiled sweets. I was to regret this, because they were useful in keeping my mouth moist.

The kasbah of the Aït-Messaoud tribe was the first building I saw (after half an hour's cycling); an eight-towered fort resembling something out of *Beau Geste*. A few kilometres further on, guarding the entrance to a narrow gorge – the N'zala Defile – is the reddish-ochre *ksar* of the Aït-Kherrou, the first of many that I was to see lining the river Ziz. The *ksour* (plural of *ksar*) can perhaps best be described as giant sand castles: much the same colour as the surrounding desert, often monumental in design, and fabulously decorated with bold geometrical patterns incised or even painted on their exterior walls and slanted towers. Many have great ramparts, with crenellated rooves and tapering turrets to protect their inhabitants against the once endemic threat of lightning-fast *razzias*, ruthless raids for which the Aït-Haddidou were much feared. Behind these imposing mud walls are entire villages in miniature: jumbles of courtyards, passageways and dwellings, large enclosures, guarded mosques and collective storehouses. I was once shown into a *ksar* after I requested some water. It was a magical place riddled with dark sandy passageways and seemingly endless tunnels of a greenish-yellow obscurity, illuminated only by the occasional door or window admitting great blinding pools of golden-white sunlight. A couple of barefoot children played with an old iron hoop in the shafts of light. Some *ksour* are large enough to permit even a small amount of cultivation within their confines. There were plots of henna, the odd fig and citrus tree, and even damask roses for making attar perfume.

The *ksour* are made of *pisé* (a form of adobe), being straw or split palm trunks packed tightly together with wet clay and then baked hard by the sun. Needless to say, this kind of structure has only a limited life span, and the ruins of older constructions can usually be seen nearby, victims to one too many downpours. There's a wonderful existential irony about these monolithic desert castles made of sand:

> We therefore commit his body to the ground; earth to earth, ashes to ashes, dust to dust; in sure and certain hope of the Resurrection to eternal life.
>
> The Book of Common Prayer

Like most things Berber, the origins of *ksour* architecture are obscure, although it is tempting to draw comparisons with the walled Nilotic villages of Pharaonic Egypt and similar constructions in Yemen (the 'ears' on the rooves, especially, are very similar). The designs may have been brought to the Maghreb by the Arab invasions, or perhaps in the Middle Ages along with an influx of rebellious Yemeni exiles. The theory that the skill involved in constructing these magnificent castles was imported from the east is supported by the name *ksar* itself, believed (like the Russian *czar*) to be a derivation of Caesar. Now, however, because of the drastic decrease in the nomad population and the eradication of inter-tribal raids and feuds, the *ksour* are in decline. Their inhabitants are largely eldery, since the younger generations tend to move away to the towns and cities, where they hope to find work and make their fortunes. It is a pattern of depopulation and urbanisation that repeats itself all over the world.

The road followed the narrow gorge, cutting through a bizarre ridge of stratified mountains, its exposed layers folded crazily one over another. At the southern end of the gorge was the village of the Aït-Labbes, a small brown stain on the gentle brown slopes of a naked brown mountain. From there, I cycled across an equally barren and brown plain, strewn with soft clay and rocks, and then on towards the next ridge, its jagged golden peaks throwing shadows over its smooth golden slopes. The vegetation was minimal, the atmosphere hot and choking. The only colours were bleached tones of khaki and ash, the dusty olive-grey of a few hardy plants, and the powdery blue of a completely cloudless sky. The lack of rain, it hardly needs saying, is an immense problem, as are the denuded and dessicated mountain sides. For the most part, there is not even any soil, however poor. There is just rock. As a result, many people still believe in rain gods. They have to, for there is no one else to help them. Sometimes, a sacrifice is made – a rain bride. She, thankfully, is not a living woman, but an unnervingly accurate mannequin – a wooden skeleton dressed and adorned in all the finery of a woman on her wedding day. Thus clothed and bejewelled, the bride is stuck into the bed of the dry river, a beautiful scarecrow to appease the spirits, waiting to be swept downriver to the joyous relief of her creators.

A few kilometres further on, the dry tributary of the Ziz which I had been following was joined by a small stream. Here, at their confluence, was another ancient *ksar*, together with a few outlying houses and palm trees. A black woman stood with a bright orange bucket at the threshold of her house, gazing expressionlessly and seemingly mesmerised at a pile of yellow maize stalks in the courtyard. On top of the house was a cylindrical stork's nest. This is always a good omen, for like the sacred ibis of Egypt, in Islam the stork is treated with a respect bordering on reverence. It is called *marabout* by the Berbers because of its habit of nesting atop saintly mausolea. Some people say that storks are men from faraway lands come to marvel at the beauty of Morocco. Others say that they fly south from Europe in winter in order to wash their wings of Christian dirt in the divinely favoured rains of the Maghreb. In Fès, there was once even a hospital for old and sick storks, established, legend has it, with money brought from a necklace that was given to a *sherif* by a stork whose nest had been knocked off its roof. If, however, a stork fails to return to its accustomed roost, then evil is feared. The Arabic word for fate is *tair*, bird.

I wondered what the black woman was thinking as she stared at the maize with the stork in her mind. I imagined that she was thinking of lands that she had never seen, and had only heard about through stories passed on down through the generations. I imagined her thinking of maize plantations and of little thatched villages, palaver and mango trees, the gargantuan roots of baobab, her roots, her black skin, and the clanking chains of the caravans that had carried her family so far away from home. It occured to me that it was I, of course, who was really imagining all this, and that someday I should like to go to the black woman's land.

Pink inselbergs ('island-mountains') rose in the distance, together with stratified escarpments. The sand encroached. Crossing over a dry river bed, the road swerved off southwest and onto yet another desolate plateau. Here and there mounds of rubble seemed to have bubbled up in the heat, mounds where once great mountains had stood. The landscape was utterly surreal, crushed and pounded as though by the steady hand of some invisible giant. I half expected to see enormous statues like those in the Valley of the Kings, but the only king here is the desert. At the turn-off to the town of Rich, 75km south of Midelt, a windbreak plantation of ailing grey poplars struggled to remain one step ahead of the desert. It seemed a rather futile gesture.

Then off towards the seemingly impregnable face of Djebel Bou Hamid. Shortly afterwards, beside the *ksar* of the Aït-Krojmane, the river Ziz itself appeared for the first time. The road swerved suddenly to cut through a short tunnel, then past a lonely army outpost, to plunge into fantastic gorge. Here, the snaking river has cut a steep and narrow valley through the orange limestone to form dizzy cliffs that resemble those found in the nearby Todra and Dades gorges, and most of all Arizona's Grand Canyon. Although the river had in places swollen to fifty yards or more across, the riverside vegetation – reeds, palms and bushes – was only intermittent, and for much of its course the river formed little more than a succession of stagnant pools, connected with barely flowing threads of water. Wheeling past a succession of riverine settlements and *ksour*, the road left the confines of the canyon to climb high up onto the surrounding mountainside, offering an unmatchable panorama over the enormous natural amphitheatre that is the gorge of the Ziz. Shortly after the climb, the last of the mountains folded away unexpectedly, to reveal nothing but a vast and shimmering expanse of sand and rock, stretching from the foot of the destitute south-facing slopes of the mountain I was still on, out endlessly towards and past the faraway horizon. This was the Sahara.

It is nigh impossible to describe on paper the full force of the emotions that hit me then, as I stared dumbfounded over the northernmost reaches of the greatest desert in the world. I was struck with a mixture of elation and excitement, pride and disbelief, awe and fright. I just stood there, on top of the last mountain of the High Atlas, gazing out over the desert as hot gusts of air buffeted me. The smell of this air, too, was something else. I can recall it even now: unmistakably thick and sweet, slightly sickly, fleshy, sweaty and alluring.

In Arabic, *el-sahra* means 'the waste' or 'the wilderness'. Spanning four thousand miles from east to west, and over one and a half thousand from north to south (an area as large as the United States), the Sahara represents almost a third of Africa's landmass. Bordering the Mediterranean, the Red Sea, the Ethiopian Highlands, the southern Tropics, the Atlantic and the Atlas Mountains, the Sahara is the largest and hottest desert in the world. It is the great River of Sand of ancient legend, the 'torrid zone' of which Pliny the Elder wrote that it was a place in 'the middle of the earth, where the Sunne hath his way and keepeth his course, scorched and burnt with flames, [which] is even parched and fried again with the hote gleams thereof, being so near.'

The Arabs know the Sahara as The Land of Fear.

CHAPTER FOUR

THE TAFILALT

The word 'paradise' is originally from the Persian *faradis*, meaning a garden oasis protected by walls.

The signs on the outskirts of Er-Rachidia welcome the tourist in five different languages. Not that there's much to be welcomed to. The town is a large, modern and ugly administrative sprawl, in many ways the equivalent of a moon base. It lies stranded all alone on the edge of a horizonless desert plateau that stretches south from the last buttresses of the High Atlas all the way to Algeria, and then beyond still further. From any vantage point one can see the sallow sand and rock that surrounds the town, much the same sober orange that plasters its buildings and barracks. The skyline is broken only by a handful of minarets, and the only vegetation – aside from irrigated palm groves to the north of town – is a smattering of roadside scrub grass, watered by occasional rains that trickle off the asphalt road. Elsewhere, the desert is too dry to sustain any vegetation, and from here on south, settled life is concentrated entirely in a chain of small oases and *ksour* that straddle the valley of the Ziz (the Tafilalt oasis). Everything else, from one horizon to the other, is wasteland.

Despite the decline of nomadism and the trans-Saharan trade associated with it, Er-Rachidia has continued to prosper, not least because of its governmental status over the Tafilalt. Er-Rachidia houses the headquarters of a substantial military garrison – intended to guard against both Algeria and the Polisario Front – and in consequence, the city often seems to give the impression of being under siege. The strategic value of Er-Rachidia – straddled across the fertile Ziz at the very edge of the Sahara – was first recognised by the French Foreign Legion, who built a fortress here at the turn of the century. From the fortress came the town's first name – Ksar-es-Souk – for it was ostensibly constructed to guard a traditionally important market site for Saharan nomads and mountain Berbers alike. However, the demise of the caravans led to the town being renamed in the 1970s after Moulay er-Rachid, Morocco's first Alaouite sultan and brother of the notorious Moulay Ismaïl.

The military apart, the most important contribution to Er-Rachidia's sustained growth has been the advent of tourism. Its proximity to the beautiful and exotic Tafilalt, to the popular oasis of Meski, and to the equally popular sand dunes of Erg Chebbi, has led to a boom in hotels and other tourist-orientated establishments. Their names say it all: Hotel Marhaba-Royal, Oasis, Meski, Rissani, Cafe-Hotel-Restaurant Renaissance... Other signs state 'English Spoken' and 'Go No Further – Fast Food Here!' Western influences are visible throughout the town, the more obvious being the quantity of advertising for corporate First World goods: Coca-Cola, Pepsi, Fanta, Marlboro, Camel, Sony, JVC, Tudor, Peugeot, Vespa, and even TOTO football pools. For some reason, 'dental technicians' seem to occupy most street corners, displaying gleaming sets of false teeth, dentures and brackets in small glass cabinets. Army fatigues and uniforms hang in the window of the 'Super Taillieur a l'impeccable: Civil et Militaire'. The display of the Studio 2000 video and photographic store is plastered with gaudy portraits of young couples nervously holding hands, of fat babies, and of soldiers posing rigidly in front of painted Alpine landscapes. There is a curious over-abundance of insurance companies, hidden between hundreds of half-built or abandoned buildings. There are dozens of opticians too. The dusty atmosphere gives the town one of the highest rates of eye disease in the country, and everywhere I saw wall-eyed or half-blind people, suffering from trachoma and cataracts.

A bare rocky outcrop a few kilometres from the city is carved with enormous Arabic script that reads: 'For God, King and Country'. Like a gold-digger's stave, it is a claim for land that has yet to repay the prospector's faith. Er-Rachidia is above all a statement. A statement asserting both Man's right and Man's ability to inhabit the hostile desert.

> Cry, you old idler of incoherent ages.
> Your pretensions will only make us laugh
> For we have made our cement
> From the dust of the desert.
>
> Paul Eluard, *Les Constructeurs*[4]

To my liking, Er-Rachidia had far too much of an outpost kind of feeling – dull, introverted, incestuous and hopeless. Fierce sand storms sweep in periodically from the desert, no matter what the time of year. There are miniature sand drifts everywhere, that no one bothers to clear away any more. Wide and dusty streets deliniate uninspiring rectangular blocks of orange-plastered buildings, three or four storey affairs in the bland and universally hated style known by architects as 'desert-utilitarian'. A few cypress, pepper and palm trees line the broad avenue Muhammad V, but the older postcards on sale in its tobacconists show a street that was once much greener. There is little ornamentation, except for a few faded posters of King Hassan II that hang from lampposts, and a couple of dusty fountains that have not seen water for years. In a way, the town itself is a reminder of the desert's destructive wiles, because many of its buildings date from after the disastrous flooding of the Ziz in 1955, a catastrophe that left over 25,000 people homeless.

I arrived in mid-afternoon. It was extremely hot. There was very little traffic: only the odd soldier on a scooter, and a camouflaged water truck that belched noxious black clouds into the sky. A gendarme paced up and down between idle Land Rovers (for tourists visiting Erg Chebbi). He looked bored and tired, and eyed me suspiciously for a while, then smiled weakly and walked away when I acknowledged his presence with a nod. A few people were sat against walls in the shade of overhanging concrete balconies, watching whatever was happening, which was usually very little. In the heat – heavy and suffocating – it was impossible to think straight. The lethargy it induced was so bad that often I couldn't even be bothered to eat, which although for fasting Muslims wasn't a problem, it was to be for me. The nights, too, were hot and stuffy, and I found it difficult to sleep. Even clambering out of bed in the morning required gargantuan effort: the heat made me so tired. Even the swarms of flies were affected by it, to the extent that they were too lazy to move when I attempted to swat them. I found it easy to understand the 'dynamics' of desert towns, to see how they have sprung up and why they have survived, for the oppressive heat crushes all desire to move or travel. It is all too easy just to wallow and do nothing, and nigh impossible to do anything else.

Er-Rachidia only begins to come to life in the evening, when the setting sun casts long shadows over dozing dogs and people alike. Shopkeepers still rubbing their eyes of sleep begin to unlock trellises, and the first tureens of *harira* are placed over the gas burners of tiny soup houses. Then, the comforting aroma of freshly baked bread drifts temptingly across the empty streets and squares, and hunger is rekindled. During Ramadan, eating is forbidden until nightfall, traditionally signalled when the difference between a black and a white thread becomes indistinguishable. Then, the drowsy silence is shattered by a wailing air-raid siren, something that scared the wits out of me the first time I heard it. As soon as the siren is sounded, all conversation and activities are abandoned as people get up and walk off in droves towards the mosques. Businesses are left unguarded, buses are emptied, doors left ajar and even the steaming soup tureens are left unattended. I found the whole thing distinctly unsettling, even frightening, especially given the wartime connotations of sirens. That there is a force so strong that it can command total subservience, that it can compel entire populations to fast for a whole month, that it can empty houses and buildings at the sounding of a siren – as an outsider, I found this nightmarish. Everyone was seen to act with identical but unconscious and unthinking reactions. For them, there was no question of whether or not to obey. For them, the question did not even exist, and should I have asked them why, they would have thought my query as pointless as asking someone why they breathed. 'Unconscious orthodoxy' is what George Orwell called it in *Nineteen Eighty-Four*.

After the prayers are over, the feasting begins, though in Er-Rachidia, even this is a subdued affair. The only spontaneous excitement came from youths cavorting about on mopeds under the orange streetlights, yelling and screaming to potential girlfriends. Bakeries and stalls opened to sell sickly sweet honey pastries – Ramadan specialities that I adored. Other stalls sold locally grown dates, which were not at their best at this time of year. Vendors with barrows and carts appeared on street corners, selling ice-cream, orange juice, nuts, sweets and chocolates, snaking reed garlands of dried figs, and 'gazelle horn' biscuits made with almond paste. The few hustlers milling around were generally slow witted, their patter old hat by now. Kids still asked me for the odd dirham or two, but were much less insistent than their Fassi counterparts, and in any case were more likely to share a joke with the *N'srani* than to treat him solely as a pliant source of pocket money. The cafes, too, opened to business, and sold the best black coffee in Morocco. Some had TVs, showing Egyptian films mingled with religious sermons. Others, frequented in the main by the younger generations, had pinball machines and were bedecked with busty posters of Madonna, Samantha Fox and Sabrina. 'Hypocrisy is the homage paid by vice to virtue', noted the Duc de la Rochefoucauld.

Wandering around one night with Dave, a thirty year old Englishman from Reigate who was fed up with InterRailing, we were accosted by a tall gangly Arab called Hamid. He was a rough and rugged character, who could have stepped straight from the pages of the *Arabian Nights*.

His face, partly swathed in a mottled blue and white Palestinian headcloth, was long and drawn, with a greying moustache and ragged beard. Hamid's eyes were intense, wildly gleaming, and unleashed the kind of the glare that penetrates right to the back of one's skull. In his right hand, he clutched a brown paper bag, containing two mouldy oranges, a small artichoke and a bottle of red wine, from which he frequently took large swigs. For over an hour he kept us trapped with his wino soliloquy in slurred and broken English, because we were loathe to walk away on account of his decidedly psychopathic appearance.

From the little that I managed to understand, I gathered that Hamid was obsessed with the idea of man as an animal. Pointing a long, bony finger at me, he asked: 'Are you a fighter?' His right eye twitched nervously, and a trickle of saliva inched down his chin. Before I had time to answer, he declared loudly: 'Ah, yes, you *are* a fighter!' I breathed a sigh of relief.

'Alas, mister fighter,' he continued, 'no Africa fighters, in Africa *no fighters.*' He belched loudly, to sniggers from the crowd that had gathered around us. On and on he rambled, every so often bellowing 'You unnerstan?' when of course, we hadn't the faintest idea.

Hamid seemed to like Dave, or rather his blue eyes, from which he inferred that he was a 'good man', because blue eyes were made in paradise. This was odd because of the commonly held belief among Berbers that blue eyes, especially those of infidels, radiate particularly bad Evil Eye. The whole conversation was a fiasco of confusion. When Hamid next stared at me and my brown eyes, I couldn't help but snigger, which provoked a prolonged fit of mock anger. 'Ah, so you are *shaitan*,' he slurred, wiping the neck of the bottle on his shirt. I replied, in my most angelic manner, that of course I wasn't, and then grinned.

'Israeli?' he asked. Many people asked me this, presumably on account of my nose.

'Humm. Then you are Merican?'

When he asked us what we wanted with Morocco, we mumbled the usual half-hearted platitudes (for me, Fès had killed all further desire to explain). 'Ah, but I have Allah,' he announced proudly, gesticulating towards a nearby minaret, at which he almost fell over. The crowd sniggered again, so Hamid bawled at them and they fell quiet.

We finally parted ways when a gendarme sauntered over to see what all the fuss was about, and then scolded us Englishmen for not having sought the services of an *official* guide.

* * *

81

I stayed a few days in Er-Rachidia, a few days longer than I really wanted to, because I needed time to find a few provisions before finally launching myself into the Sahara. I needed spares for the bike, extra water bottles (jerry cans were too bulky), plasters and aspirin, a small thermometer (for my ego), sunglasses and, most important of all, a face-muffler-cum-turban (*cheche*). One morning, on one of these shopping excursions (a few shops remained open, despite Ramadan) I met M'Hamed Ouln Hassane, a doctor at the city hospital. Because of his work, he was permitted to break the fast, and so he invited me back to his home for lunch.

Together with his wife and three children, M'Hamed lived in a small modern *quartier* a few kilometres to the north of town, reached by a gentle walk across sweet smelling plots of barley that were shaded by fig trees and date palms. M'Hamed was exceptionally polite and reserved, both prized Arab qualities, yet he was only partly of Arab extraction. Like many inhabitants of the Tafilalt and other ancient caravan termini, M'Hamed's dark, coppery skin and slightly flattened nose betrayed the fact that he was a descendant of Negro slaves kidnapped long ago in West Africa to be marched across the Sahara in the infamous 'black ivory' caravans. An estimated two out of every five slaves died in the desert before they even reached the Maghreb.

M'Hamed was uncommonly well educated, and especially loved things French: culture, bicycles, and above all, the language. This enabled us to hold a much more sophisticated conversation than was usually possible given my rudimentary Arabic. Eager for knowledge about the desert, I asked my host how, generally speaking, he viewed the Sahara. After a short pause, in which he seemed to consider censoring whatever he was about to say, he replied: 'They [speaking of his fellow citizens] regard the desert as representing everything that the Qur'an and the Way of Islam strives against. The nomads, the climate, the hardship – all are equal curses.'

'The Sahara is a land of anarchy,' he said, and he took great pains to ensure that I understood him correctly. In M'Hamed's opinion, the nomads were no better than packs of scavenging jackals.

That M'Hamed mentioned nomads first in his list of curses struck me greatly, for I had all the usual romantic preconceptions of vast, nonchalent camel trains and the like. M'Hamed, of course, had good reason to dislike nomads given his family history, and he found it difficult to forgive the past. There was something, however, that niggled my mind. Even if one were to discount the animosity caused by their ignominious past as slavers, throughout my travels in the desert fringes I was to encounter an almost universal hatred of nomads. It was a hatred that survived in spite of the declining nomad population, and the virtual extinction of their caravans. It was a hatred that had outlived the fearsome *razzias* of times past, and a hatred that seemed to take no account of the nomads' much greater poverty when compared to the material wealth of the Arabs and other settlers.

Throughout the world, people who have settled on the fringes of wildernesses have learned not only to despise but to fear the nomads, that lawless scourge of raiders and murderers that live beyond the pale of civilised society. In Mali, where M'Hamed's ancestors were born, a Mandingo proverb used to advise one to 'succour the traveller lest he return with his kindred and smite thee.' There are similar examples of this fear (well founded or otherwise) in every corner of the globe, be it fear of the Sahara's Moors or Tuareg, the Aborigines of Australia, the American Indians, the Bedouin or ancient Saracen of Arabia, the Tibetan Namtso or the Mongols, the gypsies of central Europe, or even Britain's 'New Age Travellers'. Everywhere, nomads are perceived as being uncivilised, uncouth, unkempt and immoral. Even the Qur'an condemns them: 'For they are an abomination, and Hell is their dwelling-place, – a fitting recompense for the evil that they did.'

The word *unsettled* is itself anathema to civilisation, for as well as meaning changing or moving from place to place, it means lacking order or stability, unpredictability, and emotional confusion. The nomad is fast, unpredictable, elusive and, above all, remains firmly outside the confines of civilisation.

The two ways of life seem incompatible. Indeed, even before Cain the cultivator was condemned by God to wander the earth in punishment for slaying his brother Abel, nomads and settlers have clashed in eternal conflict. To mention only a few examples: witness the Great Wall of China, built to exclude the Turks and Mongols; Hadrian's Wall to separate the northern 'barbarians' from the Romans; the fact that the Roman Empire itself stopped short of conquering the Sahara, if such a thing were possible, to avoid the fearsome ancestors of the Moors and Tuareg; and the sacking by Mongol hordes of old Baghdad in 1258, a fitting illustration of the nomads' potential power. Yet the longer I travelled, the more I came to believe that a life of wandering was somehow more natural than one spent in only one place. It seemed as though the life of city dwellers was but half a life, and that there was a great deal more that could be gained by travelling. The 14th century polymath, Ibn Khaldûn, wrote:

Sedentary people are much concerned with all kinds of pleasures. They are accustomed to luxury and success in worldly occupations and to indulgence in worldly desires. Therefore, their souls are coloured with all kinds of blameworthy and evil qualities...

[The Bedouin] are closer to the first natural state and more remote from the evil habits that have been impressed upon the souls [of sedentary people]... Bedouins are closer to being good.

Admittedly, some of this does not ring true, for who can argue that slave trading and raiding are not 'evil habits'? Nonetheless, there is much truth in what Khaldûn says. Nomadism is a mode of life that predates that of settling, in that Man progressed first from gathering to hunting, then to herding and cultivation, and finally to civilisation (and with each step, lost a little more freedom of movement). The instinct for roaming is etched much more deeply in our primitive consciousness than that for settling, and this, I believe, is the 'first natural state' of which Khaldûn speaks. This too, was how I came to justify my own roaming. Even M'Hamed could see the attraction of travel, and promised that if ever he got the money togther, we would do a bicycle tour together in South America, *Insha Allah*.

* * *

Warm, glowing shafts of sunlight splashing on my face provided the final impulse to get underway, and I left Er-Rachidia with my heart aflame in anticipation of what was effectively to be my first day in the Sahara itself. I was well prepared: I carried nine litres of water in all (contained in five plastic bottles strapped to the bicycle frame, and four 1½ litre bottles in the panniers). This was to prove adequate for two or three days on the road, which was usually time enough to bridge even the larger gaps between towns, villages or wells. I had also become the proud owner of a brand new cotton *cheche*. At first, I felt a little self-conscious wearing it, but on seeing several other similarly attired people *not* laugh at me as I cycled by, I soon got used to it.

Over on the eastern bank of the Ziz, flanked on both sides by a narrow belt of gently waving palms, the dusty tarmac road swung southwards towards an imposing nineteenth century *ksar*, surrounded by the dry remains of a moat sunk to delay any attempt by aggressors at undermining the *ksar's* foundations by diverting the river. As the shallow course of the Ziz curved away and out of sight, the land straightened out and the horizon lengthened, the road spooling out as far as my eye could see. The panorama consisted of a childishly simple play on perspective: a rectangle of land, a rectangle of sky, and the road which appeared as a grey triangle, its pinnacle a dot on the horizon. It was a landscape to which I was to become well accustomed in the weeks and months to come.

Behind me, the last of the Atlas Mountains receded into the obscurity of a heat haze, and all around now, I was surrounded with a bleak, pebble-strewn wasteland: a vast expanse of raw ochre, dirty beige and burnt sienna, peppered with small olive-drab shrubs, larger grey boulders and the shimmering mirages of trees and lakes. This was the real Sahara, for comparatively little of this desert is covered with the oceans of dunes that I had imagined. Much of the Sahara is level tableland called *hammada*, as was the case here. Sometimes, however, and to my great joy, I caught glimpses of far away dunes of red or white sand, rising from behind the surreal folds of dry river beds.

Some twenty kilometres from Er-Rachidia, still along Route P22, the road divides into two forks. The branch to the left and east goes to Algeria and the central Sahara. Its signpost set me dreaming of exotic places that I'd only ever read about: Tamanrasset, the Hoggar mountains, Niger, Mali, Ghana, and Timbuctoo. Unfortunately, I had no choice but to ignore this road, for I had been informed that the Algerian border was closed to all touristic traffic, including bicycles. Alas, I did not know that only two days later, Algeria and Morocco were to reach an agreement that was to reopen the route for the first time in years.

Shortly after the junction came Meski, a mud-walled village that lends its name to the *hammada* hereabouts, and whose 'Blue Source' attracts visitors from all around. It is a pool of seemingly miraculous water, where the Ziz re-emerges from a short subterranean journey. In fact, the pool is far from miraculous, because it was constructed earlier this century by Foreign Legionnaires, undoubtedly in dire need of some refreshment. The water is nowadays infested with bilharzia-carrying blood flukes, regardless of which, I passed dozens of men with damp towels draped over their heads thumbing languidly for lifts beside the complex's concrete gate.

A few kilometres from Meski, where the road veered to the right, the desert floor dropped suddenly away as the river Ziz reappeared amidst the hostile and scorched landscape. It was a most astonishing sight: a deep canyon, over a mile wide, carved into the desert as easily as a hot knife would slice into wax, its milky waters glinting in the sunlight. The river that had forged the fantastic gorges of the High Atlas was here enclosed by a luscious green valley, drowzily snaking its way into the quicksand marshes of Dayet ed Daura. A long series of palm groves, each one more luxuriant than the other, traces almost all of the 35 miles along which the canyon pretends that the desert around it does not exist. Irrigated by the fertile waters of the Ziz and Rheris (a smaller watercourse to the west), the Tafilalt is an ingenious spider's web of canals, conduits, field troughs, and sometimes underground channels. Double rows of aureole palms, oleander, apricot and almond trees fill the valley to choking. In the cool, tangled embrace of fig trees, there are small but regular plots of wheat and maize, alfalfa and vegetables, that are protected from pilfering goats with thick clay walls. In its time, the Tafilalt was one of the most productive regions of all the Sahara, renowned especially for the succulence of its dates. Walter Harris noted that large quantities of Tafilalt dates were shipped by Fassi merchants to the drawing rooms of late Victorian London, and so important are dates to the local economy that they have become known simply as *et-thamr*, the fruit.

As the road swooped down towards the river, I could hear once again the singing of birds and the laughing of children – this was exactly as I had imagined oases to be. I stopped at the first village, a sleepy collection of secretive *pisé* buildings called Oulad-Shahkh. It was the kind of place that, even outside the month of Ramadan, always looks as though it's only just woken up, still yawning and rubbing the sleep from its eyes. The two village stores, one a tobacconist, the other a general store emblazoned with the universal red and white legend of that a certain soft drink, were both shuttered, as were the doors and windows of the other buildings. At times, Ramadan was to make my hunt for fresh supplies extremely difficult. On the left hand side of the road stood the crumbling ruins of a small orange fort, beyond which a solitary hop-pole awaited the July barley harvest. Mercedes service taxis zoomed past, horns blaring, and dogs barked in response. Further up the road, beside a scree of rocks and boulders, sat the squat, white-tiled *koubba* mausoleum of some ancient *marabout*. The dome of the *koubba* symbolises heaven, and its cube-like interior, earth. An elderly lady slipped out from its entrance, and for the few seconds in which she did not notice my staring, her face seemed to radiate an expression of supreme spirituality. She was dressed in a pale blue robe and a voluminous black shawl, with which she briskly covered her face on seeing me.

Because of their veils, René Caillié found it impossible to describe the women of the Tafilalt: 'when out of doors they have the appearance of an uncouth mass,' he complained. The Qur'an advises men:

> say to the believing women that they should lower their gaze and guard their modesty; that they should not display their beauty... that they should draw their veils over their bosoms... and that they should not strike their feet in order to draw attention to their hidden ornaments.

In theory, those who fail to do this face public disapproval (or worse). By contemporary Islamic standards, though, Moroccan society is remarkably liberal in terms of religion, and women veiled from head to toe in haiks and *hijab* veils are very much a minority among a people who generally prefer the gaudy glory of shimmery kaftans. The Tafilalt is the exception that proves the rule, for this oasis, along with the isolated M'zab region of the Algerian Sahara, played host in the 8th and 9th centuries to the Kharijite heresy.

The Kharijites began in typical Berber fashion as fanatical religious anarchists, and rejected political government altogether saying that all authority should come from Allah and Allah alone. Like all extreme idealists, in time their uncompromising stance softened to assume a rather more practical basis, and came to embrace political ideas as well. Early in the 8th century, the Kharijites revolted against an early version of the poll tax – the *jizya* – which in theory was a form of 'protection fee' extracted only from non-Muslim subjects, a stipulation which the first Arab governors of the Maghreb chose to ignore at their peril. Shortly afterwards, in the year 740, the Tafilalt underwent a general Kharijite rebellion following the assassination of a particularly rapacious Arab governor. He had specialised in selling his subjects to slavers in distant corners of the Muslim Empire. Although Kharijitism faded within a century or two, its legacy has remained most visibly in the veils that the women are obliged to wear. Indeed, in the M'zab, women must turn their backs on any males that happen to pass them by, and are forbidden to leave the walled confines of their desert cities. Without having to go to such extremes, there is a great deal to be said in favour of wearing haiks and *hijab* veils (*hijab*, incidentally, also means a written charm or talisman – a protection). If one accepts the notion that all men have the potential to rape or be unfaithful, heavy gowns and veils have the remarkable propensity of reducing even the most voluptuous of bodies to mere anonymous bundles of cloth, of which, unless one is a particularly spectacular pervert, there is nothing even faintly attractive. As Dhou'l Rhoummah, the 'Last Bedouin Poet' who died in the 8th century, lamented:

Among all the garments, that God confound the veil!
    for so long as we live, it shall be a plague on the young.
It hides from us the beautiful, so that we cannot not see,
    and disguises the ugly to lure us into fallacy.[5]

The old lady rounded a corner and disappeared, leaving me alone save for the crazy workaholic ants and irksome flies. I cycled on. Here and there a chorus of frogs or toads joined the incessant buzzing of the locusts and grasshoppers. A lone sand-racer dashed across the road, narrowly missing my front tyre. I turned around to see it and another lizard sat gawping at me from the trunk of an old gnarled fig tree.

I passed a succession of evocatively named villages and *ksour*: Ksar Jorf, the Castle on the Cliff; Sidi-Bouabdillah, a hamlet founded by a saint called 'Father of Allah's Slave'; Oulad-Aïssa, the Sons of Aïssa; Aït-Amira, Amira's Children; Zaouïa-Jedida, the New Monastery; and Douira, the Gathering of Tents. Shortly after Maadid, the first exclusively Arab *ksar* of the Tafilalt (and thus somewhat isolated amidst the Tafilalt's Berber majority), is Erfoud, the modern capital of the oasis. Situated at the southern edge of the Tafilalt – some eighty kilometres from Er-Rachidia – the town was built by the French in the 1920s to coordinate their attempts to subdue this particularly troublesome region. The French, though, were kept at bay in Erfoud until 1931, prevented by the tribes of the Tafilalt from advancing any further to the north (the French had come from the south, via Algeria). The Tafilalt, like the Rif and Atlas, has a proud reputation for revolt and independence (of which the Kharijites were probably the first manifestation). By far the most famous example of this is the Alaouite dynasty itself, to which King Hassan II belongs. Originally from the Filal district of Arabia (hence Tafilalt, which in Berber means 'Sons of Filal'), the dynasty was founded early in the 17th century by Moulay Ali Sherif, self-styled King of Tafilalt. The dynasty became established throughout Morocco under the rule of his son, Moulay er-Rachid, usurping the Saadians in 1668. The history of the Alaouites, however, is speckled, for although they claim the honour of having finally dislodged the Portuguese, in the 20th century their rule was to see the almost total colonisation of Morocco. Yet, everywhere in the Tafilalt, people proudly pulled me aside to tell me that King Hassan himself was born in their very own village, a touching charade that was repeated on at least three separate occasions.

Erfoud itself, as is to be expected, is a pretty desultory kind of place. I was scarcely surprised to see that the French had tried to liven the place up by introducing eucalypti, but even these looked less than happy in their surrogate environment. After Erfoud the valley sides began to recede, and before long, what little remained of the river Ziz was snaking its way across open desert, for the most part too saline to permit cultivation. Henceforth, all vegetation, even beside the river, was once more to disappear: recent droughts had taken their toll. Less than a century ago, travellers to the Tafilalt mentioned an abundance of antelope and gazelle (hence the name of the river). Nowadays one would be considered very lucky indeed to see even a single specimen.

Tafilalt was once also renowned for the very fine fleece and hides of its native sheep. I saw not one, and I could not imagine how even a solitary flock could nowadays survive without devouring the precious crops needed for human consumption. The worsening situation has not been helped by the spread of *bayoud*, a disease that afflicts date palms and kills them within a year. I saw many trees that were virtually decapitated, merely trunks striking ignobly into the sun-blanched sky. In places, I could count the trees on the fingers of one hand – and then they too disappeared, leaving only a few scrawny and windblown acacia, tamarisk and dusty clumps of oleander, interspersed now and then with brittle spiny shrubs and yellow sand drifts. Everywhere, the numerous ruined *ksour* and frondless palm trees reminded me that the desert will always be king.

Of all, perhaps the greatest reminder of mankind's precarious tenure in the desert is the city of Sijilmassa – 20 kilometres south of Erfoud – whose ruins lie half-buried under great sheets of sand. The erstwhile capital of the Tafilalt, and in its time one of grandest of all Morocco, Sijilmassa was founded on the site of an ancient Roman city in the year 707 by Musa ibn Nusair, one of the Umayyad conquerors of Morocco. Situated (at that time) at the head of the Tafilalt, it soon acquired a position of great importance on the trans-Saharan caravan routes, for it was the southernmost outpost of the Maghreb el-Aqsa, a place through which all merchants and traders from the Sudan had to pass. The city was quick to exploit the lucrative rewards of this trade, and until the Middle Ages, it grew immeasurably wealthy on the heavy tributes and taxes it extracted from the caravans. The trade was indeed a rich one: slaves (including euneuchs and virgins), ostrich plumes, ivory, the horns of unicorn (probably rhinoceros), exotic woods and hides, copper, gum arabic, spices and, above all, gold. In the 8th century, the Arab geographer and astronomer al-Fazari noted that across the Sahara lay a kingdom called Ghana, a country which he called 'the Land of Gold.' Al-Fazari's contemporary, the historian Ibn Abd al-Hakam, is the first to have made mention of the trade in gold, when, in 734, an expedition returned to the Maghreb bearing 'a considerable quantity of gold'. By the 10th century, Sijilmassa had become well known as regarded that precious metal, and was mentioned in this respect by many geographers. Among the more notable ones were: al-Masudi (whose historical encyclopaedia was entitled *Meadows of Gold*); his near contemporary Ibn Haukal; the 12th century Iberian Moor, al-Idrisi; and Yaqut (1179-1229), who had been sold as a slave to a merchant of another great city of that time, Baghdad.

So great were the riches of Sijilmassa that it soon acquired a notorious reputation for greed and vice, and in consequence was sacked both by the puritanical Almoravids, and their successors, the Almohads. In spite of these set-backs, the city continued to thrive, not least because Morocco controlled the salt mines in the heart of the Sahara, and therefore a commodity that, in West Africa, was at times worth quite literally its weight in gold. But gold must be treated with respect: like wine, it is a good servant but a bad master. In Sijilmassa, it seems that gold eventually became the master, and in the 15th century, the heavily taxed nomads wrought their revenge by sacking the city. In 1818, Sijilmassa's demise was completed with its total destruction. Even the rank vegetation and weeds that once covered its ruins have now disappeared, and only a legend of a great buried treasure persists to the present day.

A few miles from the ruins rises Rissani, a city that has fared rather better than its neighbour. As a somewhat romantic place, Rissani did not disappoint me. Despite the hungry carrion crows and evil-eyed ravens that were perched on the mud walls of Moulay Ismaïl's *ksar*, Rissani exuded an oddly attractive aura. Beside the old city walls and its monumental *babs*, there were donkey carts, pink sand, blue sky, and black women dressed in black haiks. Men, too, wore in black robes, and sauntered about in face-mufflers and turbans, worn in theory for religious reasons but more practically to keep out the hot desert air and to keep in precious moisture. The face-mufflers are also said to protect the soul, for the soul is equated by nomads with breath.

Several souks (one held in honour of Moulay Ali Sherif) are held each week, even during Ramadan, when Berbers of the Aït-Hasilbiyod tribe come in from the desert to trade. There are marble trinkets; dates graded according to sweetness, dryness and texture that are weighed on makeshift scales hung from walking sticks; men squatting like strange dwarves in heavy jellabas hawking aquatic fossils that date back over 350 million years; small coloured glass beads called Mauritanian Gemstones that purport to be Phoenician; and jewellery en masse – gold and silver necklaces, bangles and filigree earrings, all of which are sold by weight. Other stalls – mainly aimed at the few tourists that hang about waiting for rides to Erg Chebbi – are laid out with rock crystals and geodes, semi-precious gemstones and 'desert roses'. Elsewhere, quack doctors exhalted the virtues of gazelle horns, lizards (dead or alive), dried birds and hundreds of herbs.

To digress: I had the pleasure, in Chefchaouen, of meeting two quacks. I was sat outside the cafe as two suspicious men with nervous, fleeting glances had stumbled past. My gaze followed them past the iron-and-plyboard tables, past the trolley that belonged to the sweet-and-cigarette vendor, past the crumbling vine-twisted archway of the ancient caravanserai, around the mountain of firewood destined for the *medina's* Turkish bath, and up the short cobbled incline that lead to the flea-ridden pension in which I was ensconced. At the time, there was nothing particularly remarkable in this, except that the shorter of the duo – fat, Teutonic-looking, bald but for sideburns and goatee, and clad in Chelsea boots, dark shades and rawhide jacket – was pushing a wheelbarrow, its jagged and lumpy contents concealed inside coarse hessian sackcloth.

The next morning, when ambling still drowsy back from an eathouse that sold only *baisa*, I saw them again. Beside the arid fountain in the centre of the square, the two strangers had unfurled a bewildering array of cardboard boxes, phials and bottles, anonymous cellophane parcels, bundles of twigs and roots, and a host of other enigmatic items. It was about 8 o'clock, yet they had attracted quite a crowd: schoolchildren on their way to school, shopkeepers with nothing else to do but wait, a few hardy regulars from the cafe, bored policemen, and a gaggle of Berber housewives on their way to market.

The couple's presence was announced with a homemade PA rig, which distorted the taller man's voice via the combination of car battery, camera tripod, and a tin baking tray to which was affixed a small loudspeaker. Of course, the amplification that this system provided was infinitely more useful in attracting attention than in faithfully reproducing the salesman's finely honed patter. With a conviction that would put an evangelist to shame, the taller man exhalted the virtues of camel teeth, of lizards fresh from the desert, and of a red powder that looked uncannily like soil. The quacks liked to call themselves 'ambulant medical specialists', although I suspected that the ambulant nature of their profession had a deal to do with avoiding erstwile customers...

They travelled the length and breadth of the Rif mountains hawking spurious potions and panaceas with which they claimed to be able to cure anything from heartburn to heartache. Their farago was a child's dream of the heavenly grotesque: various amulets and dessicated hearts, goat hooves for baldness, ground-up ferrets for depression, seeds, shrivelled barks and twigs, mouldy roots and phials of holy water... rare and expensive hoopoe feathers to guard against evil spirits, bags of desert rock salt and alum, various gall and bladder stones, strange growths, dessicated leeches, fragments of tortoise shell, and dried chameleon (not only an antidote to snake bite but an aphrodisiac too).

Well, I say *two* quacks, but in fact (as far as the punters were concerned) there was only one. The other (the Teuton) played the stooge. For the ruse to work (which unfailingly it did) the quacks were obliged to stay at least two nights in the host-town, to give the stooge time enough to enact a miraculous recovery from whatever ailment he pretended to be suffering from. But no more than two nights: their patients were rather less prone to miracles than themselves!

That evening, as I returned to the hotel, the taller quack – Nimri – simply grabbed me by the waist and bundled me into his room. At its centre (the only space not taken up by bed, bedside table, stooge or wheelbarrow) stood a large earthenware cauldron in which a goatmeat stew was bubbling. 'Hallo Nazarene!' I felt myself lurching across the room as an overly friendly hand struck my back. 'You are my friend,' Nimri stated emphatically. I was introduced to the stooge with effusive bonhomie and much-prolonged clasping of hands, before Nimri filled a plastic tumbler with a murky brick-brown fluid from a grubby jerrycan, and handed it to me.

Nimri, for professional reasons, pretended to be Indian, apparently to give him more credibility, and sported a voluminous turban of gold-laced white silk worn Hindu-style. To his credit, he did indeed attain a certain level of self-importance, and had even grown a long bushy beard for the part. If, however, one dared look closer, tiny scraps of past repasts could be seen clinging desperately from his chin, and his noble silk turban turned out to be little more than rayon. His breath, too, was rather less than saintly – an inebriating piledriver of a geyser reeking of cheap Spanish whisky, the stale deathbreath of filterless Casa Sport cigarettes, and *ashashin* opium juice. Nimri also possessed a slight squint (whether permanent or else self-abuse-induced, was hard to tell) though he was so tall that the average Moroccan would never get near enough to notice.

Nimri did all the talking – in a blend of pidgin French and English mixed up with Arabic and Berber patois. Despite the limitations of language, conversation was easy, fuelled as it was with copious amounts of alcohol, the evil juice, and at times wildly violent gestures in the universal speaktalk of sign language. Nimri was *the* male Shéhérazade if ever there was one: smooth- and double-talking, beguiling, and taken to utter the most preposterous untruths with all semblance of heartfelt sincerity. He was a pedlar of sweet lies, fifth rate buys, bane of gullible lives, harlot, conman, and first-class graduate from the university of charlatanery.

When the stew was almost ready, Nimri produced a small paper wrapper containing a Day-Glo orange powder, and duly pronounced it to be saffron. When I read him the wrapper which said 'Artificial Food

Colouring' he exclaimed 'Akh, my boy. Yes, yes, but at least it gives the *colour* of saffron, and that, my friend, is all that counts.'

Supper over, the stooge stood up and solemnly handed me an illustrated tome on the herbs and spices of the Maghreb, followed by a hefty volume on Saharan reptiles, both in Latin. As I was perusing the books, the two quacks fell suddenly silent. As I looked up, Nimri, bang on cue, produced a wallet from behind his back with obviously much-rehearsed dramatic effect. From it he extracted a battered sheet of oft-folded paper, scrawled all over with meaningless characters.

'Shush, I beg your silence,' he demanded, with as much aplomb as his inebriated state would permit. I was handed a Qur'an to swear on.

'*Bismillah al-Rahman al-Rahim.* In the Name of Allah, the Benefi-cent, the Merciful...'

'*Marabout's hijab,*' he whispered hoarsely. 'It will bring phenom-enally, nay, miraculously good *baraka.*'

'But *marabouts* are all dead!' I protested.

'Oh, of course,' said the other, and apologised profusely for Nimri's drunkenness. 'You see, Nimri's is a *maraboutic* family.'

'Ah, I see,' I said. 'So when exactly did this *marabout* write the *hijab*?' There was an uncomfortable silence, so I helped them along by suggesting that it must have been a long time ago (though the paper on which the charm was written was lined).

'Oh yes, a *very* long time ago,' they agreed readily. 'It's written in sacred human... no, no, um, sacred bird blood,' they said: parrot, budgerigar or golden eagle. Or maybe stork... (all true charms require the validation bestowed by sacrifice)

Much as humour is often the surest path to a woman's heart, it is also the smoothest lubricant of jealously-guarded pockets and purses. Sometimes, when watching Nimri and sidekick working the crowd, I had the impression of watching life enacted as theatre, or theatre as life: to sell, to influence, to amuse, to make a living – the real theatre of real life. I sensed that the quacks were consciously playing on (and enjoy-ing) the fact that they were charlatans and that everyone else knew it too. At times, it was as though they would deliberately reveal the nakedness of all their sham-scam glory, so as to soften the act, to summon an element of realism, of truth to the travesty, of honesty, before once more, with the inimitable eloquence of the skilled Arab orator, reeling in those wavering minds, exhorting and demonstrating, wheeling his arms and rolling his eyes, hinting at magical powers, at saintly effluvia, to deceive them once more into believing, if only for a few short (but lucrative) moments, into believing that all that Nimri said and claimed for his panaceas was as true as the venerable Qur'an itself.

Belief always requires an illusion.

Holding his hands up for attention: 'This, in sight of Almighty Allah, I swear by Muhammad and his gracious wife (Allah and the Prophet be praised for the Miracle of Their Creation), by Allah this is no *ordinary* length of string, oh no! No, no, no, indeed not! Is is a fact – and I know that you, my friends and fellow countrymen of this God-blessed nation of ours, of ours! – you, my friends, blessed of Allah's most magnificent virtues, that you are able to tell mere charlatanery from what is more real, indeed indisputably true, as true as the soil upon which I stand before you today, humble servant of Allah that I am, as true as the blue heavens under which today I say to you, that this [and with a sudden shout, which dwindles to a confiding whisper] this, ladies and gentlemen, *this is no ordinary piece of string...*'

Sacred string indeed, to tie around one's loved ones' wrists, or else round a barren bedpost, or to secure the plenitude of one's purse. Yes, even only a short piece of sacred string could be put to a hundred good uses. And all for a mere ten dirhams. Of course, Moroccans aren't any more or any less gullible than we are. It was the act and the dream-spinning patter, rather than the goods themselves, for which the clientele gladly parted with their money. A charm or potion, even a humble aspirin, is worthless if no effort has gone into selling it, if the chasm of credibility has not been spanned, even if only an instant, by the bewitching charm of the quack. The charms that people took home were in fact portions of the quack's own charm: his charisma, his aura, his *baraka*.

I bought the fake charm for twenty-two dirhams and half a packet of cigarettes, and thus guided by Lady Providence, was invited to divine the names of the winning horses at the next day's meeting in Tangier.

CHAPTER FIVE

THE MOROCCAN SAHARA

> geographers ... crowd into edges of their maps parts of the
> world which they do not know about, adding notes in the
> margin to the effect, that beyond lies nothing but the sandy
> deserts full of wild beasts.
>
> *Plutarch*, Lives: Theseus, *c. 100 AD*

Retracing my steps a short distance to the roadstead of El-Betorni –
known only for its gas station, the last one for over 150 miles – I turned
off the main road to join Route 3454, leading ninety kilometres due west
to the oasis of Alnif.

About ten kilometres from Rissani, abandoned sand-swept terrain
began to force itself upon the landscape: largely flat, sandstone plains
strewn with larger boulders and quartzite rocks that shimmered
blindingly in the sunlight. The little remaining vegetation faded rapidly
away, like a match that had once flared, bright and healthy, but had then
hissed and spluttered and finally lain still, sheathed only in a thin veil of
harsh but warm, lingering smoke. The lay and atmosphere of the land
changed markedly. No longer the lush irrigation and tightly spaced
inhabitations of the Ziz gorges and the Tafilalt, but a vast and empty
aspect, illuminated with a harsh waxen light, naked and open to all the
ravages of the desert. The reflected glare of the sun, especially, was
much as I imagined my vision to be on waking from a coma: a complete
white-out. This was a land of large but indistinct shapes and forms, with
few details or visual points of reference. There was an overriding
impression of a vast infinity.

The village of Oulad-Saidena is a small cluster of adobe dwellings
that straddles the brackish waters of the river Rheris. This far south,
though, the river – like the Ziz – is no more than a chalky scree of rocks
and pebbles, dry, dusty and dead. I had my dinner in the roofless
confines of a ruined house, lapped all around with a thick solemn blanket
of bleached sand and rocks that strangled a few sorrowful clumps of
parched wheat. By now the sun had been overhead for most of the day,

and for the first time I began to appreciate the difference that wearing the *cheche* made both to my body temperature and my liquid intake, for almost as soon as I removed it, streams of sweat began to roll off my brow and trickle past my mouth. In less than half an hour I had quaffed a litre and a half of water, and yet I was doing nothing more strenuous than eating.

Soon after the village the asphalt road ended abruptly, giving way instead to a faintly rutted track consisting of small dark rocks and coarse grey sand, through which the spines of desert-loving thistle protruded. All around me now, the remaining islands of cultivation vanished for good, leaving only a thin scattering of yellowed scrub grass and fragile bushes. I swallowed my apprehension. To the south stretched a vast and denuded *hammada*, a rocky plateau blackened through centuries of relentless heat and abrasion. To the north and my right rippled a sea of dirty beige sand and rock, beyond which the horizon was cut short by a looming mass of dust. To the west, where I was heading, the first eroded foothills of the ancient Djebel Ougnat rose from the desert floor, grotesquely contorted and twisted by some violent prehistoric eruptions. For the most part, the hills were a mass of lava flows, blackened quartzites, exposed reefs of grey granite, glossy mica schists, and sharp shards that cut through rubber and flesh (the rubber of my tyres and the flesh of my legs and arms) like a butcher's cleaver. In places, the stone and grit had oxidised to a dirty red, which shone obscenely in the glare of the sun. The wind rattled like rhonchus through the outstretched embrace of brittle acacia.

Many writers are tempted to compare such desert scenes with Dante's Inferno: hellish places of burning and bubbling sand under blazing mineral skies that one half expects to burst into flame. But however attractive this image may be, for the most part I found that the desert gave a sensation of having passed beyond these fiery cataclysms. The overriding impression was of a land deceased, a dust-blown corpse grown brittle through the ages, neither Heaven nor Hell, a land devoid of all colour and purpose. It is difficult to describe my feelings on being immersed for the first time in the immense silence of this strange and desolate land, the danger being that whatever I write will sound too simple, hackneyed or romanticised. The latter especially I dislike, but there are few other ways of describing the simple fact that I was delirously happy! I was happy – I suppose to my surprise – simply to be in the desert at all. To sense again the eternal fascination of the unknown. To relive my childhood dreams of innocence and naivity, and to resurrect for a while my belief in a world where wishes *do* come true, where fantasy *is* fact, and where dreams *are* reality.

The lone trail rolled on endlessly as I daydreamed, with still no sign of the absent asphalt road (in fact the asphalt was not to reappear for another 350 miles). Cycling was predictably sluggish, not least because I feared damaging the bike over the rocks were I to pedal any faster. As the sun began its westering, the hills drew near, and the sun sank beneath the ravaged peaks in hazy cascades of scarlet and violet, deepening to the blue of veiny blood, before turning still darker shades of purple in the chill of the desert night. I settled beside a low sand drift crested with a couple of thorn bushes, under which (it later became apparent) lived a colony of giant darkling beetles. Like many desert inhabitants, the beetles have evolved a peculiar adaptation to the elements: over the ages, their wings have fused with their bodies to trap a protective sac of air, an ingenious device that both provides insulation and prevents evaporation.

I awoke a few hours later, shivering, my fingers numb. I stumbled out of my Gore-tex bivouac into a sand squall to fetch my sleeping bag, only to tread on one of the beetles, which crunched with a sickening finality as the fat crescent moon flashed one of its obscene smiles across the dirty sky.

I reached the sleeping village of Mecissi at around midday, having trudged for what seemed like ages over an increasingly bumpy track and the dustblown Tikkert-n-Ouchchanem, the Jackals' Pass. A battered signpost announced the fact that Alnif was only 37km away, which pleased me no end. Even on a bad road, this should take at most two hours to complete. As I pored over my map, a large number of inquisitive children gathered around me. Unlike adults, children are exempted from the obligations of Ramadan, and in consequence they were to be almost exclusively the only people I was to see over the following weeks. It was strange to travel alone through a land populated only by children, creeping stealthily like a gold-feverish explorer through the tombs of Pharaonic Egypt. Desert children were a mixed bunch. Some wore goofy grins and gawky sneers like those of stranded walruses. Many others had blank faces that registered only incomprehension. Others looked sad and weary, often seeming to have lived through as much as a forty year old. Many were barefoot. Others wore battered plastic sandals. When trousers were worn, their flies would often be left undone (mothers, who would undoubtedly have noticed such things, were, of course, fast asleep). It disturbed me to notice that many children were cross-eyed, or blind. There was one such boy in Mecissi, who never knew exactly where to turn his head when being addressed. He was about four years old, had a snotty nose, badly flaking skin (scabies?), and had had his hair shaved off to avoid lice. For some reason, he was constantly being kicked by his two sisters. The elder wore an unusual patchwork dress, considered by Berbers to radiate good *baraka*, but by Arabs, bad. The other sister was about ten years old, and had much darker skin than the other children. She was not yet old enough to have to tie her hair back, and so instead wore it tousled and froppy over her forehead, a bit like a rag doll. She was dressed in a frilly but ragged lilac nightie, and held her hands square on her hips like an irate school teacher. In return for having helped me draw water from the village well, she demanded that I take her photograph. Meeting children invariably occasioned this request. Whereas adults (who know better) cover their faces or look away from the camera (for it is believed that the camera steals away a portion of one's soul), the children unfailingly stared straight into its evil eye, often displaying fingered 'V' signs as though in defiance.

I left Mecissi minus my last two bags of sweets, and ploughed on – quite literally in parts – through a barren landscape flanked on either side by hills and escarpments strewn black with basalt and pumice. The going was slow and the heat blistering, although my *cheche* relieved the worst of the midday heat to give my sunburnt face some respite. For most of the day, I was followed by a slight tailwind, though it served little purpose except to swirl up little *ebliss* sand spouts, at times lending quite a surreal appearance to the desert.

By mid afternoon I eventually caught up with the only person I'd seen since leaving Mecissi: an elderly gentleman swathed from head to toe in white linen. With considerable difficulty, he was pushing a moped laden with water-filled jerry cans and so I stopped beside him to ask whether he needed any help. After a lot of improvised sign language, I worked out that he needed me to kick-start the motor. Pointing to my legs, he mumbled *'bon courage'*, a phrase that every Moroccan seems to know. For a good few minutes I struggled to get even a splutter from the damn thing, until the old man helpfully pointed out that the ignition lead had come loose. The motor rattled into action and the man beamed broadly. He then shook both my hands with a steely vigour, and zoomed off and out of sight over a nearby hillock. I cycled on a little further till I came to a fork in the track. To the south I caught another glimpse of the old man disappearing over another, more distant sand hill, while to the west the *piste* clambered on past the fringes of what looked like a palm-grove, and then up into the hills. I took the former, hoping to run a short-cut around Alnif.

Before long I came to a small settlement hidden in the depression of dry river gully, its course marked only by a thin line of ragged shrubs and stunted trees. Though my map made no mention of this place, I cycled on regardless, hotly pursued by a gang of over thirty children who added the improbable 'gateaux' to the litany of the more usual demands! The opposite lip of the depression bore the track up onto the edge of a vast, wind-scoured *hammada*, strewn with a very fine layer of red stones that made cycling almost as easy as on tarmac. To the south there were no longer any hills, giving the impression that I could see half way across the desert. All around, the horizon shimmered in the heat. To say that there was not a single blade of grass or a solitary clump of bushes is no exaggeration. There was only a flat brick-brown expanse, the horizon, and the murky grey dome of the sky, over which, at its very zenith, the sun laughed mercilessly.

I cycled along increasingly hard-to-follow tracks, choosing whenever the track divided, the branch that seemed to be the most worn and frequently used. Most of the time, this was hardly at all. After an hour or so, a blood-red silhouette resolved itself from the mirages to my right – the monumental battlements of Alnif, or so I thought. The sight cheered me considerably, for I seemed to have got the knack of desert navigation, but the *hammada* soon gave way to an area of soft and in places very deep sand, which got me worrying. However beautiful to my unaccustomed eye the sand may have been, it necessitated much walking, something which very quickly dampened my confidence as well as making me tired. Surely this could not be right, I thought, for the land here seemed impassable even to the most rugged of vehicles. It was two hours later still when a brazier in a Land Rover informed me that I had somewhat misjudged my 'short cut'. If I continued southwards, he said, I would not reach another settlement for over a thousand miles. In consequence, Alnif was now at least another forty kilometres away, and I was advised to turn back and aim for that beautiful red silhouette that I had seen, for it was not Alnif but an escarpment beside the much nearer village of Achbarou (which, like many settlements, was unmarked on my map). I felt like a right fool, but the really stupid thing was that, even with the benefit of experience, I was to repeat the same mistake again in the not too distant future.

When eventually I reached Alnif – at around six in the evening – I was tired and frustrated, and in no mood to stop and talk (my mood hadn't been helped by being robbed by Achbarou's children of all my spare spokes). Situated in the valley of a seasonal stream that flows south into the desert from in-between the twin ranges of Djebel Ougnat and the grantite mass of Djebel Sarhro, and enclosed by a narrow belt of dusty palm-groves, the oasis of Alnif was a disappointment. As far as I could see, there were no pools of clear water, nor were there many songbirds to be heard, and the place had little of the feeling of warmth and sanctuary that I had expected from a Saharan oasis (in several instances, it now seems to me, I seemed to make up my mind about a place within minutes of arriving, and only rarely was humble enough to change my mind. It was as though I was too impatient to give time to places whose initial impressions I did not like).

As I wheeled the bike along the last stretch of *piste* into town, the wind picked up. With it came the sand, first in small gusts, but then gradually stronger and harder, stinging the exposed parts of my body and filling my eyes with dust. A small herd of goats being driven by a young Berber girl grew restless, and it soon became apparent that even the few birds that did reside in the village had stopped singing. The crowd of onlookers that I'd attracted scattered for the shelter of their doorways, leaving only the wind and myself in the street. Clambering back onto my bike, I made my way slowly down the gentle slope of a gully on the far side of town, my shirt flapping loudly in the wind. The soldier at the road-block waved me through with uncommon haste, though he betrayed a faint sneer as an unexpected gust of wind threatened to blow me off my bike. Now the palms were thrashing about wildly in and in the near distance the last trees of the oasis became obscured in a mist of sand and dust. Soon I reached the dry river bed itself, spattered pink with oleander, a riverine bush said to have been created by Fatima's tears on learning that her husband Ali had taken a second wife. The remaining daylight faded rapidly in the face of the oncoming storm, so I wheeled the bike down and into the *wadi* [a dry river bed]. I settled and tried to write my diary, but hardly had I put pen to paper than a large bank of nitrogenous clouds rolled in from the north, lashing out at the hills with forked tongues of light. The onset of the storm itself was sudden and ferocious, forcing me to rush about covering and securing my belongings. Then, to my utter astonishment, it began to rain. Not for long, but it rained nonetheless. Warm, dusty, Saharan rain.

* * *

I opened my eyes to see two dozen camels encircling me. They emitted an unearthly chorus of whale-like groans, and were staring at me in much the same way as I must have been gazing at them: pure astonishment. For my part – once I'd got over the surprise – I was struck not only by their otherwordly groaning and peculiar, almost condescending, expressions of superiority, but by their great height. Their long spindly legs only added to this impression of hauteur, being improbably thin except at the hooves where they flared to ̣semble the buttresses of rainforest trees. On their rumps they bore the brands of their owner, who will often allow his herd to wander freely throughout a day's grazing, knowing full well that they will return in the evening for the food and water that he alone provides. Having said this, I once saw a very red-faced nomad with streaming blue robes dashing across a rocky valley side in pursuit of one of his camels, but every time he got close, the animal bolted. Finally the poor man gave up the ghost of the chase and trudged forlornly back to the herd, hoping, I suppose, that the beast would get lonely without its companions!

First introduced into the Sahara in the 2nd century, the camel is, of course, the key to man's survival in the desert. Indeed, not just survival. Without the camel, there would never have been trade across the Sahara, and cities such as Sijilmassa, Carthage, Timbuctoo, Baghdad, Jiddah, Khartoum, Fès and Marrakesh, Damascus and Cairo, would never have grown as wealthy as they did. The camel's ability to survive without water is prodigious. With a stomach capacity of sixty gallons, and a limited ability to combine oxygen and hydrogen to make water, a healthy dromedary can cover over 40km a day for between five and eight days in high summer without drinking. In winter, this capacity doubles. The camel has other adaptations, too, to help it survive. Its toes, for instance, are webbed and hairy to facilitate walking on sand, and the hump for which it famous is used to store fat, which can be converted to energy when required. What I found most incredible (and hard to believe, it must be said) is that camels can run faster than horses. Perhaps there is some truth in this, for the name 'dromedary' comes from the Greek *dromos* meaning 'running'.

For so long indispensable, in recent decades the importance of the camel has suffered drastic decline. The shift in world trade routes and requirements is one cause, but much more damaging has been the advent of Land Rovers, of cheap shipping and of airfreight, which has rendered obsolete the caravans of old. It was sad to think that given another hundred years or so, perhaps even the camel itself will have become an endangered species in this desert.

The air hung still and warm. There was no sign of yesterday's storm. The town of Zagora, one hundred and sixty kilometres away along the southeastern fringes of Djebel Sarhro (via the village of Tazzarine) was my next goal. For a while, I kidded myself that the distance might be possible within the day. The *hammada* was good for cycling, and although some larger rocks and boulders were littered about, they lay, by and large, outside the ruts of the *piste* itself. Consequently, and for the first time since descending the High Atlas towards Er-Rachidia, I was able to keep the bike in top gear. I was also saved a few kilometres by two camel herders, who showed me a well-worn short cut around the village of Aït-Saadane, a couple of hours from Alnif. Shortly afterwards, I passed a truck that had beached itself on a large sand drift. It was a reminder that good fortune, especially in the desert, is rarely destined to last.

After rounding Aït-Saadane, the quality of the track deteriorated, once more becoming a twisted carpet of fist-sized rocks and stones that spun and slid as I tried to keep both my balance and my speed. Over confident, I misjudged a large trough in the track that jolted the bike so violently that a couple of water bottles were sent flying. At the same instant I heard a great crack, and to my horror turned to see one of my rear panniers lying on the ground beside the shattered flasks. The other pannier dangled precariously from the rack: three out of four 'guaranteed unbreakable' plastic hooks had snapped straight in two. Several minutes of anger and angst ensued, until I remembered that my otherwise useless anorak had a thick lace cord around the waist, which I used with a couple of bungy ropes to re-attach the panniers. I counted myself lucky to have been able to surmount this difficulty, and from then on I cycled at a rather more cautious pace.

Snaking through a ghostly village of mud huts and scrawny goats, the *piste* rounded a low col only to drop down onto yet another *hammada*, equally devoid of life. Only a few hardy trees, stubbornly rooted in the rocky ground, disturbed the almost moonlike desolation of this land. And so the day wore on, mostly without excitement. It was only late in the afternoon that I reached Tazzarine, tired, frustrated, and faced with the daunting prospect of still one hundred kilometres of rugged *piste* to cover until Zagora. Instead of entering the town – I still had enough water and supplies to last a day or two, and my makeshift repairs seemed to be holding – I turned south at a bizarre signpost embedded in a dry *wadi*, and began following a series of sandy tracks that in turn followed the river bed. Before long, however, the *wadi* simply disappeared, and so I was left confronted with dozens of tyre traces spreading out in as many directions. The depth of the tracks indicated that only few vehicles had recently passed this way – at least since the last sand storm – which made choosing the 'correct' *piste* somewhat difficult. Ahead of me was a small range of hills that cleaved the southern horizon into east and west. Zagora, I knew, lay to the southwest, but all the tracks veered off eastwards. My map, alas, was woefully useless, although I was beginning to be spared the anguish of consulting it because the ravages of travel and of yesterday's rain were beginning to pulp its edges.

At the small and welcome village of Timganine (unmarked on the map), few people seemed even to have heard of Zagora, whilst those who had all pointed in contradictory directions, which prompted much arguing and discussion amongst themselves. Finally, one of the village elders was summoned to resolve the problem. The *moqqadam* reassured me that I was indeed on the Zagora *piste*, but he advised me to give up cycling and to wait instead for a lift with a travelling merchant. Stupidly (with hindsight) I ignored the *moqqadam's* advice. Throughout the Moroccan Sahara, my stubbornness made me intent on proving that I could manage perfectly well on my own. On seeing my response, the *moqqadam* raised his arms up the sky, and shrugged.

Barely half a kilometre out of the village, and not yet back on the *piste*, the wind stiffened, and for the second time in as many days, the sky grew dark. Tall columns of storm clouds that simply had not been there a few minutes before, reared up and advanced from the western horizon to block out the sun. Before long, half the land was plunged into darkness, save for a few eerie islands of sun-struck desert. Still my stubbornness determined that I would not return to the village... For a moment the clouds became edged with golden glints of fractured sunlight as the low horizon flared in the glowing embers of evening, but then the clouds moved closer still so that all I could see was an oppressively sombre scene in murky shades of brown and black. A distant lick of lightning, then another, lashed out across the darkness, accompanied by dull rumbles that shook the ground and my bones. The wind blew harder, whirling and howling, lashing the desert into a fury of sand and dust – a tumultuous racket over which distant voices from the village, real or imagined, seemed to fade in and out. Soon, the village itself disappeared into the chaotic onslaught of the dust. For a while, this was the limit of the storm: merely a particularly violent sand squall, it seemed. But after ten minutes or so, I looked to the north and saw, to my horror, a simply gigantic wall of sand hurtling towards me. Now the thunder no longer rumbled but roared down in deafening peals, and I watched transfixed like a deer caught by headlights as a tree near the village caught the blue light and burst into flame, only to be swamped by the swirling sand that within seconds had reduced my visibility to only a few feet. Even my bicycle, lying a few yards beside me, was swallowed by the blackness. I cowered under my rubber sleeping mat, hoping to God that the lightning might stay away.

Then... then came the rain, torrential, for twenty minutes falling as mud from the sky. By the time the clouds had passed on and the winds had subsided, the land was left inundated, and for a few moments I seemed to be cast adrift on a vast, inland sea. It was incontestably the most bizarre sight I had ever seen. There was a disturbing stillness to the moist, cloying air, which smelt sickly sweet, of donkey or camel dung. Then, to whoops and yells of exhaltation from the village, the evening sun emerged from under the storm's stranglehold to cast long, drawing shadows across the sand, land and sky intertwined with rainbows. The sand glowed a radiant orange, nurtured under a thick olive-green sky the density and colour of which I would never have imagined possible.

I shivered as I trudged back to the track, only to find that it had been obliterated. The remaining puddles of sweet water drained away through the sand, and everywhere the desert steamed. Cycling, of course, was impossible on the damp sand which clung to the wheels and my feet, and so I walked instead in silence, pausing only to haul the bike out of the deeper drifts in which it often became engulfed. As I walked, the shadows grew longer still, before they merged with the night. After another hour of walking, I came to a sizeable sandy hillock, strewn with black lumps of coarse basalt. I had no idea where I was, nor indeed in which direction I was walking. The wind stiffened once again, and in my sodden clothes I felt cold and pathetic. I cursed the fact that I had not after all followed the advice of the *moqqadam*, and I cursed my own pig-headed stupidity. After a miserable dinner of stale bread and jam, I began restlessly to pace up and down the hillock. A stroke of luck: I saw a distant light. I rubbed my eyes and looked again, but it was still there, stationary, flickering as only oil lamps do. In a rare moment of common sense, I gathered together two mounds of rocks to point like an arrow towards the light, so that I might have something to aim at the following day.

The strategy worked, for in spite of morning revealing nothing but a sandy expanse enclosed by faraway hills and a pale blue sky, the rocks indicated a distant but distinctive mountain, which was to be my guide for the time being. At length, from the peak of a dune I spotted (to my great relief) the small oasis of Tarhbalt, whose outlying palm-groves I reached at around midday. Two elderly men in white robes stared incredulously as I approached. I must have looked like Martian dropping in from Outer Space, for as I drew nearer, one of the men excitedly jabbed his partner's ribs and started gabbling. Our gazes met, and I shouted a greeting, which elicited a couple of wide and childish grins. *Doum* palm saplings rose beside the track, while above, flocks of goldfinch and blue-rollers tumbled deliriously about the waving fronds of date palms. Eucalyptus, sweet-smelling bougainvillea, and syrupy crisscross tracks made up the outskirts of Tarhbalt. Then came a few mud houses with thick walls and iron-grilled windows, and others nearby that had crumbled to dust. A handful of well-trodden donkey tracks led up to Tarhbalt's ancient kasbah, perched at the very top of a hill like the fortresses of medieval Castile or the needlepoint monasteries of the Jura. It was a place replete in an aura of centuries-old custom and tradition, with steep muddy streets, collapsing roof beams and painted wooden doors that had probably been exactly the same over five hundred years ago. The kasbah, it seemed, had been the source of the flickering lights.

The track filed past the kasbah and down the other side of the hill to cross the dried-up Tarhbalt *wadi*. In the middle of it, a gaggle of women stood beside a well, laughing (women always seemed to be laughing beside wells). Crossing over to the other side, the *piste* then took off up the mountain that had been my guide. After about a mile, I lost the posse of children that had been following me, and I found myself alone once more. This mountain, I found out later, was the eastern embrace of Djebel Bani, the southernmost ridge of the Anti Atlas. Stretching for almost a thousand kilometres from east to west, this granite and sandstone range is the longest of all the Anti Atlas. But, unlike the High Atlas, the Anti Atlas is no barrier to the Sahara, because the Anti Atlas *is* the Sahara.

Struggling over ever more broken terrain, I despaired about the condition of my bike. In only two days, I had suffered half a dozen broken spokes, shattered water bottles, snapped pannier hooks and bungy ropes, a broken inner-tube valve, busted lights, and twelve punctures. I was also beginning to run out of water, having for some inexplicable reason not considered this in Tarhbalt. Without my mints – having equally stupidly given them away in Mecissi – my mouth soon felt like sandpaper. Without exception, all these problems had been caused by my own carelessness. With hindsight, I am thankful indeed for the healthy dose of good fortune that guarded me for much of my travels: the fortune that favours fools...

In the mountains, the heat hung heavy, and I tired quickly. The sun banged down as always, and my head began to ache. Sweat stung my eyes, and through my blurred vision, the land shimmered madly. My back and wrists complained as the track clambered inexorably upwards over still more denuded rocks and boulders. In one place, they sheltered tiny flowers, no more than a couple of inches tall, with yellow petals protected with four miniscule needles offering, I thought, no more protection than Don Quixote's buckled lance. Soon after passing the flowers I heard a faint hissing which at first I mistook for a snake. No such luck; one of those pathetic little needles had embedded itself in my front tyre! To compound my frustration, a bottle of skin lotion that I had never used chose this moment to empty its contents all over my sleeping bag. For once, I blamed myself for all my misfortune: 'This is supposed to be a bloody holiday!' I yelled out loud. 'Not some fucking assault course!' If I remember right, I think I called myself a blithering idiot.

The descent was equally diabolical, and the going was correspondingly painful as I hopped the bike down the ledges and boulders. At the foot of the mountain, where I spooked a trio of camels, an impossible hairpin in the track made me realise once and for all that I was not on the proper *piste* to Zagora (I must have missed it by not visiting Tazzarine), because the track was barely wide enough for my bike, let alone a vehicle.

At about mid-afternoon I reached a small and sleepy village snuggled in the lee of a still higher range of mountains. There was no one in sight. Glancing inside one of the clay huts, which turned out to be the general store, I saw five men sprawled asleep on the floor. I coughed. One of the men batted an eyelid, then suddenly jumped upright to stare at me in an almost apologetic fashion. His entire stock consisted of two packets of biscuits, a handful of sweets, some lentils and countless drums of cooking oil (I bought him out but for the last two). He had apparently been waiting five days for a delivery. I was told that Zagora was 43 kilometres away, and as the sun was still high in the sky, I set off with renewed hope and vigour, anxious to reach the town before dusk (why this haste, I never really knew). Repeating the pattern of the last two days, the skies once more gathered ominously in the west, although this time the desert was to remain dry. More disconcerting for me was the bleached goat skull that someone had carefully placed on a pile of bones at the junction of two rocky and uncompromising tracks. Past this worrisome sign, the track once again disappeared, leaving me to pick my way across the ankle-twisting boulders. Everything seemed to be covered in dust, even the few thistles and tussocks of spiny grass. The blustery wind blew cold, waltzing dust devils across the ravines and up the steep canyons. With the clouded sky, and therefore the absence of the sun, I once more found myself without the faintest clue as to my bearing, and at times, I really did feel that I would never escape this labyrinth of rock.

By nightfall I had reached a wide breach overlooking a spacious sand plain. For an instant, I thought that I could make out a minaret and a stilted water tower in a distant corner, but the air was dusty and my eyes were tired, and if I rubbed them the grit from my fingers only made things worse. Worst of all, my food supplies had shrunk to only two tins of oily sardines. I walked the bike down into the valley, and then on for another four hours in the dark, before giving up feeling extremely frustrated, despondent, and somewhat scared. I felt ashamed at having lost my way, but more than anything else, I felt ashamed at my wanting and needing to reach a town, to reach out for the help of other people, to sense my helplessness and inadequacy. I had been humbled, if only for one night.

* * *

One thing that I was to notice throughout the Sahara was that the desert has a particularly ironic, even sadistic, sense of humour. For instance, it is surprising to learn that most tourist deaths in the Sahara are caused not by heat or dehydration, but by flash floods which drown the unfortunate victims. I say this here because, not even a hundred yards from where I had slept, I rounded a low sandy ridge to be confronted with a wide expanse of the colour green. Behind this rose the minaret and water tower that I thought I had glimpsed in the evening. To my left loomed the conical volcanic outcrop of the Djebel Zagora, which I recognised from a postcard I'd bought in Er-Rachidia... Very funny.

I reached the eastern bank of the Oued Drâa – arguably Morocco's longest river (it is seasonal in parts) – through irrigated fields of young barley and millet, interspersed with shadowy clumps of wishbone*doum* palms and small orchards of fig and pomegranite. Here and there, small knots of indigo-robed people stood talking or gazing at the orange soil. Elsewhere, a little girl ran barefoot after a little goat. On both banks of the river, the tasseled fronds of tall date palms fluttered gently in the breeze, struck silver and gold by the morning sun. The area hereabouts is second only to the Tafilalt in renown for its dates – chestnutty, like honey – which were once regularly transported to the slaves working the salt mines in Mali. I gazed at the flowing waters obviously feeling relieved, but (I am a queer fellow sometimes) sensing a kind of anti-climax at the serene beauty of it all. After the last few days, I'd come to expect something rather more stunning and overawing, not just pretty.

Over on the western bank, the mosques of Zagora rose from behind thick battlements of ox-blood clay. Many rooves and walls were adorned with colourful rugs and blankets, hung out for an airing. As elsewhere in the Moroccan Sahara, the older buildings were made of *pisé* bricks and resembled constructions found in Yemen. Their rooves were cornered with distinctive tapering turrets, and their windows were framed with whitewash, presumably to keep their interiors cool. Behind the town the land flattened out once more, giving way to a *hammada* laced with dunes. It is not surprising, given Zagora's strategic position, that the Almoravids chose this site to erect a fortress with which to guard the precious caravan trails to the Sudan.

By the time of the first Christian Crusades, ancient Ghana – and Timbuctoo in particular – had grown prosperous on the trade in gold dust, which was bartered with the Arabs in return for salt from the mines which Morocco controlled. When, in 1324, the vast caravan of the Malian king, Mansa Musa, passed through Cairo en route to Mecca (apparently with over eight thousand retainers) he sold so much gold that the market collapsed and remained depressed for decades after his passing. This show of wealth, of course, only further whetted Morocco's appetite for gold. The golden trade reached its zenith under the Saadian dynasty of the 16th and 17th centuries, a dynasty which had originated in Zagora and the surrounding region of the Drâa. The most glorious period in this epoch was the reign of the sultan Ahmad al-Mansour, annihilator of the Portuguese at the Battle of the Three Kings. Al-Mansour presided over a rarely unified kingdom, and so was able once more to turn Morocco's gaze southwards towards the golden rewards of Timbuctoo. In Zagora, a mock-serious sign for the benefit of tourists depicts a grinning nomad with five camels, and is inscribed 'Tombouctou 52 Jours'.

Having finally disposed of the Portuguese threat in 1578, al-Mansour set about the creation of a professional army untouched by divisive tribal loyalties and disputes. With this in mind, he followed the Almohad precedent of relying on Christian mercenaries, a garrison of which was kept at Zagora. Al-Mansour also cultivated warm relations with England's Queen Elizabeth, and even suggested an Anglo-Moroccan alliance following the defeat of the Spanish Armada. All of this brought military as well as commercial security to his rule, and in the winter of 1590, a four thousand strong expeditionary force set out from Zagora to cross the great desert. Using firearms for the first time in the Sahel, victory came easily over the Songhai Empire (successor to Ghana and Mali), and the major trading centres of Timbuctoo, Gao and Jenne were quickly occupied. Although the mines themselves were never captured, the expedition greatly enriched al-Mansour's coffers. It is said that his first tribute from Timbuctoo consisted of thirty mules laden with gold, a large part of which (in addition to the spoils of the Battle of the Three Kings) he used to decorate Marrakesh's Badi Palace (which was subsequently destroyed by Moulay Ismaïl in a fit of extreme envy).

As a result, al-Mansour's name was to go down in history alongside the title *adh-Dhahabi*, the Golden One.

Not surprisingly, when the Europeans finally gained the upper hand in Africa, they too were attracted to the enigma of the African Eldorado, whose great wealth had further been embellished by such venerated writers as Ibn Batuta and Leo Africanus. It was the account of the latter, especially, that was to capture the collective imaginations of Europe's gentlemanly salons. Leo Africanus had visited Timbuctoo on behalf of the sherif of Fès in 1526, and lyricised in lavish terms on the literally massive wealth of its king, who 'hath many plates and sceptres of gold, some of which weigh 1,300 pounds.' The word 'gold' adorns Leo's description like the call of a hundred sirens, and all agreed that Timbuctoo's houses were tiled with gold. By the close of the Middle Ages, the riches of Timbuctoo had become fabled beyond the imagination:

> A foutre for the world and worldlings base!
> I speak of Africa and golden joys.
>
> Shakespeare, *Henry IV Part II*

To Europeans, Timbuctoo enshrined the essence of mystery. It was a mystery, however, that held a fatal charm for, of the two hundred explorers who set off gold-feverish to cross the Sahara in the 19th century, only thirty-five were to return alive. And not only Europeans perished in the quest for fame and fortune. In 1805, a Moroccan caravan consisting of 2,000 men and 1,800 camels perished of thirst, not a man or beast surviving. The great irony of all this (and another of the desert's jokes) was that when the Europeans finally did manage to return alive from the forbidden city, they reported – to everyone's disbelief and disappointment – that it was in fact nothing more than a large village of mud and straw straddling the banks of the murky river Niger, and that its celebrated riches were nowhere to be seen. The mines, it appears, had been exhausted over two centuries earlier!

* * *

Excepting the ruins of the Almoravid fortress and the painted sign, Zagora had little to remind me of its more illustrious past. The main thoroughfare – the avenue Muhammad V, of course – is a bland affair, lined with modern offices, an army barracks, banks, and a smattering of pretentious and expensive hotels of the type featured in women's fashion magazines (like Ouarzarzate, the town relies heavily on tourism for its continued survival). I arrived to see a few Europeans, mostly

French, strutting about arrogantly in expensive designer sunglasses, as though Morocco were merely another promenade on which to flaunt their wealthy chic. Two of them were smoking, in open disrespect (at best ignorance) of Ramadan.

I spent two days in the town, recuperating, scribbling letters, and repairing my bicycle. To my surprise, there was a shop that sold spare bicycle parts, although the snapped pannier hooks were irreplaceable, and so I resorted to tying them on with string. I even found an *amzil* (blacksmith), who was prepared to weld the pannier racks back together again, which I'd only just noticed had sheared straight in two in all the bumping and clattering of the *pistes*.

The first evening, I was cooked a ragout by a fat Bavarian named Klaus who wore a sturdy pair of (wait for it) lederhosen! The ragout, though, made me feel ill (or perhaps it was the water), and so I went to bed early. The second evening was a beautiful night of stars and barking dogs. I met a teenager, over-anxious to make new friends, which meant that he'd probably take me to the nearest bazaar, which in due course he did. The usual touristic fare was on display: carpets, rugs, teapots, slippers, green enamel pottery, ornamental daggers, and so on. I was pleasantly surprised, however – especially after having been taken for a ride in the infamous bazaars of Tetouan – not to have an intimidating sales pitch rammed down my throat, but instead to be kindly and courteously offered tea over a leisurely and unpressurized conversation with the kid's father about life, business and the desert. I was asked, quite seriously it seemed, whether I would be interested in joining a caravan that was set to leave in three weeks' time for Algeria. Like so many well-intended offers I received in Morocco, I declined, for I was warming to the idea of a pedal-powered trans-Saharan journey.

Only when the boy's father left the room did the young would-be hustler begin, rather pathetically, to spiel the usual touristic banter. I ended up getting angry with him when he called me *bourgeois*, a common enough insult, upon which his father asked him to leave, and then apologized profusely. His son was right, though, in that I was lucky in having both the time and the money to travel, irrespective of how much I was spending or managing to save every day. Towards the end of the evening, my host hurried out to fetch a small tin chest, which he unlocked and opened to reveal more hard currency than I had seen in all my life. 'For building a hotel,' he told me, *'Insha Allah.'*

* * *

The smell of smouldering charcoal stung my nostrils. It was a windless day, and time to move on again. After picking up my camera (which had needed cleaning of sand), I returned to the bazaar to barter an unused paella saucepan and a spare padlock for a couple of admittedly fake silver necklaces, inlaid with equally dubious turquoises and garnets, but pretty all the same. I set out after midday – undeterred by the heat – with Foum Zguid as my next goal, an oasis town some 130 kilometres to the west along the spine of Djebel Bani. The *piste* to Foum Zguid had only recently been opened by the military, and as a result I was able to glean very little information about its condition. No matter, for I soon found out for myself. Immediately on leaving the avenue Muhammad V, a handful of faint tyre tracks, etched in a mixture of soft sand and shale, sped off westwards, and within yards I was obliged to drag my bike rather than ride it. Past an airstrip and a few more disconcerting piles of vulture-pecked bones and cracked skulls, I found myself once again in open desert, Zagora dwindling away into a blur of hazy shapes and mirages. The bleached sky hung heavily over a wide and sandy plain, flanked on both sides with yellow hills. The horizon shimmered in the miraged reflections of distant sand dunes, and as I advanced, it unfurled only to reveal yet more dunes and empty space. There were more bones, too, strangely beautiful on the silky sand.

For the most part, cycling proved to be predictably impossible, and my cycling shoes – made only of perforated nylon – were no protection against the hot grains that burned my feet. At times, the tracks would disappear altogether under the dunes, and so I would make for what seemed to be more substantial ground. Sometimes I was lucky, but mostly I was not. I began to hate the drudge of pushing and dragging the bike over the sand, deep enough in parts to cover my calves. The temperature soared to over 45 degrees, which made the sand so hot that once, what I thought was another puncture turned out to be an old patch whose glue had melted. After three such hours, I had covered a paltry thirty kilometres. I was exhausted and frustrated at my lack of progress. Quite suddenly, I felt sick and giddy. I stopped walking, and discovered that I also had chronic diarrhoea. I sat down on the hot sand to sort out my mind, but within minutes had emptied out my stomach. I felt extremely weak and confused. My sweat ran cold, and my tanned skin looked yellow. I wondered, in a panic, whether I'd contracted cholera, about the worst disease one can get in the desert. The worry made me sick again, after which I unrolled my bivouac and fell asleep, with the sun still high in the sky. I awoke about half an hour later, only to be sick again. The second time I woke was in the evening, roused by the distant thrumming of an approaching vehicle. The throbbing grew louder, until, unexpectedly, the motor spluttered to a halt nearby. I looked up from behind the sand drift that was my pillow, to see a camouflaged personnel carrier, from which three soldiers had descended and were now walking towards me. A spasm of angst seized my insides: what if the place was out of bounds after all?

The first two soldiers walked straight past me, cradling small bundles of brittle brushwood. The third soldier almost collapsed in fright on seeing me. 'Argh!' was the first thing he said. Then, after a moment's pause, he held out his arms as if to exclaim: 'What the hell are you doing here?' but said instead, very politely: 'Ah, er, *bonjour monsieur.*' He smiled. I tried to smile back, told him I was alright (despite my splitting headache), that I was just a little tired, and, well, what a coincidence meeting him here!

'Do you like our country?' he asked, somewhat awkwardly.

'Yes, very much so.'

'And the desert?'

'Of course,' I replied. He clasped his hands together in exasperation: 'Akh, it's too hot for me.' Then someone from the lorry shouted something, and the soldier yelled back *'N'srani!'*

'N'srani?!' echoed the incredulous voice, which then laughed with a high-pitched whine. I stood up to acknowledge the voice, which belonged to a fat black sergeant. He stared long and hard at me, before saying: 'Good day, Mr. Nazarene. No worries? Then there are no problems.'

I was told that their regiment was encamped a little further up the track, although the army was unfortunately forbidden to lodge civilians. There was, however, a village not that far away in case I needed help.

'No, thank you. I'm alright,' I said, hoping that no one would notice the vomit-stained bush nearby. After they'd left, horn blaring and arms waving, I retched for a fourth time, and began to wish that I'd asked them for a lift after all.

I felt ravenous in the morning. My nausea – whatever had caused it – had thankfully disappeared, and it was with great relief that I clambered back onto my bicycle. The disparate tracks soon converged once more, dissipating my worries of getting lost again, and for the first hour or so, I sped effortlessly along. Just before the village of Bou Rbia (the Father of Spring), however, the track disappeared under a morass of rocks and boulders, and continued like this for the rest of the day, slowing my progress considerably whilst also causing another three punctures.

Bou Rbia is a small but well-spaced group of the usual one-floor *pisé* houses, with dark doorways, a well in the centre of a sandy square and a few miserable asses that were tied to a couple of bedraggled palm trees. That, I am afraid, is all that I can remember, for in the Saharan evenings – when I finally had the time and presence of mind to write – I often found that I could remember only very little of what I had seen that day. So, for example, although I remembered seeing a silted up roadside well, I was unsure as to exactly where it had been. Even my description of Bou Rbia, limited though it is, is open to doubt, for I am uncertain even as to whether it *was* Bou Rbia. Often, I would find that unless I wrote down exactly what I had seen and done within a few hours, the blankness of the desert would likely cause me to forget, to confuse places. Most of what I did usually remember was a mass of apparently insignificant details, such as the branches of a particular shrub that I'd stood over for a piss, or an arrangement of rocks not far from where I'd had lunch, or the *wadi* where I once fell off the bicycle. Almost anything that broke the rhythmic and drudging monotony of cycling seemed to me, in retrospect, to be remarkable. The thing was that day after day I would be struck by the identical strangeness of the dunes, of the barren mountains, and the boulders, and would again and again be impressed by their form and their colour, no matter how many times I'd seen them before. No matter how many times, I would always remember those odd little details much better than, say, the only village for a hundred miles. Because every day I would again be struck by the strangeness of it all, and every day I would remark on it, and so I make no apologies for my repetition, for repetition was probably my most consistent companion in the desert: the whispering breeze, the rustling sand, the unremitting heat, the blurred but shimmering horizon, the mirages, the grey flinder plains, the grey bleached sky, the sweat on my forehead, on my legs, on my back, under my chin... Perhaps it is because there was so little to see and feel in the desert, that every little scrap I salvaged from my memory became so important.

Towards late afternoon (with the worst of the heat behind me) the track swerved to the right and northwest, to cross over a dry *wadi* that I had been following for much of the day. Here, a few camels grazed on young grass shoots. Some were saddled, others burdened with sacks of grain or rice, and to my right I passed a brown tent, inside which, I presumed, the nomad and his family were sleeping off the remaining few hours of Ramadan daylight. The mountains and hills of Djebel Bani drew closer, providing a little shelter that was also the cause for the resurgence of the vegetation. There were locusts here too, sometimes in swarms so large that for hours on end the track would be totally obscured by a thick, vibrating shroud of yellow, green and brown. From a distance, they resembled a million bloated maggots feasting on a rotting carcass. Here, every river bed, dry or stagnant, played host to the insects. Locusts, it hardly needs saying, have plagued agriculture since the very earliest times (they can consume their body weight of grain each day). The Eighth Plague of Egypt, over three thousand years ago, was recorded in the Book of Exodus, and Pliny the Elder noted that in 125BC, swarms from the Sahara caused 800,000 people to perish in Cyrenaica, and another 300,000 in Tunisia. The pests returned en masse to Northwest Africa in 1986, and in places attained numbers of truly biblical proportions. But the devastation this year was to be the worst on record.

* * *

The next morning, after a beautiful sunrise over the banks of the *wadi* that I had been sleeping in, I left anxious to reach Foum Zguid as soon as possible. The track, of course, sanded up to become unrideable, and in the few places not swamped by sand, I had to cross thick areas of loose rubble and boulders. Usually, though – given either a lot of courage or stupidity – the rocky sections were just about rideable, albeit at the risk of further damaging my bike. Before long I reached the first of several small oasis-settlements flanking the narrow river gorge *(foum)* that led into Foum Zguid. As usual, I managed to greet people just as the bicycle ground to a sudden and embarrassing halt in deep sand. Worried that I was on the wrong side of the river, I approached a couple of boys to ask directions. After being reassured that I was indeed on the right side, I was asked by the elder of the two whether I would care to drink tea with him and to share his hospitality, in return for a little of my time.

Mohamed Bou Douar and I were easily able to converse because he had learnt French at the high school in Foum Zguid. He led me through a small cluster of *pisé* huts to a larger house that was faced on two sides with withered plots of corn. Behind the house was the family allotment: three tomatoes, two lettuce, carrots, and a well, around which a shackled ass trudged in a doleful manner. The garden was less pitiful than symbolic, but worth it alone for the great pride with which the tomatoes were pointed out to me. Then, I was introduced to Mohamed's family, who were especially woken up for the occasion – father, mother, brothers, grandfather and sister, all greeted me with the usual polite, if rather sleepy, inquisitiveness. I must have presented a strange sight indeed, with my battered bicycle and filthy clothes.

The formalities over, Mohamed took me to his private den, a shabby, windowless hut with walls of adobe and a roof of straw. On the floor lay two woollen blankets stained with oil and grease, sand, dried mud and dust. In one corner sat a large metal chest, which contained a clutter of greasy mechanical oddments. In another languished a rusty-looking diesel pump, which was once used to haul up water from a well beneath our feet.

'Sit down,' Mohamed insisted. 'Tell me, Yunis [the nearest Arab equivalent to Jens], have you ever drunk mint tea?'

'Of course,' I replied. Nonplussed, he continued: 'Then I shall show you how to make the *real marocci whisky*! Now look closely...'

The first problem was that he insisted absolutely on getting the water from the pump, rather than fetching it from the urn in the house, and this meant searching out a needle and thread with which to repair the rubber drive belt. The second problem was that the motor refused point-blank to work. Yet, after half an hour of patient fiddling and poking, bashing and hammering, it belched into life amidst thick, black clouds of smoke. Outside, water began squirting out of a pipe into a clay trough, before overflowing into a set of carefully constructed irrigation conduits (the ass trudged on regardless). Another ten minutes were then spent vainly trying to light a tar-coated log, until Mohamed finally resorted to pouring most of a bottle of petroleum over it. He lit a match. Instinctively, I flung myself into the nearest corner, as a large fireball blasted off towards the straw ceiling. Mohamed grinned sheepishly, then struck another match. 'No worries – Moroccan matches!' he explained amidst a cloud of black-speckled smoke. I wondered how on earth he'd managed to reach the age of sixteen at all.

For over an hour, he struggled to heat a small, soot-blackened kettle, in the end resorting once again to the trusty bottle of petroleum, oblivious to the resulting explosions. Meanwhile, we talked of many things. Mohamed wanted above all to emigrate to Europe because (like so many others) he said that there was no work for him in Morocco. He had seen many of his friends leave the village for Casablanca and Marrakesh, and had no desire to be left behind. The village, he said, was far too boring a place for an energetic young man like him (he flexed his muscles to prove the point). The problem was that in order to visit Europe he needed a banked surety of three *briques* (about £2,000), before even being allowed a visa. Who in Morocco, both of us wondered, could afford such a luxury?

Presently, the water began to boil, and the actual tea ceremony itself began. Curiously enough, the vogue for mint tea was unintentionally introduced to Morocco by the British. In 1854, so the story goes, merchants unable to offload their stocks of Ceylon in the Baltic because of the Crimean War, unloaded instead in Tangier, whence tea gradually replaced the traditional infusion of lemon verbena, sage, and absinthe.

To start with, Mohamed filled the teapot with a reasonable quantity of green China tea, along with a small amount of hot water. After a few minutes, he poured away the liquid, and once more filled the pot with leaves and water, together with sprigs of fresh spearmint and a huge quantity of (expensive) sugar hacked off a loaf (Mohamed considered it a breach of etiquette to serve tea that was too weak). The pot was then left to stand for a while, before small glass tumblers – two to three inches deep – were filled and then emptied back into the pot, an action Mohamed repeated more than twenty times until the froth in the glasses was an inch thick and sturdy, rather like the head on decent pint of bitter. The more the cycle was repeated, the sweeter and more syrupy the tea became, until once the desired sweetness and frothiness had been attained, the teapot itself was heated before the glasses were half-filled, Spanish-style, from a height of about three feet. The result of all this artistry was a golden liquid, syrupy but surprisingly refreshing considering that each glass contained barely a mouthful. And all this was just the first of three such glasses, the last of which was the most bitter: 'The first is for birth,' explained Mohamed. 'The second is for love, but the third is for death.' For some reason, he found this extremely funny.

* * *

The last dozen kilometres into Foum Zguid were dominated by clumps of palm groves, each belonging to a little mud settlement. In one I saw only an old man in a white jellaba riding a mule. At another, when I paused to ask directions, I was swamped by about fifty children, all of them grubby and wide-eyed. As had become common, at first they stared silently as though I were a vicious caged animal, until someone plucked up enough courage to tell me their name, which unleashed a flood of other hopefully proffered names. Hoots of joyful derision met my attempts at pronouncing them. At the next village, my arrival had somehow been anticipated, and so the older boys had begun bossing the younger children about. 'Photograph?' asked a little boy. I agreed, but then the older children shooed the younger ones away so that I was left pointing the camera at all the bullies. Then, a man appeared and, assuming that the kids were bothering me, hounded them all away, only to pose the same questions that the children had asked.

I stopped in Foum Zguid only to stock up on apricot jam and a roundel of Laughing Cow processed cheese – the only food that I could find – and then continued south along a rocky trail until I came to a branch in the track. To my right, occupying a prominent position on high ground, was a small military unit: a dozen tents, armoured personnel carriers, jeeps, and five entrenched tanks, their guns pointing south towards Algeria. I was summoned to the base by a soldier.

'Nazarene!' he scolded. 'Quite exactly *what* do you think you are doing here?' I told him that I wished to cycle to Tata, and did he know which was the correct *piste*? He stared at me for a few moments, then demanded my passport. 'Come with me,' he commanded, and then walked off into one of the tents. There I was given a long and detailed form to fill in, stating exactly where I had been since I arrived in Morocco, as well as my vehicle number. When I explained that my vehicle did not have a number, he frowned and stated that in that case, I would have to turn back and get one. In desperation, I gave him some production figures that had been punched onto the underside of the bicycle frame. He frowned again. No driving licence? No registration papers? I lied feebly, and explained that the numbers on the frame were in fact also those of the registration. He eyed me most suspiciously, then took my passport again and told me to wait while he radioed my details to headquarters. A cold panic set across me. Had I been misinformed about the military situation? Had I been grassed up by the soldiers in the truck I'd met after Zagora? If he refused to let me pass, then where would that leave my little Saharan adventure? It seems to me now that, the more my hopes seemed unlikely, the stronger became my resolve to see them through. As soon as I realized that I was even considering the possibility of such a crazy dream, it would not let go. Half of any adventure always takes place in the mind.

The stern-faced soldier returned with my passport. Camera? Yes, I had a camera. Had I taken any pictures of the military whilst in Morocco? My heart skipped a beat, for I had stupidly taken a photo of this very base only a few minutes before. No, I hadn't, I said, feeling my face blush. He looked me up and down once again, and then announced that the *piste* ahead was very difficult and very dangerous, and most certainly not suitable for a young Nazarene and his bicycle. I replied that I had already been forewarned, and that, in my favour, I had already crossed over the *pistes* from Rissani, which was almost four hundred kilometres.

'Then may Allah give you courage,' he said wearily (I think it must have been the absurdity of my journey that finally melted his resolve).

'If Allah wills it,' I replied, and with that, cycled away as quickly as I could.

* * *

117

I set off downhill towards the river Zguid. The bridge had been washed away in flash floods a year ago with the loss of fourteen lives (all soldiers), so I waded across instead on submerged concrete slabs. Though refreshingly cold, the water was thoroughly salty, but I filled a few empty bottles just in case.

The *piste* after the river was indeed awful, and was made worse by a constant headwind. The path rose up and far above the level of the river, eventually flattening out on to yet another barren plateau, the edge of which drooped out of sight towards the river a few kilometres to my left, leaving only sky where the horizon should have been. After a while, I came across a young boy who was sat cross-legged at the roadside, alone but for a plastic carrier bag and the flapping and fluttering of his dirty brown *cheche*.

'*Salaam Alaikum*,' I ventured, 'Peace be upon you.' I was greeted only by a heavy silence and the penetrating glare of his ruby-crazed eyes.

'*Labass*? Are you well?' I continued, after a long pause. Again silence. Then, opening his mouth to bare his rotten, shattered teeth, he said: '*Mange moi.*'

'*Mange moi, mange moi,*' he repeated in robotic fashion. I offered him some food, but he ignored it. Eat me. Eat me. That's all he ever said.

I left the boy a confused smile, and cycled away.

As the sun began its westering, a little colour returned once more to the desert. The sky was no longer flannel-grey, but a variegated wash of vibrant yellow, copper-orange and cobalt-blue. The sand, no longer lifeless, now glowed in a rich autumnal brown tinged with hints of old gold, and the long evening shadows gave back to the land some of the form and texture that the millennial sun had robbed it of. But still there was little vegetation, only the usual clumps of thistles and thorn grass. I began to feel very isolated on this exposed desert plateau.

My frustration at my slow, wind-buffeted progress was exacerbated by the reappearance of sand drifts. In places they were so deep as to swamp even boulders that would suddenly jar the bicycle and my wrists if I had the temerity to attempt cycling. Walking over one particularly thick stretch of sand, muttering loudly to myself that all this was unfair, a Land Rover appeared over a nearby hillock and sped towards me. For the sake of pretence, I climbed back on to the bike and struggled painfully to cover a few yards, before slamming my balls into the crossbar. The Land Rover, a mud-caked service taxi from Tata, stopped on a nearby set of tracks, and its driver gestured that I come over. As I did so, I saw his passengers stare boggle-eyed through the windows, most surprised at this apparition of the mad *N'srani*.

'You hiss Ingleeezh!' the driver exclaimed in a crazed kind of cackle. 'Akhaha, akhaha, akha, akha...' His voice wavered as he laughed.

'You hear onleee dogs and mad Ingleeezh-man, aheh?'

'Ahaah! You from Mansheeeesta! You hear Mansheeees Unit, aheh!' He wished me all the good fortune and courage of Allah on my journey. 'May Allah lengthen your life,' he said (which worried me slightly). He told me that I was very brave, but I replied that I was merely a little *m'zaza* (mad), which triggered another bout of giggles.

Quite a number of people I met in the Sahara had heard of Manchester, and Liverpool too. 'Football-geography', the phenomenon should be called. On the subject, I am reminded of a tale Paul Bowles recounts in his autobiography *Without Stopping*, when he had been invited to spend a musical evening with a Moroccan family whose uncle had travelled to northern England at the turn of the century. Towards the end of the soiree, the uncle unclapped the fingerboard of the prized family piano, and proceeded to pound it with his fists and elbows, apparently for almost eleven minutes. At the end of the unusual recital, the venerable pianist turned to his audience and proudly announced that that the title of his composition was 'Manchester.' The uncle's banging, one presumes, had been an interpretation of Manchester's cotton mills.

I spent the night in another *wadi*, remarkable in that every bush, tree and blade of grass was infested with locusts. Not merely hundreds, or even thousands of them, but tens of thousands. I was even woken in the morning by them, falling sleepily off their arboreal perches onto my face.

From the first puncture of the day, which I discovered on waking, things went from bad to worse. I wheeled the bike over the *wadi* and across an area of bush to rejoin the *piste* to Tata, where I sat down to patch up the flat. Half an hour later, and ready to leave, I was consternated to find the air still escaping from the tubes. When I checked again, I found four little spines embedded in the rubber, spines that I then realized were from the thorn bushes that I'd just stupidly wheeled my bike through. Another half hour later – and now in a foul temper – I left the locusts and spines behind and started along a stony track edged to the right by a slanted grey cliff, and to the left by the still gradually downward-sloping plain. Another half hour later saw me sitting in the shade of a massive argan tree, stranded alone amidst a sea of boulders. I could have dwelt awhile on the strangeness of this solitary totem of life, but the only thing that occupied my mind then was those bloody punctures – I'd missed another five spines, making ten punctures today already. Angrily, I repaired the remaining holes, only to find that the glue wouldn't set because of the heat. I resigned myself to having from now on to stop cycling every twenty minutes – throughout the remaining 120km to Tata – in order to reflate the damn tyres. It was an extra burden in the extreme heat due entirely to my own morning-drowsy carelessness.

To the west of the argan tree, the colour of the land began to deepen, from a blinding chalky white to kinder and less lonely shades of saffron and a ruddy orange, across which the track roller-coastered over ridges and depressions caused by winter flash floods. The depressions were filled with sand, which compounded my frustration by forcing my constantly having to dismount the bicycle.

Towards midday, a village appeared in the distance, which cheered me greatly. The 18th century kasbah and village of Mrimina stands alone in the desert, and consists of the usual *pisé* buildings, wide sandy squares and tiny dark alleyways, sometimes almost completely blocked by sand drifts. I was accosted by a middle-aged man who beckoned me to stay for a few days as his guest (again, I declined, hot-headed Philistine that I was). While we were completing the obligatory address swap, an old man wearing a tatty grey robe handed me a letter to read, since, although he understood French, he was illiterate. Despite being dated November 1972, it seemed to give him great pleasure as I recited the few greetings and memories contained within, and he scuttled off contentedly as I cautiously cycled away from Mrimina, aware that my front tyre was once again going flat.

My first sighting of the river Tissint was unexpected (it was not, of course, marked on my map – nothing much was). The rough plain I was following changed back to a silvery-grey colour, a wide and very bare valley littered with needle-sharp flinders and other fragments that twice burst my tyres and sent me skidding and sliding towards the river. There, the track lost itself in a compact but verdant nest of riverside plantations. The mud walls of its dwellings were mingled with reed fences and storehouses, and the alleyways in-between were thick with sand. Yet, in the shade of the palms, walking was a most pleasant experience, especially with the accompanying chirruping of birds. In the distance, the croaking of frogs and toads combined in chorus with the gentle gurgling of irrigation channels. There was no one around, just the steady *krk-krk-krk* of a few locusts, and the scampering of a rat on a pile of rotting orange peel and immature dates. It scurried away as I approached, leaving for the time being the beetles, woodlice and centipedes. The smell of this oasis, especially – even its donkey droppings – was a delight after the antiseptic environment of open desert, where I had smelt nothing but dust.

The river itself was broad and pebbly, but also stagnant. The water, where it still flowed, was salty, but helped me locate four more punctures on a spare tube. I figured that at the rate I'd been going today, I'd be needing the old spare rather sooner than I'd anticipated. From here, the *piste* threaded a northwestern path, through gently sloping valleys, again very wide and flat, and low grey hills. Despite the slight gradient, cycling was rapid on the small sharp stones, which tore at my tyres but thankfully caused no more immediate damage. Then, into a short valley whose abrupt sides of sheer rock looked like black icebergs floating in the sand. All the time, rocks small and large came tumbling down to strike the desert floor with satisfying cracks, sending miniature plumes of dust into the air. It was early afternoon, and exceedingly hot, so much so that my *cheche* seemed to make little difference to my rapidly increasing water intake. Yet, I felt exhilarated at my good workmanlike progress, in spite of perforated tyres, the awful *piste* and the heat.

Towards the end of the valley, sand drifts returned with a vengeance, sapping my strength. For a moment, I felt queasy again, but thankfully that moment passed by. Thickets, trees, bushes and grasses marked the reappearance of the river and the stagnant gorge of the Tissint Breach. Because of its steep rocky sides, which blocked out much of the sunlight, the colours here were pale and cold – tones of an overcast North Sea beach in winter: washed-out lemon rind yellow, dull green, pavement grey, and a sky the colour of luminescent ash. A Land Rover driving in the opposite direction had immense difficulty in negotiating the powdery track, which was in parts only a couple of yards wide. Below, in the river itself, lay the mangled wrecks of a lorry and a car, reminders of what could happen if concentration were to slip. In consequence, the driver ignored me totally as he drove by, his gaze fixed hard ahead.

After the gorge, over the crest of a hill, I came to an oasis of thick, green palms, verged with dry frond-weave granaries and tent enclosures, all guarded by five rambling *ksour* and the distant hilltop village of Agadir-Tissint. When I arrived, most people were still in bed. Others slept at the whitewashed portal of the mosque and at the old wooden door of an even older caravanserai, which seemed now to be used as a storage depot for several small shops. The name *agadir* is believed to be a variation of al-Khadir, variously: a mythical holy man; a psychic force; the eternal embodiment of Moses and the other Prophets; and the spirit that was said to have created the forbidden Tower of Toledo, a sanctuary for spirits and otherworldly forces. It is from the latter that the name's current usage springs, for it means a fortified granary that in the past formed the innermost sanctum of villages, a place where, when under nomad attack, the inhabitants could retreat and survive siege.

I was greeted by a brigadier, who had been driven down from the garrison by jeep, my presence having evidently been alerted by some unseen lookouts. Like the soldier outside Foum Zguid, the brigadier wanted my vehicle registration number, but thankfully left me in peace after a few minutes on discovering that I travelled in this fashion for pleasure. Madmen, by the way, are usually free to roam as they like in Morocco.

Passing through Agadir-Tissint, the track began a tortuous climb up the sides of first a mountain, and then, as the setting sun became a hazy ball of cotton wool, the southern flank of a vast canyon, the view from which more than compensated for the atrocious *piste*. Far below lounged a grey and stony river valley, very wide, and graced with innumerable palm groves. On the far side stretched a vast land of rock, carved by the waters into the most surreal molten landscape I'd ever seen. Not merely several, but scores of deep snaking gorges cut into the land, from high up interlaced like macramé. Behind this bizarre geological wonderland rose the jagged reaches of the central Anti Atlas, barren and shrouded in dust.

I awoke on a sandy desert island, adrift in a sea of hard, cactus-like thistles. I felt tired and exhausted as my recent exertions at last caught up with me. The track continued regardless, ad infinitum over back-breaking rocks and boulders. The bizarre canyon soon gave way to the (sadly) more usual monotonous plains, flanked on all sides by distant hills and mountains. The going, of course, was slow and treacherous. One short lapse of concentration cracked my front pannier rack straight in two. Another momentary lapse and I smashed my remaining bottle of fresh water, leaving me with only a litre of warm river brine (though I was near enough to Tata not to worry unduly). In addition, I then managed to break off half of one molar with a green gob-stopper that I was sucking to keep my mouth moist. Disaster is rarely sudden when it strikes in the desert. It is more likely to be a slow, gradual, almost insignificant process, that creeps up on its victim from behind and then cries 'Boo!' At least, that's how I felt, for although I was nowhere near to being in danger, my substantial collection of aches, pains and gripes, succeeded for much of the day in depressing me somewhat rotten.

Every part of my body was encrusted with thick layers of sand and dust. The sand in my ears fuzzed my hearing, not that there was very much to hear anyway, and the fingers that tried to pry out that sand were grimy, black, hard and scaly. My wrists were raw and badly swollen and my nose – oh, my nose! – was a crimson promontory protruding from a caked orange face pockmarked with beady sweat boils and flaking skin, a promontory often completely blocked up with a gooey mixture of orange sand and green mucous. I tried hard not to wipe the sweat away from my nose, because that only made it hurt more, but then the salt would begin to sting... Through force of habit, my mouth had almost developed a taste for the dust and sand that impregnated my food, regardless of anything I did to try to remove it. Flying particles also combined with the sunlight's reflection to result in more or less continuous blinking and very sore, glassy, bloodshot eyes, under which hung huge haunting black bags (I had smashed my sunglases in a crash before Zagora). Even at night, if I closed my eyes I could see almost perfect images of the desert etched on my retina. On top of all this, the glare from the sun often also gave me the first murmurings of a headache, which over time became a dull, throbbing affair. My arms and sore back were encrusted in sweat salt, as was my once blue shirt that had turned white and was starched stiff. My trousers, too, had acquired indecent rips, which I considered worrying in an Islamic country (but come to think of it, I could hardly walk down an English street with my balls dangling out of my trousers, could I?) Add to all this my thirst – which though not extreme, was uncomfortable enough – and I eventually rolled into Tata to much the same kind of reaction that I imagined would greet a zombie clambering out of a slime-filled quagmire.

* * *

I liked Tata. Surrounded by twenty or thirty *ksour* and twice as many palm groves, it is a rambling oasis town situated at the convergence of three seasonal streams. Its inhabitants are a roughly equal mixture of Chleuh (Soussi) Berbers and ex-slaves, both groups speaking the same dialect. There seemed to be little racial tension in evidence. Indeed, throughout Morocco I found that the only real racial animosity, apart from the traditional bickering of Arabs and Berbers, was directed largely towards me and other foreigners on religious grounds. If ever I had the time and the will to explain my family's long and complicated history (English-born, German, Syrio-Lebanese, French, Dutch etc) people often delighted in calling me 'a real Moroccan *tajine*' or else, a

123

hajine – a mule. But sometimes, if they refused to believe that there could be such a mongrel (and a partly Arab one, to boot), they called a dog, an infidel, *N'srani* and the like. On occasion, I was even threatened with physical violence, and I came greatly to resent the associating of my individual identity with the collective moronism of politics, religion, and prejudice.

No such problems in Tata, though, and not once did I hear the word *N'srani*. I only really experienced racism in the larger towns. Here, in the desert, the people were invariably warm, friendly, generous to a fault, sincere, and remarkably tolerant of the nutter with the bicycle! For example, when, on arriving in Tata, I asked a shopkeeper for water, I was made a gift of fresh apricot juice, several glasses of pressed orange, and three bottles of coke, and was then directed to a kind of rest-house set aside for students during Ramadan, who promptly invited me to stay for as long as I wished, and at their expense. Throughout the Sahara, it was only extremely rarely that my offers to pay for hospitality were accepted. More usually, my offer would be brushed aside as though I had commited some grave faux pas.

Along with Sadik Abdessadek, Abd Dafari from Tamanarte, and Abdenbi el-Azri from Foum Zguid (all three were grandsons of Negro slaves, and had met at college in Tata), I spent the rest of the day chatting, fasting and sweating like a pig, while listening to the hypnotic desert rhythms of the three-stringed *haejuj* of Mahmoud Gania, himself the grandson of a Negro slave. I couldn't have found a better way of relaxing and recuperating even if I'd tried.

The sounding of the siren saw the unfurling of three spotlessly clean prayer mats, all printed with images of Mecca's al-Haram mosque, which, at first, were poked and scratched with tired, dusty fingers. Then, the students removed their slippers, and washed their hands, faces and feet with a little water, in a ritual ablution demanded by the Qur'an. Facing east towards Mecca, the students stood silent and motionless. Then, one by one, they crouched to kiss their mats, then stood, and then sat with their legs folded beneath them. A pause. Then again, with their eyes closed, they stood up. Standing distinguishes rational man from animals. Then, together, they bowed, their hands on their knees, in the act of a servant to a master. Again, the mats were kissed, just once, and then, within a few seconds of each other, all three men prostrated themselves, symbolising the total abandonment of their will to Allah. They stayed like this for quite some time, reciting prayers, supplications, and the glorious names of Allah. Once again, they sat up, then crouched and kissed the ground, and then sat up again, meditating, contemplating their prayer beads without even looking at them. Sadik, though, opened his eyes, momentarily disturbed by a crash outside. For a few seconds, he seemed anxious, but then muttered a few prayers, and let the beads slip one by one through his fingers. Finally, the students clambered wearily to their feet, wiped the sweat from their brows, and exhaled.

'Food!' shouted Abdenbi. The first evening meal of Ramadan (ie. breakfast) traditionally starts with a platter of dates and olives – something easy to digest after a day of abstinence. The students also had a bowl of a curious brown powder, which they washed down with curdled milk and *harira*.

'Eat. Eat.' The students urged. When I'd swallowed several mouthfuls of the powder, my hosts suddenly fell about in hysterical laughter.

'*Jrad, jrad*!' they screamed. 'Krrk-krrk-krrk! Kri-Ket!' they taunted, which, eventually, I understood to mean the crushed abdomen of locusts. The annoying thing was that it was quite tasteless: like a mixture of flour, salt and cinnamon, or like a nutmeg concoction that is eaten in the Rif (unsurprisingly, given nutmeg's narcotic properties). Learning the meaning of *jrad* also explained why, at daybreak two days earlier, I had seen a Land Rover disgorge three men, who then shook the trees and shrubs of the dry *wadi* and then stooped to collect the adult locusts, unable to fly in the early morning chill. To some people, *jrad* is a delicacy on a par with prawns. The egg-laden females, especially, are much prized when boiled in salted water and then dried in the sun. They are eaten whole, legs and all.

After this delightful hors d'oeuvre, we hit town, an all-enveloping blackness dotted with the lights of stores and bedroom windows, lit up as in a dream, islands of warmth and humanity awash in a sea of darkness. Tata was a great place to be in during Ramadan, in stark contrast to Er-Rachidia. It was a child's fantasy: spectacular, medieval, magical, fiery, charming, and, above all, friendly. This was Ramadan at its best – not some solemn traditional ritual, but a joyous celebration of religion. Wide-eyed children tore about the streets shrieking and shouting at unfortunate mules. Some of them dangled little tin boxes with wheels on the ends of strings. Others sucked on special Ramadan treats of giant red lollipops. Smoke curled from joss sticks and candles, and figures and silhouettes gesticulated in the cool night air. Even the store that sold bicycle and moped spares was a bustling place, full of children wanting old nuts and bolts for their makeshift go-carts. How good it was to spend a night away from all that sand and dust!

Sampling street food was, for me, one of Tata's (and indeed Morocco's) greatest delights. There was anything that I might have wished for: palm-weave baskets stuffed with figs, dates, sun-dried tomatoes, pomegranates, apricots and apricot paste, walnuts and even quinces. Elderly men stood around in small knots, eagerly devouring *kefta* meat balls bought from street vendors, or else spicy *merguez* sausages. Other vendors hawked vanilla and almond blossom flavoured rock cakes, and paper wrappers containing chickpeas sprinkled with cumin and rock salt. The olive store was an Aladdin's Cave for me. On a long table placed in front of the counter, with its brass scales and weights, were fifteen large ceramic bowls, containing every kind of olive imaginable, varying in colour from almost white through shades of pink, brown, green and inky blue to black. Some were laced with *harissa* sauce (red chilli and garlic), others with slivers of preserved Marrakesh lemons, pickled peppers and carrots, or just wild thyme. As an olive-lover, I spent a small fortune here, and would have spent more had I not been dragged away by the students.

It was wonderful to see the people gorge themselves at sunset, to see their faces and expressions light up as their bellies filled up once more. Women wore their very best silken robes, and their jewellery, quantitively at least, knew no bounds. In the single-room restaurant, to which the students had been yearning to go all day, there was much animated arguing and chattering over *harira* and *tajines*. At first, tempers frayed all too easily with nothing in their stomachs. Voices and expressions rose and fell in angry gestures. Consonants were exaggerated into growls, teeth were bared, noses flared. And yet, towards the end of the evening, people were practically kissing each other through happiness! Old friends walked home arm in arm, the gendarmes smiled and patted everyone's backs, and couples could be seen canoodling in the corners (and what's more, no one seemed to care). As we walked slowly back to the rest-house, content and tired, I saw a strange sight. In a dark, unlit alleyway, the dung-eating beetles had gone crazy – rolling, falling, pushing and tumbling like drunken clowns over their moonlit feasts. A little boy with no pants on stood over them, and started pissing. A shrill giggle accompanied the poor little beasts as they sailed across the pavement and down into a drain.

* * *

I woke up still tired by the night's festivities, and only coaxed myself into cycling with the prospect of a properly asphalted road. If you'll forgive the pun, it was something that I had sorely missed!

The first twenty kilometres were indeed blissful: no fear of punctures, a good steady pace, not having to drag my bike over footloose dunes, no fear of becoming lost, and, best of all, not having to break my wrists over all those bloody rocks. The land itself, though, was still largely bare, on occasion graced with outlandish rubbery bushes bearing fig-like fruits that contained nothing but a mesh of corrosive sappy floss (possibly milkweed, or *calotropis*). The land generally had a grim aspect, rock screes tinted in shades of red and brown, but mostly in grey and black. At the oasis of Imitek, with its thick palm-groves, the road swung south, against the wind, to skirt the western foothills of the Anti Atlas. I passed two makeshift airfields en route, set up as (ultimately futile) bases for insecticide-spraying operations against the locusts. The town of Akka, reached after an easy seventy kilometres, was once, like Tata, Zagora, Sijilmassa, and the rest, a major caravan terminus. Flanked by sheer cliffs (hence its name, which means 'steep-sided ravine'), Akka was an ideal site for the caravans, for it could easily be defended against bands of maurauding tribesmen intent on redistributing the wealth of the trans-Saharan trade. Surrounded by about half a dozen crumbling *ksour*, there was little to remind me of Akka's more gilded past. Nowadays, alas, it is now only a motley collection of nondescript concrete structures, complete with the now familiar gendarmerie checkpoint (at most of which, I seemed to be detained not really for official reasons, but because their guardians were bored and just wanted a chat).

The afternoon's cycling was hindered by the wind, blowing with some force from the Atlantic (now only a hundred miles away) across monotonous valleys filled with tall, shifting dunes. I felt somewhat intrusive, passing through this forlorn land along the relative sanctuary of the tarmac road. The ride, albeit difficult (because of the wind), had little of the excitement or thrill that riding the *pistes* had offered. This place did not make me want to stay, but instead to get through it as quickly as I could, and so into the Western Sahara. My sense of intrusion was heightened on passing Talrhaïcht, a quite visibly impoverished village constructed entirely of mud. I saw no one as I cycled through, except for a couple of unusually disinterested children, who merely stared as I cycled past. The sign outside the pharmacy rattled noisily in the wind, as a constant stream of dust and sand shot through the village. Ahead, beyond a bleak and dusty plain, the tallest of the distant mountains seemed to float above the mirages. The shimmering dusty horizon that engulfed the few trees made them look short and fat under the weight of the sky. Everything seemed to be brown, even the sky, because of the dust.

At the next village, Oua-Belli, my feelings were not so much ones of intrusion, but of depression. The place was remarkable only in that it was built at the foot of a vast diagonal face of black rock, covered in loose rubble which had buried many of the buildings below. Many more lay abandoned. The road twisted up and around the low saddle breach to reach Tisgui-el-Haratine, a modern settlement that was in no danger from landslides. There was an empty school building here, its windows cheerfully plastered with crayon drawings and paintings. A few mules stood around looking sad and bored, as they always do.

I was to see no more settlements that day, although I was steadily to grow more miserable, for the wind made cycling torturously slow. The long straight road didn't help matters either, for I never seemed to be getting anywhere. Towards evening, the road twisted to enter a long (too long) windblown valley. There were bare rocky hills to my left, and bare rocky hills to my right. Even the seasonal stream that the road seemed to be following was bare and rocky, achromatic like the few dry bushes and scrawny acacia that dared despoil the land of its solemn lifelessness. The only excitement came from seeing large wild melons growing by the roadside. Their long stalks, like umbilical cords, looked like chains. I stopped to try one, not really understanding why such delicious fruits had been left uneaten. I soon found out, for their taste was indescribably putrid. The desert melon, or *Colocynthis vulgaris*, is emetic, and is therefore another of the desert's cruel jokes. It is thus also one of its rather more successful survivors. So on I trudged, hindered now not only by the wind but by an increasingly unpleasant sensation in my stomach.

The next morning, the wind continued unabated, and it took me two hours to cycle the paltry ten kilometres to the next settlement, Foum-el-Hisan. Literally 'the Gorge of the High Sandhill', Foum-el-Hisan is known primarily for nearby prehistoric rock carvings – depicting elephant, rhino, antelope and sheep-like animals – that date from between 2000BC and 500BC. There are rock carvings to be found all along the Drâa valley (Foum-el-Hisan is only 30km from the river), and also at Tazzarine, by which I had passed eleven days before. Together with the world's richest source of prehistoric art – Algeria's Tassil-n-Ajjer ('the Plateau of the Rivers') – these mysterious paintings and etchings draw a picture of prehistoric Sahara quite unlike its present state. I found it hard to believe that until about 2000BC, the Sahara as we know it now simply did not exist. Instead, amply watered pastureland stretched between the Mediterranean and the Tropics, crisscrossed with countless rivers that idled lazily into or out of hundreds of lakes. The profusion and variety of fauna that this rich land supported is staggering. Apart from a large and seemingly prosperous population of Neolithic cattle herders and hunter-settlers, there roamed vast herds of elephant, giant buffalo, hippo, lions, panthers, giraffes, ostriches, antelopes and other big African game. Polybius, among many others, records that the Drâa was once infested with crocodiles, the last of which is believed to have been shot by French hunters in 1929.

Sometime around four thousand years ago, and for a reason that scientists and meteorologists are still unable to explain, the rains began faltering. Gradually, at first, the rivers and lakes receded, shrank, dried up, and eventually disappeared altogether as the desert took hold. In turn, crops failed, animals left or died, and finally, the soil that had been the lifeblood of this ancient paradise, turned to dust and blew away.

CHAPTER SIX

THE WESTERN SAHARA

[A people] who never enjoy fresh water
And whom the grass of the fields inadequately supplies,
A country you may say ill disposed to bear any fruit,
Where the birds consume iron in their bellies,
A land suffering extreme want of everything ...

Luis Vaz de Camões, Os Lusiadas[6], *1572*

I took the turning to Bou-Izakarn, only to be stopped by two *Gendarmes Royales* who were stationed in a hut beside the junction. Border skirmishes with Algeria in the 1960s and, more recently, the guerilla war with Polisario, had for long rendered this place out of bounds to foreigners. When I asked them about Polisario and the situation in the Western Sahara, the one gendarme replied, utterly transparently: 'A war? What war? You have been misinformed, my boy. There is no war!' On seeing my expression, he started laughing.

'Hey!' He nudged the other's elbow: 'The young man does not believe me. You tell him, come on! He'll believe you – you've got blue eyes!' He laughed again. The other gendarme, who did indeed have blue eyes, leaned over my shoulder in a conspiratorial fashion, and whispered: 'You love your Queen Magritte Tattché?' At this, both of them doubled up, convulsed with laughter. A while later, the first gendarme said: 'Hey, look. Quick, over there.' He seemed to be pointing at a boulder about a hundred yards away. 'What? What? What is it? I don't see anything,' complained the second gendarme, squinting and holding his hand over his brow.

'Akh, don't you see? Look, sh-shush, over there... Now!'

The other gendarme appeared to be totally bemused, as the arm of his partner swung slowly around to point directly at his nose.

'Ha ha ha ha ha!' In between his fits of giggles, the first gendarme said to me: 'Ah, I really got him one there, eh? Ha ha ha!' He slapped me hard in the small of my back. I felt, in the company of these two gendarmes, exactly the same as though I had walked into a pub only to be cornered by its two resident drunkards that no one will talk to any

131

more. It is a strange thing, but throughout the Sahara, the gendarmes, soldiers and policemen manning the numerous roadblocks were, with only few exceptions, the craziest and funniest people that I met. Perhaps it was their job, I mused, as I cycled away. All day long, all they ever seemed to do was sit in their concrete boxes compiling useless lists of randomly chosen number plates. In Ramadan, of course, this was not exactly the most stimulating occupation in the world, and so when not considering the weather or the last plague of locusts, these two gendarmes seemed to spend most of their time placing small wagers on the colour of the next truck that was to pass them by. I gathered that they had only stopped me because I was the most interesting thing to have happened to them all week.

The road veered northwest and up again into the Djebel Bani. I struggled for two hours against a strong headwind to cover twelve kilometres, only to enter a valley that was being sprayed from Land Rovers and airplanes with vile smelling insecticide that got into my eyes and nose. Frustrated and pissed-off, I gave up the idea of cycling to Bou-Izakarn, and instead freewheeled back down the mountain to the roadblock, where the laughing gendarmes announced that they had been expecting me, and had even laid out an impromptu lunch of oily black olives and bread. Tea was served, and for once I was happy that my stubbornness had not got the better of me.

I got a lift in mid-afternoon on a pick-up truck for 35 dirhams (it's usual to pay for hitching in Morocco). I joined seven other passengers, cramped in the back alongside suitcases and a couple of goats. The scenery was beautiful. It flashed by in a cascade of colours as we more or less flew along a succession of *ksour* and villages in mountains of purple and pink rock strata, naturally sculpted rock gardens, the shrivelled branches of wizened argan, and the emetic, viciously barbed aloe cacti. We sped on past Icht and Aït-Herbil, then the promontory of Aguerd surrounded by its date palms, and then Tagoujgalte and Tarhjijt, a large and picturesque oasis with a *ksar* and an old white minaret. Then came Aït-Jerrar, and then the kasbah and fertile palmery of Timoulay-Izder, opposite the labyrinthine ruins of its twin, Timoulay-Ifla. Finally came Bou-Izakarn, a light and spacious garrison town situated at the western foot of the Anti Atlas. To the north it is flanked by forested hills, and to the south, by a large concave valley, through which runs the road to Guelmime and the Western Sahara.

I was dropped on the outskirts of town, beside its fortified exterior walls. From there, I made my way past an old Foreign Legion fortress, then through palm-shaded gardens, to find myself in an unexpectedly green land, dotted with absinthe and cypress, poppy and yellow primrose, rosemary and red-dashed eucalyptus plantations. Here, in the evening, the soil glowed in a warm shade of red, which embraced the land with a welcoming and secure aspect. The sand and rock, I was pleased to notice, had almost all disappeared. Coming from the east, this green spur of the Anti Atlas was an utter surprise, an abberation in the otherwise endless stretch of desert. In many ways, I regretted having chickened out of this last stretch of cycling, for the road between Foum-el-Hisan and Bou-Izakarn effectively crossed back over the divide from desert to pasture. Much as it had been good to cycle slowly into the desert, and to see it, ever so gradually, take a hold on the mountains, it would have been pleasing to have done the same thing in reverse.

* * *

Forty-one kilometres south of Bou-Izakarn, along Route P41, is the ancient walled city of Guelmime, in its time perhaps the greatest of all the Maghreb's caravan termini. Situated on a slightly undulating plain at the southwestern extremity of the Anti Atlas, this historic city has, like Sijilmassa, Zagora, Tata and Akka, for centuries played host to the twin worlds of the sedentary nomads and of the desert people themselves.

Guelmime is one of Morocco's oldest towns, founded in the 8th century following the first Arab forays into the Bled es-Sudan, the Land of the Blacks. In the following centuries, the town was to become by far the most important caravanserai of the Western Sahara, and was as such much frequented by Moorish traders, who came in from the depths of the desert to deal in gold, salt and slaves, as well as to acquire fresh camel stock for their perilous voyages across the interior. In later years, when European interest in the region and its links with the Sudan flourished, it became the natural base for their trading operations, and being only 40km from the Atlantic, was to provide the French and Spanish with an easily defended position from which to launch their pacifying missions at the turn of the century.

Unfortunately, the harsh post-industrial realities of the twentieth century have led to the decline of what must once have been a most magical place, although the city at the end of this millennium still has a comforting element of dilapidated (and perhaps, at the right times, chaotic) charm. The heart of the town is a curious blend of tightly packed terraces and pink arcades, through which file narrow dusty streets populated by tall, indigo-robed men and swarthy women dressed in flowing robes of burgundy or pale blue. In the evening, the circular town square plays host to a lively audience entertained by aged story tellers, beggars and *griot* musicians, and it is then, if at all, that the atmosphere is reminiscent of Guelmime's more glorious past.

Despite its unassuming veneer of modernity, Guelmime is still, in the minds of many visitors, tourists and Moroccans alike, synonymous with only two things: Tuareg nomads, and camels.

The Tuareg [singular Targui] are known in most touristic literature as the 'Blue Men', because of the indigo that is used to dye their robes and *litham* face-mufflers, a dye which rubs off onto their skins (rather like the woad-dyed ancient Britons). The indigo fad, like that of mint tea, was started by an Englishman, an enterprising Agadir-based merchant named Thomas Windham, who introduced indigo-dyed calico in the 16th century. *Tawarik*, the name given to the Tuareg by the Arabs, variously means the 'Godless Ones', the 'Abandonners of Allah', or the 'Lost Souls', on account of their lax interpretation of the Word of Islam. Caillié reported that:

> The Moors entertain a profound contempt for the Tooariks, and when they would express their utmost hatred of them, they compare them to the christians, whom they suppose to be the same kind of vagabonds and depredators.

The Tuareg themselves though, like the Berbers, prefer to be called *Imazighen* – the Noble Ones – as do many other desert people. To shatter a myth, though, the 'Blue Men' that one sees nowadays in Guelmime are not Tuareg at all, but related tribes of the Western Sahara, collectively known as Saharawis. Regarded historically as the 'People of the Littoral' (*Ahel es-Sahel*), their traditional homeland is in the extreme western stretch of the desert flanking the Atlantic coastline. The Tuareg themselves inhabit the central desert regions of Mali, Niger and Algeria, and only rarely stray into the more western lands of Morocco, Mauritania, or the Western Sahara. The Saharawis do, however, have one thing in common with the Tuareg, and indeed with the Berbers, in that their origins remain utterly obscure. From the earliest surviving Saharan cave art, it seems that the desert's prehistoric population was more or less evenly divided between Sudanic Negroes and Mediterranean Semites. As the desert expanded inexorably over the ages, however, the whites began moving to the north and the blacks into the richer lands of the tropical south, both groups, by and large, abandoning the desert. Several tribes, however, remained, preferring to roam the vast open ranges in search of pasture, than become settled. Black or white, Tuareg, Moor or Saharawi, today's remaining true nomads are the direct descendants of these pioneering desert peoples.

Like the Berbers, who have kept much of their pre-Islamic spiritual and cultural heritage alive, the Saharawis too retain many of their ancient pagan traditions, the most eclectic of which is the dance of the *guedra*. Continually repressed by Islamic reformers, the *guedra* is a hypnotic dance accompanied by the pounding rhythms of the epony-mous clay-and-skin tam-tam. It is a swaying dance, like that of the seven veils, where a kneeling woman in lustrous blue robes and black veils dances to chants and claps and the insistent drumming of the *guedra* itself. Designed to excite men before intercourse (the squatting mimics the primitive posture for giving birth), it can be extremely erotic: fertile, rhythmic, pounding, pulsating, swirling, spinning, faster and faster as veils are flung off, flung away, spinning, pounding, chanting, clapping, clapping, spinning bare face, breasts naked, pounding, drum-ming faster still, until she collapses in an exhausted heap in a great cacophony as the music gasps for breath and, presumably, her husband prepares to carry her off to bed.

Similar drum-based dances are used throughout Arab and Negro countries to exorcise demons dwelling especially in married women. They are invariably secret affairs, where the possessed similarly dance themselves into utter exhaustion. It is possible that the *guedra* is a more primitive version of the classic belly dance, both of which were carried to North Africa along with the camel caravans (in Moroccan music, especially, West African influence is very apparent).

It is the trade in camels that most closely ties the Saharawis to the Berbers. Sunday is the day of Guelmime's camel souk, when camel-breeders from the Anti Atlas come to do business with the few surviving caravaneers and saddlesmiths. The event now attracts busloads of tourists from Agadir, along with fake 'Blue People' (aka hustlers) for the benefit of the cameras. People only see what they want to see, especially tourists: in Guelmime, I heard several tales of visitors being conned into buying three-legged camels (who were kept seated throughout the proceedings), and on one occasion, even a dead one! Indeed, as far north as the Rif mountains, I saw a supposed Tuareg merchant peddling amber, desert rock salt and spices under the orange walls of Chefchaouen's Portuguese kasbah. Only then, I discovered that the Targui was actually a Fassi who commuted monthly from Fès by bus!

Considerably less prone to scams is the annual 'Moussem of the Camel Traders', held for one week each June, when herders from all over the Atlas converge on the town to conduct rather more serious business. Then, a good trekking animal can be had for £300 (white pedigree bulls cost almost £1000), and rather more average specimens can be secured for the price of a bicycle (I was sorely tempted, until I heard the three-legged stories). However, the ending of the slave trade and the advent of Berliet trucks and Land Rovers, among other factors, has prompted a dramatic decline in the nomad population, something further exacerbated in this corner of the Sahara by the war with Polisario, which has dampened the once substantial *moussem* migrations that at their peak attracted over forty thousand camels and bidders from as far away as Mali and Senegal. My journey through the Western Sahara was to be, above all, a depressing litany of dirges to famine, war, and to the death of the nomad way of life.

* * *

The desert begins again almost immediately on leaving Guelmime: a bleak *hammada* that in the past allegedly served as backdrop to scenes in *Lawrence of Arabia* (but almost every touristic rendezvous in North Africa claims this accolade). In early May, every inch of the desert floor is carpeted with a bizarre expanse of tiny brick-red shrubs interspersed with green bushes, something like a horrible skin rash. Nonetheless, this provides a much needed source of firewood for the few remaining pastoralists. The river Noun, crossed after five kilometres, is commonly taken to be the northern geographical boundary of the Western Sahara, which stretches south from here for almost two thousand kilometres, all the way to the river Senegal – where I hoped I would ultimately end up.

The Western Sahara is a bleak place, perhaps even more so than the Moroccan Sahara. Over much of the desert's one hundred thousand square kilometres, there seems to be little else than rocks and stones, stretching interminably over mountains and plains. It is punctuated only by equally dry escarpments, for there are few rivers, and none that flow throughout the year. In 1960, there were estimated to be only 130 water sources in the whole territory, and less than 4,000 palm trees, figures that are bound to have worsened in the intervening years. Evidence of a healthier past remains in the form of great *sebkha* (or *sebkhet*) saltlakes, and the eroded valleys of long-dead rivers. The little rain that does fall is quickly absorbed inland, or else evaporates within minutes. Even on the coast, rainfall rarely exceeds two inches a year, and during my visit (mostly following the coastline), the temperature rose frequently to over 115°F (46°C).

In many ways, the river Noun [so named because sailors rounding the cape at its mouth feared never to return: *Chil passa ritorna no*, he who passes never returns] shares much of its history with Guelmime, although its use as a trading post dates back much further, some say to

Phoenician times. In recent centuries, the river seems to have acquired something of an infamous reputation as a slaving port, a place where shipwrecked Christian sailors captured off the treacherous coastline were taken – if they were fortunate – to be bought their freedom by pitying European traders and consuls. That is, if the poor bewildered captives managed to survive the usual custom of being force-marched naked and barefoot across the burning sands. The tribes of the Oulad-Delim clan, in particular, were renowned pillagers, feared by other tribes for their *razzias*, and by travellers for their habit of stealing even the clothes off their backs. They justified their camel-rustling *razzias* by claiming that their own camels had a distinctive hairlip, whereas in fact, all camels bear this curious feature. In 1887, a French explorer named Camille Douls tried to pass himself off as a Muslim among the Oulad-Delim, but his pretence was quickly unmasked, and the poor Douls was stripped, beaten and then buried upto his neck in sand to be left at the mercy of the vultures. Upon which, he frantically recited all the verses of the Qur'an that he could recall, and, fortunately, was released from his premature grave, only to be strangled en route to Timbuctoo, aged 25.

Shortly after the river, the road began a climb into arid, low hills, spattered with small round bushes and sallow grasses: the last weathered foothills of the Anti Atlas before the hopeless plains of the Western Sahara itself. A little further on, I passed the last cultivated lands I was to see for over a thousand miles: yellow-beige fields of ripening spring barley and wheat. Sometimes, on the banks of dry *wadis*, I spotted the brown skin tents of pastoral nomads, their camels and goats grazing nearby. Then came more locusts, winged, and in the later, more dangerous, stages of their metamorphosis. The air was muggy and hot, the atmosphere clouded. These last hills are where the hot gusts of the desert *chagi* collide with the cool Atlantic breezes.

Before long, the valley narrowed to enclose the road and a dry river bed. A green Citroën 2CV was parked over to one side, its Italian occupants chattering with much gusto with a Moroccan youth. I arrived as they were discussing the tents pitched on the far side of an empty, stone-strewn field. The Moroccan said that they were Tuareg, although it was only later that I realised that most Moroccans tend to call all nomads Tuareg, regardless of whichever tribe they in fact belong to. Nevertheless, the Italians were suitably impressed, and wanted to take photographs. Not possible, the Moroccan said: the nomads feared Evil Eye.

A skinny young man with a faint limp, Hassan Boukhriss offered to put me up for the night with his family, if I wished, and so I arranged to meet him a few miles further down the road at the turn-off to El-Abiar (he got a lift from the Italians). It was getting dark when I met him again, sitting by the trunk of a tree sucking on straw. Until nightfall, we stayed there and talked, about politics, nomads and most of all, about sex. He could not comprehend why European families had so few children. Was it because Europeans disliked sex? Or was there a law, like in China, that prevented people from having more? He was even more shocked when I told him that in Europe one can find people who are celibate by choice. In Morocco, a man without a wife and children is not a man, he said, and throughout Africa I found that people laughed when I told them that I actually *enjoyed* being on my own. Loneliness, said Hassan, was the stuff of his worst nightmares. And the desert? Oh, he hated the desert. Hassan was also astounded that I wasn't particularly interested in sex during my travels. Moroccan women, he assured me, were the most blissful lovers in the world. 'My sister is very beautiful,' he said, 'and very discreet...' he added. 'Do you want her?' He said all this with a slight sneer at which I became uneasy. I shrugged my shoulders.

'You want sex, yes?' I shrugged again. 'Not really.' I suspect that any other 19 year-old virgin would have reacted the same. Then, to my astonishment, he asked whether I was gay. 'Look.' He said, taking my hand, which I quickly snatched away: 'Just lean against this tree. You don't have to do a thing.' I stared wide-eyed at him, shocked and scared, and wondering frantically if I had understood him correctly.

'Don't you like it?' he asked, on seeing my expression. 'But Jens, you *must* have love with me!' he declared, trying to stroke my stubbled face. He then added, in case I really hadn't understood: 'You know, I *love to fuck you!*' I blustered my excuses and edged back towards the bicycle, feeling like he'd just pulled a knife on me. Two hundred dirhams he then offered to pay, two hundred dirhams in crumpled banknotes which he waved in my face. Two hundred dirhams, and all I had to do was lean against a tree! I stared aghast, then pushed him away, which on reflection probably convinced him that I was only being coy.

'Okay, okay,' he said, this time without the sneer. 'I know what you are afraid of, but don't worry.' Upon which, I swear, from his trouser pocket he produced a limp, used condom.

* * *

I slept badly, in-between clumps of reed grass a few miles further on, and awoke soaked to the skin under a dark, overcast sky. Behind me, only a few hundred yards away, was a large village, the existence of which I had been completely oblivious to last night. Women carrying baskets of linen on their heads stared at me as though I were an alien, and I suppose with good reason! Shivering with cold, it took me three hours to reach the last craggy breach of these last craggy hills, and all the time it rained endlessly. I cycled past the *koubbas* of Sidi-Sabj and Notfia, then a couple of anonymous transmitter masts, and then down for the last time into a snaking valley, arched to my right with a magnificent rainbow, under which flew shards of orange sunlight that painted the rocks around me with a rich golden red. There was purple heather beside little bubbling streams, and birds singing to the hiss of rubber on wet asphalt. As the skies cleared and the steam began to rise, I left behind the last of the vegetation to enter a sandy plateau, past a sleepy roadblock and past the crumbling war-torn ruins of a roadhouse. Beside it, an old well had deliberately been filled with sand and rubble: an age-old military tactic designed to limit the mobility of an enemy, and a sign that until recently this area had been a war zone.

It felt good to be leaving the mountains. There was a bit more space, and a bit more freedom. I cycled over a wide concrete bridge. Underneath it was a dry pebbly river – the Drâa. Only freak rains will fill it this far, twenty kilometres from the ocean. In the winter to come, though, this in fact happened, for the first time in over a decade.

Past another checkpoint, the town of Tan-Tan snaked into view. From afar, it is not really much to look at, unless the sheer element of surprise at its very existence is seen as remarkable. Like Er-Rachidia, its relatively flat skyline of orange walls and brown buildings is broken only by a few white minarets. The town, though, is surrounded on all sides by rocky escarpments, its only defence against the ravages of open desert. Tan-Tan also marks the southernmost limit of arboreal vegetation, palms or otherwise, outside of the Western Sahara's few oases.

The town has a moderate population of about fifty thousand, mostly erstwhile nomads forced into settled life by the war and the successive droughts of the last two decades. Tumbledown mustard and blue Spanish terraces, with cracked and splintered wooden balconies, line depressingly lifeless streets. A strong colonial influence lingers. There are small ornamental squares, hot wide avenues, a few tiled shopfronts, and sad dry fountains. The town has no fresh water supply. The taps, if at all, run hot and salty, and so drinking water has to be brought in by truck from a well twelve miles away, to be judiciously hoarded in red earthenware urns. After a great deal of pleading, I managed to buy some water from the owner of a large empty cafe, who'd just received his week's supply. Because of Ramadan, almost everything was shut – in stark contrast to Guelmime – although the market inexplicably remained open. There, a few traders sat morosely behind their wares, shaded from the midday sun by a few flapping sheets of mucky tarpaulin. There wasn't much on offer though: small artichokes, broad beans, smooth skinned cucumbers, pyramids of oranges, and a few overripe tomatoes that were swarming with flies.

Tan-Tan only really comes to life during its two annual *moussems*, combined religious and commercial gatherings whose continued existence is partially indebted to the increased interest shown in them by tourists. The first, held in May, commemorates Sidi Mohamed Loghdof, one of the most revered of desert saints. It is an event that, in common with the Guelmime camel *moussem*, used to attract thousands of pilgrims, not only from southern Morocco but from Algeria, the then Spanish Sahara, Mauritania and Senegal. Born in the year 1875, Mohamed Loghdof won the respect of the people by organising *razzias* against both the French and the Spanish. Later, during the First World War, he cynically accepted payments from the latter in return for his 'allegiance', funds which later he converted into arms for use against his former benefactors! As a result of his campaigning, in the early 1970s his *moussem* became the platform for several Saharawi anti-colonial demonstrations (the Western Sahara remained a Spanish colony until 1976), demonstrations that (perversely) were put down by Moroccan troops.

Mohamed Loghdof was a son of Sidi Mohamed Ma el-Aïnin – 'He of the Beautiful Watery Eyes' – a man who has assumed an almost mythical status among the Saharawis, and to whom Tan-Tan's second *moussem*, held in June, is dedicated. As both *marabout* and leader of the Reguibat tribe, he soon became known to the French as 'our bitter enemy'. As Sultan Hassan I's representative in the South during the latter years of the 19th century, Ma el-Aïnin is famed for having led Saharan resistance to both French and Spanish attempts at colonisation in the run-up to the Great War. He is said to have learned the Qur'an by heart by the age of seven, though perhaps equally remarkable was his virility (his 26 wives bore him 68 children, and he is said to have shired many more bastards). This gave rise to a new tribe, the *Ahel Sheikh Ma el-Aïnin*. Another of Ma el-Aïnin's sons, Ahmed el-Hiba, achieved the virtually impossible in 1911 by storming the colonial jewel of Marrakesh. It is a city of great importance to the Saharawis, for it was founded by the Almoravids who came from the Western Sahara and Mauritania. Although el-Hiba was forced out of the city within a month, by his act of defiance he achieved immortality, and became known as the 'Blue Sultan'. For the next two decades – like his Riffian contemporary

Abd el-Krim – el-Hiba continued his father's work as dissident leader, fighting with considerable success in the Sahara and Anti Atlas until 1934, when he was finally beaten and the South succumbed to European control.

Despite these animated diversions, the town of Tan-Tan is depressing. It is a place where the army makes its presence felt keenly, a place which seems never fully to have achieved its independence. Red-and-green Moroccan flags flutter from lampposts and scaffolding, and portraits of the king adorn not only the interior but exterior walls of every official building. The effects of the unspoken war with Polisario are felt everywhere. For the last decade and a half, the Western Sahara has seen armed conflict between the Moroccan *Forces Armées Royales,* and Polisario, the Saharawi guerillas fighting for the region's independence. The origins of the war, like so many modern conflicts, reside in the legacy of European greed. The Spanish first colonised the region in 1884, albeit in name rather than in practice, for until the defeat of el-Hiba, Spain held only two bases in the territory. Then, in the 1960s, after the granting of Moroccan and Mauritanian independence, both countries began campaigning for control over the mineral-rich desert region which lay between them and which remained under Spanish sovereignty. Mauritania based its claim on its 11th century Almoravid heritage, and Morocco on the notion of the Greater Moroccan Cause – effectively dating back to the great empire of the Merinids (if the Greater Moroccan Cause were to be taken literally, it would mean half of Spain succumbing to Moroccan control).

In 1973, the situation became more complicated with the formation of the *Frente Popular para la Liberación de Saguia el-Hamra y Río de Oro*: the Polisario Front. On the death of Franco in 1975, the situation exploded. In a political masterstroke, King Hassan II conceived the idea of the 'Green March'. In October that year, he announced that 350,000 unarmed volunteers would march, Qur'an in hand, across the border into the Spanish (ie. Western) Sahara. On 5 November, the marchers left Tan-Tan for the south, and three days later crossed the border, at which the hapless Spanish border guards could do nothing but gape. Although international pressure forced the early recall of the marchers, the act was a great success. Spain withdrew in February 1976, awarding the northern section of the Western Sahara to Morocco, and the smaller southern part to Mauritania. Polisario, however, found itself squeezed out, and so proclaimed the creation of the Saharawan Arab Democratic Republic *in absentia*, and resolved to continue the struggle for independence. It had some success: after three years of war, its economy crippled, Mauritania was forced to pull out of its portion. But the outcome was not at all to Polisario's liking, for Morocco promptly invaded and annexed the territory, most of which it has controlled ever since.

The war between Morocco and Polisario drags on, with its propaganda, guerilla attacks, punitive raids, a scattering of major battles, brief sieges, and the like. The question is one of sovereignty, of whether the Western Sahara belongs to Morocco or the Saharawis. The cynics argue that Morocco has no valid claim, and is only interested in the territory for its potentially valuable mineral deposits. On the other hand, Morocco's defenders claim that the Western Sahara was not a *terra nullius* before the Spanish conquest, but that ties of allegiance to Morocco had existed long before (ie. that the Saharawis are in fact Moroccans). Whatever the rights and wrongs, the war has been at a stalemate ever since the construction of a defensive wall by Morocco, and it seems that only a referendum will decide the issue once and for all (a referendum that has been promised since 1976, but which has been perpetually postponed by the actions of both sides). What is certain is that the conflict has destroyed, perhaps for ever, the time-honoured nomadic way of life of its inhabitants. Age old traditions have been repressed or forgotten, boundaries that previously never existed have been fought over, past loyalties have been breached, confidences shattered, hatreds renewed, and thousands of refugees still find themselves languishing in squalid encampments on the border with Algeria.

The tribes of the Western Sahara used to have the proverb: deny me the freedom of movement, and you deny me the right to breathe.

* * *

I left Tan-Tan in the afternoon, with the temperature soaring and the morning's clouds having been dissipated by the sun. The road rose up the sides of the western escarpment, beyond which the water truck I was following turned off beside a military airfield onto the old road to Smara and Layoune, capital of the Western Sahara. From almost the beginning of the war, the road to Smara has been forbidden to all but military traffic, effectively making travel to the town impossible. Founded by Sheikh Ma el-Aïnin, Smara is of the utmost symbolic importance to Polisario, and in consequence the region around it saw the very first Polisario offensive against Spanish *Tropas Nómadas*, in 1973. Tan-Tan itself, although heavily defended, came under attack in 1979, while Haouza, only seventy miles away, came under attack four months ago. As a result, the current situation was somewhat delicate, and I counted myself lucky to be able to travel to Layoune at all. Two years earlier, even the coastal road along which I was to travel had been out of bounds.

The short descent from the escarpment brought the road down onto a placid *hammada*, where it shot away towards the coast. The landscape here was as desolate as any I'd seen. Sometimes, on the southern horizon, I thought I could make out a few tents, but then the heat haze or a mirage would cover them up, so that I was left alone, pondering whether there really were still nomads in this forgotten part of the world. When I looked back north and east – at where I'd come – all that I could see was a vast stretch of yellow sand, beyond which the last hills of the Anti Atlas dribbled into the desert. Nearer the coast, between large boulders and rocks, grew a smattering of grey bushes and tiny fleshy succulents – juicy red and green fingers that, I'd been warned in Tan-Tan, would kill me if I tried to eat them. In terms of cynicism, Sahara has it all.

An army roadblock accompanied my first sighting of the Atlantic. My God, all that water! I felt as though I was seven years old again, seeing the Irish Sea at Blackpool for the very first time in the long hot summer of 1976. Although it was beautiful (and soothing) to my eyes, there was to be one severe drawback to desert travel on the coast, and that, of course, was that it greatly increased my desire to drink. I mean, with an entire ocean of cold blue water constantly in sight, and with a difficult enough ration to keep to, it was not exactly surprising. The contrast between these twin desert worlds was at once bizarre and ironic: two oceans lying side by side, each one as barren and inhospitable as the other.

Tan-Tan-Plage, just beyond the roadblock, is the last settlement of note until Tarfaya, 235km southwest along a tarmac road that runs for the most part on top of brutally scarred hundred-foot cliffs. A road sign laconically announced the road distance to Dakar (capital of Senegal) as 2,224 kilometres. The sign was laconic because, as I was later to discover to my great frustration, there was no such road, or even a track. The war had closed it twelve years earlier.

The next day, I awoke feeling damp and stuffy, as though it had been raining again, but it was only the mist rolling in from the sea. Yet it is only rain itself, if and when it falls, that enables the full cycle of desert life to be completed. After the recent rains (some said the best since the 1950s), it was easy to appreciate the paramount importance of water in supporting life. All around me, the desert had exploded into bloom: ephemeral flowers of all kinds in bright colours, visited by hoverflies

143

and wasps; more succulents and aloe; bizarre furry cacti; vermilion grasses; purple sea lavender; and dark-green euphorbia, a spurge named after the physician of the ancient Mauretanian king, Juba II. Shortly after getting underway, I saw to my astonishment a pool of rainwater lying in a depression to the left of the road. I dismounted and walked off towards it, and, as I approached, I could hear the otherworldly chorus of hundreds of tiny Mauritanian toads, only recently changed from tadpoles, that hopped about beside the pool. There were hundreds more still in the water. I squatted at the poolside and gazed for ages at this marvellous spectacle, and at the little toads that leapt all over my hands and my feet. Their spawn can survive years of drought, buried in the dry mud of temporary pools, to await the next rains. By this miracle of nature, the croaking of frogs and toads is considered by many Muslims to be a form of praise to the Almighty.

To see the desert in the short time when it pretended to be something else, to see the pool and the toads and the flowering plants, was humbling. To see the desert when life is born, reproduces, and dies in the matter of a couple of short weeks, was something I considered to be a great privilege. But this pool had already begun to dry up, and had turned to cracked mud on its edges. Within a week, it would once again become grey and brittle, covered in dust and sand, and the desert would once again be left to the mercy of the sky.

Throughout the day, cycling was a laborious affair due to a constant headwind that reduced my speed to under ten kilometres an hour. In addition to its physical curses, the wind was also psychologically disheartening, especially seeing as I had gone to sleep hoping for a good day's cycling. It became all too easy to suspect a conspiracy of the elements, especially when motorised vehicles shot past me without a care in the world. And always the sea to remind me of my thirst. Within three hours, I had drunk half of my day's ration, and the worst of the heat was still to come.

Before long, the flowering vegetation gave way to drier and dustier terrain, littered with the more usual acacia and scaly tamarisks that evidently hadn't received any rain, and by late afternoon, I was passing only a handful of wayside shrubs along each kilometre, mostly already swamped by the hot and hostile sands. There are no permanent oases of any consequence in the Western Sahara, and even the few, small, watering holes that do exist, are rapidly drying up and dying. There are no new ones to replace them either. In the 1950s, Raymond Mauny, in an excellent description of this coastline, listed over thirty oases and wells between Tan-Tan-Plage and Dakhla (the southern limit of Moroccan rule). Thirty years on, over half have disappeared forever, whilst the continuing existence of another half dozen or so is at best uncertain. Still, sometimes I would be surprised to see a lone fisherman perched on the cliff top, usually beside a ramshackle hovel made of wooden casing and old plastic sheets. It is an irony that the coastline of one of the world's harshest lands contains some of the world's richest fishing grounds. From the Western Sahara, south along the Mauritanian coastline and down to tropical Senegal, the north and western continental Atlantic currents meet, to bring with them an astounding quantity and variety of fish. Five centuries ago, a Venetian navigator in the service of Portugal, Alvise da Cà da Mosto, spoke of immense banks of sardines, anchovy and squid. In addition, there are barracuda, tuna, blue marlin, ladyfish, white sea bream, sailfish, sole, mullet, flying fish, wahoo, shark... The list is endless.

The fishermen I saw were some of the few survivors of drought and war. They are Chnagla, erstwhile troglodytic cliff-face dwellers, who excel in the art of catching crabs and shellfish, the detritus of which litters the roadside. Although visibly impoverished, the few Chnagla that I saw seemed happy enough, waving and shouting greetings as I struggled by against the wind. Drought, however, has forced many others to abandon their traditional ways of life, and to move instead to towns such as Tan-Tan, Tarfaya and Layoune. The saddest displacement of all took place early in the war against Polisario, when thousands of Saharawis were forced to flee their homelands for Algeria. On the outskirts of Tindouf, a town near the Moroccan frontier, there is a bleak tent city, where an estimated 160,000 Saharawi refugees live in forgotten exile, subsisting on rationed handouts from international charities and agencies. It is said that sixty children died on each day of the exodus, on which some families walked over 700 miles to escape the bloodshed. It is a damning indictment on the world's politicians and indeed the United Nations that neither the plight of the refugees, nor the war from which they fled and that is still raging, has not met with more positive action.

* * *

Oued Chebeïka, one of the Western Sahara's few rivers, is a short seasonal waterway that feeds from low hills that I could see to my left. The causeway across it was flanked on either side by a crazy paving of cracked mud, beyond which the two soldiers manning the next roadblock eagerly awaited my arrival. Then came Punta del Morro/Ras Ajhennir and the mouth of the stagnant Oued el-Amra, the Red River.

Over the river the road then veered a few miles inland as the cliffs gave way to an area of silken sand dunes. As luck would have it, no sooner had I crossed the river than an old Bedford lorry carrying a consignment of soft drinks pulled up beside me. A man opened the cab door which read: 'Allah is all Wise. Allah knows all.' The man jumped out, said hello, and then asked if I'd like a lemonade. I was given a bottle of coke, then the man shook my hand, wished me good luck, clambered back into his cab and drove away. It was the last vehicle I was to see for over a day.

By late afternoon, I came to a small and utterly surreal settlement (unmarked on my map, of course) which consisted of an arcade of cafe-restaurants, a garage and a petrol station. With hindsight (and a decent map) this was Sidi-Akhfennir, a roadstead that had grown up around the *koubba* of its eponymous saint, whose mausoleum – the usual domed cube – seemed to levitate above a lake of pale cinnamon sand. The proprietors of the cafes – all fifteen of them! – gazed longingly at me. Apart from the coke lorry, I had seen no other traffic all day, and therefore any potential customers for these sad little cafes.

The next day, in the afternoon, the town of Tarfaya eventually resolved itself in the distance, at the far end of beautiful white sandy beach. Situated at the tip of Cap [cape] Juby, it is known among mariners as 'the graveyard of sailors.' In 1810, a certain Alexander Scott aboard the *Montezuma* was wrecked here, and consequently spent the next six years of his life in Moorish captivity. That same year, an American brig called the *Charles* also foundered here. The ship's crew included a certain Robert Adams (alias Benjamin Rose), who was to become the first white man since the 1630s to have returned alive from the forbidden city of Timbuctoo. He made his journey on foot, as a slave, and was held for three years until bought his freedom by the British Consul at Oued Noun. Adam's subsequent account of his visit to Timbuctoo, published in 1816, was discounted at the time – in both Paris and London – as pure fabrication. His faux pas had been that his description of the city had not once mentioned gold. Although we now know that his was probably the most accurate account of its time (the gold trade had by then slowed to a mere trickle), that it did not mention gold was seen as proof that he had never been to the city with the golden rooves. The first European to visit Timbuctoo was also wrecked off this coast. He was a Frenchman, a sailor called Paul Imbert, who was captured by the Moors in 1630. The unfortunate Imbert, however, was never released, and died as a slave in Morocco. René Caillié, who in 1828 was to receive the glory of all France for being the first white man to return alive from Timbuctoo, was therefore not the first, but only the third. The difference was that he had not been shipwrecked, and was therefore the first to achieve the feat of his own volition.

A low, sandy cape bordered by reefs, the beach to the north of Tarfaya was littered with the wrecks of five ships, the largest being the Spanish grain cargo*Monte Altube*, wrecked in 1972 and now broken into at least three sections. How appropriate, I think now, this combination of beauty and treachery.

The main reason for Cap Juby being so treacherous is that even at its highest – a hefty twelve metres! – in any sea conditions other than glassy smooth, it is invisible to sailors. And because here is the only part of the West African seaboard to run longitudinally from east to west, it is all too easy for ships sailing southwards simply to plough into the shore with their captains thinking that they are still safely out at sea. The Portuguese called it *Cap de Sabion* – the Cape of Sand – which describes it and its dangers perfectly.

Cap Juby was first settled in 1879 by the British, who needed a trading base from which to compete with the Spanish Canary Islands, seventy miles offshore. Donald Mackenzie's North-West Africa Company, which won the contract from the British government, dutifully named the place Port Victoria. Mackenzie himself was a bit of a character, and the author of a fantastical plan to dig a canal from Cap Juby all the way to Timbuctoo. It was an outlandish pipe dream encouraged by the recent completion of the Suez canal, and indeed by the support of its constructor, Ferdinand Marie de Lesseps. Mackenzie's book detailing the scheme (*The Flooding of the Sahara*, 1877) was undoubtedly a factor in encouraging the equally batty notion of a trans-Saharan railroad, reconnaissance for which led to the abortive and disastrous 'Flatters Expedition' of 1880-81, in which most of its 93 members were annihiliated by Tuareg. Mackenzie himself, though, seemed to be blessed by luck. In 1895, he managed to sell the useless and already crumbling Port Victoria to the Moroccan sultan, for the then astronomical sum of £50,000.

Next, in 1916, came the Spanish – though, it must be said, rather grudgingly – after a German UC20 U-boat was discovered offloading Turkish Qur'ans and Krupp munitions for Ahmed el-Hiba's forces. The Spanish, though, like the British, had little use for the place, and its importance extended only to providing a staging post for the pioneering trans-Atlantic *Aéropostale* service. Thus it was that in 1958, Spain abandoned Cap Juby and the surrounding region (so-called Spanish Morocco) to Morocco, leaving only a church, a barracks and a handful of moulding villas behind.

Tarfaya nowadays, I found to be not much of an improvement. It was nothing more than an ill-stocked outpost, plagued by mosquitos and infested with woodlice. Its official population is 7,000, though I found that hard to believe. Sand drifts lined the main street, a cul-de-sac, which boasted only few shops. Midday during Ramadan, and there was no bread to be had for love or money. Apparently one can buy tuna and swordfish here, but I couldn't even find a can of sardines. I also didn't like the dirty looks that the children were giving me, and so I left as soon as I found a shop prepared to sell me some peanuts.

Perhaps I am a little unkind to Tarfaya, because there was one thing that was memorable about the place, and that was that as soon as I left the town for Layoune – on the other side of the el-Gaada plateau – the northeasterly trade wind made its first appearance, something that made cycling both rapid and a pleasure in itself. Apart from pleasing odd cyclists, though, the trade wind is a curse. It ensures that Saharan evaporation rates are the highest in the world, and has undoubtedly helped a great many ships blunder their way into untimely graves. Another, more immediate, reminder of the cruelty of the wind was the appearance of Erg Lakhbayta, a narrow but tall belt of bright yellow sand dunes that flanked the coast to my right. Erg Lakhbayta was also the cause of the first proper splash of yellow ink on my map, something with which the Mauritanian border – at the very bottom of the sheet – was entirely inundated. It was something which served only to further stiffen my resolve to go there!

The road itself was perfectly engineered, which I found surprising. The reason for the extra attention became obvious as I reached Tah, 35km from Tarfaya on the western rim of the Tah Depression (fifty metres below sea level). At latitude 27°40', Tah is the site of the erstwhile frontier crossing between the Spanish Sahara and Spanish Morocco (the latter – including Tarfaya – was retroceded in 1958 to Morocco). Two key dates in Western Saharan history are commemorated here, in a magnificent monumental gateway consisting of two identical slabs of highly polished black marble. The one commemorates a visit by Sultan Hassan I in 1875. The second honours King Hassan II and the 'Green March' of 1975. It is here that the Spanish border guards gaped helplessly at the invasion of civilians. The word *tah*, rather appropriately, means 'a pouring over', a word used in the past to describe the onslaught of a *razzia*.

I spent my first night in this disputed region on a hillside beside the Sebkha Oum Deboua, and some sort of transmitter station. The only sound was that of the wind blowing against my shirt, and the occasional and very peculiar croaks of a couple of white-crowned black wheatears.

They seemed to be quite fascinated by me, and spent the good part of an hour flitting around overhead. Sunset over the *sebkha* was beautiful in its simplicity.

* * *

The masts, pipes, and exhaust flues of an oil refinery were the first indication that I was approaching Layoune, capital of the Western Sahara. The city is built on the south bank of the Saguia el-Hamra (the Red River Valley) – the Western Sahara's longest and most important river. This, however, means very little, for the river is only seasonal, and often does not flow for many years. In 1941, for instance, fresh water reached the ocean for the first time in three decades. Like the valley of the Drâa, the Saguia el-Hamra was a cradle of ancient civilisation. Prehistoric rock carvings and stone hand tools are to be found throughout the valley. Saguia el-Hamra is also the birth- and resting-place for dozens of saints, including Sidi Loghdof and Sidi Ahmad al-Rgibi, the founder of the powerful Reguibat tribe. The river is also the homeland of the pastoralist Tekna, who stem from a Yemeni tribe who migrated here in the 13th century. They had begun their great journey two hundred years earlier, as troublesome refugees who flooded into Egypt like swarms of locusts, according Ibn Khaldûn. They soon outstayed their welcome, and were hounded westwards where it was hoped that the Berbers would prove more than a match for them. This was indeed the case, and the unwanted visitors were pushed south of the Drâa by the Merinids. Their descendants remain here to this day, some of whom – until recently – bolstered their standard of living with fearsome *razzias* on caravans. In the past few decades, though, the fate of the once all-powerful Tekna has become all too familiar to the Saharawis. The war and concurrent droughts have forced many to move to the towns, where some own shops and businesses, but have little hope of ever returning to the nomadic ways of their forefathers.

The Saguia el-Hamra is, not surprisingly, of some importance to Polisario (its acronym includes the river), with the result that this region, perhaps more than any other, has suffered most consistently in the fighting. The oasis of Lemseyed, a Moroccan infantry outpost not even five miles away, was last attacked by the guerillas only a year before my visit, and Layoune, in consequence, was swarming with military. Before even being allowed into town, I was stopped on the north bank of the river by soldiers manning yet another checkpoint. For a change, the guards were in no mood for joking. Among many other things (a search of my body and my panniers, and a long questionnaire),

I had to show them my map, because those that distinguish Morocco from the Western Sahara – in addition to those that mark the disputed borders with Algeria (such as Michelin publications) – are illegal, as are guidebooks with similar illustrations, or ones with more than just a brief outline of the conflict. For once, my map – published by the Ministry of Agriculture and Agricultural Reform of the Kingdom of Morocco – served me admirably well. The soldier even allowed himself a chuckle when he saw how useless it was, and handed it back exclaiming: 'You should get a better map, Nazarene, or you may lose yourself.' He then added, as a supposedly humourous afterthought: 'And perhaps you may also lose your head.'

Official maps, such as the one I had, went so far in places that even some towns were omitted, undoubtedly for reasons of national security. Even Tah, the old border crossing, was missing, as was the defensive wall – despite which, the road across it to Mauritania was drawn on as though the war had never existed. More serious is government control of the media (with a few notable exceptions, nonetheless). The papers regularly print 'testimonies' from important foreigners, supposedly attesting Morocco's rightful claim to sovereignty over the Western Sahara. One typical issue of an English-language résumé of the month's news included the sanctimonious eulogies of the West German ambassador to Rabat, his Polish counterpart, and one article captioned: 'The Sahara Is Part Of Morocco: Said President Omar BONGO of Gabon'. He, incidentally, is a dictator known primarily for his silver-plated personal ambulance and his gold-plated Cadillac. Television confessions and denunciations also play a regular part in this diet of propaganda, usually by 'Polisario defectors'. The papers also refer to Polisario (which they try to avoid as much as possible) as 'mercenaries' or 'bandits', and say that the refugee camps at Tindouf are merely camps of torture. I leave to the back of this book[7] details of Morocco's own record on human rights, which reduces its propaganda (like all propaganda) to the level of sick farce.

Although Layoune was founded in 1932, it is the war that has spawned the growth of this strange modern city of the desert. Still a small outpost in 1975, Morocco, when it came to occupy the region, decided to make of Layoune the jewel of the Western Sahara, living proof of Morocco's generous patronage. Layoune is the Moroccan dream of modernity set into concrete, a triumph of man's industry over the brutish and inhospitable desert. The money that was sunk into Layoune helped to pay for the contruction of an entirely new part of town, as well as an airport, a Grand Hotel, and a royal palace, the latter built especially for the king's visit in 1985. Layoune is forever being expanded: new buildings, roads, schools, a stadium, another hospital, another mosque for the faithful... Layoune, like Saudi Arabia's neo-modernist desert cities, is a place that is both arrogant and woefully lacking in character. To be fair, perhaps this is a phenomenon common to all newly-built cities, and one that can only be remedied only through the passing of time.

Like all concrete towns built in, or on, the edges of great wildernesses, Layoune sustains a healthy element of the absurd. One evening, in the dying embers of sunset, I saw a middle-aged man who had erected a wooden-framed glass panel in the middle of the street beside the Souk el-Djemal (the defunct camel market, now occupied by greengrocers). The man bore an uncanny resemblance to King Hassan, with his fat but dignified blue blood nose, his red fez and his cream-coloured jellaba (perhaps the effect was intentional). He began his patter – like the TV ads for Royal Air Maroc – with exhortations to Allah (it seems as though Allah can sell anything). Brandishing a bundle of xeroxed sheets in one hand, with the other he was eagerly (and anxiously) demonstrating a patent rubber squeegee. Handing a foam-filled plastic bucket to a lone housewife, he urged her to have a go herself, to *feel* how effortlessly the new invention glided over the window pane – splosh, squeak, squatch, screech! And then, as if to demonstrate the efficaciousness of this gadget, he ran his thumb nail across the glass and then beamed triumphantly as we cringed. Unimpressed, the housewife walked away, leaving only me to keep the man company. It appeared that a medicine man nearby had robbed him of his punters.

I found a hotel that was both cheap and quiet, a rare combination. I was initially offered a windowless room inhabited by cockroaches, but ended up plumping for a three-legged bed and a slanting floor overlooking the busy Rue Mouhamed Salm. The concierge was teenager called Abdellah Ali el-Hajji, who, like Hakim of Chefchaouen's Pension Kasbah, had a very coquettish giggle, and the habit of tilting his head to one side whenever he spoke or was embarrassed. Unlike Hakim, however, Abdellah was notorious among his friends for being a womanizer, who, whenever his charms were found wanting, indulged in a special half-price deal that he had negotiated with Aïsha, the hotel's resident whore.

I was invited to spend one morning with his family for a traditional dinner of couscous (dinner, during Ramadan, is taken before sunrise, while breakfast, confusingly, is served at dusk). On this occasion, the couscous was served with lamb, pepper and onion, with a side dish of cumin and salt to rub into the meat. The el-Hajjis were devoutly Muslim and, needless to say, had not the faintest inkling of what their son got up to behind their backs. I also suspected that they were none too pleased to see the filthy *N'srani* that their son had dragged in.

The meal began with the ritual purification of hands and faces, using lavender-scented water poured from an ornate silver jug. For my part, I had also to wash my hair, which was fair enough given the state it had got into. Then, a simple grace was offered – *'Bismillah'* (In the Name of Allah) – before we all tucked in. In keeping with tradition, eating with the left hand was strictly frowned upon (it is used in the toilet), so that when I once absent-mindedly held a serving spoon in that hand, I was given a dirty look from father el-Hajji, whilst his wife got up to fetch another spoon. I apologized profusely, and from then on, followed precisely the movements of my hosts.

Both Abdellah's parents had been on the Hajj, the pilgrimage which all Muslims are expected to complete at least once during their lifetimes. It is performed during the second week of Dhull-Hijja – the 12th month of the Hejiran calendar – and represents the fulfilment of many a pious Muslim's dreams. Whosoever enters Mecca and touches the Black Stone of the Ka'bah attains eternal security. As a result, the el-Hajji family were well entitled to their name, which means 'the pilgrim'.

The el-Hajji household was only modestly furnished. Abdsalam (the father) only just made a living from his store, selling anything from Butagaz cannisters to nylon stockings. There were a few family photographs hung on the walls, although pride of place was given to two framed portraits of the king and his father. The el-Hajji's were staunch royalists, and had *willingly* emigrated from Casablanca to aid the re-population of 'Our Sahara'. I suspect that they considered themselves and their duty in much the same way as the Quakers might have felt aboard the Mayflower. Abdellah shared little of his parents' puritanical enthusiasm, and longed instead for the cosmopolitan pleasures that had been left behind.

We talked little throughout the meal, except towards the end, when both parents politely urged me to finish the enormous quantity of couscous that remained. The meal ended with the usual *alhamdulillah* and the regulation three glasses of mint tea (during which the conversation died completely). Finally, and to everyone's relief, I made my excuses and walked back to the hotel.

* * *

Just past Layoune airport, dominated by three camouflaged Hercules transports and a couple of Sikorsky gunships, I was stopped at yet another roadblock. 'Do you *have* to cycle to Dakhla?' the soldier asked wearily, not, I sensed, out of any concern at my imminent kidnapping by Polisario, but because he was incredulous that anyone would actually *want* to go there. With hindsight I can well understand his astonishment.

The exact distance between Layoune and Dakhla (erstwhile capital of the former Mauritanian-occupied sector) is something of a mystery. My map indicated 580km, although for the most part the road was marked only as a dotted line, and a seemingly random one at that (as though the cartographer had simply got bored with accuracy). The Michelin map of Northwest Africa states 559km, and another one omits the road altogether. Even stranger was a roadsign I passed outside Bou-Izakarn, the distances of which I'd scribbled into my diary. By subtracting the figure it gave for Layoune from that to Dakhla, I arrived at 697km, which was the same as that given by a similar roadsign near Tan-Tan. Whatever the distance, the actual route that the road took was quite unlike anything marked on any map, past or present, although in the event, the trade wind succeeded in turning what had at first seemed a daunting prospect by bicycle, to be as easy as a Sunday morning ride around the streets of Manchester.

For the first 20km – the only stretch that all the maps agreed on – the road ran westwards across the dunes of Erg Lakhbayta to rejoin the coast. Cycling across the dunes, I had to keep my eyes half shut to avoid the windblown sand. Huge sand breaks were ineffectual in preventing the southward march of the dunes across the road, which in parts was totally swamped. A couple of sand ploughs struggled gamely to keep the road open – an endless and thankless task. Although sand was to dominate the landscape for much of the day, Erg Lakhbayta itself was left behind as the road hit the coast and turned south again towards Boujdour and Dakhla. Shortly after Layoune Plage – swamped by sand and choked of all life – the road swung round a huge phosphate factory, the last building I was to see until evening. From the mines at Bou Crâa – one hundred kilometres inland – the ore is transported along the world's longest conveyor belt all the way across the desert and straight into the heart of the factory. Bou Crâa started production in 1972, but had to be shut down in 1975 because of Polisario attacks. It had only recently resumed production, and I was stopped at two seperate checkpoints where my papers and bags were scrutinized with uncommon meticulousness.

The war meant that there was more traffic in these parts than further north: invariably military. By midday (when all traffic ceased), I had seen seven Land Rovers and four trucks, driving south in two convoys. Towards evening, I settled down behind a clump of acacia, having heard the approach of another convoy. Crouching alongside a helmeted gecko, I saw nine lorries pass me by, loaded with guns, personnel carriers, and the dreaded *Stalin's Organs* – multiple missile launchers made in Ceaucescu's Romania.

Roughly one hundred kilometres from Layoune is Lemsid and the *koubba* of Sidi Mohammed Bou Gambour, which, like so many other Western Saharan mausolea, was destroyed in the war. Lemsid was the smallest settlement that I was to see in all my travels and, to my utter amazement, was marked on my map! It consisted of precisely two huts and one cafe-cum-restaurant. The latter was painted in gaudy two-tone pink and caramel, and the sand around it was littered with rugged piles of blown-out and shredded tyres, smashed hurricane lamps, various engine parts, broken axles and a rusty 1950s petrol pump. There was no one about. This, to the best of my abilities, is an exhaustive description of Lemsid.

* * *

The following morning, at a roadblock just outside Boujdour:

'Ah, *N'srani!*' exclaimed the soldier manning the barrier, who later asked: 'You *do know* what is *Nooo-sra-ni?*'

'*Nooo-sra-ni,*' he explained pedantically, 'is an infidel, a dog, a woof-woof! You understand? *I*, however, am not a dog. I am *Musulman*, a servant of Allah. Allah who is the most merciful. Allah who is the most high...'

I was obliged to endure this irksome man for over an hour, since I was to be escorted into town for further questioning. Once there, in the army headquarters, I was subjected to half an hour of suspicious interrogation by a fat and heavily bearded gentleman, who sat behind a typewriter throughout. Using one finger, he laboriously thumped out my details on a xeroxed sheet of paper, as I stood in front of his desk like a naughty schoolboy.

'How long have you been in Morocco?' asked the commissioner.

'What are your motives for coming here?'

'Where have you been in Morocco?'

'How long do you intend to stay in Boujdour?'

'How long do you intend to remain in Morocco?'

'Where are you going to afterwards?'

'What is the maiden name of your mother?'

'What is her nationality?'

'Where did she study?'

'What colour are her eyes?'

'Do you love your mother?' All the time, he assiduously typed down my responses.

'Ah, that is good. Very good. And your father?'

'Hmm, yes…'

At last, he stood up, shook my hand very firmly and painfully, and said: 'Very good, you may go now, *N'srani.*' He even allowed himself a glimmer of a smile. Perhaps the Nazarene was not the devil in disguise after all. But the oddest thing was that, as I was leaving his office, I caught a glimpse of the sheet that he had been typing on: '0rtksvh FFTHY fdkytu…' [etc]. He had covered it, from top to bottom, in utter gibberish!

Apart from the military presence, the one-street town of Boujdour has an unexpectedly attractive air about it. Perhaps, though, it was my mind playing romantically with its history. The triangle of ocean between Cap Juby, the Canary Islands and Cap Bojador (Boujdour) is the southern limit of the variable Atlantic winds, meaning that from here on, the trade winds dominate exclusively. It is for this reason that in the age of sailing ships, Cap Bojador came to be the absolute southernmost limit to which sailors dared venture, for fear of being blown so far south by the trades that returning to Europe would be made impossible (as the two unfortunate Vivaldi brothers found out in 1291, who were never heard of again, and were presumed to have been blown off the edge of the world). In addition, sailing was rendered treacherous by a strong offshore current, as well as the risk of frequent and unexpected storms. Neither was the confusion surrounding the etymology of Cap Juby and Cap Bojador any great help. As early as 1375, the Catalan World Atlas of Abraham Cresques mentioned a cape called 'buyetdor', only it was marked at Cap Juby, a confusion that prevailed until the last century.

In many ways, the Atlantic was as formidable a barrier to African exploration as was the Sahara: the ultimate frontier beyond which it was impossible to venture, the 'Land of the Setting Sun' where Sidi Uqba ibn Nafi rode his steed into the ocean to proclaim, in the sight of Allah, that he had conquered all the land that there was left to conquer. South of Bojador, legend had it, lay the dreaded 'Mare Tenebrosum': in al-Masudi's words, 'The Green Sea of Darkness', which was worshipped out of dread by the early Saharawis, who made sacrifices and offerings to calm its frequent rages. Alexander the Great is said to have built a tower in this 'Foetid Sea' engraved with the words 'Let whosoever cometh to this place with the intention of sailing over this sea know that I have locked it up...'⁸. The Greeks believed that the Pillars of Hercules (Djebel Musa and the Rock of Gibraltar) guarded the passage to Hades and the 'Exterior Sea', and perhaps even to the lost kingdom of Atlantis.

> I and my companions were old and weary, when we reached the narrow strait where Hercules set up his boundary-marks, to the end that no man should proceed beyond
>
> Dante, *Hell*, Canto XXVI

As time went on, the fear of this ocean became more embellished in fable. The Atlantic beyond Bojador was commonly believed to be an all-consuming sea of liquid fire where only those who had made a pact with the devil could sail. Tales abounded of monsters and demons that inhabited the seas beyond the Canary Islands: seven-headed dragons, the leviathan, and man-eating sea serpents. The conqueror of the sea and its legends was Gil Eanes, equerry to Prince Henry the Navigator of Portugal (in whose honour Boujdour's ancient lighthouse is dedicated). In 1434, enticed by rumours of a legendary 'Golden River' that lay further south, Eanes became the first sailor to round Cap Bojador and return alive to tell the tale. The secret, he found, was to return to the north not along the coastline, which was more or less fatal, but in mid Atlantic, where the trade winds subsided and the currents from the Americas flowed north.

The rounding of Cap Bojador was an achievement that changed the entire course of world exploration. The Gold Coast (modern Ghana) was discovered in 1475, the Congo in 1482, and in 1487 the Cape of Good Hope was rounded for the first time by Bartolomeu Dias, who called it the Cape of Storms. Ten years later – barely half a century after rounding Cap Bojador – Portuguese caravels under Vasco da Gama had reached India and all its riches. Thus, it can truly be said that the dawning of the new modern era began not with Columbus' 'discovery' of the New World in 1492, but with Gil Eanes' rather more humble voyage 58 years earlier.

* * *

The soldier at the next roadblock, a few miles to the south of Boujdour, was fast asleep when I arrived. A scruffy man, with a beard as scrappy as mine, he kept saying how kind I was for actually having bothered to wake him up, for otherwise he might have got into trouble with his superiors. When I asked him whether the road south from Dakhla to

Mauritania was open, he replied with the stock excuse that the immediate region around it was still mined with explosives, that the road was still being surfaced, and that it was therefore out of bounds. I didn't want to believe him, and said so, but he just shrugged and said that he looked forward to seeing me again when I came back up north. He added that I should count myself fortunate enough in being able to travel to Dakhla at all, because the road had been closed until only the very week before.

The sky was muggy, the air humid, and the heat feverish. By mid-afternoon it had reached 55°C (131°F), and I was thankful for the good road. Throughout the day, the scenery changed very little. The rocky ground, and sometimes the road, was covered with sand, in places thick enough to merit being called dunes. There was, as usual, very little vegetation that could survive in this waste. One of the few exceptions – and the most noteworthy – was *Acacia radiana*, a low bush which, as its name suggests, grows in ever expanding circles, so that from above it would look like an archer's target. At first glance, the wildlife too was nonexistent, but that was not entirely the case. Insects and arachnids, especially, thrive in these conditions. Flies were the most irritating, and followed me everywhere, sometimes riding pillion on my panniers or shirt. They had the annoying habit of getting trapped between my face and the *cheche*, and then panicking. Ants, too, were regular companions, often hiding away in the round loaves of bread that I carried along with me. To my relief, though, I never once saw a scorpion (whose venom can be as poisonous as that of a cobra) – mainly because I made a point of not sticking my hand under rocks and in crevices. There was also a wide selection of beetles and cockroaches, although locusts, this far south, had virtually disappeared – a telling indication of the sparsity of vegetation. Snakes, though, were common, either buried like coiled ropes in the sand, or else squashed flat by vehicles, as were a variety of lizards, frogs and toads, jerboas (the desert rat), and hares. There were strange white skinks too, their shiny fish-scaled skins splattered with bright red blood. A few decades ago I might have seen gazelle, wild camels, ostrich, fennec (desert fox), oryx and addax antelopes. Nowadays, they are endangered or else already extinct.

The desert seemed as hostile to me as an ocean would be to a shipwrecked mariner. The land was eerily silent in its vastness, and yet, it was a beautiful silence. The Arabs tell a tale about Allah having created the desert so that He could be at peace with Himself when reflecting on the world that He had created. I imagined that if He were to spend too long a time in all this silence, then He too would begin to go slightly mad. I remember once picking up a pebble that was more or less the exact replica of a nearby mountain, eroded to reveal layer upon layer of stratified rock. I put it in my mouth, chewed it for a while, and then spat it out. I also recall laughing for a good half hour at the thought of darkling beetles and the droning *bukhakes* bumblebee-beetle of the Rif exploding, caused by the air in their pockets overheating: *Bzzzzz, bzzzzz, bzzzzzzz...* BANG! I also recalled English pop songs, that whirred endlessly through my head as the wheels whirred through the sand, though the thing that annoyed me most was that I could only ever remember two or three tunes, and so for hours I would whistle and hum the same piece over and over again, until I became so sick of it that I condemned my physical struggles to silence.

About fifty or sixty kilometres south of Boujdour I came to an area of wind-scarred ruins, interlaced with barbed wire and anonymous mechanical contraptions that were scattered around. As far as could make out, this was the abandoned settlement of Aoufist [though it may have been Hassi Aouziouah – curse my map!]. Here, an earlier part of the Moroccan defensive wall drops down all the way to the coast. The beach to my right was barred with wire, concrete and mounds of rubble. From Aoufist, all maps were ignored again as the road started up the valley of the dead river Assaq, where in the year 1500, the Spanish – who had wanted to construct a fort at its mouth – were massacred by local tribes. The river hasn't flowed for decades. The land hereabouts consisted of bizarrely eroded tufa – a porous rock made of calcium carbonate deposited from ancient springs – which crumbled like meringue if ever I touched it. On leaving the valley – some way inland – the colour of the land turned to a violent orange, a maddening Martian landscape that contrasted starkly with the bright blue sky. Mile upon mile of flat orange desert followed, devoid of any wildlife whatsoever, flattened or otherwise. The infinite disc of the rusty horizon was interrupted only by lazy mirages with blurred edges that floated across my vision. In places, not a single twig or blade of grass could be seen, and the only relief for my sun-broiled eyes was the blue sky. The early morning clouds had been blown swiftly away in the hot and dusty wind, but this only made the heat bite still more keenly. My nose once again got red and burnt, as did my cheeks and forehead, despite the protection of the *cheche*.

For much of the day, the only living creature that I saw was a solitary cream-coloured courser, huddled in the scant shade of a small bush. I was surprised to see such a delicate little thing in such a harsh place, and so I stopped cycling and walked towards her. At first, she feigned death, but was given away by the shrill cries of her distant chicks. Then she flew about in short leaps, hoping to lure me away from the nest (the courser is one of the few birds to nest in the desert). It is odd to realise that birds are in fact the last surviving true dinosaurs. I suspect that they have survived so long because of their mobility, their migrations. In a way, I had followed them down all the way from England (several species nest there and fly across the Sahara to spend their winter in Senegal). The Arabic verb 'to travel' (*safara*) is related to the word *saffat*, which describes the soaring of flocks of birds.

To travel with the wind is something truly fabulous, especially on a bicycle. On the newly-built road, the going was easy, and the kilometres fell quickly away to the sound of hissing rubber on smooth asphalt, and to the sound of my body: inhaling, exhaling, inhaling... the only rhythm that I could hear. There are no limits to the wheel. No top and no bottom. No one point that is forever rooted to the ground or yearning for the sky. A wheel can only turn, turn around and around. The bicycle was perfect in its simplicity – the perfect machine. When it behaved, and didn't cause me too much anguish with punctures and squeaks and jammed gears or chain, it was almost an extension of my body, and no longer a mechanical 'thing' on top of which I had to fight and curse in order to get somewhere. At times like these the whole world seemed to be a perfect kind of place, and I was happy.

Heat and monotony mesmerise the traveller. All deserts have unusually high rates of road accidents (in spite of there being little to collide with). A particularly gruesome sight was the aftermath of a crash that had involved a lorry carrying a load of goats. Although the vehicle had been towed away (I saw its remains in Dakhla, and was told that five people had been killed), much debris remained, in addition to sixteen dead goats, some bloated in the heat, others dismembered, their limbs and other pieces of flesh scattered over the road: bloodied ears, legs, heads, and guts. The stench made me sick. When I turned to look back at the scene, a couple of miles afterwards, I saw a jackal flitting between some nearby boulders. I was pleased to have seen a live desert mammal, and the jackal made me smile. At least someone had gained from all the carnage, I thought, as I headed off towards Dakhla.

Eventually, in the evening of the third day from Layoune, I reached a road junction. The left branch ostensibly led to Mauritania via the bordertown of Lagouera, 400km to the south. The other fork went to Dakhla, situated at the very end of a 40km peninsula (hence its full name, Ad-Dakhla, which means 'the Bay's Mouth'). Beside the junction were mounds of rubble and grit, rolls of barbed wire, geometric concrete castings, and a couple of large bulldozers. These, I was told later, were for building the road to Lagouera. The barbed wire and concrete blocks, however, led me to the conclusion that these materials were being used only to bolster the defensive wall that runs alongside the Mauritanian frontier. The sixth and final stage of this project was completed in April 1987, after heavy fighting. The wall stretches over 1500km, and is made of sand, rubble, barbed wire and land mines, and is protected by electronic sensors, radar, tanks, and 160,000 troops. The cost of these defences were estimated in 1988 to run into the order of one million US dollars each and every day.

For a while, I was tempted to try the Lagouera road regardless of what I had been told, until a passing police car stopped and warned me of land mines south of the village of Al-Argoub (40km away). Reluctantly, but not overly willing to risk being shot at or else blown sky-high, I took the road to Dakhla. Not even two minutes' cycling brought me to yet another roadblock: the old and once picturesque settlement of Tamayya, which now houses a small barracks to guard the neck of the peninsula. Bleached and threadbare flags fluttered atop a couple of very tall poles, and the soldiers looked meaner and altogether much more serious than elsewhere. I was ordered to stop with machine guns pointed at my chest, and it took quite an exhaustive show of friendly smiles, humouring platitudes and solemn assurances for the soldiers to drop their suspicions, and their weapons. Again, I was recounted the official excuse that the road south had not yet been properly asphalted, and was therefore out of bounds, which was plainly nonsense. Pleading for a lift on some army truck was no good either. When I asked how the people in Lagouera coped with not being able to travel up to Dakhla, I was bluntly told that there no longer were any people in Lagouera.

'You, mister...' He burbled my name as he read it from my passport. 'You, *monsieur*, are going back to Layoune. You are going back *now*. *Yallah*, be off with you!'

After a good deal of pleading (I was damned if I was going to cycle back up north against the wind), I finally got permission to travel as far as Dakhla, on condition that I reported immediately to the chief commissioner of the gendarmerie, and to ensure that I did this, he radioed through my details. I was bitterly disappointed as I left the *barrage*, knowing that Dakhla was the end of my travels in the Western Sahara. I was especially gutted by the thought that to reach Mauritania would have only required another three days cycling, and that, instead, I would have to pay my way there via Layoune and an expensive flight via the Canaries. At least I could console myself with the fact that I had been luckier than some. In Boujdour, I'd seen a couple of Frenchmen turned back by the military. They had hoped to go sea-bass fishing off Dakhla.

The panorama from the neck of the peninsula was beautiful. The dusky pastel light, so soft and yet so bright, seemed to stroke the silvery sand flats, velvety dunes and sapphire sea. To my right lay the crumbling white ruins of an ancient tufa fort or barracks, it was hard to tell which. In the bay to my left, dolphins and seals bobbed about and played. There was a slight breeze, which made the atmosphere most bearable, and the chalky tufa clearings caught the setting sun with a deepening glow of warmth. But there was also a sinister undercurrent to all this. After all, I was in a war zone. This knowledge was hard to reconcile with the beauty of the land. It was also difficult to tell whether the ruins of the fort really were ancient, or whether they had, in fact, been bombed to the ground only recently. There were also a few fire-gutted vehicles lying about, and the masts of wrecks protruding from the bay. On the mainland, I thought that I could just make out a faint line of fortifications near Al-Argoub, but perhaps that was just my imagination. Beyond the village is the Tropic of Cancer, south of which is no-man's-land, out of bounds even to the Moroccan military.

The road passed along the remaining thirty-odd kilometres on a sandy causeway only a few feet above the water. To the left and east, between the mainland and the peninsula, was the lagoon of Rio de Oro, sheltering a dozen sandy bays and the island of Kerne (or Herne) where, in 420BC, Hanno the Carthaginian's galleys put in on their journey around Africa (ironically, the Atlantic was navigable in those days, because oars were used instead of sails). Rio de Oro is one of only two important gulfs on the Sahara's Atlantic coastline (the other being the Baie du Lévrier, 400km further south on the Mauritanian border). As its name betrays, European interest in Rio de Oro stemmed from the mistaken belief that there was gold to be had here. Hanno's mission, if his *Periplus* is to be believed, was to establish coastal settlements with the purpose of preserving direct trading links with West Africa, which, according to Herodotus, supplied much of North Africa's gold (West African gold is believed to have been used to cover the Phoenician Temple of Solomon). In the late 14th century, Abraham Cresques' World Atlas mentioned a sea voyage in quest of the *Rio do Ouro*, although nothing more is known about it (perhaps it was a reference to the Vivaldi brothers?). Like those of Timbuctoo, the legends surrounding the mysterious River of Gold grew from strength to strength. According to Yaqut, gold sprouted on its sandy banks like carrots. Others believed that gold grew like coral, renewing itself with the turning of the seasons. Richard de Haldingham's 13th century Mappa Mundi even mentioned the celebrated legend of gold found in the nests of ants, ants – according to Herodotus – 'bigger than a fox, but not so big as a dog.' It now seems incredible that such tales were taken seriously at all, yet even the Genoan secret archives, which determined their goals of exploration throughout the Middle Ages (and which Colombus consulted before chasing his American Utopia), mentioned a river in which:

> one may gather patines of gold... the larger part of the people who inhabit the region are employed in gathering gold from this river which, a league across, is deep enough for even the world's largest vessels.[9]

The Portuguese sailor, Alfonso Goncalves Baldaia, is believed to have been the first European since Hanno to 'discover' Rio de Oro when, in 1436, he returned from the lagoon with the first shipment of black slaves ever brought back to Europe. Gold too, was obtained, though it had to be bartered from the Moors who, with hindsight, had transported it by caravan from the mines in the Tropics. Rio de Oro is, of course, a complete misnomer. Not only is it not a river, but it has absolutely no gold of its own. The Portuguese had mistaken the bay for the river Senegal, seven hundred miles further south, and even it was to disappoint. And with no gold to be found, European interest in the Western Sahara dwindled, to be next rekindled only during the frantic Scramble for Africa in the run-up to the Great War.

I was waved through the last checkpoint – they'd heard that I was coming – and made my way past a massive infantry barracks into the centre of town. Dakhla is a city of long anonymous avenues, cinemas and whores. There is a seaweed processing factory, built in the 1960s, and mile upon mile of tall, unforgiving walls, with few windows or entrances to betray any secrets. There are posters everywhere, advertising Indian love-epics and popular kung fu films, as well as pro-government May Day demonstrations. Because this city is the southern headquarters of the Royal Moroccan Armed Forces, civilians are vastly outnumbered by the military. In any case, most of the original inhabitants fled Dakhla at the outset of the war, and the civilians nowadays are mostly Moroccan settlers. Most of the buildings are official, festooned with flags and the ubiquitous portraits of the king. The beach is a military scrap yard, strewn with old signposts, engines, tattered uniforms, wheels and other mechanical parts. There is a constant flow of tanks, gun-trucks, armoured vehicles and jeeps.

At the *commissariat*, I had to pass three further checkpoints and their sour-faced denizens before being allowed to speak to the commissioner himself. He gave me precisely one day to get out of Dakhla, or else. That was alright, though, because I didn't much want to stay. When I enquired about possible boats to Mauritania, he grinned weakly and shook his head. 'Not possible, not possible,' he sighed. 'The mercenaries, you see. I'm sorry, you had better go.' Nevertheless, I tried the port, but was hounded away by other gendarmes who threw stones and hurled obscenities.

I cycled back to the checkpoint just outside town, and introduced myself, in the hope of catching a lift back to Layoune (from where I would fly to Nouâdhibou via the Canary Islands). The two guards, a soldier and a gendarme, were a peculiar pair. The gendarme resembled Rowan Atkinson both in looks and in his little pernickety mannerisms. For instance, when he sipped tea, he used only his thumb and index finger, the other three fingers pointing away as far as possible from the glass. Then, he would tilt his head right back to reveal his hairy nostrils, before delicately slurping the liquid down his throat to a sound like the last few inches of bathwater disappearing down the plughole.

The soldier was a scatterbrain. He looked permanently dazed and confused, like a child transported into an adult's body. He kept asking the same questions of me, repeating them in an endless dirge. He never managed to grasp the fact that I lived in England and not in France or Spain. He also had the habit of frequently gargling his saliva before spitting it out onto the floor (for strict Muslims, fasting forbids even the swallowing of saliva, and hence kissing). He was also completely entranced by my bicycle, and repeatedly asked whether he could have it as a present. On failing that, he tried everything to get my camera, my anorak, my water bottles, and even my diary!

'Ignore him,' advised the gendarme when the soldier wobbled uneasily away on my bicycle, swerving erratically past a laughable concrete wall built to deter guerilla attacks. 'He is only a small child,' he continued as we heard a distant thud followed by a short yelp.

In the evening, a jeep passed by the checkpoint. On spotting my bicycle, it howled to a halt and disgorged a small man with a mustache. The two guards saluted. Colonel Mahmoud bel Souza wanted to know how the *N'srani* had managed to get here with a bicycle. When I explained that I'd cycled from England, he smiled, and then grinned: 'Yo, boy! You betcha goddam ass you sure am one cooool kat!!!' What could I say? He offered me his hand, then explained that he had been stationed in the States in 1952, and had loved every minute of it. It seemed that the only English he knew was some kind of crazy southern slang, complete with the accent.

'Marine Corps, Louisiana, U. S. of A. D'you know it, boy?'

'No shit, kick-ass! Those goddam sonnovabitch mudderfuckers sure got huge knockers boy!' And when he saw the kilo of dried figs that I'd bought in Dakhla, he exclaimed, 'You sure gonna have one goddam fiery asshole tonite, you betcha goddam ass boy!' He then wished me the best of luck for the rest of my life, saluted and left. The two guards looked on speechless.

Dinner was served at sunset. I was famished! It was a rushed affair of sorts: bread, *harira*, a gloopy rice pudding, mint tea and processed cheese, all in all not bad considering it came courtesy of the Moroccan army. Soon after, the soldier was replaced by another, and immediately, I noticed a degree of animosity between the newcomer and the gendarme. When the former sloped off somewhere, as he often did, the gendarme would lean over the table and confide, rather too theatrically, that the new guy was with Polisario, oh yes, because he was born in Tan-Tan. Despite his overly royalist leanings, though, I quickly got to like the gendarme – he made me laugh. The soldier, too, was okay. He was intelligent, nimble minded, and for his part confessed his belief that the war was futile. He was a fountain of information. Apart from confirming the little I knew about the wall and the no-go areas, he also recited a sad litany of what newspapers would call 'tragic human interest' stories: families who had been ruined when their fathers were killed by land mines; horrific injuries; friends missing in action, and so on. He also pointed out presently 'problematic' zones on my map, meaning areas of ongoing hostility or places under constant threat of guerilla attack. In particular, the region around a village called Techlé, near the Mauritanian border, he called Hell. It was the first time that I had heard the word used in Morocco. Last July, Polisario seized 40km of the wall near Techlé, and the ensuing battle had claimed 275 Moroccan lives. According to the government in Rabat, these were 'sustainable losses'.

As he continued, the soldier became more and more downcast, and no longer criticised only Polisario in his stories. Some of the things he said were disparaging even of the Moroccan army. In particular, he told of one colonel who had forced his prisoners to sweep a minefield by walking across it. It soon became obvious to me that the soldier rarely had the opportunity to talk to someone who wasn't about to report him to the court martial, and several times I got the feeling that he was only telling me all this to alert me to the fact that there *was* a war going on. He wanted to tell me of a war that most of the world prefers to ignore, and that war meant horror, destruction and death. 'Please remember what war really means,' he seemed to be saying across his stories.

The gendarme, on the other hand, believed vehemently in the God-given right of Morocco to occupy the Western Sahara. 'The reason is simple,' he explained: 'this *is* Morocco.' In the gendarme's opinion, anyone who disagreed with this deserved whatever punishment was meted out to them. The original citizens of Dakhla – those who had not joined the exodus to Tindouf – were, in the eyes of this man, traitors, informers, scoundrels and dogs, no better than Christians or other forms of dirt.

Thus counterpoised, the soldier and the gendarme were, in essence, the embodiment of Morocco. All its wisdom and stupidity, its tolerance and bigotry, its contradictions, its generosity, and its naivete contrasting with its intellect and pragmatism. Yet only here, in the war zone, at the very southernmost limit of Hassan's power, did people deign to talk about such matters with an outsider. The soldier even joked about the pictures of the king that adorn every public building in the realm – something that I'd grown quite accustomed to – by saying that he couldn't even pick his nose without Hassan knowing about it. 'Hassan knows all,' he said, leering at the photograph, and that was that.

It was funny to think how perfect a clichéd outpost this little concrete shack was, stuck in all isolation at the end of the world. Even Dakhla was out of sight, no more than a gloaming in the pitch black sky. The wind brought with it great washes of sand and dust that rustled gently over the cabin. Later on, in the silence – the wind now dead – there were bobbing lights of trucks, both military and civilian, little ships sailing a black ocean, riding like brave cavaliers off into the unknown (or so the drivers liked to believe, who festooned their cabs with great twinkling garlands of fairy lights). At night, the stillness overwhelmed the conversation, and we sat, not really thinking or feeling anything, just watching the darkness ebb and sway, at times tense, and then, at other times, welcoming. The air smelt of gasoline and burnt rubber. A praying mantis skidded across the road, in hot pursuit of an unseen insect.

At one point, the soldier wearily heaved himself up and started dancing an improvised jig, his heavy boots kicking up great clouds of dust as he swirled and feigned swoons, flung off his imaginary veils, then grabbed me along too, so that finally we both lay quite still, panting, giggling, spread-eagled on the sand. The gendarme, who had almost fallen off his stool through laughing, then lay down beside us, convulsed in fits of hysterics.

CHAPTER SEVEN

MAURITANIA

...the lande of mauritania [is] a province that hathe been gretelie
named by cosmographours past, for thei take this place for the
ende of the worlde.

Roger Barlow, A brief summe of geographie, *c. 1540-41*

This is Mauritania: the end of the world. It is without doubt the most
amazing place that I have ever seen. Sometimes, on being asked my
impression of it, I reply with only one word: sand. Although only a fifth
of the Sahara lies properly under the stuff, Mauritania does more than
most countries to uphold the commonly held notion of deserts being
limitless oceans of undulating dunes, rolling endlessly unto shimmering mirages under the sweltering gaze of a merciless sky.

With the exception of the eroded Adrar mountains at the heart of the
country, and a thin strip of cultivated land straddling the river Senegal
in the south, much of the 'Vacuum' – as the French referred to
Mauritania – consists of dunes. Covering an area of over a million
square kilometres, Mauritania is a huge and empty land, a desolate and
disconsolate place of burning sands, hopeless plains and blazing skies.
Mauritania is a land of hyenas and jackals, lions and leopards of old, of
holy lizards and accursed locusts. It is a land where bird song is rarely
heard, a land whose dust fills the eyes and heart of man, a land punished
by the perennial trade winds that carry the desert inexorably onwards.
Medieval maps of the region are adorned with the wild beasts and
monsters of fertile imaginations: snakes as long as rivers; dragons and
devils and demons that live beyond the pale of Allah's ordered realm;
armoured dogs whose horns are impaled with human heads; and the
terrible mantichora, a man-eater with the body of a lion, the face and
ears of a man, the quills of a porcupine, and the fatal sting of a scorpion...

> So geographers, in Afric-maps,
> With savage-pictures fill their gaps;
> And o'er unhabitable downs
> Place elephants for want of towns.
>   Jonathan Swift, *On poetry: a rapsody*

Mauritania is also a land that has been raped and pillaged by the droughts of the last two decades, a land trampled under the bloodied boots of poverty and famine. In summer, when for much of the day the sun hovers directly overhead, temperatures commonly surpass 60°C (140°F). In winter, they plummet to below freezing. There is little in the way of tall mountains, or even vegetation, to halt the lethal wind, and rainfall, of course, is almost nonexistent.

Yet this apparently hellish land is home to over two million people, a figure set to double within the next twenty years. The great majority are Moors [*Maure*, from the Phoenician *Mahour*, Men of the West]. Their origins, like that of their Berber, Tuareg and Saharawi cousins, are shrouded in confusion. Of what can be garnered as fact, it seems that three major displacements brought about the existence of these remarkable people.

The first took place in the 7th century, when the first southward Arab-Berber migrations took place, mostly traders and Muslim proselytizers leaving the comfort of the Maghreb for the geographical Sudan, an area corresponding to Mauritania and part of Mali. The subsequent intermarriage of the indigenous Negroes with the white Semite settlers produced the first true ancestors of the Sahara's most important ethnic groups: the Tuareg, the Tibbu, and the Moors. The Moors themselves claim descent from the Sanhaja tribe of Berbers, founders of Northwest Africa's first Berber dynasty, the Almoravids. The next influx of new blood took place in the 15th century, when Yemeni pillagers belonging to the Beni Hassan tribe were hounded out of Morocco by the Merinids. They, in turn, intermarried with the Sanhaja's descendants, and imposed their own language upon them. Hassiniyah, a dialect of Arabic closely related to the classical, is still spoken today. In contrast to the sometimes harsh accents of Moroccan Arabic, Hassiniyah has a soft and pleasant rhythm, easily lending itself to poetry and song. The last great input came in the 16th and 17th centuries, when descendants of the Moroccan sultan Ahmad al-Mansour's army of conquest (many of whose soldiers had settled in the Sudan), shed their past to merge with the nomads.

Not surprisingly, this rich racial heritage is still very much in evidence, with a roughly equal proportion of light and dark skins, and a similar blend of Caucasian and Negro features. The swarthy Moors of European legend are very much a generalisation.

Like the Tuareg, the Moors were – and a minority still are – an essentially nomadic people. But here the comparisons end, for there is one important difference between the two peoples, and that is Islam. As the Arabic language spread westwards from the Middle East, and then south along with the Maghrebi migrations, so did Islam, and in consequence we find that Moorish history runs almost parallel to that of the religion in North and West Africa. The puritanical Almoravids were the first heirs to this legacy, zealots who were to conquer not only Morocco, but the Iberian peninsula and the ancient empires of West Africa. Without the Almoravids, it is possible to argue that Islam would never have survived as long as it did in Spain. Whatever, when Moorish influence in Europe began to wane in the 15th century, many Moors returned to the desert and have lived there to this day.

In the 20th century, the Moors stand alone among other Saharan nomads not only in their religious fervour, but in the fact that they have succeeded in creating their own independent state.

Indeed, until the 15th century, no European (excepting Hanno the Carthaginian, the unfortunate Vivaldi brothers, and a remarkable foray by the legions of Julius Maternus) had even ventured further south than the Maghreb. Even Hannibal, who had dreamed of conquering Europe, never once considered the continent whence he came. Naturally, the desert itself was a formidable barrier to overland conquest, and furthermore, the Moors and the Tuareg (and their ancestors) had acquired awesome reputations for warlike savagery. The Victorians used the fearsome spectres of the moor and blackamoor, alongside that of the bogeyman, to frighten naughty children into behaving. As nomads, the Moors were long regarded by Europeans as being somewhat less than human. According to Dom João de Castro, writing in 1541, they were:

> wild men, amongst whom is no civill societie, no truth nor civilitie... above all other People they are given to Stealths and Rapine; they eate raw flesh... their habit is vile and filthy.

Even Walter Harris, who on the whole seemed to respect the Moors, wrote:

> the Moors are not far removed from savages. They possess very little feeling of any sort; love little but their women – whom they treat as an English costermonger treats his donkey...

Not surprisingly, quelling these people was long deemed both impossible and futile, especially when given that most sub-Saharan goods such as gold and slaves were in any case freely available in the souks of the Maghreb.

European involvement in Mauritania dates from 1441, when Portuguese mariners reached Cap Blanc, a narrow peninsula now forming the northernmost extremity of Mauritania's Atlantic coastline. Nearby, on the tiny isle of Arguin, traders established a *factoria* in anticipation of a massive trade in gold dust. In time, though, the *factoria* was to prove rather more useful in trading gum arabic and slaves. But despite the florid and often exaggerated claims of contemporary historians, European influence was at best negligible beyond the confines of coast, and its few inland adventures invariably ended in disaster, cursed either by the desert or its unruly inhabitants. It is a measure of the Moors' power to remain independent that it took the French until 1934 – 117 years after the Treaty of Paris which had granted her the territory, and not even thirty before independence was regained – to achieve their 'pacification'. In consequence, both the land and its people remain to this day largely untouched by external influences.

For my part, I am ashamed to admit that it was only until halfway through my stay in the country that I even managed to recall, spell and speak the name of Mauritania. I sincerely hope that the following chapters in some way atone for my initial ignorance.

* * *

Las Palmas International Airport, Gran Canaria:
Innumerable strange voices swelling and falling like the surface of a deep ocean, filled the waiting lounge for the delayed twice-weekly flight to Nouâdhibou. It was a soothing hubbub to while away the long wait. Despite being in the Canary Islands, I seemed already to be back in Africa, and the Spanish announcements over the tannoy sounded alien and out of place. The majority of the travellers were Moroccan, invariably wealthy businessmen. Most were dressed in the traditional jellabas (despite the heat), but the younger among them wore loosely-tailored suits and ties. The Mauritanians, both black and white, wore *boubous*, looser and lighter versions of the jellaba which, when indigo-dyed, closely resemble the garb of the Tuareg. The other passengers were mainly Negroes from the sedentary Tukolor and Wolof tribes of the very south of the country. The Tukolor spoke a dialect of Fulfulde, common throughout Senegal and southern Mauritania. The language is easily distinguishable by its typically sub-Saharan glottal stops used in

the pronunciation of some consonants. A man called N'dour amused himself no end with my attempts to pronounce his name, the 'N' being articulated at the same time as clicking one's throat. The Wolofs, for their part, gabbled non-stop, the women clucking and tutting like hens. The Wolof are known throughout West Africa for their garrulousness, and who were they to disappoint me? For some reason, they were all travelling with their families, and their conversations were punctuated with searing peals of laughter. It is said that Africa boasts over one thousand languages – the richest and most vibrant oral tradition in the world.

Eventually, we were herded on to the tarmac and into a sweltering forty-degree heat, whereupon a handful of passengers produced prayer mats and knelt down beside the bedraggled Air Mauritania Fokker F-28 to offer their prayers to Allah. The rugs disappeared as the cabin door opened, and in the crushing surge of ninety people, all shouting and pushing with their mountains of hand luggage, I somehow managed to worm myself up the steps and into the plane. There was no air-conditioning, which seemed to suit only the flies, and so, with my clothes sodden with sweat, I sank wearily into a too-soft seat on the portside aisle, feeling most uncomfortable.

Once inside, the passengers became distinctly quiet and subdued, and with good reason. Three passenger planes had so far been downed by Polisario, and six months later an American insecticide-spraying plane was to be accidentally shot down over the desert. A thin young Moor sitting to my right was nervously rubbing his hands together. Trickles of sweat from his brow ran down past his eyes and angular Roman nose, to drip off his pointed goatee (the goatee is typical among Moorish men). The man returned my greeting with a wavering smile, under which a gold-capped tooth struggled to be seen.

In the row in front, a black Wolof girl from Senegal – about seven or eight years old – stared at me with inquisitive brown eyes through the gap between the seats. Her hair was woven into five thick plaits, each threaded with a dozen colourful beads. Like her mother, she was dressed in a glistening ochre robe mottled with saffron and overlaid with olive-green leaves outlined in a rich earthy brown. She gazed unflinchingly at me for over ten minutes, until the plane dipped suddenly in an air pocket and she started crying.

Across the aisle and further back sat a Berber salesman I had seen at Layoune airport. There, he had kicked up a fuss with the customs officials about having to unpack and repack each one of six large bundles of carpets, destined for the Canary Islands. A small and wiry man in his late fifties, at the time I had wondered at his deceptive strength in being able to carry the bundles at all. His worn and wrinkled face – a weather beaten bronze finely beaded with sweat – sported a small ashen goatee and narrow moustache. He wore a battered but dignified grey jellaba, from under which protruded a new pair of bright yellow slippers. He wore his white turban like a doughnut about his crown, and a shiny balding head poked out from above. Small beady eyes were busily scanning *Le Monde*.

As the plane cruised away from the civilisation of the Canary Islands and took me across the Tropic of Cancer, I experienced a sense of anticipation to the forthcoming adventure that I had not felt since crossing over the Atlas mountains and into the Sahara for the first time. I was hungry for the solitude, the desolation, and even the hardship that desert travel had brought me so far. Yet, I had no real idea as to what awaited. I was going with eyes and heart open into a land I knew next to nothing about. With hindsight, it was a wonderfully childish thing to do (as well as being potentially stupid), simply to go into the unknown to see if it really was as I dreamt it would be. Dreamy desert images filled my mind. Hazy pictures of cycling over silky sand dunes; days on end without seeing any form of life; vast camel trains snaking from the mirrored horizon towards the alluring greenery of imaginary desert oases; the feeling of the desert heat burning my nostrils; the astounded expressions of nomads mounted on camels as they would confront me and my bicycle... I remembered staring at the bottom of my Moroccan road-map, adorned not merely with splashes but with a great wash of yellow ink. This was Mauritania, and for the first time it dawned on me that I might actually succeed in my crazy dream. I had begun to realise that I was no longer *going* to cross the Sahara, but that I was already in the act of doing so.

'*Le déjeuner, m'sieur?*' A pretty air hostess, her veil worn only loosely, interrupted my reverie. I gazed back vacantly at her smile, momentarily confused.

After barely half an hour we reached the southwestern coastline of the Western Sahara and proceeded to follow it southwards. From an altitude of twenty thousand feet, the view was simply awe-inspiring. Although aerial views are always stunning, perhaps even clichéd, this particular panorama held an especially dreamlike quality. To the east and my left spread a vast blanket of featureless orange-beige sand, sprawling beyond the murky horizon and punctuated only by scattered patches of deep ochre on the few remaining hills. Stretching all the way from the Red Sea in the east to the Atlantic in the west, here, below me, the Sahara ended in spectacular and abrupt contrast with the turquoise depths of the ocean. The constant northeasterly trades threw up the surf so that the water sparkled. Once or twice, ships could be made out, given away by long and wispy tails. As the plane began its slow descent towards Mauritania, the harshness of this rugged landscape became more visible, and at the same time more enticing, alluring. Vast crescentic *barkhan* sand dunes sharpened into focus, their starkly outlined claws pointing south towards the now unmistakable shape of the Cap Blanc peninsula. The *barkhan* are unique to the Atlantic coast of Mauritania and to the Borku region of Chad, and are among the most rapidly moving dunes in the world. They are therefore also the most destructive. The scars of the clasping dunes and exposed rock were all that now remained of once endless forests and a lush agricultural land, long since overwhelmed by the burning desert sands.

Four hundred kilometres south of Rio de Oro, Cap Blanc represents the westernmost tip of the Sahara. Fifty kilometres long, and ten at its narrowest, the peninsula typifies the Western Saharan conflict. Nominally, it is halved laterally, albeit contentiously, between Morocco on the west and Mauritania on the east. Morocco, however, has been unable to station troops there, and in consequence Polisario at one time used the peninsula to launch attacks on Morocco-friendly shipping. But the recent completion of the defensive wall has more or less eliminated such activity. The western slice of Cap Blanc is now no-man's-land.

The peninsula's only settlements – Cansado, Nouâdhibou, and Lagouera – are situated at its southern end. Nouâdhibou (the Jackal's Well, or the Desired of the Fox) is Mauritania's second largest city, with an official population of around 30,000. It began life in 1907 as the major fish processing centre for French West Africa, and today survives as Mauritania's only significant port. By the 1960s and the birth of the new nation, both Nouâdhibou and its port were massively expanded in order to cope with what was hoped would be Mauritania's key to future prosperity: iron. With it lie Mauritania's hopes of material wealth, of self-sufficiency, and industry. It is the dream of almost all Third World countries. With the tenacity of a spider clinging to her web in a sudden downpour, two thin slivers of steel skirt the sandy wastes of the frontier between Mauritania and the Western Sahara. Upon them, runs the world's longest train, commonly hauling a retinue of over two hundred carriages, rumbling and rattling their way across the interminable desert. The iron ore train is the modern-day incarnation of the camel trains of yore. The first to have mentioned the metal in Mauritania was el-Bekri, who in 1067 referred to an 'Iron Mountain'. Several similar reports followed, but it was only in the 1930s that attention turned seriously to this hidden wealth, when mail pilots flying south towards Dakar reported that their compass needles went beserk over the region.

To the east of the railway on the peninsula lies an abandoned road, once leading all the way to Nouakchott, Mauritania's capital. The road lies forgotten, eroded and half-buried under the dunes. It is still land mined, as the English traveller Quentin Crewe and his companions found out in 1982, by managing to get themselves blown-up! Similarly, the few kilometres between Nouâdhibou and Lagouera (on the Moroccan side) are also mined. Almost everyone in Nouâdhibou had a story to tell about some distant friend or relative having been killed trying to cross the divide. Lagouera was evacuated – some say massacred – during the first engagements with Polisario, and is now inhabited only by a colony of monk seals and a few fearless (or foolish) fishermen. Several young men were to offer to guide me across the minefields to see the ghost town, but I had been warned by others that my guides would in all probability demand extra payment once there in order to bring me safely back. What is certain is that Cap Blanc is more or less isolated from overland contact with the capital, and that my journey to Nouakchott was going to be harder than I had anticipated.

I had heard that the only way to reach Nouakchott nowadays, without using camels or reliable high-axle-clearance four-wheel-drive trucks along the risky coastal road, was to take the iron ore train north along the peninsula, then due east along the frontier for four hundred kilometres to the first village – Choum – where the railroad veers north again and a road apparently heads off south towards Nouakchott.

The plane circled the peninsula in order to land against the wind. At its southern tip, and at the northern end of the rich fishing grounds of the Baie du Lévrier (Greyhound Bay), the sand continued its southward march into the sea, destroying the otherwise razor-sharp coastline with a melee of silty sand banks. In consequence, the bay was dotted with shipwrecks, dozens of them beached or grounded on the submerged sands, some of them deliberately scuttled in insurance scams. I was later told a rather dubious theory about all the captains having been drunk, but being the Islamic Republic of Mauritania, this story sounded rather more like a useful yarn to warn people off alcohol than anything else, especially as the Moors say that: 'wine is the key to all evil' (the only places in Mauritania legally permitted to sell alcohol are a handful of extortionately expensive hotels in the capital, well out of the reach of ordinary people).

The plane spluttered to a halt in front of an angular concrete building. Windowless and with ageing whitewash yellowed and flaking, it had nothing to distinguish it from any other construction save for an old battered sign that read 'Nouâdhibou International Airport' in both French and Arabic. The control tower was little more than a shed on stilts, crowned with a frayed orange windsock. My first impression on stepping out of the plane was of extreme dryness, dust and heat, an atmosphere altogether much harsher than in the Moroccan or Western Sahara. It was an all-consuming heat, so overwhelming at first that I felt as though it would swallow me up there and then. As my body recovered from the initial shock, I noticed that the landing strip was covered with a sheet of airborne sand, several feet from the ground, that was being blown south from vaguely outlined dunes to the north.

Along with the other passengers, I ran towards the building, my eyes streaming in the assault. Within minutes, the plane's wheels had acquired miniature sand dunes of their own, whilst the runway could hardly be distinguished at all. As usual, there was a massive crush, even though only twenty passengers had disembarked (the plane was flying on to Nouakchott). The same heated arguments over queue jumping and pushing ensued, and again the same solution, more queue jumping and pushing. The ability of Africans to transform even the smallest group of people into a heaving swelter never ceased to amaze. But slowly, the throng advanced into and through the single door in the side of the building. In all the commotion, a young Moor behind me accidentally struck an old woman's face with his suitcase, and still managed to look mortally offended as she swore and cursed at him whilst theatrically clasping her flushed cheek. I offered to let her pass in front of me, but she just stared back, bemused at my gesture.

Out of the crowd, a benevolent hand reached out, waving a piece of paper that turned out to be a stencilled customs declaration. Suddenly, a middle-aged Wolof man leant forward and gestured that I use his back to write on. The man disappeared before I'd even had time to say thank you, and so I smiled instead at the immigration officer, who eyed me suspiciously.

Customs consisted of a muscular black man in his late twenties, his thick neck bulging with blood vessels. He was dressed in a myrtle green uniform adorned with a colourful array of military stripes, a peaked cap with a chrome badge reading 'Commissariat des Douanes', and the obligatory (in West Africa) pair of dark sunglasses – the inevitable caricature of some banana republic dictator. I offered him my passport, which he snatched away before striding off in the direction of a similarly attired colleague. He, looking simultaneously both at the passport and me, only shrugged his shoulders and skulked away into the gloomy far side of the room. The first dictator returned and queried, in punctuated French: 'What is your business in Mauritania?' I tried my best to explain that I was sightseeing. He was incredulous. 'Here? In *Mauritania*?'

'Why not?' I replied, to which he paused, and then, to my relief, handed me back my papers and said: 'Yes, why not. You may pass, *Toubab* [the West African version of *N'srani*]. Come along. Please be welcome in our country... *Next*!'

The exit seemed to be through a grey-curtained door in the far corner of the room. This door, however, turned out to be the entrace of a converted photo booth where a short, squat elderly woman was being searched in the gloom by the second dictator, still wearing his shades. I apologised for the intrusion but they took no notice, so I clambered over them and into the equally gloomy foyer, where the other passengers were already being accosted by a dishevelled assortment of beggars. To my surprise, my arrival warranted no extra attention whatsoever. Perhaps a detour to the strange white *Toubab* wasn't worth the effort, since the beggars seemed to be doing quite well without me. It stands to logic, because, afterall, the other passengers too had been able to afford the equivalent of six months' wages – $200 – for a ticket to fly to one of the world's poorest countries.

A broken conveyor belt poked into the room through an opaque plastic flap in the wall – baggage reclaim. The toilet door was boarded-up with what looked like driftwood, and in front of it, squatting in the corner, was a hefty pair of baggage scales. On it, someone had placed an empty crate bearing the immortal Coca-Cola legend (the bloody stuff gets everywhere). As I watched the commotion, a large brown rat scurried unnoticed across the floor and darted under the conveyor belt. On it, my bicycle had just appeared, along with heaps of sand.

I was still busy tying the panniers back onto the bike when one of the beggars approached. With only a stump for his right leg and the bones in the other bent forward at an impossible angle, he moved himself around by sliding face down on the sandy floor, propelled by his stringy arms. His skin was flaking badly, although his face remained somehow little touched by his overall wretchedness. He spoke in a soft but broken French lilt, and didn't ask for money, but just wanted to talk. Messmoud Ould Mohammed had contracted polio when he was five years old, and had consequently been abandoned by his parents. His only 'family' now were the other beggars who lived beside the airport, and against whom he vied for the attentions of the guilt-stricken passengers. In spite of his pathetic condition, Messmoud maintained a solidly determined disposition, and asked of me a lot of questions. They were simple questions, concerning my name, my family, my country, my home, my brothers and sisters...

'Are you here to help us?' he asked, not understanding why else I might have come to this drought-riven country. Simple questions, yet I could answer only with great difficulty. I felt damned even in my modest wealth, and felt patronizing as I looked down into his eyes, pleading pools at the bottom of deep wells that brimmed full with questions. I tried, in vain, to place myself in his position, to understand his thoughts and to wonder at his dreams, if he dreamed at all. Again, he asked me why I had *chosen* to come to Mauritania. He could (and would) never comprehend my desire to see the desert, never mind my intention to cycle through it, and all the more so when I told him that I'd already seen the Moroccan half. Sahara – a land of no shadows in the heart of darkness – figured only as hostility in Messmoud's imagination. If I really wanted to see the desert, he suggested, then why did I not simply go and buy a jeep or a truck? Was I sure that I hadn't got off the plane by mistake?

'Sir, my friend, there is nothing here. Nothing but sand and rock. Why do you want to see nothing?' Then he hesitated (for the first time in our conversation): 'Sir, from where you come... is it true that there is snow?' I felt as though I had been given the task of informing a condemned criminal that his last appeal had been rejected. Of course, I replied. He nodded, thoughtfully, as though pieces of a mental jigsaw were falling slowly into place, a jigsaw that would never be completed. Then he would ask another question. I gave him my Berlitz phrasebook for Morocco, full of pictures of the snowy Atlas mountains in midwinter. I felt awful. With each answer, I encouraged and strengthened his dreams still further, but what galled me most was the thought that they would never be fulfilled, a truth which contrasted painfully with mine. I felt a dreadful emptiness inside of me as I left Messmoud and his dreams in the concrete shade of the airport. Messmoud was fourteen years old.

* * *

Nouâdhibou is a motley collection of early 20th century French colonial buildings, bland post-independence offices, and shabby alleyways cramped to overflowing with squalid and decrepit huts. Except for a mosque minaret, a handful of defunct telegraph poles and the cranes in the port, the town is almost completely flat. There is a single dusty tarmac road running from the airport through Nouâdhibou to Cansado,

177

but there are hardly any cars. Sand breaks have been constructed on the northeastern side of town to guard against the dust-laden *Harmattan*, but with little success. Small dunes rise on almost every street corner and the road is often completely buried, as are the once-green gardens of boarded up tumbledown French villas. The construction of Nouâdhibou was financed by foreigners, and the town now depends on foreigners to buy its iron ore and fish. But even the fishing is done mainly by foreign fleets, and once the fish and the iron have been exhausted, there will be nothing left.

Nouâdhibou exudes a lumbering end-of-land sadness. I suppose that any town situated at the end of a peninsula is bound to be a dead end in some way or other, but Nouâdhibou is worse than that. It has no history of which it can be proud, no culture, no customs, no past and, arguably, no future. It does not even have a hospital to cure the sick, though it does have a burgeoning population which is both hungry and thirsty. Neither is the peninsula able to grow food to feed its people, for it has no natural water supply. Cap Blanc receives only an inch or so of rain every year, and so supplies have to be brought in by train from Bou-Lanouar, a deep well ninety kilometres away. The irony of all this is that prior to 1960 – the year Bou-Lanouar first started being heavily exploited – water was distilled locally from the sea, which did not deplete the precious underground reserves. If the present arrangement continues, we shall find that within a few decades, the short-term interests of economy will have bled dry the wells of Bou-Lanouar, and there will be no more water left at all.

In the sweltering afternoon heat, the task of obtaining water was utmost in my mind, for I didn't much feel like rushing about madly the next day trying to fill my bottles without knowing when, if at all, the iron ore train was due to leave. A tall and handsome black youth said that I could get water at his home not far away. We tramped past a school. At first glance it was not too dissimilar from my old junior school in Manchester: an austere building with a yard enclosed by iron railings, and children's paintings and drawings stuck to the windows. The railings, and the old inscriptions on the gates – one for 'Garçons' and the other for 'Filles' – placed the building in the 1930s during the period of French colonisation. Nowadays, the majority of girls are withdrawn from school at the age of fourteen. As we passed by, most of the children in the yard – grubby and skinny ten year olds – ran out and started following us, much to the dismay of their teacher. His futile shouts faded away as we rounded the next corner into a dark passageway littered with broken bottles and cans, bits of plastic laundry baskets and dog shit. The youth stopped and suggested that I stay the night with his family. Normally, I would have accepted, but having just arrived in Mauritania, I felt that I needed some time alone, away from the pressure of new people and new places, and so I declined. We carried on walking, but he seemed to feel ill at ease with the train of children following us, and repeatedly told them to go away, slapping one of them. As I couldn't understand why the children should bother him so, I grew suspicious. Again, he asked if I would spend the night with him, and again I declined. Then he asked whether I had any money on me. I lied, and said that I hadn't. He then became visibly nervous, insisting that I could not sleep rough and that I *had* to accept his hospitality. He stopped and moved in front of me, blocking the passageway, and demanded that I pay him twenty dollars whether I wanted a bed or not. Trying to remain as calm as possible, I told him that there was no way that I would spend that much for a bed anyway. He scowled and moved closer. I looked round at the expectant crowd but they just stared back in silence. Dredging the depths of my French and Arabic, I let loose a violet tirade of abuse and threats, much to the delight of the onlookers. We stared at each other for what seemed an age, until he turned, pushed through the children, and slunk away under a hail of pebbles and insults.

Shaken, I turned to the children. One of them had taken an empty water bottle from my bicycle and was motioning 'drink'. I nodded, and almost immediately a mass of children surged forward, each trying to take one of the remaining bottles away for filling. In the end, they had to satisfy themselves by holding the bottles two or three at a time and a few minutes later, seven bottles complete with grinning faces traipsed back, dribbling dark patches over the sand. I walked the children back to school, thanked them for everything, apologized to their irate teacher, and shook goodbye with thirty little pairs of bony black, brown and white hands.

By late afternoon, I was feeling drained. I needed to rest, but as the three hotels in town were all too expensive for my budget, I decided that the best place would be the beach beside the bay near the airport, a couple of miles to the north.

Coming off the road, the only way to the coast without a substantial detour was through a makeshift *bidonville* [literally 'tin-town'] of slum dwellings on the southern skirts of the airfield. The *bidonville* sprang up during the drought of 1968 to 1973, as people sought refuge from famine; the desert having completely destroyed what little remained of Mauritania's agriculture. Following independence, and in the heady spirit of unity and modernism, the government had proudly adopted the proverb: 'Men resemble their times much more than they resemble their fathers.' In these slums, it was so true as to be perverse. Threading the bicycle through the shacks, I was knocked senseless by the saddest and most pitiful sights I had ever seen. Packed into an area not even one kilometre square lived at least ten thousand people, of every race and generation, all of them in the most abject poverty and disease ridden shambles imaginable. The once sandy path along which I was passing was choked ankle deep in excrement, broken bottles, mud, odd pieces of metal and wood, dead dogs and rats festering with maggots, and rotting food: rice, rancid meat, peels and skins of all kinds, and discarded fish offal, all swarming in flies and mosquitos. The claustrophobic squalor gave the wind no chance of ventilation, resulting in an foul and all-pervading stench. The dwellings, if one can call them such, were made from anything available. Many were constructed simply from cardboard packaging, either washed up, or somehow obtained at the port. The boards were held together with bottle tops and old nails or wooden sticks, the bottle tops acting as rivets when driven through with the nails. Many other huts were merely adapted nomad tents. Ideal in the desert, here they stood no chance of ventilation and provided little protection against anything. Even the occasional whiff of boiled goat meat or fish only slightly disguised the reek. More saddening still was the despondency of the people. Old men squatted against the more stable structures, fiddling idly with pebbles or beads, and children, instead of shouting or chasing after me as in any other African town, sat or stood still, their tiny naked limbs hanging motionless, and their small weary eyes gazing sadly at the passing European. They stood frozen, barefoot, clasping their hands behind their backs, their bellies faintly distended, and just stared and stared, devoid of any emotion.

The children are the disinherited generation. Their clothes were rags: shirts torn down at the shoulders, trousers missing a leg, the skeletal remains of T-shirts... Many – usually the youngest – went about naked but for an old pair of much-darned underpants or a scabby cloth wrap, flies clustered around their noses and eyes and mouths. Not even thirty years after the hopeful dawn of independence, Mauritania is on the brink of disaster. Average life expectancy is 42 years for men and 46 for women. They wait, trapped, as their world, their civilisation, collapses about their feet. The story is the same throughout the Sahara and the Sahel. It is estimated that over the last twenty years, a quarter of a million people have died from starvation, as well as three and a half million cattle. Poverty and racial strife, too, have become rampant in recent years, although, unlike other African countries, it is not the legacy of colonialism that has destroyed the ancient status quo, but rather the unstoppable expansion of the desert. Over the last two decades, the once creeping advance of the Sahara has become a stampede. Countless wells have been lost to the sands, agriculture has been destroyed, and hundreds of villages lie abandoned and in ruins. By tradition, the Moors are nomadic. The land of these people is the Sahara. They are Saharans first and Mauritanians second. Yet they have been forced to leave their desert and their nomadic ways of life to seek refuge instead in the towns. Towns with very little work and towns that have very quickly become overcrowded. In 1960, over 80% of the population was nomadic. Now it is about 20%, a figure that dwindles from year to year. During the worst times, it was not unknown for mothers to rent out or even sell their daughters in return for a little rice or sugar. It was saddening beyond words to realise that I was witnessing, in effect, the death of a way of life that dates back tens of thousands of years, older even than the first settled civilisation. I was witnessing not only the death of a nation, but, I truly believe, the death of humanity itself.

* * *

Between the *bidonville* and the bay lay a short stretch of windswept sand, known locally as *la Table Remarquable*. Like the landing strip nearby, sand was blowing over it at waist height, forever extending the desert into the bay, and where I was standing would have been water a few years ago. In the bay rotted the corpses of the wrecks that I'd seen from the plane, though what I hadn't noticed before were the masts and bows of other ancient ships protruding from the dunes ahead of me, like huge sundials, far from the sea. The debris cast long, doubting shadows across the sand. At some angles, the old ships' wheels and broken masts resembled graveside crosses.

In July 1816, in apparently calm weather, a brigantine called the *Méduse* foundered on hidden reefs some ninety kilometres off Cap Blanc. It was one of a flotilla of four French ships carrying future colonists to Senegal (including a young René Caillié). The officers of the *Méduse* took to the lifeboats, leaving 147 people to save themselves on a makeshift raft. By the time they were picked up, thirteen days later, only fifteen remained alive. When news of the disaster broke in France, the harrowing (not to mention salacious) tales of death on the high seas – drowning, murder, suicide and cannibalism – captured the public imagination, and inspired the artist Théodore Géricault to paint his masterpiece, *Le Radeau de la Méduse*.

As I moved closer to the shore, patches of quicksand became visible, given away by tell-tale white crusts. I skirted these, but still managed to cover the bicycle chain with a soggy goo of salty sand. Half in and half out of the water lay a rusty iron trawler, coated and tainted with the same sand that embraced it. I scrambled on to the deck, and eased myself tentatively down a hatch in the centre, landing on a soft pile of silty sand. From the inside, the hull resembled the belly of the whale in *Pinnochio*, all black and ribbed. The sea came in through a gaping hole in the bow, and settled into small pools. I stared at a few small fish for a while, before I got depressed and climbed out to sit in the shade of the hull, gazing out over the bay. The setting sun struck low, starkly illuminating the ships against a deceptively alluring backdrop of sapphire, shot through with streaks of gold.

To my left a small group of fishermen worked the evening catch. Three lines, about thirty metres long, stretched out into the bay. Several vividly painted wooden bobs bounced about on each, betraying the poisonous traps hidden below. Every so often, a naked black boy with thin limbs and shorn hair would wade out along one of the lines to check the nets. It was a sign of the times that even the smallest fish would elicit a great commotion amongst the fishermen, whereas a few decades ago, vast shoals could be caught within a matter of minutes.

Nevertheless, at Nouâmghâr, a small and isolated village on the coast half way between Nouâdhibou and Nouakchott, there still exists a most fantastic tradition, unparallelled anywhere in the world. In an act of the most exquisite symbiosis between man and animal, dolphins and men work together to reap a rich harvest. Responding to the vibrations of sticks beaten on the surface of the water, the dolphins round up and then chase shoals of fish towards the shore. Whereas the fish would normally skitter away to safety in the shallows, on seeing the approach of the dolphins, the fishermen of Nouâmghâr rush out into the sea with long snaking nets, trapping fish not only for the villagers but also for the dolphins. The fishermen are the Imraguen, and are considered by the Moors to be society's outcasts, similar in status to the former Indian caste of untouchables. Yet, like so many 'outcasts', the Imraguen have lived in this land well before the Moors even came about, and are believed by some anthropologists to be their proper ancestors. Like the Chnagla fishermen of the Western Sahara, the Imraguen have distinctly Negroid features. And like the Chnagla, the Imraguen are proud of their pariah status.

A while later, night creeping up fast, the fishermen collected their nets and made to leave. The few fish that they had caught were threaded together by their tails, perhaps to be dried out, or perhaps to make *tie-bou-dienne* (Wolof for rice-with-fish), a traditional West African dish made with huge quantities of peanut oil that is eaten at lunchtime. The men, though, looked sullen, and walked towards me with their heads bowed. As they passed, one of them – a withered old man in the ubiquitous white *boubou* and turban – turned to me.

'Hey. *Toubab*. It is not safe in these parts, I think. Why do you not go home?'

'I have no home,' I replied.

'But the wild beasts,' he retorted. I relaxed, for I had thought at first that he meant maurauding bands of robbers or murderers, but the prospect of vicious animals seemed rather tame and unlikely in comparison. Still, just to make sure, I moved back over the quicksand to one of the larger dunes near the airfield, and chose a welcoming sandy hollow to sleep in, overlooked by the protruding masts of a buried ship. The light faded to leave only the twinkling of the stars and the ships in the bay. Although I was naturally excited to be back in the desert, I could not help thinking of the contrast between the noble life of the nomads and the pathetic squalor to which they had been reduced in the shanty town only a few hundred yards behind me.

* * *

Nouâdhibou was deserted in the morning, just empty shadows and the stench of drying fish wafting through the thick air as I cycled past the naval base to Cansado to catch my train. A battered road sign read: 'Cansado / Ville Neuve / Vous Souhai…' The rest of the greeting had vanished over the years.

A largely residential town, Cansado (which means 'tired' in Spanish) was built jointly by the French and Mauritanian governments in the late 1950s and early 1960s, to house the new generation of miners, railwaymen and dockers that were needed to turn the Mauritanian industrial dream into reality. Thirty years on, that dream has become a nightmare. Half the houses are shattered, and the others are either massively overcrowded or else occupied by various governmental functionaries and secretive European 'technical advisers'. Modest concrete blocks rise to three storeys, aligned in neat and antiseptic rows as ugly and monotonous as anything that the Man of Steel, Joseph Stalin, ever provided. Of necessity, the doors and windows are tiny to protect against the dust and the sand and the heat, a feature that only adds to the stifling austerity of the place. Still, I was surprised to find, tucked away amongst all the greydom, a French-style supermarket owned by 'la société industrielle de la grande pêche', known, like everything else

183

in Mauritania, by its acronym, SIGP. To my horror, the prices of the pitifully few goods on sale were astronomical. Cans of sardines cost over £2, a small can of Ivory Coast pineapple slices cost £4, and a bottle of French mineral water would have set me back by a fiver. On seeing the only well-stocked shelf crammed with caviare and fish roe, I turned tail and headed back out into the relative sanity of Africa.

The heat was considerable and clung cloyingly to my skin. As I'd already drunk two litres of water, I asked a bunch of nosey children where I might find some more. They showed me to the house of a French doctor, where I knocked and waited. After a few moments, a makeshift shutter cautiously opened, and a white woman's face appeared at the slat.

'*Oui*?' I said hello, and all the usual stuff, and asked whether I could come in.

'No. The doctor isn't in,' she snapped. 'He won't be back until Wednesday.'

'Oh, I see. Well, I was wondering whether I could have some water, you see, urm, I…' The shutter closed and I waited some more, much to the amusement of the children who were keeping a polite distance. Then, the door opened, slightly, and an arm beckoned me in.

'I just *hate* this place,' she said, as she secured the last of four metal bars across the door.

'Oh.' She was middle-aged, grey haired and extremely paranoid.

'There's nothing that works in this *pays foutu*,' she said as I entered the kitchen. 'I cannot wait to get out of here. It's driving me mad.'

In one corner stood a shiny white fridge with a freezer placed on top, and under the small shuttered window was an electric cooker with an oven. Beside it, and combined with a neat set of fitted drawers, was the kitchen sink, complete with two taps, one painted red and the other blue. None of which worked. I was given a bottle of that expensive French spring water, along with a curt smile, and was then ushered back into the street. The door slammed shut behind me to hoots of appreciation from the waiting children, who had obviously been thinking of something else.

Back to the road fork, and then south for a few miles, was the entrance to Point Central, the iron ore terminal. It was marked by a concrete sculpture not unlike the three-legged Manx emblem. It was inscribed: 'Société Nationale Industrielle et Miniere' (SNIM). About half a mile past the junction were two whitewashed cabins, each protruding a frail red iron barrier. The checkpoint seemed to be deserted, but I stopped anyway, not wishing to complicate matters later on. The two guards were fast asleep on the blind side of one of the boxes, their revolvers lying on the ground beside them. The older guard, a black Moor with fine facial features that betrayed a nomadic background, wore a simple grey-green *boubou*, blue plastic flip-flops, and a turban dyed batik-style in orange, maroon, sky blue and white. The other guard, a Wolof or Tukolor, seemed more urbanised in his tastes, and wore an amazingly thick fur-lined leather jacket, black tailored trousers with worn out pleats, black patent leather shoes and a white woollen hat. His face was muffled in a green blanket that was slung over his head.

'*Salaam Alaikum!*' I shouted. The younger man immediately jumped to his feet, and was about to salute when he realised that it was only a teenage *Toubab* with a bicycle who was stood grinning at him. Meanwhile the older guard, who had almost fallen off his chair, slowly got up and held out his hand.

'*Alaikum Salaam.*'

'*Salaam Alaikum,*' I repeated, determined for once to get the hang of the customary greetings.

'*Labass*? No evil?'

'No evil,' he replied, violently shaking my hand. 'Allah is indeed merciful, *alhamdulillahi.*'

'No evil? Ah, praise be to Allah,' I reiterated.

'*Akh, labass… Ash halak?*' he continued: how are you?

'Fine, thank you. Praise be to Allah. How are you?'

'May you only be burdened with light loads!'

'May no one intend to harm you!'

'*Akh*, Praise be to Allah! May only good things happen to you!'

'Praise be to Allah, Allah the Merciful, the always Merciful…'

The greetings eventually returned to the more usual rounds of '*Labass*' and '*Yak labass*', and I lied and said that I was still fine, although I was sure that my crushed hand was beginning to turn blue under his vice-like grip.

'And your children?' I asked, dredging the phrase from some murky shelf inside my brain. 'Are they fine too?'

'They too are fine, *alhamdulillahi!*' and I was chuffed that he'd understood. 'And *your* children?' he asked. I started giggling, whereupon he thankfully loosened his clasp and allowed a bucktoothed grin to spread wide across his face. He then continued, in French: 'I am Bâ Oumar, and this is my colleague, Abou Gueye.' More handshaking and greetings followed.

'Do you want to see my passport?' I asked, after the introductions had fizzled out. Bâ pondered this for a while.

'Erm… No, not really. Unless you *insist.*'

This roadblock marks the boundary of Point Central. Almost half a billion tons of iron ore – half of Mauritania's export trade – are processed here every year. The roadblock is consequently of the utmost national and strategic importance, to which, inexplicably, the gendarmerie had managed to post two utterly incompetent (if wholly charming) guards. All the time that we conversed, my impromptu hosts paid scant if any attention to the vehicles driving by on the other side of the road. Occasionally, as though to impress me, they would try to flag down a car or a truck. Most of the drivers, though, would ignore them completely, although some would have the courtesy to wave back, or else pull a silly face. But nobody ever stopped. The normal routine was something like this: waving his arms wildly in the air and shouting 'Stop! stop! stop!' Abou would then exclaim: 'Hey, he isn't slowing down!' to the inevitable sight of a passing car showering him in clouds of sand and dust. He would then continue: 'By Almighty Allah, the cheeky runt didn't stop! Hey, Bâ Oumar, did you get his number?' But by the time that Bâ Oumar had wearily heaved himself up to look, the car was no more than a rapidly disappearing speck on the hazy horizon. Usually though, they couldn't even be bothered to get up, but instead cursed dutifully whenever a vehicle sped by.

Presently, the phone in the hut rang. There are only 5,200 working phones in Mauritania, and this was one of them. Bâ, who had meanwhile sat down again, leapt to his feet to pick up the receiver, carefully wiping and dusting it before holding it to his ear and answering. As he listened, his face clouded over and became more serious, and as he put down the receiver, he said: 'The Chief.' Suddenly, the slackest checkpoint in all Mauritania became magically transformed into the most efficient. Barriers were lowered, vehicles were stopped and papers demanded. The boots, luggage and even undersides of the cars were meticulously checked and examined, to the intense fury of the frustrated drivers who swore and cursed angrily at the guards. But only when Bâ was completely satisfied, or more likely became sick of the insults, did he let Abou open the barricade to let the vehicle through. Meanwhile, I had had to hide myself and the bicycle, since my presence would only have complicated matters for the two guards. Squatting inside the cabin amidst clouds of flies, I could see the road reflected in a grimy cracked mirror on the table beside the telephone. Shortly, a well-maintained Citroën – and as such, rare in Mauritania – appeared in the distance. As it approached, the barrier was raised, as were the hands of Bâ and Abou in salute. The Chief nodded in acknowledgement as he drove past the two motionless guards, but as soon as he had sped out of range, Bâ muttered *'Espèce de con!'* – probably for my benefit – and once more the checkpoint reverted to its old happy self, oblivious to any vehicle that happened to pass it by.

Bâ told me that there were two trains a day, one at four o'clock, the other at half past six, and confirmed that the trip was free if I rode on an open waggon. However, he stressed that these were merely *official* times, and so were prone to vary. As it was already two o'clock, I decided that it would be wise to leave for the railyard as soon as possible, and so I bade the two guards farewell, and cycled off towards the end of the peninsula, though not before I had been cajoled into taking a picture of them *in action*!

* * *

Despite being situated on the beautifully named Pointe des Mouettes (Sea Gull Point), Point Central is just as ugly as any other large industrial combine. It processes all the haematite ore (63% pure and therefore top-grade) mined in Mauritania and as a result, sky-high corroded funnels spew dark noxious fumes, coolers belch great clouds of grey steam, and the sound and sparks of welders escape from hangars. On the far side of the complex, across a log jam of rails and pipes, a strange contraption was tipping rail waggons upside-down to empty the ore onto a conveyor belt that snaked around virtually all the site. As I arrived, workers were busy pouring molten tar on to the railroad to keep down the dust that billowed everywhere.

I was greeted by a welding foreman who handed me his face mask. His digs consisted of an old rusty container crate, propped up at each corner with a pile of rocks. The gap this created between the sand and the base provided a storage area where water and cartons of UHT milk were kept. Two bunk beds took up half the room. In the other half were sat about a dozen bloodshot-eyed workers about to start their shift. They sucked nervously on the cardboard roaches of their last joints. The foreman said to make myself at home, and then disappeared, only to return with a bowl of steaming rice and goat meat. I wanted to pay, but he refused, saying that it was his duty as a good Muslim to offer me hospitality, and that Allah was Great.

As I clambered awkwardly on to the open carriage, my gaze was met by eight other pairs of eyes, not hostile, but then not particularly friendly either. They were already perched precariously alongside their baggage on a consignment of gas cylinders bound for the mines at F'dérik. I sandwiched the bike between the two pyramids of cannisters, hoping that they would neither fall off, nor roll together to crush my bike.

Making myself comfortable wasn't easy either, balanced on top of the cylinders, hessian sacks, mysterious wooden boxes, suitcases, and various other containers, all of which were secured with tangled green netting. There was also an albino billy goat, tended by a young pale-skinned girl.

At first, conversation proceeded extremely slowly and monotonously. I greeted an elderly black man who was staring at me with piercing eyes.

'*Salaam Alaikum.*' A pause.

'*Salaam,*' he eventually offered, but only grudgingly.

'How are you?' I asked. He grunted.

'Where are you from?' No answer.

'Where are you going?'

'Mali,' he mumbled.

'What were you doing in Nouâdhibou?'

'Business,' he said abruptly, and then looked away, seemingly offended. I felt stupid having to ask the same, tiresome questions that were usually demanded of me, and so I gave up trying conversation and started rummaging through the bicycle panniers in search of my diary. On seeing that my flow of questions had dried up, one of the men, ditching the usual string of formalities, asked whether I travelled with them because I was too poor to take the aeroplane. I shook my head, so he continued: 'Then what, by Almighty Allah, are you doing here?' and then added, almost as an afterthought: 'On *that* thing?' He pointed to my bicycle. Pleased that I'd attracted some attention, I shrugged, and lifting my arms up skyward replied: 'Allah only knows. I wish to travel to Nouakchott, *Insha Allah.*'

The man introduced himself as Diur Fall, a Saharawi.

'I am the son of the desert,' he said proudly, and indeed, he looked the part. He wore by far the largest turban of all the passengers, and his face was sharp and gaunt. He looked at me through the same piercing eyes as that of the old man, and so I asked Diur why the old man seemed so aggrieved. Diur explained that many nomads disliked *Toubabs* because they thought that the *Toubab* did not like the nomad. I told him that that was ridiculous, because I wouldn't be wanting to speak with him otherwise. Diur turned briefly to say a few words to the old man, who then smiled an uneasy smile at me.

'*Ingleez?*' Diur ventured unexpectedly. What else? Apparently the last *Ingleez* he had seen was in the late 1960s, when a couple on motorbikes had crossed the Sahara from Algeria. It was a thought that conjured up images of two groovy and spaced easy-riding hippies freaking out and digging those mellow far-out cool desert vibes, man.

If I ever cross the desert again, I swore, it would either be by camel or motorbike.

The old man, meanwhile, had clambered off the cannisters in order to inspect my bicycle, and was gesturing at the water bottles strapped to the frame. He looked puzzled, so I said that he could have some if he wanted. But still he looked baffled, as though he expected them to be full of petrol. I tried to explain the bicycle to him (how does one explain a bicycle?) and pointed to my legs. To prove the point, I clambered down and took a sip from one of the bottles, before offering it to him. It was hardly surprising that he'd never seen a bicycle before. Most 'proper' nomads rarely if ever leave the desert fringes. The few that do manage to see the larger towns more often than not go in connection with smuggling: diamonds, gold and weapons.

Diur got up to examine my pedal machine when, at that very instant, the train jerked into motion and sent him sprawling into the goat and the girl, who started giggling. For a moment, Diur lay unceremoniously spread-eagled on the floor, his turban caught on the goat's horns. The rest of us, including the old man, started laughing. Diur picked himself up gingerly, his sheepishly grinning face flushed and embarrassed. Retrieving his turban in as dignified a manner as was possible, he turned to us and exclaimed: 'In the name of Allah the most Gracious and most Merciful, I hope that you are all pleased now!'

Over one hundred and fifty waggons long and capable of carrying twenty-two thousand tons of ore, the train's full length of two and a half kilometres only became apparent as we snaked our way slowly around the circular track at the southern end of Cap Blanc. Soon, we were passing again through Point Central, the clouds of thick grey dust from the waggon tipper still billowing over the complex and into our faces. But the dust from Point Central paled into insignificance compared to the sand and dust thrown up by the howling wind and the speeding train. I was watched with intense curiosity as the *Toubab* draped his face with his turban, but even with the *cheche* wrapped tightly, there was little I could do to avoid the incessant onslaught. After an hour or so of tying and retying turbans, we all resigned ourselves to the fact that, for the next day at least, our eyes would be almost constantly streaming and sore, and that there was nothing that could be done about it, for even closed eyes were found wanting.

Looking at the other passengers – who were all coated in the same drab dust as me – I was jolted to reflect on why I was actually sitting there as a stranger amidst all these strange people in this strange land. Simply saying that I hoped to travel through the desert to get to Senegal was an insufficient explanation. I found that as I had slowly travelled further south, and therefore further away from Europe and home, that travel per se had become not only a source of great pleasure, but something that was now necessary for my continued well-being. Even the five days that I had spent in the Canary Islands had found me bored and impatient, and only too anxious to be off again. Travel, like a virus, had infected my blood. Much as a junkie gets his fix of 'security' from the tip of a needle, I got mine from the road, from the constancy of movement. 'Our nature consists in motion;' wrote Pascal, 'complete rest is death.' Similarly, the Arabs advise: 'Change your dwelling place often, for the sweetness of life consists in variety.'

In Mauritania, I was to be pleased to find that I had lost my hectic haste. I no longer felt the need to charge blindly across the kilometres as I had done in the Western Sahara. I had decided that I was here to enjoy myself, to listen, to see, and to experience: to soak up experiences like a sponge soaks up water. I'd done enough already to absolve myself of my insecurity, and so I now felt refreshed, even innocent, and yet I was conscious that I was actually living out a dream. To live out a dream. Perhaps that was why I found myself here.

For whatever reason, I was once again travelling through hot and hostile desert. The same old descriptions, the same old desert. Screwing up my eyes, all I could see was a vast, flat void of sand, occasionally strangling an isolated tree or bush. With my eyes fully open, the desert was only an empty blinding pallor, enough to dazzle even the fiery bloodstone eyes of the Medusa herself, perpetually shocking one's mind and one's vision. Again, I felt the apprehension that one feels before launching into the unknown. As such this was adventure in its starkest form. The prospect of travelling alone through Mauritania excited and intimidated me – that blank corner which on ancient maps had been adorned with dragons and demons to signify the end of the world.

I was writing my diary when, out of the wind, I heard: 'Excuse me, Sir, are you acquainted with Chelsea?' The sudden appearance of outlandish English startled me greatly. A short, plump, middle-aged Liberian sidled up to me and introduced himself.

'*Mister* Jacob Clarkson, Sir, but please call me Clarkson.' Clarkson bore none of the features that distinguish the black nomadic Saharans from other blacks. The long gaunt faces, the wary penetrating eyes and the tight lips have all softened south of the desert. Clarkson's best friend, it transpired, had emigrated to London a few years earlier, to Chelsea, in fact. I was informed, rather proudly (and with no hint of irony) that Clarkson heralded from the 'Great Urban Metropolis of

Monrovia', a place that had already variously been described to me as an infernal nightmare, hell on earth and, worst of all, as bad as Lagos.

Clarkson was astonished that I, as a city dweller too, did not find nomads necessarily crude, vulgar, uncivilised, uncouth, primitive or even just plain stupid. 'Do you mean to say that you actually *like* these people?' As our conversation continued, I found Clarkson's seemingly irrational hatred of nomads increasingly irritating, as well as embarrassing. He represented everything that I was fleeing from, whilst to him I must undoubtedly have represented all the things that he craved. It was as though we had met along the same road, travelling in opposite directions. I have to admit, though, that it was only much later that I realised that Clarkson could hardly be blamed for his prejudice. For hundreds of years, long before the Europeans even set foot in Africa, both the Moors and the Tuareg had actively been engaged in the slave trade. Over the centuries, tens of millions of Negroes had been sold into shackles, to work not only for the Moors and the Tuareg who organised the hunts, but also for the Arabs of the Maghreb. By the time the Europeans arrived in West Africa, the practice of slavery was far from new, though colonial rule did help establish the trade more permanently and thoroughly than it had ever been before. In Mauritania, slavery was so well established, in fact, that it was only officially abolished in 1980! Even now, there are still an estimated 100,000 slaves in the country. It is hardly surprising then that blacks whose parents, or even themselves, had once lived in perpetual fear of the slavers, have reacted against that racism and violence by using it themselves. In Mauritania, the years since 1980 have seen an upsurge of racial tension between the Moors and the Negro communities in the south. After all, Mauritania's present frontiers were decided not by tribal, nor even by national or geographic considerations, but by the interests of colonial France. The racial problem was highlighted in October 1987 in an attempted coup by Negro army officers against the predominantly Moorish government, and thereafter, in bloody race riots and murders, which culminated two years after I left with Mauritania and Senegal severing both diplomatic and physical ties. But as I talked then with Clarkson, I found him stupid in his bigotry, and so (in *my* ignorance) I returned to my diary as soon as I could.

Towards evening, as the sun began its rapid flight from its daytime perch, Diur clambered over to talk me. With a dramatic flourish, he removed his turban to reveal a large oval scar on his forehead. 'A present from Morocco,' he said as he showed me the offending bullet, now hung on a chain. Then, in a deliberately dramatic whisper, he confessed that he had once fought with Polisario. That is, until the day he woke up in a linen-bedded hospital, having miraculously survived that bullet.

That was in 1978, or so he said, for how it was possible to survive a bullet to the head that left such a scar was beyond my comprehension. 'I still fight in the Polisario,' he said, to my surprise. Rather than fight militarily, he was now on what he euphemistically referred to as *service diplomatique* for the Saharawan Arab Democratic Republic, the exiled Saharawi government based in the refugee camps at Tindouf. It was Diur's job to secure contacts, to organise the supply of school and agricultural materials, and to provide arms for the guerillas in the desert. It would not surprise me if half the baggage that we were sat on had contained munitions or other military provisions. It was probably also part of Diur's job to talk to foreigners. The war in the Western Sahara has dragged on for almost as long as the troubles in Lebanon, and yet whereas almost everyone is aware of the latter, hardly anyone in the West is aware even of the former's existence. It is not in the West's interests to let us be aware of this conflict, because Morocco is an ally, and a useful one at that. Morocco buys Western arms, leases bases to the United States and NATO, stands against communism and Islamic fundamentalism (and therefore Algeria), and, most recently, provided forces for the war against Saddam Hussein's Iraq.

Until his injury, Diur had fought against both Morocco and Mauritania, but now that Mauritania was no longer involved, he told me that he considered the Moors to be both his friends and his comrades. Then how, I asked, did he feel about still fighting fellow Arabs and Muslims? 'They have occupied my country,' he said curtly, 'so how can they be my fellows?' The official Moroccan line, of course, is that they are not *occupying* the Western Sahara at all, but that they are historically entitled to it as part of Greater Morocco. That is to say, that King Hassan's government believes the Saharawis to be Moroccans, though that does not disguise the fact that most Saharawis do not see themselves as Moroccan, for surely then they would not have fled or have been expelled? Indeed, the guards that I had spoken to at the roadblock in Dakhla, all told of the general feeling among Moroccan soldiers that they had been posted in a hostile land. Playing the devil's advocate, I put it to Diur that the Moroccans were surely still good Arabs and good Muslims, irrespective of their government, and that therefore they were in the same boat as himself. 'On the contrary,' he replied, 'the Moroccans despise the nomad, and therefore they cannot be good Arabs or good Muslims.' Mauritania, he said, was to her credit one of the few countries where the nomad was not just tolerated, but welcomed. Why else, he asked, had Morocco built the system of defensive walls in the desert, if not to keep out the nomads?

The sun sank like a drop of blood into the sad Saharan night. The train rumbled on, and after a few hours, a few flickering lights appeared in the distance. The lights grew brighter, the train slowed down, and then stopped. Silence. This was evidently not Choum, for it was too early, and even in the dull obscurity, there was nothing at all to be seen except for the now huge outlines of the Azeffâl dunes, the train already having passed through a two hundred kilometre stretch of low, wave-like *méréyé* dunes. No one got off. Then, suddenly, the lights reappeared, this time unmistakable as the dancing headlights of vehicles driving alongside the railroad. Two open-topped jeeps drove slowly by, each containing eight men. Some wore light turbans, all wore khaki battledress and all were armed with kalashnikov AK-47s. A couple of rocket-propelled grenade launchers were also visible. As they saw us, they stood up and shouted greetings, raising clenched fists into the cool night air. The old man, Diur, and most of the other passengers on our waggon, did likewise.

'They are my brothers,' said Diur, after they had passed. 'May Allah give them strength and be with them always.' I only found out later that it was the fifteenth anniversary, almost to the day, of the first ever Polisario offensive (against an outpost of Spanish *Tropas Nómadas* at El-Khanga in eastern Saguia el-Hamra).

The train trundled off once more, and conversation dwindled as tiredness set in. I yawned, turned and tried to fall asleep at the same time as keeping a hold on the green netting to stop myself from falling off the train. I'd been told that Choum would be reached after midnight.

I awoke suddenly, sweating and covered in sand. The steady rumbling and hissing of brakes had stopped and three hurricane lamps were burning in the distance. The only other light came from the stars, but the dusty sky made them indistinct. This didn't seem to be Choum either, but when I turned around, there remained only one other passenger.

'What's up?' I asked. He shrugged his shoulders.

'Where are we? Is this Choum?' Again, he shrugged his shoulders. Then he pointed to his chest and, apologetically, said 'Guinea.' Guinea Bissau, south of Senegal, was a Portuguese possession until 1974, and this guy spoke only pidgin Portuguese and Mandingo. Realising the futility of asking him, I shouted the same questions to a group of figures huddled beside the train, but heard no reply. And then, with a jolt, the train started off again, veering to the left and straightening out towards the Pole Star. Damn.

I moved to sit cross-legged on the floor beside the Guinean. He had an amiable face, small, round and cheerful, topped with short black hair. His head looked like it was supported by his turban which was coiled like a snake around his neck. We decided that the best thing was sleep.

The train had stopped again. The sun burned my skin. I tried to open my eyes, but found that dust had fused with my tears to stick my eyelids firmly together. I rubbed them with my knuckles, and stared out at the blurred desert. About thirty carriages had been uncoupled overnight, and we were left stranded in a siding somewhere between Choum and F'dérik. Or, to be more precise, we were sandwiched between the northernmost spur of the Azeffâl dunes and the southernmost spur of the El Hammâmi dunes, surrounded by nothing but bright orange sand. For a while, I considered cycling the two hundred or so kilometres back to Choum but, on reflection, decided against the idea, for the sand was both far too thick and too soft to cycle over, and there would be no guarantee of water. In 1963, the year the railway was completed, these naked sands were covered with grasses that provided enough grazing for thousands of camels and goats, and the road that straddled the railway was proudly known as the 'Trans-Mauritanian Highway'. It was said to be completely passable by all kinds of vehicles in all kinds of weather. Twenty-five years later, the road had vanished into oblivion and there was not a single blade of grass to be seen. Even the rails were only just peeking out from beneath their sandy shrouds. Moreover, the railroad was supposedly still mined in parts, and was littered everywhere with viciously large fragments of metal from abandoned vehicles, from the construction of the railway, and from the war. It is a graveyard of man's iron machines in a fluid desert of sand, and a poetic justice of sorts.

The sun shot up quickly, that blasted sun, and the Guinean and I soon found ourselves sheltering in the gap between the waggon and the raised base of a container crate. There was no sign of a locomotive, and we began to get worried. A short while later, and to our surprise, we were joined by a thin black man with long frizzy hair who had been sat on another waggon but had seen me pissing beside the train. He introduced himself by holding out his hand, saying: 'I am Mahmoud. I am Mauritanian.' I responded in kind, we shook hands, and that was that. Although Mahmoud didn't look Mauritanian, and his greeting was certainly somewhat shorter and more to the point than was usual, he lived in Choum and offered to put us up if we needed to rest. Apart from that, he didn't say much more except to express his relief at having found some other people on the train. He too had missed the stop the night before.

At around midday, with the sun blazing down from directly over-head, a locomotive appeared from the north to couple with our stranded rump of train, shattering the strange silence of the desert. The two-tiered diesel-electric loco was brightly painted in green, yellow and white livery, and bore the name 'Alsthom'. Before long the train jerked into motion and we were off again, but to our dismay in a northerly direction. Even Mahmoud didn't know why. Before long, the train slowed and then stopped. We clambered off to see what was happening. Nearby, a small group of workers were busy hauling wide plastic piping towards a container waggon further down the train. Once attached, the distant and muffled thumping of a motor started up. We were told that we were near Touâjîl. With the notable exception of Chinguetti, there are few other significant oases in Mauritania. Those that do exist are either pumping stations such as Touâjîl and Bou-Lanouar, or else simple hand-dug wells that quickly become silted-up or else collapse in on themselves. Even so, water can generally be found in most areas of the Sahara, if one digs deep enough, though in most places it is too salty to be drinkable. Criminally, however, the massive overuse of this invaluable and irreplaceable underground resource by shortsighted irrigation projects – notably those of Algeria and Libya – is fast reducing the water table. At Al-Kufrah, in Libya, irrigation projects are conserva-tively estimated to be reducing the water table at the alarming rate of 35 metres every forty years.

The train itself was taking on supplies for settlements of nomads-turned-railwaymen along the line to the south. The railway is laid over both 'active' and 'stabilised' dunes, and therefore requires constant maintainance to prevent its erosion or undermining. Water is given to the new railway people as a form of payment by the mining company, SNIM, in return for the maintenance of part of the track. During the day, we stopped numerous times to give water to these settlers – small and invariably glum-looking groups of people who would crowd beside the water waggon with various receptacles, and who would offer us, as travellers, the traditional Arab gifts of sun-dried dates and the deliciously refreshing *zrig*, a mixture of cold water, sugar, sour milk culture and milk. Their kindness was all the more touching because we were only passing by on the train, and had no real need of their hospitality. Their kindness was such that we felt as though we had been invited into their dwellings as honoured guests of the family. I felt sorry that these people had been forced to give up their ancient existence in return for dependency on the mining company. Desertification, com-bined with the power of SNIM (which controls the wells), has effectively rendered these people powerless to choose their own destinies, for they have all long since sold or lost their livestock, which makes returning to a nomadic existence near impossible. It is said that only the richest can still afford the *luxury* of being nomads, for nowadays, a life of wandering is indeed a luxury.

A few hours later, the train stopped again, this time in the middle of nowhere. A few minutes later, as we were beginning to wonder what had gone wrong, a company of eighty or ninety soldiers appeared in unison from behind some sand dunes to the left of the track, also to refill on water. Mahmoud anxiously advised me to hide on the blind side of the train because I might cause trouble with them. After all, we had passed a Polisario unit the night before. Instead, I just readjusted my turban to cover my face and neck. So long as I didn't speak, I reckoned I could easily pass for a white Moor, or so I flattered myself in believing.

This was the aptly named oasis of Châr, which, in Hassiniyah, signifies an armed conflict bereft of religious significance. Châr is an important and abundant source of brackish water. It is adequate for most purposes except drinking, and hence the need for the soldiers to fill up on fresh water from Touâjîl. The importance of Châr stems not only from its abundant water supply, but from its position. Fifty kilometres north of Choum, during the war with Polisario it was of great strategic importance (though admittedly of little effect) in protecting both the railway and the Adrar massif (further to the south) from guerilla attack. Nominally, it is still important in ensuring that Polisario units do not pass through Mauritanian territory in their raids against Moroccan bases, but the effectiveness (or indeed willingness) of Mauritania to prevent Polisario's incursions is at the very least questionable. This was well illustrated by the fact that the Polisario jeeps of last night would have passed very near here, and had evidently not been challenged. The Moroccan government has frequently accused Mauritania of actively allowing Polisario guerillas free passage across its territory, and has threatened in the past to pursue raiders across the border. On the question of aiding and abetting the guerillas, Mauritania has always claimed that with only about ten thousand soldiers, airmen and sailors all found, it can hardly be expected to prevent *all* incursions (the Polisario fighters are estimated at 15,000 to 25,000). More to the point, Mauritania can ill-afford to once again become embroiled in the conflict, for the country is bankrupt. Indeed, hardship caused by the war led directly to the 1978 coup d'état that installed the military government presently still in power. Having subsequently survived two more coup attempts, the political situation in Mauritania is hardly one that can support another conflict.

CHAPTER EIGHT

THE ADRAR MOUNTAINS

The desert road is a giant that casts no shadow

Moorish proverb

Shortly after midday the train finally swung westwards and drew up in Choum, a once moderately prosperous trans-Saharan staging town. It was no wonder that we had missed the place last night, for even in the light of day most of it remained hidden from the track, lying instead in a shallow depression ringed by a low curtain of dunes and sand drifts. To the east of the village rose a stark sandstone escarpment, at the base of which I saw the remains of fortifications and embankments built by Morocco to keep out Polisario – Choum lies only a couple of miles from the border. Beyond the escarpment is nothing but El Djouf ('the Belly'), Mauritania's frightening 'Empty Quarter', a region utterly devoid of any form of life. One would have to travel eastwards for over a thousand kilometres, over desolate and scorching terrain, before reaching the next settlement, Taoudenni. It is the site of Mali's legendary and equally notorious salt mines (once controlled by Morocco), which were until recently worked by slaves (and since then, it is rumoured, by Tuareg 'political prisoners').

Although an estimated five thousand people live here – or did – Choum shows little outward sign of life. There are precious few stone buildings to speak of, and not even a mosque minaret to call the faithful to prayer (at least that I could see). The village has only a handful of wells, and these draw the same brackish water as that of Châr. Except for a few isolated acacia and withered tamarisks, there is little natural shelter from the burning sun. The reasons for the demise of Choum are many and varied, but perhaps most damning has been the decline of the trans-Saharan caravans, a trade that was at one time the linchpin to the survival of virtually all the North African nations. By the 7th century

197

and the advent of the camel, the Berbers were in almost total control of the trade, dealing primarily in salt, slaves and gold. Then, as the Arabs moved westwards in their great migrations, another, shorter route across the desert was founded. The *Tariq el-Lemtuni*, or 'Mauritanian Way' as it has become known in more recent years, stretched for fifty days from Morocco to the gold-rich headlands of ancient Ghana, passing en route the Idjil salt flats, near the iron ore mines. At the time, salt was a commodity worth its weight in gold because, like water, it is essential to life. Perversely, then, it is the trade in salt that for centuries paid for the black African slaves that were then transported back over the Sahara to the Maghreb.

The decline of the *Tariq el-Lemtuni* began in the Middle Ages, following the arrival of the Yemeni bandits, who brought great insecurity to the region with their habit of raiding caravans and killing its occupants (they were also rumoured to eat their own children). European colonisation also helped reduce the importance of the caravans, because slaves and other goods were then transported by sea. The French occupation of the Adrar itself (1909), effectively closed the route to the then still rebellious tribes of the Western Sahara. Subsequent attempts at industrialisation and modernisation, and the drawing up of latterday North African boundaries, has also affected the caravans, although the most decisive factor has been drought. As I had already seen in Nouâdhibou's *bidonville*, drought and famine together have drastically diminished the number of nomads plying the ancient routes. The final deathblow for the 'Mauritanian Way' was the conflict in the Western Sahara which, since 1975, has barred the northern reaches of the route. Indeed, Choum itself came under attack in 1977, when suspected Polisario positions were strafed and bombed by French Jaguar fighters, in retaliation for the kidnapping of a number of French technicians and advisors. And so with war, drought, and the extinction of trade, people have left Choum in their droves. Its complete demise has only been prevented by the fact that the town is used to house railway and mine workers, and acts as a sort of stepping stone for the handful of travellers that interchange each week between the railway and the *Route Nationale* that goes south towards Nouakchott.

* * *

As I hauled my bicycle from the train, I noticed to my dismay that the rear tyre had somehow punctured. Much worse, however, was that the constant bumping and clattering of the train had dislodged the pump from the bicycle frame, and it had disappeared into the desert somewhere between Nouâdhibou and Touâjîl. The problems and fears that this engendered were all too obvious. Mahmoud assured me that he could get his hands on a foot-pump, but he wasn't too sure about one for a bicycle, mainly because it was the first time he'd ever even seen one. Along with the Guinean, we walked past the railway and down into the village, an unremarkable collection of mud, stone and tin huts, a number of which doubled as restaurants and crash-houses for railway passengers. Most of the dwellings were wide and breezy nomad tents enclosed with crumbling stone walls, remnants of the more prosperous times that had graced the construction of the railway in the 1960s. Unlike Nouâdhibou, where space is restricted by the geography of Cap Blanc, here, in open desert, the village had been allowed to sprawl, which meant that the dwellings were reasonably well spaced out, and without any of the squalor that had been so evident in the city.

Near the western edge of the village we arrived at the home of Mahmoud: a couple of old clay walls surrounding an acacia tree, topped with tent canvas to keep out the sun. Aïsha, his wife, and his sons Djibril, Hasni and Fadel, had been worried sick about Mahmoud, and were more than pleased to see him again. 'May Allah be thanked, praise be to Allah,' Aïsha repeated, over and over again. Aïsha was very beautiful. Tall and slender, she had dark, sable-coloured skin, and a walk like that of a cat.

We sat barefoot and cross-legged on a dusty grey blanket, and awaited the inevitable glasses of mint tea that were hastily being prepared. Then a meat and potato stew called *bonava* was served in a large enamel platter around which we squatted. Having already been through Morocco, I prided myself in my proficiency at being able to use small pieces of bread to shovel up mouthfuls of food without making a mess. Until, that is, I realised that my hosts were using a completely different method that involved using the bread rather more like a pincer than a scoop. My resulting efforts at imitation ended in having to eat off the palm of my hand, much to the amusement of the three sons who received frequent and icy glares from their father to stop them laughing. Save for their muffled giggles, the dinner was a serious enough affair. In the desert, people do not dawdle over their food, for it can never be taken for granted.

After lunch, the boys disappeared and Aïsha retired to her personal corner of the tent to brew yet more tea, leaving me to converse with Mahmoud (the Guinean neither spoke nor understood a word of French or Hassiniyah). Again, I asked him whence he originated, and again he answered, with a wry ironic smile: 'Mahmoud, *il est Mauritanien.*' There was something odd about this that I couldn't quite grasp. It was not just the way he said it, but also that the fact of his saying it was strange enough to be remarkable in a country where everyone else I met invariably mentioned some tribe or other that they belonged to, rather than the nation. In fact I can't recall anyone else who actually admitted to being Mauritanian. When I changed the subject to his work, Mahmoud explained in the same matter-of-fact way that he was a miner at Zouïrât. In vain he had travelled to Nouâdhibou in order to find another job because, he said, the miners were paid a pittance and the conditions were bad. The subject prompted a rare glimpse of emotion.

'They take us for... [he paused to grasp the word] They take us for dogs,' he said eventually as an unguarded scowl flickered briefly across his face.

'*You* know perfectly well that I am not a dog, and yet *they* treat me as though I were.' He closed his mouth and clenched his jaw. His nostrils quivered. Many workers had died in accidents, he said, of which several had been his friends. Many more now had bad coughs from the dust because they were not provided with protective masks. In Mahmoud's opinion, the bosses were all crooks and wanted the work done for next to nothing.

As we talked, I noticed more and more the pessimism and despondency lying beneath the anger in his voice. His face, too, was sullen, morose even, and when we'd finished, he was talking mostly with his head bowed. He said that he was not allowed to talk to strangers about the mines, but that he didn't care for the company's threats. 'Nobody ever takes any notice of *haratin* anyway,' he said.

To explain: until recently, Moorish society was organised in a rigid and hierarchical caste system. Seeing as the system still survives to some degree, I have used tenses as appropriate in what follows. At the top of the pyramid are the two noble (*bidan*) castes: the *hassanes* and the *marabouts*. The *hassanes* were effectively a warrior class, who extracted or extorted tributes from all and sundry in return for their dubious protection. They claim direct descent from the Beni Hassan, and therefore consider themselves to be of more noble blood than any other caste (they are indeed invariably pale-skinned). René Caillié, though, found them 'idle, mendacious, thievish, envious, superstitious and gluttonous; they combine in short, all possible vices.' The *marabouts*, for their part, combine the roles of teachers, sages, givers of hospitality, and merchants, and were frequently exploited by the *hassanes*. Below these two noble castes are the *zenaga*, semi-nomadic herders and cultivators who were tributaries of the *hassanes* and were often little more than skilled slaves, rarely if ever allowed to keep the fruits of their labour. Lastly, at the bottom of the social pile, came the Negro *abid* and *haratin*. The *abid* were the proper slaves, whereas *haratin* were/are mulatto descendants of Moorish men and Negro slave girls, whose slave status was often unclear. Mahmoud used *haratin* to mean a freed slave rather than a half-caste.

When I questioned Mahmoud about the *haratin* I was told (to my astonishment) that he and his family had only been freed in 1983, three years after the abolition of slavery in Mauritania, and fully thirty-eight years after the United Nations' Declaration on Human Rights. Sceptics argue that had the economics of drought not forced the freeing of Mauritania's slaves, then slavery would never have been abolished. It is ironic, then, that the demise of the nomad, however much that is to be regretted in itself, has released hundreds of thousands of slaves from their shackles.

But why, I wondered, was Mahmoud the free man and husband of the beautiful Aïsha, so sullen and so depressed? As *haratin* go, he was moderately well off, and was lucky enough to have found a job at all. I tried to put myself in his situation. For all those years that Mahmoud was forced to work like an animal for a master who scarcely acknowledged his presence, Mahmoud had also lived a life of hoping and dreaming of the day when his chains would finally be cast off, when he could walk away from his past a free man. Of course I would be happy. But would I then be happy to find myself as an adult, with no past of which I could speak, flung suddenly into a strange new world that knew no future but only the past? Would I be happy to all of a sudden be released from a lifetime of knowing that my future, however bleak, was secure and certain, to be pushed into a world that guaranteed nothing? Would I be happy to find all my hopes borne of a lifetime of toil, my hopes of equality, of fortune, of peace, of the true inviolability of the individual, suddenly dashed by the cold harshness of reality? Like societies the world over, Mauritania does not treat kindly its most recent converts, especially the *haratin*. Mauritania already has more than enough poverty. It has prejudice, it has hatred, and it is hard enough surviving without having the extra burden of *haratin* to bear on one's back. Worse still, society will never honour nor even recognise the need to compensate those that it has abused. It is not in the nature of society to consider whether it has wronged its individual constituents, but rather to consider the welfare of society as a whole, or at least the welfare of its masters, its creators and patrons.

Perhaps you are thinking that I am mistaken in assuming that Mahmoud's slavery was as miserable as I make out, even though he repeatedly refused to talk about his past. So let us imagine that his former master was a most kind and generous person, and that under him, Mahmoud's life of slavery had actually been bearable, perhaps even enjoyable. But in such a situation, Mahmoud would have mourned the loss of his chains even more than he would have celebrated the bitter-sweet taste of his new found freedom, for the society in which he would have found himself is precisely that which I have just described. The chains of slavery are not merely physical. They scar the mind and the spirit forever. There is no comfortable middle-ground in slavery. Slavery is either total or absent. The irony in all this is that although it is chains that tie the slave to the yoke, the man who is freed of his chains is still enslaved. The loss of the spirit, like the loss of life itself, can never be regained. What else was there for Mahmoud to say, except 'Mahmoud, *il est Mauritanien.*'

* * *

Mahmoud disappeared briefly, only to reappear holding aloft a heavy car pump that he had somehow managed to wangle. I knew, however, that without a pump to carry with me, I would be running the risk of puncturing irreparably somewhere along the 120km between Choum and Atâr, the first town on the road south to Nouakchott. I left Mahmoud and his family towards three in the afternoon, the hottest time of day. There was no wind, the escarpment saw to that, though the air was dry enough to contain some of the heat that would otherwise have been intolerable. I walked the bike back to the centre of the village with the Guinean, in the hope of finding him a lift to Nouakchott. For my part, I need food, water, and a few extra water bottles.

Most of the stores in Choum are collected together in two makeshift arcades, and are constructed of various sheets of scrap metal and wooden mining struts bound together using rope, nails and even netting. The arcades make up two of the four sides of what might be called the village square, most of which is sand strewn with broken glass, plastic bags, bottles and tins, empty oil drums and small strips of discarded acacia bark that is used to make rope. Without exception, all the shops were closed, though their owners, who were usually sat outside their shacks, were helpful enough. With their aid, both water and extra bottles were easy to find. Food, though, was another matter. As far as I know, Choum does not have a public baker, and so bread has to be brought in by train, but as the train would at this hour only just be leaving Nouâdhibou, there would be no bread until midnight. This arrangement was especially annoying given that most of the other stuff sold in the stores, like pulses and rice, needed to be cooked, and the only food available that did not need cooking were small bags of tasteless

Algerian biscuits. I bought these nonetheless, much to the chagrin of the shopkeeper who was trying his level best to sell me a drum of Chinese gunpowder tea.

By now, a large crowd had formed around us. Children shouted and grinned and laughed. Teenage girls not quite old enough to have to wear veils, fiddled self-consciously with their glossy black braids. One girl carried a handful of writhing lizards' tails. Later, I saw her throw the whole lot at a boy who had been pestering her! A lot of the children wore Western cast-offs, probably donated as aid: an assortment of baseball caps, cardigans inscribed 'N.Y.', faded and ripped T-shirts, jumpers with holes in, oversize shorts, and scabby patent leather shoes. In the distance, a donkey cart laden with scrap metal floated by, the kid who was driving it struggling to keep his mule under control. To my amusement I saw a group of kids fighting, because one of them couldn't get a good enough view of me. As they punched and kicked each other, they would glance over as though hoping that, like Caesar overseeing his gladiators, I'd somehow favour one or the other.

There was a sizeable contingent of adults, too. There were men holding hands (a common sight in Mauritania), others showing off by smoking expensive American cigarettes, some chewing sticks, and all staring at me. One man, who wore a horrendous blue tracksuit, assigned himself the task of 'protecting' me from the children, and clobbered them if they got too close. Thankfully, he was soon overwhelmed by sheer numbers. It felt good to be surrounded by so many people, and seeing that I didn't mind the attention, it didn't take long for enough courage to be plucked up by those nearest to reach out and touch the bicycle. The saddlebags, the frame and especially the tyres were all touched, prodded, poked and generally inspected to approving oohs and aahs. A small girl then started touching and squeezing me in much the same manner as people were touching the bike. First my legs, then my arms and shirt. Finally, on tiptoes, she started tugging gently at my hair and began trying to untangle it, occasionally poking her head round my neck to elicit an approving grin! Amidst all the commotion, a tiny and extraordinarily grotty toddler somehow managed to wheedle himself past the leggy jungle towards his sister, who indicated that she would look after my bike if I would give her brother a piggy back. So I lifted him on to my neck, and then waded through the crowd, everyone by now laughing and shouting at this extremely strange white man.

Somewhat inevitably, the crowd attracted the attention of the local gendarme, at whose appearance the throng dispersed. Forcing his way through the last stragglers with a truncheon, he accosted me, his face visibly livid. '*Toubab!*' He screamed like a teacher. 'What... What do you think you are doing here? Why have you not reported to the police? Where is your passport?' I handed him my papers and grovelled my apologies, claiming ignorance.

'Everyone knows that visitors have to report to the gendarmerie the first thing,' he snapped back. 'Even *Toubabs*. These are the regulations. *Everybody* knows that.' I grovelled some more, reiterating my ignorance of the rules, and soon he calmed down and began to relax. So much so that a few minutes later we were engrossed in a conversation about his family, about how wonderful Mauritania was, and so on. I asked him where I might find some bread for the journey to Nouakchott.

'Some *bread*?' he joked. 'Bread, my friend, is the food of the women!' Nevertheless, he managed to unearth six stale loaves, for which I was allowed to pay for only three.

After the gendarme had disappeared, the crowd reassembled, inquisitive as ever, from which one man, wearing a voluminous green turban, extricated himself. He was perhaps only about forty, though his moustache, drooping over thin, tight lips, had long since greyed. The usual piercing nomadic eyes were accentuated by dark eyebrows that tilted up from the bridge of his nose. He greeted abruptly, and then asked where it was that I intended going. Senegal, I replied.

'By Almighty Allah! You are surely insane!' he exclaimed, playing to the crowd with grandiloquent, sweeping gestures.

'Insane? Then may Allah be thanked!' I replied, grinning. He grinned back, and scowled, and for a few seconds I was unsure as to whether he was going to hit me. Then, he proceeded to empty out the contents of a tricolour bag into my hands: two cans of sardines, a can of skipjack tuna in tomato sauce, a can of pineapple chunks, a packet of peanuts, a carton of Austrian pasteurised milk, and even a small bottle of Perrier!

'*Monsieur le Toubab*, you have the good fortune to have the eyes of a madman. May Allah give you strength, and give you health.' With that, and before I even had time to consider protesting, he turned and walked away through the gaping crowd. A moment later, one of the shopkeepers ran up to me and explained (almost apologetically) that the man himself was a little *m'zaza*, though I needn't worry about accepting his gifts, because the madman was also quite a rich man!

As we walked off to find a truck, we were stopped by a plump, middle-aged *bidan*, whose face I cannot recall, but whose pot belly I can.

'Hey, *Toubab*, where are you going with that bicycle?'

'Nouakchott.'

'Look here, do you not understand that there is no road to Nouakchott?

Toubab, I have a taxi, look...' He took the Guinean aside, apparently to fix a price both for he and I.

'I will do you a favour,' he continued. 'Five thousand ouguiya. Only.' I smiled, but shook my head.

'But the sand comes right up to here,' he protested, as he levelled a hand at his waist. 'You cannot cross *that* on your bicycle. Come with us, come.' He made to walk off, but still I shook my head. He wanted me to haggle, but my mind was made up. Instead, I asked him directions for the road to Atâr and, sensing that I was serious, he acquiesced and pointed to one of three distant mountains rising out of the afternoon haze. It looked like a breast. All I had to do was cycle towards it for about twenty kilometres. Then, if I was going in the right direction, near the mountain I would see the ruins of the village of 'Aggui and four nearby *balises* (erratic road-markers not unlike telegraph poles). 'It is easy to find,' the taxi driver assured me, though that much, I knew, I doubted.

I left Choum pursued by hordes of children, all yelling and shouting and screaming at me to stop. I suppressed my haste and turned round to yell farewells and good wishes, greetings that echoed back from a barrage of frantically waving arms. I looked at the children for the last time and then, with the biggest grin in the world, I turned round, climbed on to the bicycle, and pedalled away.

* * *

The distant breast-shaped peak by which I was supposed to navigate rose like an iceberg above a shimmering sea of mirages. The sky was still and clear, the plain that surrounded me flat and featureless: a stony *hammada* dusted with a carpet of pebbles and sand that made cycling luxuriously easy. The ground skimmed by effortlessly to the sound of gently stirred gravel and the smooth oily whirring of gears and cogs, and for an hour the whole world was perfect in its simplicity.

Neither simplicity nor perfection, however, last forever, and as I cycled, the ground began gradually to sand over. With the passing of each kilometre, the effort required to keep the bicycle moving increased. I started sweating, and in the dry air my mouth soon became parched. Here and there sand drifts had begun to form around dead bushes, scrub that years ago had flourished in the ample waters of a now completely dessicated stream. The dunes of Erg Akchâr were beginning to dominate. Rising near Choum, the *erg* stretches southwest along much of the five hundred kilometres to the coast around Nouakchott. As I advanced, the mirages receded to reveal the gently undulating forms of sand dunes proper, stretching around and past that

205

mountain. The shroud of sand grew heavier, and vague vehicle traces appeared, more often than not going in every direction *but* the mountain I was heading for. Yet more sand and yet more tracks, dozens of them, each one unique to a particular journey in the past. Although the divergent tracks did nothing to reassure me of my own bearing, there was something satisfying about ignoring them all in order to leave behind my own.

In places, the *piste* consisted entirely of washboard corrugations – a series of compressed troughs lying sideways across the track, each measuring up to a foot in depth, and placed within a foot or two of the next. The corrugations demanded a reduction of speed to walking pace, lest the unavoidable pummelling damage the bicycle, myself, or both. In consequence, cycling rapidly became frustrating. Hour after hour of bouncing in and out of endless ruts with the bike lurching like a seesaw as the wheels alternated between trough and ridge, was not my idea of fun. Hour after hour of seemingly getting nowhere, and with no alternative but to walk. Hour after hour of not even being able to sit properly on the saddle without being thrown painfully onto the crossbar... Despite it being late afternoon, the heat was oppressive, and I was sweating profusely. Even the slightest additional effort would result in fresh beads of sweat forming on my brow, that would then splash down over the dusty handlebars and onto a couple of water flasks, already empty. In my frustration born of tiredness, I just stared at the ridges passing hypnotically beneath me, counting them in between the distractions of avoiding particularly deep troughs or isolated boulders.

My trance was shattered by a small explosion, followed by the flapping of my front tyre... and no pump either. I cursed my lousy luck, though I had absolutely no intention of returning to Choum. Apart from the humiliation, I figured that the possibility of another flat was overwhelming, especially given the dozens of punctures I'd already suffered in the Moroccan and Western Sahara. Foremost in my mind, though, was the belief that if I couldn't even surmount this relatively minor obstacle without outside help, then I might as well give up. So thinking, I remounted the bike and rode off, or at least I tried to. The puncture made keeping the bike steady extremely difficult, for the wheel rim could now slide about freely on a wide strip of rubber, without the tyre itself slipping on the ground. This often resulted in the bike veering unexpectedly, and sometimes violently. The flat also placed the brunt of the shocks from the uneven track onto my wrists and back, and both became sore.

The ruins of 'Aggui huddled on the sand at the foot of the mountain. Except for a few low walls that delineated the husks of what were once houses, the old village had been reduced to piles of shapeless rubble. The blackened chassis of a 1940s Renault stood incongruously among the stones, a reminder both of colonialism and of the graveyard that the desert has become. Past the village, a short line of wooden *balises* did indeed point the way to the *Route Nationale*. It is a grand name for something no more substantial than an infrequently used track, which often vanished altogether under the sands. Nevertheless, the *Route Nationale* made off into a wide and sandy valley. The sand was much thicker here, which forced the track into two deep ruts [*ornières*] which were impossible to cycle on. The landscape, though, was beautiful, with its soft and sensuous cusps and curves. As the sun sank deeper into the obscurity of the hazy horizon, a cascade of rusty iron reds showered the distant, broken-backed hills, their bases still separated from their jagged peaks by mirages. I stopped to look back at the way I had come, but all I could see were my own half-engulfed tracks stretching far out on a flat sandy plateau, tracks which for a while were etched in the soft sand with long, sharp shadows. Somewhere in the distance was the village of Choum, lying prostrate next to the rails and already far, far away. It was strange to consider that I'd effectively followed the same track all the way from England. But it wasn't like a railroad, travelling along a predetermined line from A to B. Rather, I was laying my own tracks, and I was leaving behind my own traces. The thought pleased me.

The first stars were beginning to pierce the sky when I noticed the flickering of a lantern on the opposite flank of the valley. In the nascent obscurity I could make out the outline of a tent, pitched beside the low silhouettes of a couple of acacia trees. Standing still, the gentle whisper of the evening breeze seemed to me to caress the shrill bleating of the nomad's goats. In the usual custom of camping near others (to dispel suspicions of impending *razzias*), I left my bicycle under a lone thorn bush and walked over to introduce myself. I was greeted warmly and with much aplomb by an amiable old man with hollow cheeks and spindly hands, these almost as black as his *cheche*. Along with his two teenage sons, he insisted vociferously that I should stay with them a while to talk and eat. The tent was surprisingly simple in construction. It was like a miniature but skewed circus big top: a large canvas sheet strung over an off-centre shoulder-high stave, secured with numerous guy ropes. The sides near the ground were left open and could be closed with flaps to protect against the elements. There was very little inside, save a large sack of rice reading 'USE NO HOOKS' that doubled as a cushion, two thick cotton blankets, and an anonymous metal chest upon which various cooking utensils had been placed.

We sat outside the tent to a meal of boiled rice and camel meat, huddled around the comforting amber glow of a lantern. Accompanied by the plaintive bleating of goats and the gut-wrenching growls of camels, we talked. Tarkhit, a *zenaga* of the Tajakant group of Moors, began the conversation with a flood of questions, rather in the manner of an interrogation. It was an impression that was accentuated by his eyes, which glared at me as he spoke in needle-sharp flurries of French. In between his initial over-inquisitiveness, I managed to interject a few questions of my own. Tarkhit had two wives in Atâr, six children (he wanted more), and a herd of over a hundred goats and two dozen pack-camels that he grazed in and around the Adrar's foothills. His life was a constant search for water and pasturage. In winter, he followed the rains north, and in summer he followed them south, a continuous search which has prompted the ever-poetic Arabs to call the pastoral nomads 'the sons of clouds'. In the past, tribes were known to ride towards grass that had sprung up over two hundred kilometres away, but the past few years, complained Tarkhit, had been unusually harsh. The rains were dwindling, and were coming later each year. There was now very little grazing land left, even in the once lush Adrar, which was almost threadbare as a result of overgrazing. It is estimated that over half the Adrar's cattle perished in the droughts of the 1970s, and then again in the early 1980s, and I cannot recall even once having seen cattle in Mauritania. At times, the situation became so bad as to provoke bloody quarrels and raids between rival groups of nomads, who were forced to graze their herds on the same land. With this in mind, I was proudly shown a gleaming antique rifle with which Tarkhit claimed to have foiled two bands of armed raiders.

As a result of the worsening situation, Tarkhit had decided to sell most of his camels as and when the opportunity arose, probably in Atâr or the famous oasis town of Chinguetti. The prospective sale depended on the arrival of a group of Malian caravaneers who, he had heard, were looking to buy replacements for animals lost over the last few months. Indeed, Tarkhit himself had lost over two dozen goats and half a dozen camels over the last year alone, and the meat that we had just eaten was from a bitch that had died only three days earlier. The caravaneers themselves, said Tarkhit, would almost certainly have lost more animals when crossing the wastes of El Djouf.

To my mind – from a European perspective – Tarkhit was surprisingly fatalistic about the future, and the phrase '*Insha Allah*' tended to follow a good many sentences. All the same, his fatalism was certainly not resignation, but rather a philosophical and theological acceptance of some greater and unknowable force, the Will of God. Tarkhit believed that his fate ultimately resided with Allah. If his herds and therefore his livelihood were to survive, then that was only due to Allah, whereas if his herds were to perish through lack of water or grazing, then that too was the Will of Allah. As Albert Hourani, the Lebanese historian of the Arab peoples, commented: 'belief in a God who created and sustained the world could give meaning to the blows of fate.' The attitude is prevalent among most nomads, among whom I found little of either pessimism or optimism. There is no need for these emotions, for everything is predetermined by Allah, or, in the case of non-Muslim nomads such as the Tuareg, by some superhuman abstraction of Nature or Fate.

Towards the end of the evening, I told Tarkhit a story that I had often recounted in Morocco. It is the true story, as far as I know, of the son of some French tycoon, who had rebelled against the wealth of his family when young by giving away his not-insubstantial pocket money to school friends. In the same way, the family fortune, when it eventually passed onto him, he also wanted to give away. By ridding himself of the burden of his wealth, it seems that the young man hoped to achieve his freedom. The problem was that the money was in held stocks and shares, and by the terms of his late father's will, he was only able to squander a comparatively small amount each year. The poor wealthy son soon grew desperate at the irony of his situation, and apparently, the newspapers said, he'd even contemplated joining a monastery in order to rid himself of his unwanted riches! He was desperate, that is, until he struck upon the brilliant idea of trading his original shares and certificates for ones in companies reckoned to be on the verge of collapse, for such a manoeuvre was permitted by the terms of the will. Thus, the problem of discarding his money seemed to be over, until, by some horrendous twist of fate, some of the bad apple companies that he'd counted on doing badly began unexpectedly to do well, and before long he had even more money than he'd started off with! All this had happened before the crash of October 1987, and so, tragically, the young man was so distraught at his ill luck that he flung himself off the top floor of the luxury Marina Baie des Anges in the Cote d'Azur.

'What?' exclaimed Tarkhit. 'That is all? He *killed* himself!' Tarkhit's initial consternation dissolved into helpless roars of laughter. 'Ha ha ha! Too *much* money! By Allah, he killed himself? Hoo-hoo-hooo...'

In return for my little offering, I was treated to half a dozen traditional tales recounted in a mixture of French and Hassiniyah, wonderful stories and fables that help keep alive the nomadic tradition of each tribe, preserving an oral continuity with ancestors that binds people much more strongly than the dusty leaves of leather-bound books. The fable I recall the clearest is the following, of which countless versions have been told:

'This story, and Allah knows that I speak the truth,' began Tarkhit, 'this story took place many, many years ago, at the time when the desert was a paradise of cold rivers, rolling meadows, and aromatic forests, where there lived one thousand different kinds of animals, and the skies were always full of birds. These were prosperous times and there were many large towns, of which the one called the River of the Great Stork was by far the most beautiful and pleasant. Its houses were large and spacious, and were decorated with beautiful murals that depicted each family's proud past. Yet, amongst all these beautiful houses, one in particular stood out from the rest, for this was the house of the sherif who lived with his seven wives and seven sons. By all accounts, they were happy together. All, that is, except for the mother of the second son. She was an exceedingly jealous woman, for she saw that it was the eldest son who, as heir to the sherif's title, received all the attention. So jealous did she become that one fateful day, when by chance she was alone with the eldest son (who was still young) in a forest, she conspired to sell him as a slave to a passing merchant. After much heart-rending searching, the family became resigned to the fact that the son had fallen prey to a lion or some other wild beast, and so the inheritance passed on to the second son. For many years thereafter, the evil woman lived happily with her sordid secret.

'As the years passed by, the tragedy was slowly forgotten, although the town was never quite as happy as once it had been. Then, another fateful day, in a far away city at the other end of the land, the merchant, now on his deathbed, confessed the whole sorry tale to his faithful manservant, who was, of course, the eldest son. Though the merchant could no longer recall the name of town, the son resolved to return to his family, and after many years of roaming the country like a beggar, he came to the River of the Great Stork. By a divine stroke of fate (Allah has His Ways) his mother happened to set eyes on him, and she immediately recognised him. Imagine the joy when the news was broken: the whole town celebrated with one hundred days of festivities, so happy were they at this miraculous return.

'But let us not forget the fate of the evil stepmother, for so ashamed was she of her wicked deed, that she ran away into the forest and was never heard of again. It is said that the forest demons punished her by turning her into a fly.'

A large black fly,
Hideous and agressive,
turns and turns
above the water lilies of the mysterious pond.
Is she born of jealousy?
Or is she born of sadness and envy
For her to dare not land
on the white petal crown of the lily?

Moorish poem[10]

* * *

I slept badly, and awoke as the last of Tarkhit's animals were being driven northwards down the valley towards Choum. I could hardly have felt worse: stiff limbs, swollen eyes, sore back and wrists, and a dull headache. I was hot, sticky, knackered and still sleepy, the latter because of one particularly large darkling beetle that had kept me awake for much of the night by clamping its sizeable pincers firmly around my nose. The third time that I'd felt a sharp pain coming from my proboscis, I launched my assailant into orbit, reckoning that I would have made good my escape by the time it managed to crawl back and disturb me again! My panniers, incidentally, and therefore my food, had become infested with a colony of ants, and as a result, the first hour of my day was spent picking them off my bread and sifting my peanuts. Another half hour was spent repairing the bicycle. I tried to soften the shocks of riding on a flat tyre by stuffing an old T-shirt between the rim and the tyre, but the shirt tended to bunch up and so made cycling even bumpier than it had been before.

I left several hours after dawn, the white sun already blazing down from its zenith. The broad valley that had begun past the ruins of 'Aggui continued southwards as far as I could see, rising gently all the time. There was sand everywhere, though there were sporadic patches of rocks and vegetation, roughly defining the path of some ancient stream or river. For the first few hours the vegetation survived, albeit sparsely. The sand, however, remained – a torrid river of yellow grains flanked on either side with a low line of serpentine hills. The *ornières* along which I was travelling became deeper and softer, forcing increasingly frequent bouts of walking. Sometimes, the sand gave way to short stretches of corrugations, making it difficult to decide which of the two I hated more. Tracks appeared and disappeared, in places completely obscured by deep sand drifts that not only forced me to walk but carry my bicycle, all forty kilos of it. I learned a lot about cycling in sand in

211

those few hours: the tell-tale signs of colour, of ripples, and the engulfed vehicle traces that warned of impending quagmire. In places, the roots of decapitated acacia were visible and meant firmer ground, albeit at the risk of more thorns finding their way into my tyres. As the day wore on, however, all the vegetation vanished.

Late that morning, a Peugeot 504 station waggon roared past me, only to skid to an abrupt halt amidst clouds of dust and sand. It was the taxi driver from Choum.

'Ah, there you are, my insane friend! Radiance be upon you! You okay? I hope you have not been thirsty?'

'Of course not,' I replied, and then asked him if he could spare any water. He leaned back into the car to confer with his passengers, and after long deliberations gave me two litres.

'They did not want to stop for you,' he confided, 'or give you any water, but I told them that you were my mad *Ingleezi* friend!' In the back of the car, ten passengers busily pretended that they hadn't seen me. With a cheerful *'B'slama, Ingleezi,'* the driver clambered back in and drove away.

By midday I had already drunk the taxi driver's two litres, but felt still thirstier. My frustration grew hourly as only more sand appeared on the horizon to compensate for my progress, and my exhaustion, and indeed my anger, increased as my water supply dwindled. The thermometer stuck at 52°C. Twice I fell off the bike, and I stumbled as I walked, swearing and cursing the desert. Yet, passing over one sand dune, my gaze met with a most astonishing sight. Stretching as far as the horizon, where the sand merged with the sky in a flurry of mirages, was a veritable forest of surreally weather-beaten boulders, tossed about a flat and pebble-strewn plateau as though by some gigantic, cataclysmic mind-storm. Huge rocks stood isolated like those in the metaphysical gardens of Japan's Zen Buddhist temples. The place was beautiful, and would have been most meditative had it not been for the scorching heat. The boulders reminded me of Henry Moore's sculptures, possessed of a most sensual beauty, shaped and honed to perfection by the endless abrasion of wind and sand and water. My imagination, numbed by the monotony of the day's cycling and long-since starved of even the slightest glimpse of another naked human form, revelled in the inherent sexuality of these deliciously moulded rocks. Soft and rounded female torsos, convoluted and provocative, powerful and eternal like the desert of which they were born.

The track wound its way around these strange monoliths in great fluid arcs, infinitely more aesthetic than travelling in stubbornly linear fashion. These rock-strewn lands are known locally as *Turab el-Hajra*, the Land of Stone. Despite the absence of life, it was a strangely reassuring land, and for a while I quite forgot my tiredness and thirst. But the stomach is never one to feast merely on emotion, and so I stopped beside one particularly large boulder for lunch, squeezing myself as best I could into the few inches of shade it afforded from the sun. Several handfuls of peanuts and a can of sardines later, I stood up and was most surprised to find myself reeling in the heat. Suddenly, I felt drained, and the thought even came to mind of giving up and waiting for a lift. This much I can't explain. Maybe I had rested too long? Perhaps I was experiencing the beginnings of dehydration? Or perhaps it was the sudden shock of the heat? Whatever it was, it had crept up unawares and I was now worried at my sudden physical deterioration. The temperature still hovered around fifty, and I realised that at this rate I would not reach Atâr until the following day. Worse still was that my water and food supplies were beginning to run low, for I had not counted on the extra day that I might need to reach the town. Wearily, I slumped over the bicycle, oblivious now to the beauty of my surroundings. The salty sweat from my forehead stung my eyes and blurred my vision. Past the last few boulders, the tracks started down into another sandy valley. Again, the impossible-to-cycle *ornières* and again the reappearance of a few thorn bushes and clumps of grass that seemed to be floating on the sand like gulf-weed on the Sargasso Sea. By now, my thoughts were directed almost entirely by my frustration. The monotony of alternately cycling and walking, together with the heat and my tiredness, served only to blight still further my hopes. 'Oh, to hell with it,' I thought, as I foolishly carried on drinking my precious water, though I was to find out to my cost that drinking too much in extreme temperatures only makes one hotter and even thirstier than before. Another hour passed with no sign of the mountain pass that according to my map lay on the road to Atâr.

Sometime in the afternoon my hopes were lifted upon sighting a few skin-and-bone donkeys stood beside the track in a clump of thicker vegetation. Their presence seemed to indicate the proximity of nomads, although I could see nothing to betray human presence. I shouted a greeting, but heard nothing but my echo returning unanswered from the flanks of the valley. Depressed, I walked on, feeling hotter than ever, even though the sun was beginning to relax its hold on the day. Mid afternoon is the cruellest time because the midday heat still lingers and your bones begin to fry in their burnt sleeve of flesh and skin. Whenever I touched my forehead to wipe away the sweat, I experienced the uncomfortable sensation of seeming to rub holes into my skin. The sand also was hot, and baked my leaden feet as I walked. Mid afternoon is a hopeless time of day, half way between the clarity of dawn and the calm reflection of dusk. Mid afternoon is the time of day when hope turns too easily to despair and you begin not to care anymore about the day, which can be fatal.

I was about to give up when I spotted a small white building in the distance, a sight that gave me renewed energy, though it still took a good hour to reach it. My arrival startled a slight old man who had been sleeping on a woollen blanket.

'*Marhaba w'sahala,*' he greeted: be welcome and feel at ease.

While Caucasian in feature, the old man had very dark skin and a surprisingly sonorous Negro voice. The racial legacy of the Moors has certainly produced some strange mixtures. As is customary in the Sahara, I was offered a bowl of *zrig* and a handful of dates. The man insisted that I stay until evening.

The hut – a one-room shelter typical of the Sahara – was constructed of plywood sheets and corrugated tin, but had no windows save for three shutters arranged like cat flaps near the ground. These were intended to allow cool breezes into the building whilst excluding the sand, in spite of which the inside of the hut was sandy anyway. The plywood gave the hut a pleasurable musty odour, and the glow of daylight filtering through the gaps in the roof and the shutters made it quite cosy, if a trifle hot. The hut was devoid of any furniture, save for a few rickety shelves that were nailed to three corners of the room. On these were arranged an assortment of tools, cooking utensils, car spares, and food. In the other corner stood three butane gas cylinders and a goatskin butter churn, over which, to my amazement, hung a red and white Manchester United F.C. scarf! As far as I could gather, it had been presented by someone on a 1974/75 British Joint Forces Expedition to the Sahara.

Because my host spoke only Hassiniyah, we resorted to sign language. Conversing in this way was surprisingly easy, even for explaining quite complicated matters, though the conversation tended to take the form of simple questions and answers. Naturally, my host wanted to know where I'd come from, but when I unfolded a map to help explain, he didn't even recognise the outline of his own country. So instead, I pointed north, and then, describing the arc of the sun to mean a day, I indicated 140 on my fingers and pointed to a drawing of a camel on my notepad (I reckoned one 'camel-day' to be approximately thirty miles). The old man was astonished – the furthest he'd ever been was ten 'camel-days', from the Adrar to Nouakchott in 1960 to witness the Independence Day celebrations.

For over ten years now, the man had made his living by supplying petrol, soap, food and other essentials to passing motorists. He also cannibalised any abandoned vehicles in the vicinity for spare parts, which were then sold to passers-by. The untethered donkeys that I had seen were used for this purpose, as were four camels that were presently being grazed by his son.

As we were conversing, there was a terrible scream outside the hut. I turned to see a small girl come tearing inside to hide trembling behind the old man. Then a little boy, also screaming, came running in, and then another. Finally, another round of shrieks and shouts were unleashed as a man of about thirty – presumably the old man's son – came in laughing through the door, holding in front of him a rake upon which was perched a two-foot long spitting *dhab* lizard.

'Grrrr!' he taunted, to another salvo of screams.

The lizard, needless to say, was not overly impressed with all this, especially when it was accidentally dropped onto the floor, at which the young man himself screamed and ran out of the hut. Spitting some more, and with the children still screaming, the lizard scurried off to take refuge under a rug, by which time the old man and myself were in hysterics. It took almost a quarter of an hour for the son to pluck up enough courage to creep back into the room, tie a rope around the lizard's tail and drag it outside. The Moors, for all their fighting prowess, are scared stiff of lizards.

I left the old man, who was still giggling inanely, as the sun was setting. I had been forced to accept a good few litres of water, a dusty carton of milk and some biscuits, gifts for which, as usual, I was forbidden to pay. In the stark evening light, I could now see clearly the mountain pass – Aouînat et Mlis – that I had worried about missing: the first ascent into the Adrar itself (literally 'the Mountains'). The track, no longer as sandy as it had been, consisted once again of corrugations, made harsher than before due to a lack of cushioning sand. There were also more thorn bushes, the odd severed branch of which lay across the track. The sun set when I was half way up, and so I settled down among clumps of spiky grass. The half moon rose soon after dusk, gliding into the sky with the silent grace of an ocean liner coming into berth. The sand around me was lit with the eerie yellowish glow of waxlight, and a few delicate cloud sylphs in electric-blue swam above me, teasing. As I had progressed through the Sahara, I had come to appreciate that one of the desert's greatest attractions is the poetry of its night, its cool tranquillity, its silence that seems never to have been broken. As though I were mesmerised by a film, or entranced by a concert, I would sometimes stare for hours at the colours in this darkness, listening to its silence and losing myself in a wonderful feeling of well-being. From the tree of silence hangs its fruit, tranquillity – an Arab saying – and often, I never felt more alive than when enveloped in this shroud of silence, this pensiveness, my thoughts and my dreams. It is dreams that make Man great, and not necessarily their fulfilment. Dreams give hope, for they give one something to live for.

The Arabs also say that day effaces the promise of the night. Morning, and I still hadn't managed to sleep properly. Worse still, I was struck by a most fearsome lethargy, which was to make the day's travel exceedingly difficult. Thanks to the old man in the hut, food was no longer a problem, although the biscuits had been reduced to powder by the corrugations.

As I was packing away the last of my things, I was startled to see a man walk up to me. 'Drink?' he motioned. Bemused, I followed him over the rocks to the right of the track, and down into a rocky depression that I had not previously noticed. At the bottom of a narrow gorge, only a couple of hundred yards from where I had been sleeping, was a well. Crowded around it were perhaps two hundred camels, complaining like cantankerous old colonels, as half a dozen nomads relayed themselves in the tiring task of filling a couple of clay troughs from two skin buckets. The nomads were too busy to talk, so I filled my bottles, thanked them, and returned to the bicycle.

At the top of the pass – a stony and windblown ridge, slightly convex in shape – stood a few stone walls. This was a seasonal *n'zala* for pastoral nomads. For a few weeks each year, while their flocks and herds graze the surrounding hillsides, a nomad family or clan pitch their *friq* here. The ground was strewn with oxidised stones, baked black by the sun and polished by the wind.

I walked the bike down into the next valley, a basin filled with sand that was studded here and there with a few flat-topped acacia. In the centre of the valley was another well, from which six nomads filled goatskin *guerbas*. The well was surmounted by a wooden pivotal arrangement that enables water to be drawn using animals. I arrived as a woman and her daughter, both veiled from head to toe in black, were walking three donkeys to a *friq* beside the next ridge of mountains. Each donkey carried six or seven bulging *guerbas*, painting trails of water on the sand. The track continued along a mixture of corrugations and sand drifts before winding up towards the next pass, Te-n-Zâk. Again, the heat was seething, and I was beginning to feel the worst of it. The climb up the pass took over two hours, including several rests to catch my breath, and by the time I reached the top I was exhausted.

Once over the col, and fed-up with walking, I resolved to cycle the rest of the way to Atâr, irrespective of my stricken bike. This decision was stupid, but typical of my stubbornness, since the rocky descent made my back and wrists even more sore. Steering was hard with the puncture. Twice the bike veered unexpectedly, and twice I fell off. Twice the bike was jolted so violently that bottles were sent flying and I lost three litres of water as a result. Sweat poured off my face and I was beginning to feel dizzy and nauseous. The carton of milk was already rotten, and the heat was so severe as to have melted the insides of my plastic water bottles so that the liquid had turned a dirty brownish red and tasted sour.

Towards early afternoon, I rounded the peak of a small hill to be confronted with an expanse of vegetation and dwellings. But as I approached, it became apparent that this was not yet Atâr, since there were no more than a dozen stone-and-straw huts in all. This was the once-fortified oasis settlement of Ksar-Torchane. Straw-woven sand breaks protected small plots of millet, and corn and grasses grew in the shade of several towering date palms that followed the underground course of the Séguélil *wadi*. The crops were protected from maurauders and other scavengers with a vicious barricade of thorn brush and barbed-wire abatis, as were the village's wells. But even in the relative verdancy of Ksar-Torchane, the recent droughts had left their mark. Patches of greyed and withered millet interspersed the healthier crops, and the only wells that were not barricaded with thorns or fences were bone dry. Yet, it was the inhabitants who, more that anything else, betrayed the lasting effects of drought. Their expressions combined amazement with condescension, and they refused point-blank either to give or to sell me any water, saying that Atâr was only 20km away.

This was unfortunate for me, since my remaining water was so hot and putrid as to be undrinkable. The heat and the corrugated track, my hunger and generally bedraggled physical shape, exacerbated my nausea and compounded my exhaustion. Although I knew that I was near Atâr, I felt as though this whole heap of human and bicycle would sink without trace into the voracious sand, and I swear that the next twenty kilometres felt at least like two hundred. My legs cramped up (which they had never done before) and the pain was searing. My eyes hurt. I felt sick. A cold sweat broke out on my face, and I realised that I was shaking uncontrollably. Then, I threw up. My head whirled. No longer able to be supported by my aching neck, it was slumped over the handlebars, straining my bloodshot eyes still further as I tried to see where I was cycling. As a result, I just stared at the ridges moving hypnotically beneath me, battling to keep my lacerated eyelids from drooping over my stinging eyes. I looked up, but my head was spinning, hallucinating. The striations of the track drifted up to become superimposed on the sky, which turned from grey-blue to purple, and then green. The shimmering white sand turned into a boiling mass of red liquid. I stared again at the hazy horizon, but it had vanished. My eyes closed, at last, even though I knew I was still cycling. Many were the times I deceived myself into believing that what were in fact old gnarled scarecrow trees were groups of waving people running towards me. Then, my shivering returned, and I had to stop cycling to prevent myself falling off or from being sick again. In this feverish state, I was both shocked and scared, especially after what should have been – in principle at least – an easy ride.

After what seemed like an age, I rounded another hill to be welcomed by the jumbled silhouetted skyline of Atâr. I had lost all sense of time.

* * *

I stopped beside a small grey hut on the right hand side of the road, and gazed, mouth agape, at a lush field of green millet. Over it, jets of water scattered their precious life. The millet stalks stooped gently in the breeze, and between them, I caught glimpses of dark-skinned girls wandering about hand in hand, their skins glistening across the rainbows. On impulse, I left my bike and dashed off to join them under the gushing water, and for several minutes I stood there, motionless, feeling cold wet fingers caress my sunburnt face and outstretched arms.

I turned round to see two girls in their late teens, smiling coyly.

'*Salaam Alaikum.*'

'*Alaikum Salaam.*' I was too drained to smile back. All that I felt able to do was stare, hoping that the girls would understand how I felt. The last two days had virtually petrified the flesh on my face, and for the first time I felt that I could understand and relate to the hard-faced, minimalist expressions of the nomads, expressions that relegated all but the strongest and barest feelings to the back of the mind. Without a word, one of the girls disappeared into the nearby house, and reappeared a moment later carrying a ceramic bowl filled with fresh *zrig*. I mustered a half-smile and thanked them, before lifting the bowl with trembling hands to my chapped lips. I closed my eyes to take a sip, letting the cool liquid trickle slowly across the base of my sandpapered mouth, soothing and embracing it, before easing itself down my throat. Then another sip, and another, until I was pouring down the rest almost laughing.

Both sisters – Aïsha and Aïssata Mint Allaf – were slender, and cut tall and graceful figures. In my state of mind, they were, at that moment, the most beautiful things in the world. Aïssata was the eldest, and wore a colourful robe of gold, earthy brown, and olive green, splashed with red. Her sister, who was rather shy, wore a similar robe, but in shades of saffron and cobalt blue. She soon disappeared into the house, leaving me alone with Aïssata. I didn't and couldn't really say very much, so instead I stared hypnotised – or rather, exhausted – at her. Around her neck, she wore a cross-like pendant that reflected shards of sunlight. Large urn-like beads were threaded into her hair, around which she had wound a loose, black cotton shawl. Her earrings consisted of several golden pendants threaded together, their motifs being a fusion of a ring and a triangle, a fertility symbol that is found even in Asia. Still she smiled, and then motioned for me to follow her indoors.

A few nervous questions established the fact that the sisters were originally from Oualata, a town in south-eastern Mauritania that lies on the ancient salt road from Idjil to ancient Ghana. The town is apparently renowned for the beauty of its women. Exactly what this means, though, is difficult to say, for both the Tuareg and the Moors – especially the Brakna of the centre and south of the country – have a penchant for fat women. Plumpness, or preferably gross obesity, is considered by many to be a sign of great wealth and fertility.

'The largest and fattest are the most admired. To be a real beauty with them, a woman must have such a degree of obesity as will render her unable to walk without two assistants', noted René Caillié of the Tuareg. Of the Moors, he mentioned that their conception of beauty: 'consists in enormous embonpoint; and the young girls are therefore obliged to drink milk to excess... At twelve years old they are enormous'. It said that some women are so fat that they become bedridden, a (desirable?) effect similar to that produced by the old Chinese tradition of foot-binding. All of which, I suppose, means that Aïsha and Aïssata were probably considered to be monstrously ugly. I also learnt that being Muslim didn't prevent Aïssata from asking, quite unabashedly, whether I would marry her or her sister! I tried to explain that I was only nineteen years old and that marriage might be just a little premature, but judging by their giggles and awe-struck expressions, I suspect they understood that I was betrothed to nineteen already!

* * *

The town of Atâr lies on the western cusp of the Adrar massif, of which it is the regional capital as well as its largest settlement (it has a population of around 20,000). The Adrar, together with the adjoining Tagant mountains, is the historical heartland of Mauritania, and effec-

219

tively shelters Atâr from both the trade wind and the *Harmattan*, and therefore from most of the sand. Until the droughts of recent years, the Adrar received an average of about seven inches of rain a year, and every autumn the Séguélil*wadi* on whose banks Atâr rises, would flood to fertilize the soil. The Adrar is one of the Sahara's six major microcosms, and is without doubt Mauritania's most important agricultural region, producing dates, millet, sorghum, barley, watermelons, tobacco and vegetables, albeit in quantities nowhere near large enough to make any impression on Mauritania's massive import requirements.

Despite being surrounded by hills, Atâr is a flat and broad town. The only things, beside the mosques, to breach the skyline are the occasional acacia or dalm palm that peek out from between the buildings, and the telegraph poles, devoid of wires, that stand to pointless soldierly attention. The roads – wide and sandy thoroughfares – are flanked with terraces of one or two storey houses whose uncluttered decor, red clay plaster, and false battlements evoke some of Marrakesh's architectural simplicity (that city, after all, was built by the Almoravids). Most of the dwellings are made of clay-clad stone, and are strung together in rows of up to a dozen houses, all doors and no windows. The doors and shutters are often brightly painted in red, green, yellow and blue, and add a touch of gaiety to the otherwise featureless town.

Two white-skinned Moors in flapping white *boubous* stand hand in hand in the main square, staring saucer-eyed at the arrival of this very odd-looking European and his even stranger wheel-machine. I wave and they wave back. There are people everywhere, in dozens of small groups and clusters, standing, sitting, arguing, laughing, chatting, and all, it seems, converging on me. Old men in floppy indigo or black turbans sit in front of their shops fiddling with white prayer beads while waiting for business or the next call of the muezzin, whichever comes first. In the distance a man stares. A blue veil is draped across his face so that only his eyes are visible. Similarly veiled women walk around in pairs, with huge bales of straw balanced on their heads, or else baskets filled with branches for turning into charcoal. It still amazes me to see how they can perch anything from a small urn to a billy goat on their heads, and still be able to walk, turn, twist, bend, run and defy the laws of gravity in such a graceful manner!

Two young black girls in white frilly dresses, also holding hands, run barefoot across the sand to avoid a dusty Peugeot station waggon that careers blindly towards them. The older girl has a funny little cherub's face, and screams. Her skin shines in the sunlight and she has a long flowing mane of thinly braided hair. The little girl is snot-faced and has her free hand stuck in her mouth. Her hair is shorter and frizzy, and she seems scared on seeing me. In one corner of the square there is a clump of gnarled palm trees, providing dubious shelter for an old battered Land Rover and a truck with no wheels. If it wasn't for the motor vehicles and the constant throbbing of a distant generator reverberating throughout the town, one could quite easily believe oneself to be in another century.

I soon enlisted the help of a few nosey villagers to try and locate a bicycle pump, though with mine being the only bicycle in town and with today, May 25, being African Liberation Day (ie. a holiday), I despaired somewhat at my chances of success. For the next few hours I wandered through Atâr with my youthful guides. It seemed as though everyone we talked to knew somebody else with a bicycle pump, but when we found that somebody else, they would invariably direct us to yet another person. Dozens of houses and almost every shop on the way were visited, including those in the smith's quarter, where finely incised silver jewellery, copperware and saddle fittings are made. More than once I managed to get ejected from a shop by its owner who was annoyed at the thirty or forty children who were trying to squeeze in.

Then, miracle of miracles, someone appeared with a Chinese 'Squirrel Brand' bicycle pump. It cost me a small fortune, but who was I to argue? The next item on the agenda was food, meaning bread and peanuts – for they were the only cheap provisions not requiring cooking that could last several days in the desert. Again, the same problems with the shopkeepers and my over-enthusiastic entourage, the size of which was growing by the minute. Constant chattering. Faces: suspicious, grinning, joking, finger-biting, apprehensive, inquisitive, happy and sad, confused, bold... Grown men stood around on the peripheries, chewing profoundly on sticks whilst contemplating the spectacle. Like in Choum, children touched or just stared at my smashed bicycle, pointing out helpfully that one of the tyres was flat. Others stared in bemusement at the crusty remains of what were in fact still my cycling gloves tied around the brake-levers. One group of old men shooed us away like flies because we were disturbing their peaceful afternoon's rumination. I sympathised, having the same problem myself, for I was again beginning to feel my tiredness, and my patience with the crowd was wearing thin. All I wanted was to be left alone in peace, yet I felt like a zoo animal cooped up in a cage with a thousand fingers pointing and five hundred faces leering. Whenever I stopped, the crowd closed in and began pushing and shoving to get a better view. I could hardly breathe, let alone move, and the sun glared. There were just so many people, too many people, especially after the stillness and desolation of the desert, hateful and exhausting though it had been. Everyone touching, squeezing, groping. Three hours had brought me one bicycle pump, six small baguettes and severely frayed nerves. I still needed to find water and peanuts, to get some rest, to eat and to repair the bike. In peace. But there was none to be had, not even the faintest glimmer.

The crowd had ballooned to over a hundred people – if anything, an understatement – and not just children. I wanted to escape. I wanted to be able to fill my aching lungs with fresh air, but instead I breathed in a stuffy mixture of dust and the smell of the crowd. I felt suffocated. Claustrophobic. Trapped, like in the web of some giant spider, invisible. The heat seemed to increase interminably. I felt dizzy again and my head started spinning. I began trembling once more, shaking. I turned round to see yet more stares and laughs and fingers pointed, and in the distance even more people were being attracted towards the spectacle. I turned again. Yet more stares and laughs and hands pointing.

Out of the corner of my eye, I caught a glimpse of a shiny Land Cruiser that had just appeared at the far edge of the square. To my surprise, I saw that I was being filmed by a European who was perched atop it. I took my chance. With the intention of momentarily distracting the crowd with the new arrival, I walked up to the vehicle. The man was still filming as I greeted him.

'*Bonjour.*'

'Err, *bonjour*,' replied the Frenchman. 'Are *you* the madman with the bicycle?' he asked. He'd evidently heard about the nutter in Choum.

'You look remarkably well,' he lied (I know this because I later saw my reflection in a mirror). 'How do you feel?' he asked, still talking from behind the camera.

'Hot.'

'Any problems?'

'Yeh, punctures. And you?' He shrugged. The crowd was even larger, and a background patter to our conversation had started: '*M'sieur, gimmoi un balong.*'

'*Viens, viens m'sieur...*'

'*Attention!*'

'Hey, *Toubab...*'

'Do you always talk from behind your camera?' I asked as I pulled a grotesque face at it. This seemed to prompt an old lady – wonderfully cross-eyed, toothless, and grinning – to examine the camera.

'Ah, *la télévision*?' she asked, still grinning. I told her that it was Moroccan TV. 'Ah,' she said thoughtfully as a grubby finger reached out to touch the lens as she read out the 'C.C.D.' logo, much to the annoyance of the Frenchman but to the delight of the crowd.

The Frenchman invited me back to the Hôtel de Marie so that I could wash and have a rest, and he kindly ended up paying for me to stay the night. He, along with another nineteen people, had each paid over twenty thousand francs, plus petrol and expenses, to spend two weeks driving from Paris to Dakar in a convoy of ten 4WD Toyotas. The convoy had arrived in Atâr last night, and had presumably passed me lying asleep and unnoticed at the foot of the Aouînât pass. It seems as though they had been delegated in Choum with the unofficial task of assuring that the madman was alright – a veritable motorcade of baby-sitters!

So far, they had covered 4,000 kilometres in eleven days, whereas it had taken me almost three months to cover the same distance. Most galling for me was not that they had done all this in luxury (I felt perversely superior to them in having done in the 'proper' way), but that they had somehow managed to wangle permission from the Algerians to travel via the usually closed northern section of the 'Mauritanian Way' accompanied by Polisario guides. Being the 15th anniversary of the Front's formation, the French had been made guests of honour at the celebrations held in Tindouf. By all accounts, the organisation of the event had been impressive, and had even included a brief sortie into Moroccan occupied territory, where a few symbolic mortar salvos and bursts of machine gun fire were offered in the name of Allah.

The hotel (its very existence surprised me no end) was situated on the western outskirts of town. A modern concrete structure, it made every pretence to appear both affluent and traditional, but failed on both counts. It is said to have been a fort for the French Atâr Camel Corps, though this seemed most unlikely given both its size and its garishly painted false brickwork. Its windows were secured with grills of butterfly motifs, and a tall unfriendly wall shut off the hotel and its grounds from the inquisitive eyes of Africa outside. A couple of other Land Cruisers were parked in the yard beside a clump of pitiful shrubs – the rest of the French party had gone on a two-day trip to Chinguetti. Inside, the lobby was bare but for five chairs, a wobbly table and a bar. The latter housed very expensive French mineral water, a few bottles of Orangina, and the exceedingly grumpy maître d'hôtel. He was middle-aged, short, and balding, and had been nick-named *'Monsieur Non'* by the French on account of his inability to say anything but 'no'. The most amazing thing about him was his fantastical plan to build a swimming pool beside the hotel!

* * *

Because of its plentiful water supply, and comparatively agreeable climate, the Adrar has been populated since prehistoric times. In parts, the desert floor is strewn with Stone Age tools and spearheads, and there are several mysterious stone circles (similar to ones in Senegal and other parts of West Africa), together with hundreds of examples of prehistoric cave art. The most enigmatic of these are a few equine engravings belonging to the so-called 'chariot period'. Horses, I was surprised to learn, had thrived for centuries in the Sahara, having first appeared around 1200BC (a thousand years before the advent of the camel). Though no longer to be found in the desert, that they had once lived in the Sahara was a sign of the great climatic changes that have occurred over the intervening centuries. Chinguetti (Shinqit), the name of the celebrated 14th century oasis town 120km to the east of Atâr, means 'the horse's springs'. It is by far Mauritania's largest oasis, and perhaps for this reason is often said to be the seventh holiest city of Islam. The oasis lies on a now almost defunct caravan route from Atâr across El Djouf to the salt mines of Taoudenni. It is a route that once provided the only direct means of communication between the Moors and their Tuareg cousins, and in its heyday, Chinguetti was considered so important that all of Mauritania was known as the *Turab Shinqit*, the Land of Chinguetti.

The most puzzling aspect of the horse-engravings is the depiction of chariots, which has led to speculation that there may once have been a couple of trade roads reaching across the great desert, perhaps several millennia before the arrival of the Arabs and the subsequent establishment of the camel caravan trails. Herodotus, writing two and a half thousand years ago, spoke of mysterious Garamantian nomads who: 'have four-horse chariots, in which they chase the Troglodyte Ethiopians, who of all the nations... are by far the swiftest of foot.' At the time of Christ, Strabo – another great geographer – mentioned that chariots were ridden by the equally mysterious 'People of the Sea', presumably Berbers from the Mediterranean.

These early trading routes, in addition to the spiritual purity of the desert, were crucial to the success of the Almoravids, which were founded in the cradle of the Adrar early in the 11th century. Within the space of twenty years, they had succeeded in expanding from an initial band of around 500 puritanical ascetics, to ruling over an empire that stretched from West Africa to Spain, and from the Atlantic to parts of what is now Tunisia. Their first sultan was Yusuf ibn Tashufin, born in the Adrar and leader of the powerful Lemtuni tribe (hence the ancient name for the 'Mauritanian Way', *Tariq* [Way of] *el-Lemtuni*). The rekindler of the flame of Iberian Islam, and vanquisher of El Cid, ibn

Tashufin had in the years before the Almoravid jihad resided in a small *ribat* (fortified monastery) ten miles from Atâr. The Almoravids, it is certain, could never have achieved their success had it not been for the then already extensive trading routes that radiated out from the Adrar. The foundations of Atâr itself (the name means 'the road') were laid at about the same time as the forging of the *Tariq el-Lemtuni*, and the subsequent establishment of other roads either passing through or starting from Atâr secured both its and Chinguetti's future as important trading towns. By the time the Portuguese led an expedition to the region in the 15th century (to procure gum arabic for the use of drapers), Atâr was evidently a centre of some renown. It appears that the town continued to flourish, to such an extent that in the late 17th century an English bounty hunter named Cornelius Hodges opined that Atâr was 'very neare as bigg as ye Citty of London'.

Atâr and the Adrar remained important enough for the French to fight a long and bloody campaign at the turn of this century in order to secure its trade. Resistance to the French penetration and their policy of 'civilizing the savages' was so fierce that total 'pacification' of the ungrateful and anarchical Adrar tribes was only achieved in the 1930s, three decades after the first French incursions and only two before independence was gained.[11] As a result, very little remains to remind one of the French occupation, with the exception of a handful of military advisers and doctors, and the spectacle of a group of old men who daily played a version of petanque in the sandy hotel courtyard.

* * *

The morning air reverberated to the dull but reassuring rhythm of a distant tam-tam, once used to relay messages but now only played for tradition's sake. The sky had clouded over during the night, and hung grey and heavy, hot and sticky. Breakfast was a joke: a cup of coffee, a slice of bread, and a blob of apricot jam. By now, my metabolism had speeded up to such an extent that I was easily devouring over four pounds of bread and a pound of peanuts a day, as well as anything else at hand, and so I sought to supplement breakfast by unearthing the baguettes I'd bought yesterday. To my dismay, I found that they had also become infested with ants. I would have to wait until late afternoon to buy some more, but, as I didn't want to waste a day (my visa had only six days to run, though in fact this wasn't to be a problem), the ant-bread would have to suffice. In any case, Adem, whose room I had shared (and who had refrained from the Chinguetti excursion on account of his driving partner being a lunatic), had kindly offered to bring some extra provisions with him when the expedition left the next day, in the hope that we would meet somewhere along the road.

I spent the rest of the morning cleaning the bike and patching up my inner tubes, one of which had mysteriously gone down overnight. The spectacle of a white man sat on the ground repairing a bicycle proved to be a source of endless entertainment for the local children, who sat with me, cross-legged, in the hotel courtyard. Whenever I rose to move the bike or to pick up a tool or take a drink, I would find a dozen pairs of hands already there to help me.

As I was securing the panniers for the journey ahead, someone grasped my arm from behind.

'Ah, so it is *you* ze mad Engleeshman wiz ze bicycle!'

'Let me see...' My arm tightened in a squeeze.

'What? No bites of scorpion! 'ow about snakes, 'ave you been attacked yet? No? Ah, you are too lucky. 'ow do you do it, levitate?'

It was Giles, Adem's driving partner, on his return from Chinguetti. His bloodshot eyes had almost dropped out of their sockets, and he spoke with a heavy Marseillais drawl, interspersing every other word with dopey sounding expressions like *beh*, *urr*, *oue* and *err*. He had left the rest of the convoy near Chinguetti and had instead taken a 'short cut' back to Atâr across the mountains. He was stoned out of his tree.

I sympathised with Adem, though I could also easily see the attraction of driving stoned across unmarked desert tracks at a hundred miles an hour.

CHAPTER NINE

CHASING THE LIZARD'S TAIL

It is man, not the desert, that eats you.

Arab proverb[12]

I left Atâr in the afternoon. I figured that the 440km to Nouakchott would take about four days, a higher daily average than I had achieved between Choum and Atâr, but one I thought reasonable because I had been told that the road from here on was well surfaced. Both me and my bicycle were in good shape, and my water supplies were back up to nine litres. I also had the five remaining loaves of ant-infested bread, two pounds of pink Senegalese peanuts, and a few cans of sardines. Supplies along the way, I was told, were easy to find, for there were several roadsteads set up for the express purpose of catering to travellers' needs. I was also told that there was a military roadblock thirty kilometres down the road, where I would be able to refill on water, and that there was the possibility of another roadstead one hundred kilometres further along. In any case, the copper-mining town of Akjoujt lay just 180km away – at most two days' cycling – and from past experience, there was usually at least one vehicle a day that I could flag down in case of an emergency.

The forty-degree heat and the stifling grey flannel sky colluded in the absence of any breeze to deprive me of even the faintest illusion of coolness usually afforded by the northeasterly trades outside the sheltered hills of the Adrar. In almost suffocating humidity, and with my already sweat-stained trousers clinging like leeches to my legs, I slowly threaded the bicycle though the remaining dilapidated huts and shacks to the south of the town. Passing the last few clumps of irrigated date palms that hung motionless like spiders in the thick webbed air, I found myself once again alone and in the comforting desolation of the desert. Although I was sweating profusely and felt clammy, it was good to be on the road again, to be moving. Atâr, like Choum, had been little more than a brief interruption in my journey across the desert.

Before long, I came across a small group of workers 'resurfacing' the corrugated road, using gigantic sand ploughs that spouted clouds of orange dust. An impromptu diversion veered off into the surrounding hills, strewn with coarse but yielding sand. True to form, everyone preceding me had beaten their own tracks, irrespective of where others had travelled before (a practice common to all desert tracks that results all too often in 'roads' spreading sideways over several kilometres). In consequence, a plethora of tyre traces scattered off into the hazy distance. For once my luck held firm, for as I pondered the way, a heavily laden goods truck appeared on the horizon behind me. Waiting till it had passed, I continued roughly in its direction and then, when the lorry itself had disappeared from view, I followed the dust plume thrown up in its wake. When that too had vanished, the welter of tracks had reduced considerably, leaving just a couple of well-grooved tyre ruts and a set of camel hoofmarks.

The two tracks, entwined and twisting, snaked around and through the dull weather-beaten granite hills, sometimes rising to avoid wispy sand dunes to the west, sometimes falling to avoid the boulder-strewn wastelands of the east. On and on the lonely tracks meandered, past the occasional acacia, dusty, grey and brittle from months of drought, and past ragged clumps of equally dessicated thorn bush grasping with exposed gnarled roots at the bare rocks and boulders. Sometimes the tracks would merge before plunging deeply into the unseen gorge of a long-dead river, before climbing steeply back up onto another plateau, only to plunge down again after a few more kilometres. Sometimes, the tracks would disappear altogether under the sand.

Some hours later – it was hard to tell exactly because the sun was still shrouded by the blanket of cloud that made everything look a muggy and dirty orange – I rounded the side of a hill buttress to see a small building in the distance: the military outpost. The building – a small hut of whitewashed stone with a corrugated iron roof – nestled forsaken on the outside curve of a sharp clockwise hairpin; the start, I hoped, of the descent to the silken sand plains of the Mauritania-Senegal basin. The checkpoint was established in 1976 during the first conflicts with Polisario, ostensibly to protect the important oasis springs of Terjît, a few kilometres into the hills. A decade after the ending of hostilities, the ever tightening noose of drought has drastically diminished the size of the oasis and so the checkpoint is now mainly used for the extraction of much needed taxes from the few remaining merchants and travellers.

Beside an orange barrier that hung limply across the track, the occupants of the lorry I'd followed were embroiled in a vociferous dispute with a scab-faced soldier, who leant casually on the open cab door, ubiquitous kalashnikov hanging from his neck on an old battered leather strap. His 'uniform' consisted of standard-issue khaki trousers and a dirty pale blue T-shirt bearing a faded logo of sorts. As the travellers shouted at him he would turn nonchalantly away to gaze instead at his dusty boots that were idly kicking about pebbles at his feet. Only when replying to the tirade of insults with a string of his own did he ever look up. As far as I could gather, the argument centred about the lorry, which was piled sky high with precariously balanced crates, boxes and about two dozen people. In itself, this was hardly an unusual sight in the Sahara, but this particular soldier was evidently not prepared to let the lorry pass unless he was paid a tax or a bribe. As I approached, the soldier glanced briefly over at me, before turning back to continue the argument. Bemused, I walked up to the building instead.

Inside its sticky, windowless gloom, a fat Negro soldier sprawled, snoring heavily on a bed of straw-covered clay bricks. An old rifle and an empty bandoleer were lying on the ground beside him. I noticed with some amusement that he wore the other half of the thinner soldier's uniform – an army jacket emblazoned with colourful honours, and a misshapen olive-green kepi that shielded his face from the flies. A magazine cutting of the Mauritanian flag was stuck on to the otherwise bare wall over the bed, the yellow crescent Ramadan moon embracing Venus on a background of Muslim green. Various other objects – a small gas burner, a blackened ceramic teapot, a bag of sugar, four miniscule glasses, a bag of China tea and a large blue and white enamel bowl encrusted with rice – rested on a soiled prayer mat by the door. Sensing my presence, the man grunted and opened one eye, and then closed it before asking gruffly: 'What do you want, *Toubab*? There are bandits and criminals here.'

The water was contained in a hairy goatskin *guerba* suspended by a nail on the rear wall of the building. It was cold and tasted curiously sweet due to the expensive luxury of argan oil. I filled my bottles and returned to the front of the building where the argument had flared up upon the arrival of the Negro soldier. Above angry shouts and furiously waved fists, I thanked both guards, who continued to ignore me, and cycled away.

Happy in the knowledge that I was making good progress, I began to dream of Senegal and Dakar, and of all the things that I had heard about them. Then I thought of home, and I was pleased that I wasn't there. The Sahara was fine, absolutely fine, not to mention a hell of a lot easier to cycle across than I would have thought. According to my information, the next roadstead was now just over a hundred kilometres away, two thirds of the way to Akjoujt. With a full three days' supplies remaining, one hundred kilometres was a pushover, I told myself gleefully, and, as I had hoped, the track swerved strongly to the southwest and I soon found myself bouncing effortlessly down rocks and boulders. Although the murky atmosphere still abounded, it was hot and so it didn't take long for the water to heat up and acquire the plastic taste of the bottles. As I descended, sand began to fill the ruts that I was following, slowly burying the stones and pebbles of the higher Adrar, and made cycling in many parts a good deal smoother and easier than before. But the sand also made my already sore eyes stream tears. Occasionally, *ebliss* dust devils would appear from nowhere to whip up swirling, opaque columns, sometimes 30 or 40 feet high, which would suddenly disappear, leaving a gentle shower of grit to rain delicately back onto the ground.

After a good hour's cycling, the track turned sharply. Beyond the bend, a battered Mercedes truck bearing a blackened cylindrical tank had crashed off the road. Mangled pieces of metal and shattered windscreen littered the diesel-stained rocks between the track and the lorry. All four tyres had burst. I clambered onto its rear. The lid of the tank had been thrown off in the crash, revealing a small murky puddle of discoloured and putrid water. Inside the cab, the steering wheel and dashboard were covered in dry blood. I thought it extraordinary that the driver's personal effects had still not been removed: a blurred photograph of a pretty young woman, a small tattered copy of the Qur'an, two cigarettes and a magazine cutting of Mecca's al-Haram mosque.

The track continued roughly southwards along two, by now largely rock-free, tyre ruts, with puddles of rusty beige sand lapping the boulders at the sides. The temperature cooled and swarms of flies and midges congregated above my head. Flies are especially irritating in the desert as there are not that many other things to stimulate one's mind. Flies up my nose, on my eyelids, in my ears, down my mouth, flies everywhere – bloody things! A few kilometres further on, still pestered by flies, I found a large sand dune to settle behind, and decided to call it a day. I stared at the blank page of my diary. It needed filling but I was unable to concentrate, so I stared instead at the mute grey sky. Eventually, the sun broke through the dust on the western horizon, briefly swamping the desert with warm shafts of light that danced mysterious shadows on the sand. Today, I mused, had marked the completion of three months on the road (only three months! – it felt like twelve). Three months of travelling, three months of living my life the way I wanted to. The tour was no longer the mad venture I had once thought it to be, but had become a way of life, as normal as working nine to five from Monday to Friday. The last colours of evening faded away, and I found myself staring at the blank page of the dusty sky.

I was woken abruptly by the angry buzzing of motors, and turned my head to catch a glimpse of the last of the French Land Cruiser expedition speeding over a nearby ridge, leaving a plume of dust shimmering brightly in the rosy morning sunlight. The beetles and bugs burrowed back into the sand, and as the throbbing of the jeeps faded into the distance, I was again left alone. Then I cursed, for I realised that I had missed the extra food and water that Adem had promised to bring.

The clouds had cleared overnight in the renewed trade wind. This was a mixed blessing, for although it dissipated the stifling humidity, the clear skies would result in much higher midday temperatures and so I would feel more thirsty. I was also feeling slightly sick, probably because of the various bits of the deceased goat of the checkpoint *guerba* that floated around my water bottles. It was late morning when I finally clambered on to the bike and pedalled wearily away. According to my map, the rocky foothills of the Adrar were today to give way in the southwest to the relatively flat and featureless terrain of the sand plains between the Akchâr and Amatlich dunes, which flank much of the road to Akjoujt. The road did indeed continue southwest for a while, but then veered sharply and into the blinding glare of the sun.

This easterly bearing did not make sense, for I was now travelling away from the *Route Nationale* and away from Akjoujt. Yet I *had* passed the military outpost that I'd been told about, and the French expedition had also passed this way, so I tried not to worry. My map, though, was too simplified to be of any use, and so I was left with no real choice but to continue along the track, hoping that it was merely one of several mapping errors or part of some detour. However, the further I cycled the more worried I became, especially as there were no real features in this monotonous land to distract my mind. Neither, come to think of it, could I see any trace of the Frenchmen's vehicles. Always, the same hills to my left, always the same dunes to my right, and always the same track taking me towards the same hazy mirages in the distance. Always, too, the same blazing ball of white fire that hung like a curse above my head, leaching all colour from the desert. Sandstone mountain edges drooped like half-closed eyelids, naked as on the day of creation, and naked now, dead. Is this the fate of the earth, that it will have been and gone in a solitary batting of an eyelid, unnoticed and inconsequential?

Hours slid by, with only my tiredness testifying to the passing of time. I began to worry about comments I'd heard in Atâr along the lines of: 'No way, it is *impossible* to cycle to Akjoujt.' Perhaps I should have paid attention to these warnings, rather than have taken them as further encouragement.

Several hours later, as the temperature touched fifty degrees, the track had still not changed direction, and, to deepen my dismay, had become fainter and seemed less frequented by both camels and motor vehicles. Surely this could not be *La Route Nationale*? According to both my maps, it should almost certainly have veered to the west long before now. There was, however, a thin little line printed on one of the maps that went southeast. If I had somehow got onto this track, then I would eventually find myself on the fringes of El Djouf! Even so, the only thing that was certain about the maps was that they were both inaccurate, and so, armed with this valuable piece of knowledge, I decided that it would be wisest to keep on going, for the track, I figured, had to lead *somewhere*.

Still feeling unwell (my head was spinning slightly), I cycled indifferently through the sand and rocks. On and on in the unrelenting heat I travelled, sweating profusely, cursing profusely and worrying more and more that I might have to retrace my steps to Atâr. But then, I wasn't at all sure that I would be able to retrace my steps, for the wind was making them indistinct, and in places invisible.

After another hour's dejected cycling, the mirages melted away to reveal a bend in the track. A few kilometres further on, I started around and down the last few grotesquely folded layers of exposed hill buttress. As I descended, the soft shapes of sand dunes became visible on the near horizon to my right, peering alluringly from between the depressions and troughs of the surrounding rock. The track twisted down precarious bends, and clung ever tighter to the prehistorically etched mountainside. Then I spotted the fringed fronds of two palm trees peeking out amidst a cluster of boulders and sand drifts. I ditched the bike, and walked over to the edge of the crag. I saw several more clusters of palm trees. There is an Arab proverb that says that the palm tree must have its head in fire and its feet in water, and so, determined to prove my hunch correct, I heaved myself down the rock face, and continued along what would have been the bed of a stream. A little while on, the pebbles and boulders fell away to the skeleton of a dry waterfall, and in the splashpool ten metres down, sheltered from the wind and sand, I saw water.

Whooping with joy, I clattered and clambered noisily down the rocks, dislodging an avalanche of dust and stones. At the bottom, I found myself facing a couple of miraculous pools of water. The smaller one was turbid and stagnant, but the larger one contained water of such crystalline clarity that the rock forming the pool effused a most delicate tinge of amethyst. Small lizards lounged lazily in the shade of a few boulders, and a couple of eight-winged dragonflies honed in to inspect the visitor. As I moved closer, I heard a rustle at my feet and glanced round to catch the black tail of a viper disappearing into a crevice. Among the reeds in the pool swam tiny blood-red and brown fish, along with tadpoles and beetles and camel-spiders. I cupped my hands and took a sip. It was fresh and cold, and tasted faintly of mint. It sparkled brilliantly as it flowed from my hands and back into the pool. A handful of tiny saffron-yellow chaffinches, desert warblers, and a turquoise trumpeter finch chattered excitedly, as an acid-green gecko eyed the scene suspiciously from under a palm tree.

After all the sand and dust, to see the colours, to taste the water, to smell the scents and to breathe the dustless air – everything that one would normally take for granted, existed here as a microcosm of paradise. There were even a few tufts of grass growing in the mud between the two pools. It was ages since I had last seen green grass. I stood and gazed dumbfounded at this beautiful aberration, listening to the birds and the locusts and the dragonflies.

> Until the Desert knows
> That Water grows
> His Sands suffice
> But let him once suspect
> That caspian fact
> Sahara dies.

Emily Dickinson, Nº.1291

* * *

As I walked back to the bicycle, I saw a nomad walking towards me. Behind him and next to my bicycle were stood three enormous bull camels with ratty tails, and another nomad. The men were dressed in tatty loose-fitting riding trousers, over which they wore sky blue smocks tied loosely with simple belts, into which silver daggers were thrust. Both sported voluminous dark green turbans, tainted orange by the dust. The face of the man walking towards me was a soft hazelnut-brown, though his hands, like the thorn bush, were black and gnarled. On seeing my dripping water bottles, he smiled, greeted unusually abruptly, and then walked on down with his companion towards the pools of the *guelta*. I sat down to eat. Before long, the nomads returned. The first was muttering and shook his head. He explained that he had been to the village of Oujeft at the foot of the hills and was looking for somewhere to water his herd of a hundred camels (waiting a few kilometres back).

News of the village relieved me enormously, and I was assured that it was possible to rejoin the *Route Nationale* by going via the village. The nomad then mumbled something about the villagers being crooks, the reason being, as far as I could understand, that they were charging him an extortionate price to water his camels, but that he would have to accept because the herd had not drunk for four days.

The road to Oujeft continued down several hairpins, each one revealing just a little bit more than the last of the huts and palms below. In the ravine off one particularly severe bend, lay the gutted shells of a bus and several other vehicles, deformed and twisted. I heard later that the bus had claimed seven lives. It seems that the road from Atâr to Akjoujt is famed, even feted, for its fatalities: accidents due mainly to freak sand storms caused by the *Harmattan*. It is ironic that this once prosperous caravan route, once an artery of life across the desert, should now be remembered primarily for death. It is also sadly apt, for drought has rung the death knell for the village of Oujeft.

Situated at the foot of the southernmost skirt of the Adrar, sixty kilometres from Atâr, Oujeft is a small village that has been almost totally abandoned. The village has an aura of having fought a battle and lost. Most of its buildings have been left to crumble, and those that remain are shuttered and closed to the hostile ravages of the outside world. There were few people to be seen. The fate of Oujeft is the same as that of thousands of similar settlements across the Sahara and the Sahel. A well fails and sand drives in. Then another well fails and the crops won't grow. The trees wither and die, the young people leave and never come back, and the door is left open to the desert.

Two decades ago, Oujeft was entirely surrounded by a green belt of palm groves. It had even been possible to cultivate the hillsides, those same arid hillsides of rock and sand that I had just descended. In better times, houses were built using carefully-chosen rocks that were meticulously pieced together in the manner of English dry-stone walling. The walls were then plastered with laterite mud gathered from the river bed during the *hivernage* (the winter rains). Mud would also be used with palm tree fronds or millet stalks to make the rooves. Year after year, the walls and rooves would be repaired and then replastered with fresh mud, often mixed with cow dung or straw. But the recent

spate of droughts made replastering impossible, and in consequence
the rooves had begun to cave in and the walls began to fall. Many of the
buildings abandoned in the famine already lay as crumpled heaps of grey
rubble, barely distinguishable from the rocks and sand to which they
were returning.

Cycling through the village, a couple of children appeared from out of
nowhere and started chasing me, making grabs at the water bottles on
the back of the bike. As they ran, they shouted to unseen friends who
appeared from dark huts and alleyways to join in the chase. This I didn't
need, for it was too windy and the track was too rocky to outpace them.
But then, I didn't much feel like having to run after my water bottles
either. I carried on cycling, hoping that they would tire before me.

'*Bonjour, m'sieur!*' they cried cheerily. 'Stop!' I carried on stubbornly, pretending not to hear. 'Hey *Toubab, arrete!*'

Briefly, I glanced round, and saw that my spare tyre, usually hooped
around the rear panniers, had been pulled off and was lying on the
ground amidst a small cluster of grubby children. Fed up, I stopped
cycling and dismounted. I was tired and that made me feel angry at
having been forced to stop by a bunch of insolent kids. I walked back
towards them, thanking them sarcastically for having stopped me, but
they just stared back silently and my words floated harmlessly over
their heads and away in the breeze. I gave up being angry. It wasn't
really in my nature anyway, and the little bastards looked too innocent!
I tried a goofy grin instead, which elicited a fit of giggles from a girl who
had both her thumbs stuck in her mouth. She almost choked.

The children smiled sweetly, before unleashing a flood of questions
and demands to drown me in: '*M'sieur, voulez vous me donner* ouguiya...
un stylo... un cadeau...' and even '*un gateau pour moi*' (it seems they
confused *gateau* with *cadeau*). I gave them some money but they just
asked for more.

At the end of the village, several workers with cranes and trucks
were sinking a well. Both it and the old well beside it were in the centre
of a dry *wadi*, which in times past would have supplied the mud for the
buildings, and fish and water for the villagers. One of the workers, a
burly *haratin* with arms like bulldozers, explained that the old well had
silted up and was beginning to cave in, and so it had been necessary to
build a new one. The French expedition, the worker said, had passed by
earlier in the day, and they had apparently heard mention that Choum
had miraculously had rain the day before. The *haratin* hoped that Oujeft
too would get some rain before long. '*Insha Allah,*' I replied, looking up
at the dry sky.

As we were talking, one of the sand ploughs that I had passed near Atâr trundled past and continued straight on towards an area of dunes. The well digger explained that these dunes were covering what had been, until a decade ago, the *Ancienne Route Nationale*. This information finally made sense of my maps, for they showed only the newer route from Atâr, from which I had been diverted because of the resurfacing.

The track from Oujeft headed south, and soon deteriorated into waves of corrugations, this time made trickier to cycle because the troughs were filled with an extremely soft cinnamon sand that would all too frequently grind the bike to a sticky halt. I couldn't even try to avoid the ruts, as the surrounding sand was far too soft for any kind of cycling at no matter what speed. Out of frustration, I started pushing and pulling on the pedals as hard as I could, mindlessly ignoring the ridges. Within twenty metres, one of the plastic water bottles bounced out of the rear panniers and smashed on the ground, and I watched helplessly at the water draining into the sand. Worse still, a few minutes later I discovered that another bottle had cracked and shed half its load, soaking my diary and a precious loaf of bread. Standing there beside my bike, there was nothing but silence screaming mockingly at my stupidity. Worst of all, I was now only carrying six and a half of my initial nine litres of water, and I figured that the remaining 150km to Akjoujt, given my unforeseen detour, would still take another two days. The only permanent settlement on the route of which I knew – the supply hut that I'd been told about in Atâr – was still some eighty kilometres away, and even if I were to find water elsewhere, my reduced water-carrying capacity made getting to Akjoujt or the supply hut a rather more urgent matter than before.

About an hour later, the track veered sharply to the right, almost cutting back on itself. To my intense relief, I was travelling westwards and, as far as I could see, the track continued all the way towards the flat horizon over which the sun was gradually sinking, the horizon where tomorrow I should hopefully rejoin the proper road to Akjoujt. Taking advantage of the cooler evening air and my rediscovered high spirits, I cycled on until the remains of the day were swamped by the night. I lay down next to the track under a myriad stars and felt my body heat slowly dissipate into the sand. I closed my eyes and let my memory tumble into a morass of images and sounds, colours and feelings tangled in webs of darkness, all confused and all forgotten as I drifted peacefully into sleep.

There is a sudden flash of light. Startled, I open my eyes but it is still dark. The moon has disappeared. It is cold and I hear a slow and ghostly drumming resonating in the wind. For a moment I am confused, not knowing where I am or what is happening. There is another flash of light, this time accompanied by the low rumble of distant thunder. The drumming increases with the wind, tearing up sheets of dust and sand from the plain that come crashing painfully over me. Faster and faster the furious wind blows, lashing and whipping the sand into a spinning, howling, yelling and chaotic frenzy. Abruptly, the confusion subsides, and within a matter of minutes the atmosphere has become heavy and sombre, presiding claustrophobically over a thick, violent silence. There is no sound. I wait, but nothing stirs, not even the wind. I dare not breathe. The world has been frozen by this absolute silence.

With a deafening scream, an electric blue spear of light hurls down from the heavens to strike the desert about half a mile away. I try to run from the bicycle, for it is the best conductor for miles, but before I have time to get out of my sleeping bag another bolt explodes nearby, accompanied by even fiercer gales and the renewed drumming of the madman. The storm rages briefly, and then, as quickly as it arrived, it vanishes. The clouds part to reveal once again the naked brilliance of the stars and the full moon. For a while there is an eerie silence in the now still air, broken only by the occasional and distant rumble of departing thunder. Still there is no rain. The Moors call the drumming the Spirit of Ghaul, for he is the drummer of death, an evil, wandering *djinni*, ever eager to snatch away the weary traveller's life, should he ever pay too much attention to his desires.

* * *

Morning smiled sweet and innocent under sparkling skies of azure. There was no sign of the storm except for the track having sanded over, as had my bicycle. With the absence of any wind the temperature rose considerably, soon taking the edge off the freshness that the storm had brought, and before long the atmosphere once again was thick and syrupy. Nonetheless, the brief spell of freshness had brought new vigour to my tired body, and for a while cycling was easy and relatively painless. Soon, though, the track was overwhelmed by sand, and the going correspondingly grew slow and difficult.

The track crossed back over the Tayaret *wadi*, that pretended to have snaked through Oujeft. Here, no longer sheltered by the Adrar, it was marked only by a thin and perfunctory line of more or less dead acacia, blackened and brittle and only still anchored in the sand because of their long and wiry roots, most of them already exposed like the naked aerials of banyan trees. Sand dunes had begun to form around them, and it was only a matter of time before the last of them would be devoured by the voracious sands. It is said that the acacia can tolerate dessication so extreme that its branches become brown and brittle, and are still capable of recovery. The acacia can also reputedly withstand fire, but most remarkable is its ability to survive interment for several years, eventually to be exhumed by the relentless southward march of the same dunes that had once buried it. Nevertheless, all living things need water, even the sturdy acacia, and sadly there may well be no more water left by the time that these particular dunes have moved on.

Within seconds of crossing the *wadi* my front wheel began to soften to the delicate tune of a puncture. Sitting down wearily on the sand, I mused that I had at least been fortunate enough to have found a pump in Atâr, and that I was lucky to have been able to cycle here at all. Waiting for the glue to set, I gorged myself on some peanuts and the mouldy and still ant-infested bread. The water was hot and tasted sour – the bottles had not been cleaned for weeks. Soon after leaving the bushes and their thorns, a distant lorry crossed my path from right to left, north to south. It was the proper track to Akjoujt. The two tracks intersected a few kilometres further on beside a canvas awning and a small, tin-rooved hut. Its occupants, a disagreeable middle-aged man and his wife, scurried out of sight when they saw me approach, and I had to search around to find them. The man was dressed in the traditional blue *boubou* and white smock, the woman in a black gown and black yashmak. Both treated me with the utmost suspicion. I was told that I was at the village of Agrour Sfaya. Glancing outside the hut at the tent canopy and the sand, it was evident that I was at best at the *remains* of Agrour Sfaya. Was this the supply hut that I had been told about? It seemed to be much nearer than I had imagined, and that would mean that there might not be another supply hut at all, a thought that I would rather not have had to contemplate.

Unfortunately, the couple could not clarify matters over whether there was indeed a hut further on, or how far I was from Atâr or Akjoujt. Of greater concern to them was the task of selling me something, anything: petrol, rice, a plastic laundry basket, a barrel of tea, as well as a packet of those dry Algerian biscuits. I bought the biscuits and was given three litres of water from a chipped blue urn inside the furnace-like hut, bringing my supplies back up to six and a half litres. The woman then replaced the lid, held out her hand, and scowled.

Preparing to leave, I discovered that the front wheel was flat yet again, and so to repair it I installed myself under the canvas awning. I should have guessed that there had been *two* thorns stuck in the wheel, and not just the one that I had already removed. To my dismay, I discovered that my penknife had disappeared. I had probably left it on the ground while repairing the last puncture, and I cursed at the prospect of having to walk back to find it. Grudgingly, I heaved myself to my feet and turned around to see the man standing behind me. He held my penknife in his hands, hands that were idly cutting slits into the tent posts while the man stared coldly into my eyes. 'It slices well,' he said.

The tracks converged and headed out southwest towards a shimmering expanse of sand. As far as I could see there was nothing but a vast expressionless gulf, reaching far out towards and beyond the murky horizon. It was ringed in places by the tall shimmering mirages of sand dunes, blurring the distinction between land and sky. For the second time since leaving Atâr, I got worried. For sure, I had expected to see sand along my journey – indeed I had quite looked forward to it - but this was plainly ridiculous! With the exception of myself and the bicycle, everything but everything under the sky consisted entirely of sand. My map hadn't shown any significant dunes actually *along* the *Route Nationale*, and the road itself was classified as 'improved', whatever that meant. Here, it was patently no such thing.

The task of finding the supply hut was also beginning to worry me, for assuming that Agrour Sfaya had not been it, I reckoned that I was still a good day away, and getting lost after the impromptu diversion had screwed up any notion I had had of how far I was from Akjoujt. I had further reason to be careful, for already today I had drunk two litres, and the midday temperature was only just peaking, at 52°C. Thankfully, the track in most places was still just about rideable, so long as I kept up a reasonable speed and avoided particularly soft patches of sand, given away by the deepening or disappearance of the vehicle tracks. If the avoidance of the softer patches was impossible, or if I noticed them too late to take evasive action, then a burst of speed would usually gather enough momentum to carry me across.

As the day wore on, I found that more and more walking was required. Perhaps because of this I felt the dry atmosphere all the more keenly. Pushing the bicycle tended to exhaust me much more than cycling, and the scorching sand came into direct contact with my feet. As I walked, I mused on my own insignificance in the face of all this desolation. Cast adrift in a sea of rolling waves, hot, uncaring, faceless and overawing. I was helpless, and yet somehow happy that I was entrusted to the mercy of this great void – Mother Earth, if you will. I was happy to be embraced by this vastness. Yes, I am insignificant, but perversely the revelation of this strengthens self-respect rather than destroys it. The wind whistled softly. I trudged on, half the time cycling and the other half walking, yet happy, despite everything. The singularly beautiful sight of a bird high in the sky, flying south, made me even happier. Senegal, I thought, here I come.

Some hours later a Land Rover sped towards me, the noise of its engine muffled in the wind. I jumped onto the bicycle, ashamed to be seen walking, and struggled off towards it. A very startled European leaned out of the window.

'*Salut. Ça va, non?*' he asked in bewilderment. I guess he half expected me to groan and ask for a lift, but instead I smiled and nodded, and asked the same of him.

'You must be mad!' he exclaimed. 'What are you doing here with your bicycle? *Mais dites donc*, you really *are* mad!' He later explained that on first seeing me he had thought that I was a stray camel, but then, on reflection, and as the mirages around me cleared, he'd decided that a camel wasn't so short and narrow, and so I became a donkey. Only as he drew closer had he realised that the donkey was in fact a cyclist!

'*Anglais?*' he asked, like everyone else.

'*Naturellement,*' I replied.

Albert introduced himself. He was Belgian, lived in Nouakchott and worked for a charity that constructed wells in the desert. He was on his way to inspect a series of projects all the way up to the ancient ruins at Aghouedir (300km northeast of Atâr), including the well at Oujeft. Albert's anonymous companion was middle-aged, balding, and wore – of all things – a pinstripe suit, shirt, and tie! He was the Belgian ambassador's aide-de-camp in Dakar, and, it seems, had just come along for the ride.

If I managed to make it to Nouakchott within a week, Albert kindly offered to put me up and also to take me to an exclusive restaurant called El Frisco. All I had to do was ask for someone called Naf, who would introduce me to the chef, Bhoo Nomdu, who would organise everything.

As we said goodbye, Albert apologised for not having any water, but instead gave me a packet of biscuits, a carton of apricot juice and a bottle of coke, which I quaffed in seconds. It all tasted the same in the heat, and in any case, all that my taste buds had tasted over the last ten days was sand. The biscuits were even less palatable than the ones I'd bought in Agrour Sfaya, being inedible without copious amounts of liquid to wash them down. I junked them. Meeting the Belgians, though, made me hopeful that I would soon reach Akjoujt. If Albert was correct in his estimation, the town was about 60km away, and so, with luck, tomorrow I would find myself its star attraction.

It was already dark when I came to a stop at the lip of a gentle sand crater, up which I had been struggling for the best part of an hour. I wheeled the bike off the track and parked it behind an incongruous boulder, lit up eerily in the lime-glow of the moon. I lay down on the sand, too exhausted to untie the kipmat from the bike. I had drunk relatively little today, but my body still felt alright, albeit tired and sore, as was now usual. Before long, the headlights of two trucks appeared in the distance, bobbing and partially miraged by the lingering heat haze. The vehicles stopped some two hundred metres in front of me. I heard voices and could make out three figures. Suddenly, the talking ceased, doors slammed and the trucks drove off.

I awoke late, extremely tired, with the sun already thumping heavily (for some reason, the desert sun always seems to thump at its hottest). It was a windless day, still and quiet, and by the time I was packed and ready to leave, the temperature had shot well over fifty degrees. A mile or so ahead, and partly hidden behind a small dune, I passed the sand plough that had passed me in Oujeft. One of its giant tyres had exploded, and the driver was nowhere to be seen. I presumed that he had been picked up by the two lorries last night. Before me sprawled an imposing tract of wasteland, the same as yesterday, only more impressive in the relative mental calm of morning. The land seemed more belittling. Masses and masses of beige sand, and nothing but. Absolutely nothing else, not even the faintest trace of vegetation, present or past – just sand. Stretching off into the distance lay vast cradles of sand, like gigantic flattened egg trays with their dimples not quite squashed flat. Dunes about 150 feet high ringed the near horizon, coming closer to my sides and thus effectively enclosing the length of the route. I say 'route' because there was nothing left that could even vaguely be called a 'track'. Strong winds overnight had obliterated the remaining vehicle traces.

The thick sand necessitated walking, and within a few minutes of surprisingly difficult slogging, any aspirations that I had entertained of reaching Akjoujt within the day evaporated. Given this, my priority was now to find water, which meant reaching the supply hut, the existence of which I was beginning to doubt. If my calculations were correct, I figured that it was about fifteen kilometres away. As I cycled, the mid-morning heat, which had initially been a pleasurable glow of warmth seeping gradually through my body, became uncomfortable, and then unbearable. By midday, the thermometer strapped on the handlebars had breached 55 degrees, and was still rising. The skin on my face, in spite of the *cheche*, was hot and sore, and my hands were hard and scaly. At first imperceptibly, the heat sank deeper towards my bones as my skin grew hotter and hotter still, until of a sudden I shouted out in pain. I stopped cycling and unwound my turban, clasping my left cheek so that I could feel the heat transfer onto the palm of my hand. I soaked the turban in some of my remaining water, ran it over my arms and then wrapped it tightly and securely around my head.

Sometimes I would manage to keep to a rhythm of sorts. With every down stoke of the left pedal, I would breathe in, and then with the right stroke, I would breathe out, and so on until it became hypnotic, whereupon I would invariably grind to a halt. For hours I struggled on like this, exhausted, sweating and cursing over the too-thick sand that was holding me prisoner. I was beginning to wish that I was back over the corrugated ruts, for at least they were just about rideable (if uncomfortable). Although the crusted surface sometimes held my weight, most of the time it cracked to allow the bicycle to sink through to a soft and deep undersurface, forcing me as usual to get off and push. The charade of mounting and dismounting in the sweltering heat repeated itself endlessly and pitilessly. Heaving myself off the crossbar after a typically short but exhausting slog on the pedals, I would need to rest a few minutes to regain my breath and drink a little water, before having to push on with forty kilos of baggage and bike. Pushing was infinitely worse than cycling. The soles of my shoes were no match for the burning sand on which they trod, and it would always get into my shoes. My feet began bleeding through their many blisters.

As the hours passed, I felt more and more distraught. Surely I had now covered the fifteen or so kilometres to the hut, for even in the desert I could manage a paltry five kilometres an hour. Yet still the hours passed. Only when the sand was thin or compact enough could I empty my shoes, remount and ride off – usually only to have to dismount another fifty metres further on. I sat down on the hot sand to eat: peanuts, the ant-infested bread, and hot water. By now, I'd given up picking out the insects from the bread but just ate it as it was, regardless of my silly qualms. I sat eating with my head between my knees, pondering what lay ahead of me as I stared and fiddled with the stones at my feet. It was unbearably hot. I might just as well have been walking naked, for in this temperature my clothes and turban gave me little protection. The skin on my nose was peeling every twelve hours on average. Even my fingers were crusted hard and scaly and were themselves also peeling badly, probably due to vitamin deficiency as much as anything else.

At one point, the front wheel sank suddenly into a trough of deep sand, sending me sprawling across the handlebars. I still remember approaching the ground in graceful slow motion, and then cursing aloud as I landed face down on the sand. For once, I didn't leap up to check that the water bottles were still intact, but instead just lay there, exhausted and motionless and my eyes closed. I tried to convince myself that I was comfortable lying there, and, to my surprise, I found that I was. In fact, I was so tired that I toyed with the idea of simply falling asleep there and then, but then the sand started burning my arms and face and made me jump up. I righted the bike and set off again, only to come to another grinding halt a few metres further on. I started walking.

Here and there, the bleached skeleton of a camel or a goat or a donkey protruded from the sand, though I was still spirited enough to take a self-exposure photo of myself next to a camel skeleton, using three bottles and my diary as an impromptu tripod. Despite the heat, I had restrained myself sufficiently to have four litres of water remaining by mid afternoon. All the time now, I had to wear the turban wrapped tightly across my face to prevent excess water loss from my mouth and nose. Though this made me appreciably hotter and made breathing more difficult, it kept my throat moist and that was what really mattered. By late afternoon my mouth was parched regardless, and there was still no sign of either the hut or Akjoujt. I began to despair a little, especially at the sluggish pace, and yet it was my anger and frustration that for the most part fuelled my determination to continue no matter what.

Determination notwithstanding, I began to experience the first symptoms of dehydration: extreme exhaustion, my willpower becoming harder to sustain, reality becoming harder to cling onto. The mind starts playing tricks and your imagination goes haywire. I looked around me. The dunes rose and fell, like the sun over broken-back landscapes of shattered dreams, overlaid by the imaginary strands and clusters of rocks and shrubs. Intertwining, interlocking, but always abrupt, the dunes end as they begin, caught in the paradoxical violence of the desert calm. I imagined trying to outstare the glaring sun, but for all its brightness I couldn't see a thing. One day, I shall win, I told myself as I fumbled around blindly for a water bottle. Like me, the water was hot, but I drank it anyway. Then I felt sick. I heard the brief cry of a bird, but it was far away, and its song was drowned out by the wind, warbling, distorted, failing, falling... I was alone, yet the bird carried on singing inside my head. Let me free, let me free, it cried. You are free, I thought, and it flew away. I was staring at the sun when I realised that I had been hallucinating. Shocked by my sudden dehydration, I drank a little more water in the hope that it would go away. It didn't. I simply could not believe that this was happening to me. Dehydrated hallucination, I had thought, was something that one only ever read about in books or saw in cheap Western flicks. All those images of lost desert travellers crawling on all fours, face in the sand, crying 'Water! Water!' – in my more lucid moments, I felt like a living cliché, a thought that brought a smile to my bleeding lips.

As evening drew close I felt my hope gradually slipping away. I was confused at the absence of the supply hut, at the absence of Akjoujt, and at the fact that nothing seemed to make sense anymore. Although I knew that losing hope was fatal, I could not prevent it trickling slowly out of my grasp. Dehydration, in addition to its physical effects, destroys the higher emotional passions. Even dreams become perverted and confused, frightening, all the time sucking off what little spirit remains in both mind and body. One deception trails into another, leaving little room for reality to reassert itself. It is self-deception, nourished by dehydration, that more than anything diminishes the will to continue. My desperation and confusion continued until the relative clarity of the desert night gently eased my senses back into my bedraggled mind. 'Happy the Sahara, where day and night swing man so evenly from one hope to the other,' wrote Saint-Exupéry. As I lay down on the sand and took stock of the situation, I realised that the supply hut, if ever it had existed, had probably been hidden behind a sand dune on some separate stretch of track. I had three litres of water left, enough for one day at most, but well below the six litres that I had usually been drinking. I also realised that I could have asked the drivers of the two lorries last night for water, and I felt stupid at my thoughtlessness. I fell asleep knowing full well that I would have to reach Akjoujt the next morning, for otherwise the midday heat would further worsen my dehydration.

* * *

For once I awoke early, with a little renewed hope born of the peace of night. Yet, as the first few hours passed by to reveal nothing more than the same timeless sands spread, as always, to all four corners of the world, I began once again to despair. I felt an old recurring wrist injury return, which if it got really bad would rule out cycling altogether. My hands were now badly cracked and covered in open sores, as were my lips. I had also begun shaking uncontrollably and, perhaps most tellingly, was sweating nowhere near as much as I had been, a condition that leads to hyperpyrexia (hyperthermia). Worse still was that the mental effects of dehydration returned with a vengeance. To save what little water I had remaining, I promised myself not to drink anything for the first few hours at least. Yet within an hour I found myself involuntarily drinking from a bottle. Much as I tried to stop myself virtually committing suicide, my body would not listen. In vain I tried to tell it of the crime it was committing, but my hands listened only to my immediate thirst...

I felt so angry at my helplessness. 'You stupid bastard,' I yelled after I'd eventually managed to wrest the now empty bottle away from my lips. Dehydration slows the mind. At the same time, the body becomes deaf to it, and because the mind has become slow, it can't react in time to what your body might be doing. Mind and body become two separate entities. Any break in communication between the two necessarily results in two states of being, a form of non-clinical schizophrenia. As a result, I was now down to two litres, having been awake for only an hour. I was utterly disgusted with myself.

I absolutely had to get to Akjoujt, but in the still swelter of the desert day, I found myself increasingly desperate. Akjoujt now seemed little more than a figment of my imagination. I had been underway from Atâr for almost five days, and still there was no sign of the town (God, I was supposed to have reached Nouakchott by now). I was worried that maybe I'd overshot Akjoujt as well, but surely that wasn't possible? I felt anger and frustration at being so physically helpless, and that all that I could do was plod on regardless, and all that I could see was yet more sand with no sign of life anywhere. The vehicle tracks had more or less disappeared and so I was left following merely my instincts and the ever-vaguer promise of eventual sanctuary. I felt so angry. Angry at being cheated, though by whom or what I did not know. I just knew that I had been cheated. And yet there was nothing at all on which my anger could be vented, and in consequence it grew and grew, feeding off itself to such an extent that at several times in the day I had to stop walking just to shout and yell myself hoarse, simply to prevent myself exploding. All that I could think about was the great injustice of it all. Why me? Why me, of all people? Why was it that *I* should suffer so much? I had not harmed anyone, so why me? But I could think of no answer.

As the sun increased in intensity, my frustration and anger turned again to despair and hopelessness. *Silent* despair and hopelessness. Rather than feeling overawed by the desert, I now felt cowed by it. I was utterly helpless and utterly isolated. I had not seen a single living creature for over two days – I was scared. I felt, and was, quite simply, pathetic. Once, I stumbled and hit my ankle on a pedal. I cursed. I cursed the desert for doing this to me. I cursed the fact that I had no water. That I was exhausted. I cursed that I was stupid enough to be here in the first place. I cursed the fact that I couldn't give up. Then I smiled, for indeed I had a choice. On the one hand I could give up, and wait for the off-chance of a passing vehicle, or else risk dying, defeated within myself. On the other hand, I could risk being killed by the desert. Perhaps I didn't have a choice after all. I clambered on to the bicycle and started pedalling. But then, a few minutes later, I would again start cursing, and would find myself once again entertaining the idea of giving up. As the afternoon temperature breached 55°C once again, thirst had taken over my thoughts.

Over a distant cluster of dunes, I saw a clump of welcoming palm trees, their leaves hanging limply in the stifling air. At last a sign of life, although I couldn't yet see whether the trees marked the outskirts of Akjoujt or an unmapped oasis. Either way, I was as relieved as I was happy as I left the *piste* and pushed the bicycle towards the trees across the soft hot sand that enveloped my feet, only to realise as I approached that they were merely boulders playing tricks on my tired eyes. Dejected and shocked, not least because of having succumbed to a cliche so hackneyed, I turned to push the bike back to the *piste* along my already melted tracks. My shoes were full of sand that burnt my feet, and so I sat down and emptied them, staring entranced at the bloodied grains falling from my shoes as through the waist of an hourglass. I stared at an ant climbing my leg, but it fell off and scurried away to the shade of a stone. I recalled my feelings on leaving Manchester, cycling down the A34 on a drizzy and overcast February morning, wondering what would replace the gloomy Cheshire plains as my horizon. I righted the bike, and tried to imagine the wet tarmac skimming underneath, but all I could see was sand.

The hallucinations returned. I imagined that the sand was drinkable, although I knew perfectly well that it wasn't. Then I started considering how many steaks I could make out of my arms, depending on how I carved them. I worked out ways of amputating them without it hurting, without it bleeding my insides too much. How to stop the inevitable gangrene from setting in, how to deter any interested vultures. When you're dehydrated, your mind wanders without your knowing it. But when you're really dehydrated you start believing all this shit. Your body completely takes over from your mind. Then you've got to fight your body because it doesn't like all these stupid things you're forcing it to do, like live. Your body just feels like lying down and stopping. Not dying, just stopping, resting. You, however, your poor dehydrated and hallucinating self, somehow you know that you can't just rest because if you do you'll probably never want to get up again. On the other hand, the thought of just lying down for a while becomes so tempting, and for a minute you almost succumb… I craved nothing more than to be embraced, held tight, reassured by something secure and dependable. Even so, I realised the futility of my daydreaming, and again all I thought of was water. Then I tried to block this from my mind, because it was making me thirsty, but in vain. Water was now all that I wanted, indeed, all that I craved. Everything that I had ever cared for was now represented by that barest of necessities. And a hundred times again I would deceive myself into believing that what was in fact a boulder was a well or an oasis or a settlement. A hundred times again I would resolve never to deceive myself. The agony of false hope is the greatest curse of the desert, its sickest joke, and perhaps that of life too. Still more walking and still more cursing, and by the evening, my thoughts were simply going round and around, repeating themselves, repeating subjects, repeating words, repeating noises, repeating themselves. And in that way, by coming almost to ignore the world outside the cocoon of my mind, I survived the blistering day to walk into the cool of night.

The descending sun resembled a red Chinese lantern, briefly returning some of the colour and music to the desert that it had taken away during the day. The sky darkened, and the colours faded away to be replaced by the ghostly charm of the rising moon. Still there was no sign of Akjoujt, not even the faintest gloaming of hope in the murky darkness. I had just over one litre of water left, enough for about four hours if I ignored the fact that I was already dangerously dehydrated. I stood still next to the bicycle, gazing at the void ahead of me. Again I was overawed by the stark beauty of this empty and monstrous land. I listened to the silence. It was playing a fine line between tranquillity and violent agarophobia. I was but a tiny drop in a vast ocean of barrenness, a solitary grain of sand amongst all these dunes. I was a human being, nineteen years old, weighing seventy kilos and five foot nine tall, all but engulfed by the Sahara. Millions have died in it, and no one, not even the nomads, trust it. Yet here I was, stranded alone and quite possibly lost in the middle of the world's harshest desert in summer, exhausted, dehydrated, hungry, with precious little water and food remaining, and with only a bicycle as my sole companion. I started laughing. Then I started dancing. The more the situation struck me as being ludicrous, the harder I laughed and the quicker I danced, until, in shrieks of helpless laughter, I was so tired and hot that I just had to sit down, my lungs shaking, and tears running down my face. For the moment at least, my thirst and all my worries and feelings of anger and frustration and desperation and helplessness were forgotten. I fell asleep with sand drifting over me like a gentle shower of rain.

It was late morning, and I was already exhausted. My mouth was dry and the sores on my lips had opened up again. I felt so tired that for a while, the effort required even to stand up and fetch water and food from the bike was too much, and so I stared skyward instead. The sun above me shone a brilliant silky white, obliterating the blue from the sky. I could see points of light flitting across it like sperm, first a handful, then hundreds and then thousands of them, all spinning and rushing about in the hallucinations of my deadened mind. Soon there were so many of them that I could no longer even make out the sky. Everything grew darker and darker, and yet my eyes were still wide open.

A while later, I don't know exactly how long later, I realised with a start that I was still staring at the sun. I stood up, shaking from both the shock and my hunger, and tried to snap myself out of my daze, but my eyes merely locked on to a nearby sand dune and so I stared at that for a while. I managed eventually to eat the remaining loaf of bread and to take a sip of water, though by now even eating had become a painful affair because of my lips and my sandpapered throat. Still dazed, I climbed on to the bicycle, only to fall off the other side. I was neither shocked nor scared at my state. Not even confused, but just dazed like a drunkard. I realised that I wasn't feeling particularly well, but then I didn't much care either. In fact, I no longer seemed to care about anything. I just picked myself up from the sand, took the bike and started walking away into the silence. I never looked back, but just carried on walking through the desert, my feet still bleeding. At first, I stumbled frequently on my leaden and numbed legs but then, as I continued, the walking became a little easier. A world of shimmering mirages filled the world in a blazing vision of madness. Relentless, merciless, the sky spat fiery curtains upon insanity furiously pumping, bubbling. I no longer knew, nor even cared, about death. My head contracted, pounding, heavy, thoughtless, devoid of feeling, plodding relentlessly onward. The sand bubbled and swirled. I gazed too long and stumbled. There was no pain, there were no feelings. No thoughts, floating, marching hypnotically into oblivion. I thought of nothing as I pushed the bicycle slowly along the track. I felt no mood or emotion. I felt no pain or sensations. I thought of nothing. Thought had become irrelevant. So on I cycled, saying nothing, thinking of nothing, and doing nothing except struggling, until it seemed that there was nothing left in the whole world but this huge dumb emptiness and me.

Sometimes, my mind would slip back into a few moments of lucidity, as though to reassure me that it was still there. I vividly remember talking to myself about chocolate bars, but invariably my mind would just ignore my words and shut itself off from the outside world. So my words would then trail off into a sad swirling wordstring of nonsense and then I would stop talking and stare instead at the sand passing beneath my feet as I plodded slowly onwards and back into my senseless daze.

Other times I would kid myself by staring at a distant dune and thinking 'when I get to that dune, I shall almost be there.' But of course, when I did eventually get to the dune there would be nothing to see but yet another one, even further away, and so I would think again 'when I get to that dune, I shall almost be there.' Unnoticed, I would stare again at my plodding feet. First the left, then the right, then the left, then the right, until, again, I caught myself in a trance and no longer realised that I was still staring at my plodding feet.

Once, towards midday, I sat down on the sand and asked myself what the hell I was doing here. I stared glassy-eyed at the sand at my feet without bothering, or half an hour later even remembering, to answer my own question. There no longer was an answer, and half an hour later, back in my dazed, cotton-befuddled mind, having forgotten what it was that had made me want to sit down in the first place, I got up and carried on. After a few kilometres, I stopped for a piss, my first in four days. I pissed barely half a litre of dark fluid into a spare bike bottle.

I did eventually succumb to the temptation of lying down at the side of the track. With the tranquil and unhurried repose of a man lying on his deathbed, I felt my life ebbing ever so gently away from me and back into the earth. Without my even knowing, I was finally at peace with myself. No longer confused, no longer despairing, no longer frustrated, I accepted fate without so much as a whisper of regret or self-pity. I cannot pretend to any courage or bravery, though, in the face of my imminent demise, for I was no longer conscious of it. In my advanced stupor, emotions such as caring and fear never crossed my mind, having long since faded into the obscurity of the past. Moreover, it was no longer even *possible* for me to care or fear. The possibility of finding myself on the brink of life and death had already been considered many weeks before. Anyhow, my transition from the temperate climate of northern Morocco to the searing heat of Mauritania had been gradual. In a way, I was already immune to the fear and panic that I would undoubtedly have felt had I suddenly found myself in the desert without food or water. My absence of fear was characteristic of all such situations. By all accounts, fighter pilots under heavy enemy fire rarely if ever confess to having been scared. Likewise, a man condemned at the gallows does not usually portray fear but, rather, stoic acceptance of the *fact* of death. Captain Oakes, when facing certain death in the Antarctic, did not show fear, neither did Kitchener in Khartoum, or Nelson at Trafalgar. It is not, however, that these men displayed particularly exceptional heroism or gallantry, but that all fear is ultimately the fear of the unknown. Once one's fate is recognised, it is no longer unknown and so there is no longer reason to fear it. The spectre of my impending demise was in fact almost too easy to rationalise. Fate had become fact and that was that.

By mid afternoon my eyes were extremely sore, both from sweat and the reflected glare of the sun. I closed them. The horizon, a hellish fusion of red sand and black sky, spread slowly to cover everything that I could see. On and on I pedalled, sand and dust now stinging my face in the rekindled trade wind, arriving hot and dusty from the north. Then the imaginary haze of a distant mirage, dark and luminescent, appeared over the crest of a dune. Hypnotised, I plodded on, the mirage looming ever larger as I approached. And then, as quickly as it had appeared, it disappeared, water sinking into sand and leaving nothing behind but a bare grin on the desert floor. I opened my eyes to find that I was still walking. I walked like this for most of the day, until the sun sank down over the western sky.

Darkness had already fallen as I wearily pushed my bicycle off the camel tracks, only to settle a couple of yards away in the imaginary shelter of a small sandy copse. Even at night, I had little respite from the blazing midsummer heat. The night-time temperature kept well over thirty degrees due to the trade wind that blew in from the Western Sahara. I collapsed with throbbing head onto the sand, too tired to bother about untying my kip-mat or bivouac from the back of the bike. I was exhausted to the point that I was too tired even to fall asleep. I had a paltry three quarters of a litre of water remaining, having drunk almost nothing during the day. The only advantage to my dazed state was, I suppose, that I was no longer having to battle with my body to stop it from finishing my remaining water. It was as though it too had given up the ghost of pretending to life. My poor lips, though no longer bleeding, were shrivelled and felt brittle. My hands were in a similar state, but still bled occasionally, as did my feet, though I did not even have the energy to take my shoes off for the night. My back and wrists were sore and swollen, and the skin all over my body flaked rapidly and painfully. My eyes ached, and I could no longer spit out the phlegm that was blocking my throat, making my breathing harsh and painful. For the first and only time in my life I considered that it was quite likely that I would never see the sun set again.

And yet, my tiredness was one of the most beautiful and intimate feelings that I'd ever experienced. The exhaustion was of the purest kind, brought on solely by physical exertion, and it challenged incessantly both the innermost mental and outermost physical limits of my body, and then passed beyond still further. I just lay there, between sand and stars, motionless with my legs splayed-out, arms flung behind me and my parched mouth gaping up at the sky. A dew-like crust of delicate sweat beads formed on my frown and chest, occasionally letting loose trickles of salty liquid, which wound their way teasingly down my skin before disappearing into the sand. A fly hopped about restlessly on my belly. During the day, the only assaults on my senses had been of the most basic and extreme nature – thirst, hunger, heat, incessant physical work and my already strained tiredness – and their collective effect had been to clear my mind of all thoughts except those necessary to the basic task of surviving. Consequently, when the struggle was given time off at night, my mind, stripped of every trace of superfluous emotion, was left free to re-enter a higher plane of thought, which this time reasserted itself in a completely fresh way, uncluttered by any triviality of thought or emotion. I couldn't decide whether it was total sensory deprivation or overload that I was feeling, for they both seemed the same to me.

As I lay prostrate on the ground, my spine started to tingle, the sensation creeping up my back and then down into my legs. I felt my nerves sparkling, my every muscle twitching and each and every pulse from my heart radiating gently outwards through my body until I felt that I was conscious of even the very last cells in my toes. The throbbing pain of exhaustion gradually ebbed away as my thirst became tolerable and my fantasy finally became utterly tangible reality. I had stared at the sky a thousand times before, yet this night, it possessed the most captivating brilliance. Above me hung an intricate and glorious tapestry, intricate in its minutest detail and glorious in its overwhelming vastness, a vastness matched only by the desert. The haloed moon's lips smiled serenely across unimagined billions of stars, and I felt as though I could reach out and touch each and every one of them. The bright constellations of Cassiopeia, Ursa Major and Orion had long since been engulfed in a myriad other stars and galaxies, all equally as bright and awesome, shining in every colour and intensity conceivable. The Milky Way slit the desert sky with a luminescent carpet of gently twinkling gemstones, from bloodstone to emerald, aquamarine to moonstone. A giant meteor flew blazing across the sky, exploding near the horizon in a gentle sparkle of confusion. It was the first time I'd ever seen a meteor.

I closed my eyes. Except for my own breathing and the occasional howl of a lone jackal in the distance, the world lay shrouded in silence. Intently, I listened to the air rush down my throat and plunge into my lungs, only to linger a while before slowly being expelled back up into the sky. My breathing slowed and my mind concentrated ever more intensely on the phrase that I had most often heard in the Sahara. You're mad. You're mad! The accusation replayed itself faster and faster inside my head, like reverberations from an iron bar being run along railings, until the phrase became nothing more than the distant silent echo of something that I no longer was. I saw milky ripples on a pond after the first drop has fallen.

After a while my lungs ached so much that I unconsciously reversed my breathing and began hyperventilating. The faster and deeper I breathed, the more I became hypnotised. It was like two people sucking and blowing down both ends of the same straw, sharing the same airs of hope and friendship. Images of the last few days flashed before my closed eyelids – flickering candlelight moonscapes – the nomad camel-herders whose lives I was briefly sharing – a young child grinning a gap-toothed smile – incandescent skeletons – an oasis and its crazy profusion of life – a grave strewn with thistles – the feelings of desperation, of frustration and of a great excitement – the leer of a camel – images of endless tracts of sand – of my sweat playing on the handlebars – of laughing and dancing and shouting – of the sun beating relentlessly down from the merciless sky... Faster and faster and faster these images of madness came flooding back, until my body was left quaking in the spinning reflections of the shadows of my mind. I stopped, suddenly, panting, and opened my eyes to gaze once more at the heavens as my pounding heart raced oxygen through my veins and I realised that I was crying, and I realised... and I realised that I was laughing.

I felt as though I were leaving behind some uniquely earthbound force called gravitation, called insanity. Insanity was no longer even relative but hopelessly irrelevant. In its place was an intense love of life, a love that, far from being passive, had as its heart the childlike fascination of the unknown. Without my love of endless self-exploration, and exploration of the world I find myself in, the very foundations to my life would become stale, rotten, rancid. I felt that if I died that night, it would have been the most perfect ending to anyone's life.

For three hours I lay thus awake, too engrossed even to reach over to the last full bottle of water to ease my throat. Then, all of a sudden,

I felt sleepy. I rolled over on the sand, closed my eyes, and fell asleep.

The sun rose quickly over the eastern sands, blinding my vision in a kaleidoscope of shimmering yellow and golden rays, throwing long pointed shadows over the dunes. Although today I had especial reason to dread the sun, there was something very reassuring about it. I remembered thinking last night that the sunset might have been the last that I would ever see. I looked again to my left and saw the blazing sun rise once more up into the sky. The sun rises and the sun falls, but then it rises again. The sun, for all its brutal harshness, represented the only constancy over all the formless madness of the desert. It is the cruellest of all paradoxes.

Breakfast consisted of the remaining peanuts and dry biscuits. I had half a litre of water remaining, half a litre of urine and no food, and yet I felt strangely calm and relaxed, even lucid. I not only realised my own insignificance, but that the responsibility for my life lay entirely in my own hands, my own legs, my head and my heart, and in nothing and nobody else. I realised that I, and I alone, held the responsibility for my fate and my future. That only I had the power to continue my life. The strangest feeling at that moment was to realise that the only reason remaining for my existence was quite simply to survive.

I felt an immense pride. There was no way in the world that this bloody desert was going to claim me without a fight. I was on my own. It had been my own decision to cycle here, on my own volition, my obsession, my pride, and it was entirely up to me to succeed. I promised myself not to drink anything until my collapse, and felt then that I could do anything in the world, anything at all. With a final defiant shout to the desert and the sun (in fact, it was probably rather more of a croak), I climbed on to my bike and started pedalling towards the south. The ground seemed to speed past as I flew over it, and I was surprised at my temporary and final burst of strength, the last reprieve of dehydration. On and on I surged, ploughing through sands that would yesterday have been impossible. For a change, I was moving at much the same speed as the following wind, which made for a deathly silence superimposed only by the whirring and clicking of the bike, my own grunting and panting and the occasional rustle of pebbles being thrown up in the air behind me.

The sun had been directly overhead for quite some time when a white speck slowly appeared from out of the mirages on the horizon. I stopped cycling and stared in silence, as disbelieving tears trickled down my cheeks.

CHAPTER TEN

Nouakchott and the Sahel

Nothing but a handful of dust will fill the eye of man.

Arab proverb

The three men in the hut seemed as elated at seeing me as I was at seeing them. We hugged and embraced each other at great length, as though we had been long-lost friends. They smiled, grinned and laughed, slapped me on my back, and pinched my burnt cheeks as though to remind me that I was back amongst human beings. My God, I felt wonderful in my exhaustion. The unutterably blissful feeling of knowing that my downward mental spiral, my hellish hopelessness, my solitude, had finally come to an end. I was utterly ecstatic, or as much as I could be given the state my body was in. I punched the walls, thumped my head, and beamed impossibly wide grins. My hosts looked on open-mouthed as I yelled my head off, just so fucking happy to be alive! *So fucking happy!*

How to describe my delirious sweet ecstasy? I was just so fucking happy to be alive! It was not so much relief at not being dead, but positive, childish joy and bewonderment, bewilderment, sweet confusion, endless days and endless nights now behind me, part of self, memory, recollection, never to be lost... Fuck, was I happy.

I was given a bottle of soda pop, and then another, and my body screamed in pleasure as my skin opened up, my pores unclogged, and I sweated like never before, gorgeous sweat. Then two large bowls of cold *zrig*, my body subsumed in perspiration, my body once more allowed to breathe. I lay exhausted on the bed, flooded with indescribable emotions and feelings. My kind hosts seemed to understand, and left me alone with my thoughts for a few hours, interrupting my reverie only to refill the bowl or to hand me glasses of steaming mint tea. I stayed until the evening, first resting and sleeping, and then talking,

255

listening to Bob Marley on their battery-powered tape player, playing poker, eating, grinning and just so fucking happy to be alive, and I know I repeat myself, but how else to express my joy?

Besides all this, however, I was also to experience a nagging sense of anticlimax, which I suppose wasn't entirely surprising. My recovery from dehydration was rapid (perhaps too rapid), lasting only a matter of days rather than weeks, and from Akjoujt onwards (then only twenty kilometres away), the road to Nouakchott was asphalted and made cycling easy, and therefore also unremarkable. Perhaps more important was the curse of forgetting, the ease with which I became re-acclimatized to reality, the little I thought of those days between Atâr and Akjoujt, and the accursed ease with which my experiences were catagorised and neatly filed away in my memory, and then forgotten. Once more, the ever-poetic Arabs have an epigram for this: in the desert, one forgets everything and remembers nothing any more.

The days from Akjoujt were bound to be days of anticlimax, and of disbelief tempered by the grey monotony of the desert. From here on, the Sahara was a vaguely undulating landscape of dust, nothing more and nothing less. The weird contradiction in my mind was that cycling was just easy. A half-decent road, a good mileage each day, little thirst and no hunger. These few days to Nouakchott were remarkable in that they were the only times throughout my travels that I was to feel properly lonely. With both land and sky devoid of colour and life, cycling was repetitive, even boring. The mornings shimmered like ghostly shrouds, and for most of the way the horizon was cut short by dust, which at times reduced my visibility to no more than twenty or thirty metres. The only vegetation for over two hundred and fifty kilometres was a few equally ghostly acacia and the occasional clump of omnipresent thorn grass. All colour, except greys and drabs, was absorbed by the wizened sky, rumpled with pleats of dust that obliterated even the evil sun. It was a windswept place, lifeless, and with none of the desert's more sensual charms.

I cycled with the wind in my back, and was pleasantly surprised at the ease with which the kilometres fell away. Apart from the dull aches and pains of my body, there was little sign of the exhaustion that my body had undergone over the last week. It was almost too easy. The temperature, regardless, continued to peak at over fifty degrees, despite the wind, and it was a relief to find roadside huts dispensing food, water, and shelter. At one of these roadsteads – a couple of huts beside a large blackened water tank – a goat was tied to a solitary post. Inside the smaller hut were four children, huddled asleep amidst an assortment of pots and pans and soiled Persian carpets. Their mother, a wrinkled but elegant *bidan* dressed in a black cotton wrap and loose headscarf, was weaving with green wool on a wooden loom inside the larger hut. Beside her were piles of ripped cardboard for her children to play with.

The woman insisted that I stay a while, if only to talk to her husband who spoke French. He was in a small side room, curtained-off from the rest of the hut. She called him, and then we waited. In the meantime we tried to converse, although I suspect that neither of us had the slightest idea of what the other was trying to say. When I mentioned Nouakchott, her ears pricked up a little.

'Ah, you have been to Nouakchott.'

'No, I'm *going* there.'

'Oh, what was it like?'

Before long, a small, gruff-faced black man emerged from the curtains, spanner in one hand and spliff in the other. He had been repairing a gear box, and was covered head to toe in engine grease. As he wiped his face on a flannel, I noticed that he was actually pale-skinned, which contrasted oddly with his tightly curled black hair, thick lips and flattened nose. He told me that his family, like all the other inhabitants of the roadsteads, had once been herders, but due to the droughts and the extermination of Mauritania's grazing land, they had settled into the business of providing food and water, petrol and mechanical expertise to the passing traffic. He prided himself on his skill as a mechanic, and proceeded to explain in great detail the inner workings of some gadget that I supposed came from a car or a truck. Although the volume of traffic was low at present – perhaps only a car or two a day – he said that business picked up considerably at the time of the *guetna* date picking festival, and also in winter when the few surviving caravans return to Mauritania, which means businessmen travelling up to the Adrar from Nouakchott.

I was given some rather green water from the tank. Its colour was hardly surprising given that there is only one well between Akjoujt and Nouakchott. On reflection, it still worries me to think of all the shit I drank in the desert. Speaking from personal experience, I am quite certain that given no other choice, the human body will adapt to almost anything you might care to sling at it, if only for a short period of time.

As I cycled, the air became dustier and the sand whitened, spattered here and there with ancient chalky seashells. Although it was a gradual thing, by mid afternoon I was cycling through what could only be described as an achromatic dust storm, my visibility down to ten metres. Nothing at all broke the cast-iron monotony of the place. Kilometre after kilometre, hour after hour of the same unbroken sameness made for gloomy cycling. Only the relentless song of the desert gave any variety: hiss, growl, whoosh, silence, the sound of sand marching to the tune of a military tattoo.

At one point, a large black shape loomed out of the gloom, which turned out to be an antique car husk like that at 'Aggui. As I drew close, a wall appeared, and then another, and then a well, filled almost to the brim with sand. These ruins, I was told later, were the site of an abandoned French farming project from the 1940s. To think that not even fifty years ago the desert that I was now crossing could have been farmland was a sobering thought.

I passed another roadstead, but this time didn't stop as I had plenty of water. Two small children were chasing each other around the hut. They froze and stared at me as I passed. I waved and grinned, prompting much yelling and shouting. Like many Moorish children – especially young boys – their heads were shaved but for a Mohican kind of tuft, something that their heavenly protectors can grab hold of to pull them up to heaven in time of disaster.

Towards late afternoon my boredom was eased by a loud throbbing. The vague silhouette of a vehicle appeared from the dusty haze. As it sped past I could make out American plates and white faces staring at me. It screeched to a halt, and reversed at full tilt until it was in front of me again. Then the doors of the brand-new state-of-the-art white Chevrolet 4WD opened, belching forth the portly frames of five American tourists. Never mind my seeming alien to the desert nomads, this, I thought as I grinned at them in disbelief, was weird! Two shiny spare tyres and several metal hampers were strapped to the roof, and a big sticker reading 'Air-Conditioned Environment' was stuck on the windscreen.

'Bon-joo-er, vooz ate Fransayze?' said the fat driver in a blurred Texan drawl.

'Err, no. I'm from England actually.' I smiled at the bleached, middle-aged strangers.

'Oh, England!' he boomed enthusiastically. 'We're from Austin, Texas. The name's Flannigan. How d'y do?' He held out his hand and we shook.

'I'm Earl, and this is my wife Avril,' he said, pointing to a short, fat woman with an endearing grin. 'And you are...?'

Earl and his four companions were *the* archetypal American tourists, the eternal cannon-fodder of travel writers. Plump, greying, middle-aged, and in all the right clothes. Earl was wearing a garb of white tennis shorts, Nike sports shoes, short grey socks and a large red and white 'I love Dallas' T-shirt. A bulky camera hung about a protruding gut of generous proportions, and his reddened rotund face was topped with one of those shapeless cricket hats. The other four were similarly attired.

I was told by Earl, somewhat proudly, that it had cost him a minor fortune to airlift the vehicle from the States to Dakar, but that after only five days in Africa, he could see that the expense had been well worthwhile. Presently they were off on a two day trip to Chinguetti. The other woman, Vera, who I'd heard exclaim 'Gee whizz, it's hot!' on getting out of the vehicle, said: 'You know Gentz... It is Gentz ain't it? Well, Gentz, would you believe that we thought you were one of those nomads! Until Joe saw your face, that is!' Joe beamed broadly under his saggy hat.

'Tell me,' Vera continued, grimacing in the glare: 'How d'you cross the desert on a push-bike? Ain't it too sandy?'

'Yes, I suppose so,' I replied. 'That's why it's called a push-bike.'

As the chit-chat began to falter, Joe produced an outrageously large camera and started focusing it on me. Avril noticed, and added that perhaps they would all like to have their photos taken with me, and would I mind. Of course not, and so in turn, each of the five were photographically immortalised beside me. Both Joe and Earl put their arms around my shoulders as though we were great buddies, and grinned triumphantly into the lens while I tried my best to look like the real life adventurer that Avril wanted me to be. After the impromtu photo session, Avril and Earl asked for my autograph!

After a final round of handshakes, they piled back into the Chevrolet and drove off, horn blaring, into the obscurity of the dust. It took me some time to recover from the experience before I could remount and cycle away. I couldn't believe that I just had met these people, and I looked again at the packet of U.S. Army ration peanuts that they had given me, just to make sure.

The hazy sun set slowly (for a change) behind a nearby sand dune, in its own way a gentle farewell for the time being. I slept behind a clump of prickly spine trees, on which I managed to gash my forehead, and woke to a beautiful sunrise, the bright crimson disc of the sun at first only just peeking over a salmon-pink landscape of gently undulating dunes, speckled all over with crooked acacia and smaller but equally gnarled thorn bushes. The wind, and therefore the dust, had settled overnight, resulting in a visibility of about four kilometres. The sky was a crisp blue canopy, gradually seeping away as the calm dawn was overwhelmed by the acrid magnesium sun. The wind picked up, and within an hour the sun and the sky and the horizon slipped once more behind the suffocating monotone dust.

A couple of hours later, I reached the outskirts of Nouakchott, mostly silhouetted slum dwellings rising inconsequentially from the flat and gloomy desert, devoid of any colour except for miserable greys and blacks and browns. Here and there grew a dusty palm tree or an acacia, chiaroscuro caricatures without shadows. There were a few dogs and donkey carts, and anonymous matchstick people who shuffled around in the dust clutching empty plastic baskets or cloth-wrapped bundles. Opposite a junk yard, piled high with mangled vehicles, was a roadblock.

'You must be crazy,' said the gendarme.

* * *

Nouakchott, wrote Quentin Crewe (he who got blown up near Nouâdhibou), must be the favourite in a contest for the most irrelevant capital city in the world. Starting life as a French Foreign Legion outpost, it was chosen in 1957 by *bidan* elders to be the capital of the nascent Islamic Republic of Mauritania. Its name means either 'Place of the Wind' or 'Place of Floating Seashells'. With hindsight, it should more accurately have been called the 'Place of Dust'. The site, five kilometres from the Atlantic, was chosen for its then relatively cool and healthy climate, as well as for its proximity to the agricultural lands along the river Senegal. In recent years, however, the desert has expanded so much that dunes are now threatening large areas of the city, including, ironically, the presidential palace. A cemetery to the north of the city has already succumbed to the sands.

Originally built to accomodate 30,000 people, it is now home to almost half a million, a quarter of the country's population, and as a result is grossly overcrowded. There is little water, and in the slumtown, where the majority reside, there are sometimes hundreds of families sharing the same standpipe. Yet, in spite of its huge population, the centre of Nouakchott is notable only for its lifeless sterility. Originally intended to be the visible centre and symbol of the nation's bustling modernity, it consists largely of a few perfunctory blocks of shops, three and four storey offices, clumps of wasted palm trees and windblown rubbish. The architecture, though officially Moorish, is in fact 'desert-utilitarian', the euphemism for concrete slabs strung together in monotonous rectangular grids. In the wide and dusty streets, drowned rather than bathed in sunlight, there is little traffic: only the odd green and yellow *Transports Urbaines* minibus, the zippy jeeps that belong to international aid agencies, and a few angry, low-horsepower Suzuki motorcycles. The so-called Chinese Mosque is perhaps the most interesting sight – its tall minaret sparkling in the sun. On looking closer, however, it is an ugly affair with fifteen zinc domes, mock battlements and a series of ungainly arches. Many buildings still stand unfinished, their ground floors often used as a shops whilst the concrete pillars and struts overhead slowly crumble away. Like Cansado, Nouâdhibou and to some extent Akjoujt, Nouakchott resembles more a gigantic Legoland than a real city, one whose impersonal nature is epitomised by the alphabetical numbering of its *Ilôt* housing blocks.

On the hot pavements, old men squat around in the dust, swaying gently as they move their pebbles or walnuts in makeshift games of draughts. Younger men stand around holding hands in greeting or friendship, wearing loose white turbans, blue *boubous* and white smocks with large embroidered breast pockets. On one street corner there are stalls selling French-style loaves of bread, and others peddling expensive imported fruit: oranges, mangos, guavas, pineapples, melons and the like, around which mill knots of envious black-veiled women with dark puckered lips. Their blackened feet are hennaed like their hands, and their fingernails are painted bright red. At another corner is a shoeblack, presumably servicing the footwear of government functionaries, bank clerks and the resident diplomatic community. Nearby are a couple of old scribes, one of whom is deaf, sat behind their typewriters. They also sell stamps and paper, biros, envelopes, bleached postcards showing bleached desert scenes, and the national daily which has a circulation of three hundred.

As I cycled around town, killing time before my planned reunion with Albert (I was a few days late, but no matter), I was hailed by a shopkeeper on the junction of the city's two main thoroughfares, Avenue Abd el-Nasser and the Avenue Kennedy. Mahfoud Ould M'Hamed Hassani, a cheerful thirty-five year old *bidan* Moor, was a devout Muslim, and supported his three wives and nine children by selling butane gas, various hair dyes and skin ointments from Asia, and rice, dates, peanuts and flour contained in large cardboard barrels. After a sweaty lunch and the requisite three glasses of mint tea, during which he closed the shop, he spent the best part of the afternoon trying to convert me to Islam. For most of the time he gave the impression that it was his duty, as a good Muslim, to rescue me from the infidelity of the Christians. His favourite means of attack was mentioning Cat Stevens' conversion, saying that since he had managed to embrace Islam, then there no reason why I should not also. When I eventually informed him that I'd never heard of Cat Stevens, he took great pleasure in citing Mohammad Ali as another example.

Mahfoud then added that Islam was the most tolerant of religions, something I might have believed had it not been for Mahfoud so insistently tried to convert me that I felt victimised, and most certainly not the recipient of the tolerance that he so forcibly preached. When I queried the position of women in Muslim society, he became defensive and after much goading admitted that it was wrong to oppress them, but he then added that the Qur'an itself did not advocate the superiority of either sex, which was true. Later, Mahfoud changed tack to propound the more liberal side of Islam, saying that so long as I believed in God there was always hope, and even went on to say that I didn't have to become Muslim in order to enter heaven, but that it would be better. He believed that heaven was a place *beyond* the universe, because all life and time would cease on the Day of Judgement. At one point, when a few customers were in the shop, Mahfoud asked me, with a sneer: 'Do you know where paradise is?' I thought for a moment, and then mumbled some or other equally unmemorable response. Thinking about this some time later, I decided that I should have said: 'Inside your mind.' As George Orwell's interrogator in *Nineteen Eighty-Four* put it: 'Nothing [is] your own except the few cubic centimetres inside your skull.'

My host persisted regardless with his proselytizing, and in exasperation, began to pray for my salvation.

* * *

I eventually met up with Albert at El Frisco's, an expensive and pretentious expat restaurant guarded by three stone-faced bouncers, intended to deter inquisitive locals. After talking myself past these gorillas, my filthy and bedraggled appearance was greeted by the rather shocked expressions of a dozen or so dinner jackets and accompanying *haute couture* gowns. Following a cursory wash in the toilet, I sat down at a table laid with silver cutlery and bone china, to a meal of shark steak, langouste, shrimps, stuffed avocado, mango and guava salad, and a bottle of smuggled wine – ah!

Nouakchott's European community is, understandably, very isolated. Geza was fed up with Mauritania, saying that the people were lazy and that the government was corrupt. It was a view similarly held by a group of aid-workers I met at a barbecue later that evening. Aid workers, no matter where they are, always seem to grow disillusioned with time. Albert's main grudge, though, was the ban on alcohol, even for Europeans, which meant that half of his diplomatic luggage was taken up with bottles of Irish whiskey. The strain of the place seemed to show on a large burly Dane I met at the party, whose catchphrase was: '*La vie est belle, mon ami, que la vie est belle.*' He had suffered his third nervous breakdown two weeks earlier, and wanted out.

Albert's villa was on the northwestern outskirts of the city, beyond the last of the slums. Alongside was Mauritania's only stadium, home of a fledgling football league. Opposite was the new Novotel, at which the pleasure of spending a night in an air-conditioned room costs upwards of a hundred dollars. For most of the day its gates were besieged by an army of hawkers, selling anything from neolithic spear heads to gold painted 'nuggets' at a fiver a throw. I was to spend four days at Albert's, largely uneventful save for a large bougainvillea hedge with green leaves and aphids which made me realise for the first time in weeks that I was once again able to smell, a sensation that had been totally absent in the desert. Except for the fine-mesh mosquito netting strung over the windows, there was no indication whatsoever of the continent that lived outside the walls and iron gate of this villa. There was electricity and running water, and *all* the kitchen appliances were in full working order. The larder was full of canned produce shipped in from Belgium, and the walls of the living room were hung with prints of Vanderbilt's steamships, Jean-Michel Jarre posters and postcard views of grassy North European landscapes.

Although I had experienced great relief on reaching Nouakchott, within days I was again feeling restless and frustrated, all the more so because the only thing that was keeping me here was trivial money hassles. Foolishly, I had changed £150 into ouguiya, in order to buy a plane ticket to Paris, the idea being to return to Mauritania after having visited black Africa. Only then I discovered that no such flight actually existed, and so when I tried to change the ouguiya into CFA – the common West African currency – the banks refused on the grounds that Mauritania was poor and that I was rich. This resulted in three intensely irritating days of to-ing and fro-ing between banks and institutions in order to obtain the necessary permission for the transaction. I knew what I was trying to say when I told the director of the Banque Centrale de Mauritanie that he would be acting idiotically if he let rules be more important than the people they were supposed to protect, but he misunderstood and took offence. 'From now on, I will ignore you like you are not here!' he exclaimed, and emphatically turned round on his swivel chair to shuffle some papers. And ignore me he did, but only for three hours, after which his resolve weakened and I was grudgingly handed the relevant papers and forms.

I was finally kicked out by Albert when his blonde girlfriend came to stay (his Belgian wife lived in blissful ignorance). Although I had hoped to leave that day anyway, my financial troubles forced me to stay on for another few nights. Frustrated at my first taste of intransigent bureaucracy, I spent much of the day sitting with the scribes outside the bank, who also dealt in old Asian magazines, cigarettes, digital watches and shades that few could afford. There, I met Oumar Niang, a tall black youth who kindly offered to put me up for as long as I wished. He had the sort of handsome features that would make him look very dignified in his old age. His great dream was to become a fashion model in Paris, and so follow in the footsteps of both his sisters. In the meantime, he worked in a hardware store that sold Sony TVs, Atari computer consoles, diamond necklaces and Christian Dior perfumes.

Nouakchott has been called the world's largest refugee camp, and not without reason. It is a city hemmed in by a sprawling grey *bidonville* of unbelievable proportions. Galvanised iron, ripped hessian sacks, crudely sewn linoleum awnings, old mouldly packing crates and tarpaper, form the tiny shacks that often house families of ten or even twenty people. As I walked my bike with Oumar to his family compound, little children came out onto the dusty alleyways to stand and stare, yet not a word was spoken. What struck me most was the dull lifelessness of it all, murky black and brown dwellings rising from the pale grey sand under the pale grey sky. The nomadic past of many of its inhabitants was still discernible in the thousands of tents that make up part of the slumtown. Some had even sprouted in the gardens of larger buildings and in the shells of others unfinished. The place was stricken with poverty and, to some extent, fear. Most children forgo the opportunity of education to become beggars, thieves or prostitutes. Or else they die from disease. There have been cases of ex-nomads going mad in these shantytowns: flipping out, killing randomly, or killing themselves. Suicide, which until 1975 was absolutely unheard of among these people, has become commonplace. To add to these already horrendous problems, the combination of extreme poverty and varied ethnic composition has resulted in the slums becoming a hotbed of racial and political foment. Although the majority of Mauritanians are, of course, Moors, there is a substantial minority of Negro sedentary tribes living in the south in the precious cultivated lands of the river Senegal: Tukolor, Fulani, Sarakolé, Marka, Wolof and Bambara, all of them with their own languages, customs, traditions, histories and lands. And here in Nouakchott, to an even greater extent than Nouâdhibou, these many disparate people find themselves forced to live together. The greatest agency of change was the disastrous drought of 1968-73, when a high proportion of pastoralists – even from the Senegal valley – lost their herds and were forced to flee to the towns.

The predominantly *bidan* government hasn't helped matters by openly and often contemptuously referring to Mauritanian blacks as 'Senegalese'. A one-party state since 1964, the government's policy of enforced 'arabisation' was greeted with riots on its introduction, and still causes considerable animosity between Moors and Negroes. In 1983, the clandestine *Forces de Libération Africaines de Mauritanie* (FLAM) was formed to campaign for black rights, but was powerless to prevent the imprisonment, in 1986, of twenty Negroes accused of 'attacking national unity'. Then, in October 1987 (the year before my visit), Mauritania saw its first coup attempt to have been entirely racially-provoked. In the aftermath, three Tukolor officers were executed, and five hundred black NCOs (a little less than 10% of the total number) were ejected from the armed forces. That, in turn, led to minor school strikes that ended a month before my visit, and on the day I left, two Moors and a Senegalese taxi driver were murdered in Nouakchott, presumably in racially motivated killings. In April and May 1989, the year after my visit, the tensions escalated catastrophically, when two hundred Senegalese died in riots in Nouakchott, and an unknown number of Mauritanians were killed in Dakar. It was an outburst of violence that led both countries to the brink of war. Altogether. some 300,000 Mauritanians fled or were expelled from Senegal, with untold consequences on the already dire situation in the slums of Nouakchott and Nouâdhibou.

Oumar – a black Moor – was surprisingly optimistic about the future. It was an attitude, I suppose, well in keeping to the character of a country that can call the road to the drought-stricken east of the country, the 'Road of Hope'. Indeed, the Niang family seemed to have made the best of the generally atrocious conditions in the slumtown, having travelled the 'Road of Hope' five years earlier, all of seven hundred kilometres from a village near Koumbi Saleh (site of the ruins of the capital of ancient Ghana). The Niang family compound – five adjacent huts – was well kept and as clean as conditions would allow. Oumar's room, which he shared with two brothers, was decorated on two walls with Senegalese tapestries, and with a tattered poster of Bob Marley on another. In the corners were cushions on which to sleep, or relax to the rather distorted strains of a battery-operated stereo. Outside, in the narrow dusty yard, lived two chickens and a goat, which would be slaughtered come the feast of Aïd el-Kebir. Oumar's parents were very sweet and gracious, always at pains to ensure that I was well fed and content, and were almost embarrassed by what little disorder there was in the compound. They were very proud of their son being able to speak French, and my presence seemed to confer some kind of status on the family as a whole.

I parked my bike, washed in the slimy cubicle that doubled as the toilet, and was then dragged off by Oumar to be presented to some of his friends. They lived in one of Nouakchott's few five storey blocks, built in the 1960s but already decrepit. It gave the appearance of being at least a hundred years old. Inside, I noticed at once that its roof was missing. Shards of stark sunlight baked the miserable crumbling concrete staircase and its flaking, rot-ringed green and blue paint. The walls, once white, were now yellow or brown, and its wooden bannisters and window frames had long ago been used for fuel. As we slumped up the stairs and into a dark tiled room, Oumar was assailed by questions regarding the *Toubab*. Two girls, wearing orange and pink dresses respectively, were reclined on an old brown couch, watching what was left of the TV. On the walls hung a couple of the ubiquitous Marley posters, one of them saying 'Exodus'. I remember feeling slightly awkward, even ridiculous, when Oumar loudly announced that I was an adventurer all the way from Manchester United! He then pinched my calves to show the girls how fit I was. In the evening a few male friends turned up with some dope, and the conversation turned to alcohol and sex, except for one guy who was too far gone and kept smiling and exclaiming '*C'est extra!*' Oumar, who didn't smoke, quickly got offended, and later apologized (needlessly, I thought) for his friends' behaviour.

Later in the evening, we paid a visit to the wife of his elder brother, a beautiful young woman with high pronounced cheekbones, who was pregnant for the first time and had been suffering from a splitting headache. We arrived as she was still in bed, lying on her side and groaning loudly. Oumar surprised me. As we entered the room, the family moved aside after the perfunctory greetings to let him through to the bed, whereupon the woman sat up and Oumar began to mutter a strange litany of what could only have been spiritual incantations. Then, placing both his hands on her scalp, I saw his arms tense and his eyes close as he began to concentrate. The incantations grew louder as his grasp became firmer. Then, slowly but still powerfully, he began running his fingers up through her hair, pulling at the roots as he dragged the demons out of her skull and flung them away into the air. Then again, and the tension in her face was seen to ease. Finally she smiled, and told Oumar that the pain had gone. More incantations followed as the floor was wetted to keep the exorcised demons at bay, and finally she grinned, albeit weakly, and held Oumar's hands between her palms to thank him. There is a similar ritual among the Lébou people of Senegal's Cap Vert peninsula. *Ndeup* is a mystical faith-healing ceremony held in the open, and is performed to extract the evil spirit from a person. It is often conducted by women, and involves much dancing and drumming.

Oumar later told me that back home in his old village his family had for generations been able to cure illnesses with their hands. But he then asked me not to mention this to anyone else in Nouakchott, because they might become suspicious...

The last evening was spent at the Maison Française, which was holding some kind of cultural soiree. Oumar made a special effort, and was dressed in very chic Parisian style: smart white shirt, silk tie, and carefully pressed slacks. For my part, Oumar was so embarrassed at the prospect of being seen with a dirtball whose only trousers no longer had a backside, that he gave me an old pair of jeans to wear. We bluffed our way in by saying that we'd been invited by the ambassador's wife (she was apparently well known for liking young men). Following canapes of smoked salmon and liver paté, the gathering of assorted dignitaries and clandestine gatecrashers made their way into the main hall, where the evening's distraction was the screening of a dire Bourbon romance, complete with crinolines and whalebone frocks, the talc-besmirched Marie Antoinette in an array of bouffant coiffures, pompadours and frills, and transparent intrigues galore! Given that we were in Nouakchott, I considered all this to be highly amusing, as did Oumar. Most of the Europeans, though, did not share the joke, and stared accusingly at me each time I sniggered. It was an absurd and wholly enjoyable evening, one that was at once hilarious and sad.

* * *

Having finally ironed out my financial problems, I left Nouakchott for the river Senegal, the southern boundary of the Sahara. Needless to say, I felt extremely excited. As to the north, the southern outskirts of Nouakchott consist of a sprawling expanse of ramshackle huts and tents, on the periphery of which rises a waist-high rubbish tip consisting of stinking rotten food, jagged metal, broken glass and dead dogs. A flock of screaming seagulls circled above, preferring this dump to the nearby Atlantic for their source of food. Unfortunately all too memorable was the pitiful sight of an elderly, veiled woman scavenging through the rubbish for anything remotely of use, while her children kicked saggy footballs and bottles around in the dirt. For me, the rag-picker epitomised Mauritania, both her dreadful plight, and her steady resolve and determination to overcome even the most shameful adversity.

The desert here was flat and, except for a few withered shrubs, featureless. The road itself had recently been tarmacked, and so had not yet had a chance to break up, which, with the strong tailwind, made cycling easy. The sand was a drab, ashen colour, peppered with shiny pebbles and white oyster shells left over from long-gone days of tropical mangrove swamps. Miniature clay mounds moulded by the gradual erosion of sand and wind and flood water rose almost guiltily from the omnipotent sand, sheltering a spattering of compact bushes and shrivelled thorn grasses. Some of the mounds harboured the crumbling entrances to abandoned jackal or hyena burrows. Cracked and splintered branches surrounded these pitiful remnants of life, waiting to be carried away in the next deluge, or more likely, by nomads searching out firewood. The wind howled.

As I cycled, the left horizon shrank closer as large dunes came into view – the western periphery of Erg Trarza. Further on, a dry water course appeared, a flowing river of soft white sand, straddled on the one side by half buried tamarisks and acacia, and on the other by the road. Beyond the old stream rose a belt of beige dunes, and behind this an altogether more imposing ridge of dunes, violent amber in colour. The road skirted these for much of the day.

There is only one major oasis along the road to Rosso (on the banks of the Senegal). Yet even quite recent maps show the latitudes between the river and Nouakchott to be sub-Saharan savannah – the Sahel – which stretches for three thousand miles along the southern fringes of the Sahara to the Red Sea and the Indian Ocean. The name Sahel derives from the Arabic for 'coast' or 'plain' and, in effect, the Sahel is the coastline between a sea of sand and the lands of the Tropics. Until the 1960s, the Mauritanian Sahel supported a thriving population of pastoral nomads, and provided ample grazing for large herds of cattle, sheep and goats. In the last century, the area was part of tropical Africa, and giraffe, cheetah, lion, leopard, antelope, ostrich and even elephant roamed the land. Today, however, the Mauritanian Sahel has been replaced by a flat, arid wasteland, for the Sahara has moved on. Although the expansion of the desert is in part due to natural causes such as drought and the windblown sand from the north, much more damaging has been the human element. Most of the big game, for example, was exterminated by indiscriminate or naïve hunting, and more recently, selective irrigation has deprived much of the land of flood water, destroying first its flora and fauna, and then the irreplaceable top soil and humus, thereby turning good farmland into desert in a matter of years. More than anything else, it is ignorance of the dynamics of deserts and of the needs of the savannah that has hastened the destruction of the Sahel. By way of example, in 1959, the outgoing French authorities, in cooperation with the fledgling Mauritanian government, determined to wage war against what they perceived as being the greatest threat to their agricultural programmes – birds. Altogether, an incredible forty million 'millet-eating birds' were destroyed across southern Mauritania and northern Senegal, using a burlesque combination of explosives, nets, and flame throwers. Needless to say, this farcical operation did nothing to prevent the desert from advancing, and in actual fact, the agriculture that it was supposed to protect itself played a part in quickening the onset of desertification. Indigenous vegetation was destroyed both to make way for the planned millet fields and also to provide firewood for the new settlers. The new deep wells in turn encouraged the proliferation of animal stock, which led to overgrazing.

The figures speak for themselves. In 1963, the Sahara covered an estimated 5.6 million square kilometres. By 1988, the area had almost doubled to 9.1 million, and still the desert grows. In Mauritania, 80% of the country's grassland has been destroyed over the last two decades, and on the rare occasions when it rains, over ninety percent of the water evaporates.

The fate of the area that I was cycling through was starkly illustrated by the sight of a complete camel skeleton lying bleached and half-buried in the sand, exactly as the poor beast had fallen. Its head was bent back in a contortion of agony, and several of its ribs lay scattered around, presumably having been dragged there by vultures or other carrion-eaters. The skull still had all its teeth, and around the eye sockets, small patches of dry parchment-skin flapped in the wind. A small token of hope: two dusty myrtle saplings sprouted from what would have been the camel's underbelly, nurtured in sand fertilized by flesh and blood.

Towards evening the bright orange sands of Erg Trarza dominated completely. The wind had by now blown away the dust, washing the sky bright blue for the first time in days. The road veered eastwards towards the small village of Tiguent, once an important trading centre in gum arabic, which was collected from *Acacia arabica* by Brakna and Trarza Moors. Here, thick orange sand crept over the road, although the tarmac underneath still made cycling possible. I reached the village as the sun was setting. It was a disconsolate place. There were no palm trees, no pools of fresh water, and only a few concrete shacks and tents scattered on the sand. To the north and east, dunes loomed ominously. Some distance below their surface lay the remains of fences that had been hastily erected a few years ago, in a futile attempt to prevent the sand's relentless march. In places, roof tops were still visible, but only just. Southern Mauritania once consisted of 'stabilised' dunes, in parts conducive to cultivation. In many areas now, however, the dunes are reactivating, like skeletons rising from their graves, and are even threatening to cross the river into Senegal.

To my left, a couple of goatherds in indigo robes were walking their animals back to a *friq* pitched in the distance. At the end of the village, I came to the 'Poste Gendarmerie Nationale Tiguent': two concrete pillboxes, hardly five metres square, with turquoise venetian blinds that hung limply from gaping holes that were once windows. A couple of gendarmes greeted me. Thiam Youssef, the older of the two, was a tall and skinny Moor with unkempt hair, scraggy goatee, moustache and sunglasses. The other, a Negro named Diallo Adama Yero, never stopped grinning, despite the desolation. Both guards wore the usual green battledress, boots and berets. They were very friendly, and invited me to stay for the night. I accepted. As we talked, we were joined by one of the blue goatherds, and the conversation switched to a discussion of goats. Manga Suba, the shepherd, and his brother, owned about twenty animals. Like many Sahelian herders, Manga believed that goats are testimony to the wisdom of Allah for having created such a wonderful machine that it can transform waste paper and other refuse into good milk. The guards thought otherwise, saying that goats were a nuisance because they ate anything and everything, including Thiam Youssef's beret a few months back.

* * *

The desert rain fell stealthily that night as I walked sleeplessly around on the hot sand. The drops fell like a million tiny crystals, glinting in the starlight.

* * *

The morning air smelt fresh and sweet as it drifted gently about my nostrils. The sand was still wet. Shards of glistening water hung from my bicycle's frame. The sky was a rich ultramarine, reflected in a large shallow puddle which had formed on the road between the two huts, and from which a goat was drinking. The guards were hunched at the door of the other hut, joking bawdily as they ate from a large tin pot.

'The rain! The rain!' exclaimed Thiam Youssef as I appeared. 'Allah is indeed great, praise be to Allah!'

He said a prayer.

Within an hour, however, the desert was once more dry and dusty, and nothing remained in testimony to this most precious desert rain except the grins that remained fixed on the faces of my hosts. For them, the years of drought were almost at an end.

Breakfast consisted of half-cooked camel stew. The meat was sandy, tough and difficult to chew, but it made a welcome change from stale bread and peanuts. Under great protests from the guards, who wanted me to stay with them a few more days, I said goodbye and started off on my final day in the desert, not entirely oblivious to the irony of leaving it on the occasion of the first rain.

A few kilometres from Tiguent, the orange dunes cascaded onto and over the road. All the time the dunes were growing taller and larger. I stopped at the foot of one particularly high ridge to climb the 200ft to the top. Its surface was unreal: perfect ripples gently stroked by the shadows of the wind that had formed and moved the dunes at its will. They were the most perfectly formed dunes I'd ever seen. A single thorn bush was growing half way up, drawing water from deep aquifers. At the top, sand was being blown horizontally off the edge dividing northeast from southwest, slowly pushing the desert further south still. The view was stunning. To the north and east, the dunes rolled on like clouds over valleys, endless. To the south, a belt of orange dust ringed their periphery, and beyond, over the dry watercourse, spread a grey expanse mottled with dull green shrubs.

The road wound on through more and more bushes, some growing in distinctly brown patches of clayish sand. Then a few old trees appeared, and the road crossed firmer hillocks and troughs of rock and soil. In the hollows on either side of the road the odd well stood guard over small patches of vegetation, patches that were to grow larger and greener as I sped on south. Then, at around midday, and some forty kilometres from the river Senegal, low tussocks of prickly-seed grass appeared. This *khram-khram* grass is generally taken by geographers to mark the end of the hyper-arid desert and the beginning of the true southern Sahel. I had come to the Sahara on a sudden impulse. I had come to the Sahara wanting to see a land of sand and camels and oases, but I was now leaving it having encountered the desert of the mind of which I had been so ignorant, and the desert of dust of which I was made and would in turn become. It was hard to believe that this part of my journey was nearly over, and I could not help but feel a sense of anticlimax. My home for the last two months was rolling gradually away under the wheels of my bicycle.

The first of several settlements appeared, either temporary or abandoned. Several were little more than a few oddly placed rocks with clusters of collapsed reed fences. Further on, I passed larger villages, with perhaps a hundred inhabitants in each. The dwellings were made of reed or matted woven grass, strung over wooden hoops that rose from the smooth sandy soil like bronze igloos. Some had branches placed on their rooves to secure the huts in high wind, and many had fences, not only around the few pitiful vegetable and sorghum plots, but around the huts themselves to keep away the pilfering goats. Stick-legged children with shorn scalps, long sad faces and protruding bellies walked about somewhat rigidly, wearing plastic sandals and torn and very dirty hessian smocks. In the 'gardens', fenced with the old sacks of aid-donated rice and flour, their mothers tended plots of vegetables, watering them lovingly and perhaps vainly from blackened kettles. Not only is their work hindered by the arid conditions and the hungry goats, but by plagues of rats and locusts, and the risk of freak, cruel rainstorms that can flatten and destroy crops within minutes.

Here and there a few donkeys stared indifferently at my passing from the shade of palm trees growing on 'stabilised' dunes. I saw no new saplings, though, and so once these remaining dusty trees finally collapse to the ground, and the remains of the settlements are blown away, there will no longer be any reminder of the greenery and the villages that once were – all will have been reclaimed by the desert. Already now, some trees were half-buried by the sand – trees of twenty or thirty metres buried up to their necks, with only a few branches protruding to remind one of the past. The Tagant region to the east has suffered similarly. Its name, ironically nowadays, means 'forest'. As I passed through the villages, no one would appear to cajole or chase or shout, no one to smile or to cry, to remind me that they were my brothers and sisters and that they too were still alive in this stupid and confusing world.

Further south still, the once sporadic tussocks of grass, clumps of acacia and palms began to get more frequent. I saw two donkeys trying, unsuccessfully, to mate under a clump of spiny trees, whilst a group of children laughed and prodded them with sticks. I was finally entering the valley lands of the river Senegal. But the river level over the past 30 years has sunk by over half, to the lowest since records began in

1904, and the river has not flooded for decades. Only within a few kilometres of the river was there really anything of consequence. Here, its waters were being used to irrigate plantations of sorghum, for a while thwarting the evil ambitions of the Sahara. This is the land of the black sedentary tribes. Their homes, so typical of black Africa, are made of straw and stone, topped with thatched parasol rooves. It was the first time I'd seen 'proper' reed huts. I came finally to Rosso, capital of the Trarza region. The town is situated near the mouth of the river Senegal, and – along with other riverine towns such as Keur Massene and Kaedi – in the old colonial days supplied food to much of French West Africa. In the years following independence, however, Rosso and the Trarza region have suffered acutely from the droughts, and in consequence Mauritania now only produces about five percent of its own food requirements, the shortfall being imported from Senegal and elsewhere. Yet Rosso was a lively place, even in the midday heat. There were people everywhere, the majority of whom were black. Veils were a rare sight, and women sauntered about almost flirtingly. A lot of care seemed to have been lavished on appearances: an array of skillfully sculptured hairdos, heavy jewellery, brilliantly coloured scarves and body wraps, semi-precious stone necklaces, gold chains and other jewellery.

An old Fulani sage walked past, followed by a cringing and downcast young man. The sage, all of seventy or eighty years old, had a knotted and wrinkled face, and a rubbery nose that he picked at with his fingers. Under his tattered oily turban and mushroom straw hat – a smaller version of the Riffian sombrero – he wore a broad but toothless grin, and a blue denim shirt. My remaining ouguiya bought a bottle of fizz and a bag of peanuts, leaving a few coins which I gave to a fat grinning dwarf who'd insisted on following me throughout the town singing: '*Toubab, Toubab, m'sieur le Touba-beu!*' Having spent all my money, I made my way to the river. It was a brown sliver whose northern shore was festooned with stinking lines of drying fish. A few lazy boatmen wandered around, touting for business. Above it all, seagulls cried or wept. Standing on the clay bank, gazing out at the murky waters sifting slowly by, at last I allowed myself to be overcome by the most absurd realisation that I had actually crossed the Sahara on a bicycle!

CHAPTER ELEVEN

SENEGAL

Passing the desertes is the land of the sileos and the nomades
which be people bestiall without forsyght and goes nakyd...

Roger Barlow, A brief summe of geographie, *c. 1540-41*

'Welcome to Senegal!' boomed the customs officer. Playfully, he
punched my chest, before slapping me on the back with a hand the size
of a saucepan. I winced.

'Yes indeed, *monsieur*, it is true that we are in fact the most
wholesome country of all Africa. Oh, do relax, *monsieur*, relax.'

My ignorance of Senegal, as I wandered aimlessly around the frontier
town of Rosso (it shares its name with its Mauritanian counterpart on
the opposite shore) was astonishing. The little I did know was the
universal stereotype of reed huts peopled by naked tribes of cannibals
who, when not busy firing poisoned arrows at pith-helmeted explorers
in steamy jungles, would be the hunters of vast herds of African game
that thundered across endless prairie. Senegal, I had imagined, was a
place where I would hear the pounding drums and strange chanting of
skeletal witchdoctors dressed in reed skirts, swirling and stamping
their feet amidst great clouds of dust. The rest of my pitiful knowledge,
I'd picked up in Mauritania, viz: a disquietingly large number of tales
concerning corruption and bribery; of roadside strip searches by hu-
mourless soldiers armed to the teeth with automatic weapons; and of
a continent almost constantly embroiled in revolutions, coups d'états,
civil wars and dictatorships. The Africa of my mind was also a land of
extreme poverty, synonymous with drought and famine, cholera and
malaria, and a thousand other diseases with unpronouncable names.
That much is true. In the Canary Islands, whilst biding my time before
the flight to Mauritania, I had met a Scot who had just returned from a
six month trek around West Africa. He told me of having been robbed

at gunpoint in Nigeria and, another time, at knifepoint. I ignored his advice not to travel here at all, though, because he seemed to be the kind of person who inevitably attracted trouble and misfortune. He was currently recovering from his sixth bout of malaria, and as a result his skin had a deathly pallor to it, tinged with green, and for three days he'd trembled like a leaf.

In common with other Sahelian countries – sandwiched between fiery desert and steamy tropics – the topography of Senegal is largely devoid of extremes. Much of it is flat and featureless; bush-speckled savannah that covers an area about the size of England and Scotland put together. Yet for all its visible poverty, the gods have blessed Senegal with four large rivers, where the low-lying plains and semi-arid scrub give way to more archetypal African terrain of tropical mangrove swamps, exotic palms and impenetrable forests of bamboo, mahogany and silkwood. The rivers – Senegal, Sine-Saloum, Gambia and Casamance – are the lifeblood for over two and a half million pastoralists, one third of the population. Without its waters, Senegal would undoubtedly be as barren as Mauritania.

The Senegal, of course, is the largest and most important of the four rivers. It rises in the Fouta Djalon highlands of Guinea, and flows for over a thousand miles to the charming colonial city of Saint-Louis, founded in the 17th century by Louis XIV. On the northern shores of the Senegal, the dunes of the Sahara finally end their death-dealing march, their sands and dusts flowing downstream into the Atlantic. The Senegal is the fabled 'River of Gold' that European explorers sought for so long, and ultimately in vain. In ancient times, river tribes both feared and worshipped the spirit god Nyamia Ama, Lord of rain, storms, lightning and gold. Bondou, a tiny mud village 300 miles upriver past the Devil's Gorge, was where, according to Arab legend, gold sprouted like maize every August at the moment when the river was in flood. The river Senegal is not only a gift from the gods, but is itself a god, to whom sacrifices were once offered, much as ancient Saharawi tribes prostrated themselves to the might of the ocean-desert.

West Africa is rich in legend. To European minds, the greatest of them all was that of the fabulous Malian city of Timbuctoo which lured, like moths to the flame of a candle, so many explorers to their doom. Ever since the Portuguese landed here in the 15th century, West Africa has been a land much stumbled across by incompetent explorers and adventurers, many of whom had come in search of Timbuctoo. Almost without exception their forays were disastrous affairs, manifestly cursed by their woeful knowledge of the land, by disease, by tactlessness and arrogance which inflamed native passions, and by roving

Moorish and Tuareg warriors from the desert. Contemporary maps were necessarily works of fantasy and conjecture, and Timbuctoo – that false Eldorado – drifted aimlessly and uselessly. The only anchor to Europe's knowledge of this corner of the Dark Continent was the fact that Timbuctoo was known to nestle on the banks of the Niger, but this only added to the confusion. The river that the Tuareg called *N-ger-n-gereo* – the 'River of Rivers' – was a mystery almost as unfathomable as the golden city itself. Herodotus, the Father of History no less, began the confusion by wrongly stating that the Niger was a branch of the Nile, while Pliny the Elder believed that the Nile had its head in a 'mountain of lower Mauretania, not far from the [Atlantic] Ocean'. The Arabs only added to the confusion by calling the Niger *al-Nil al-Kebir*, the Great Nile. To further muddy the waters, Ptolemy fathered another fallacy by stating that the Niger flowed westwards, and by the Middle Ages and the time of Leo Africanus, it was commonly believed that both the rivers Gambia and Senegal were its mouths. Alas, it was a falsehood that brought dozens if not hundreds of expeditions to a bloody and ignominious end. As the Huguenot John Barbot recounted:

> through continual toils and hardships the best part of the sailors sickened and dy'd, whilst others perish'd by the intolerable scorching heat, which threw them into burning fevers; and those who had been proof against that intolerable fatigue, were destroy'd either by the vile perfidiousness of the native Blacks of the country, or devoured alive by alligators...

Only in 1796 was the riddle of the rivers finally unravelled, when the indefatigable Scottish explorer Mungo Park reached the Niger and correctly reported its eastward course, thereby proving conclusively that it could not possibly also be the Senegal or the Gambia. Few, however, chose to believe him (Park was only 24 at the time), and as late as 1820 the *Proceedings* of the African Association of London still blithely reported the Niger's westward flow.

The confusion and ignorance was encapsulated for all time by Senegal's very name. According to an apocryphal Wolof tale, it was an anonymous – but above all witless – explorer in the mould of Livingstone who, on reaching the bank of the river, pointed across it and asked some nearby fishermen what it was called. *Li suñu gal le*, they replied: 'that's our boat.'

* * *

Rosso's market swarmed in a profusion of colours and forms, sounds and smells. I was stunned at the contrast with Mauritania's dusty and dirty austerity. There were shops and stalls everywhere, in a curious blend of concrete shacks and thatched mud-walled huts that epitomised the clash of the Ancient and the New. Vendors of medicinal roots and potions squatted beside facades bedecked with great piles of garish laundry baskets and Taiwanese flip-flop sandals, which Moorish merchants bought by the sackful to transport back to Nouakchott. From China, hi-tech electronic gear shared pride of place among barrowfuls of gnarled ginger roots and much prized (and narcotic) kola nuts. From rafters hung shiny aluminium saucepans and kettles, strung together on chains that rattled loudly in the hot, summer breeze. Old men, serene in voluminous white cotton, sat or stood impassively, observing with wry smiles the shuffling cross-border trade.

A fat, harrassed-looking businessman, with blackened rotten teeth and a small suitcase perched on his shoulder, grinned inanely at the itinerant dentists, trying as best he could to avoid their sarcastic goads and offers. Elsewhere, drapers dealt in colourful *faneaus* (textiles) smuggled in from the Gambia and Guinea. On every street corner, down every dark alleyway, by the police station, in the middle of the street, hawkers stood and shouted out their wares: cashews and caramelled peanuts, mangos, biscuits, soda pop and ice, stamps and envelopes, grilled fish, and even sulky budgerigars. There was a choice of German or Austrian UHT milk, sweet white potatoes, over-ripe aubergines, sweet peppers, squash, okra, sun-dried tomatoes, onion tops, and fat chickens – ripe for the plucking – which squawked disconcertedly from trussed-up bundles of feathers.

The disparity with famine-struck life a mile or so across the river was glaring, and it was shocking to discover that much of the staple foodstuffs, such as rice and flour, actually came *from* Mauritania, as illegally smuggled foreign aid. It was a perversity that helped to explain recent fighting that had flared along the fertile river frontier. The violence had arisen over disputes concerning the allocation of the ever-dwindling waters, which in turn led to bloody land feuds and a spate of cross-border raids. In reponse, both nations imposed punitive tariffs and quotas, resulting in the decline of Rosso's importance on both sides of the river. In 1989, bloody racial clashes in Nouakchott and Dakar led to the neighbouring states severing all links, diplomatic and commercial. As I write, I find it hard to imagine Rosso devoid of people. Perhaps it is because it was the first Senegalese town that I ever set foot in, that my strongest image of it has always been one of a great, bustling warmth. Five years on, the border remains impassable, and the river

Senegal, no longer an artery of commercial and cultural interchange, now serves only to divide.

* * *

I bought a few apples and headed off in the direction of Saint-Louis, one hundred kilometres downriver. It was late afternoon, and the road was occupied only by a handful of lolloping donkey carts and the odd bush taxi. These were dilapidated Peugeot 504s, seemingly held together only by lengths of rope and vinyl sheeting. They spluttered and swayed drunkenly under rocking towers of luggage.

From Rosso, the road hooks away from the river to avoid the marshland Djoudj National Park, a wildfowl reserve created in 1971 on a large delta island between the river and the Gorom stream. In winter it is home to a kaleidoscopic cornucopia of migratory birds, recently arrived from across the great desert: pink flamingo, enormous flocks of white pelican, crowned cranes, yellow-billed storks from Morocco, bustard, spoonbill, wagtails, garganey ducks, and a whole lot more. I could easily see what attracted them. The land was lush: grassland streaked with sparkling streams, sugar cane plantations edged with tall aureole palms, and other trees hung thick with creepers and vines. Between then stretched immense fields of wheat and barley, over which flocked countless thousands of birds. I started whistling, and it occured to me that it was the first time that I had done so for over a month. There were birds everywhere, in velvet and scarlet, gold and purple, amber and blue. The last straggler sandmartins darted between nine foot tall reed beds, along with weavers, red bishops, and a solitary long-legged lily-trotting jacana. My vision was overwhelmed in a flood of radiant myrtle, jade and emerald greens, shades to which my eyes were so utterly unused after so long in the Sahara. The air, no longer dusty and harsh, was scented and sweet. The evening hung pregnant with moisture, crackling with bird song and the chirruping of grasshoppers in the reeds that verged vast rice paddies. The sun – a rich, simple red ball – was obscured by a hazy mist that swamped all but the northern horizon.

A couple of firefinches took interest in my passing, darting after me for a while, ducking and swooping, dancing and singing. There were flowers also, with butterflies and spectral dragonflies. Everything was so tranquil, so peaceful, with the reassuring rustle of wind-stirred leaves as the setting sun flickered through gently swaying treetops. It was everything that I had ever imagined a savannah evening to be, and it represented everything that I had ever desired in the desert. The mood of the place was that of an autumnal wave-lapped beach, with its gentle breeze and the pebbles murmuring on the sand. I cannot describe the elation I felt when I finally settled down beside one of the many irrigation canals skirting the Lac de Guiers, with my head resting in the cool, fresh grass.

The smoky morning air drifted lazily by, the mist shimmering golden on the tarmac under a bright, flaxen sky. The birds refound their voices and the crickets stretched their legs. In the distance, a hyena let loose a short howl. I yawned, a sleepless owl hooted, and slowly another day on the African savannah gathered its relentless pace. Cycling, though, was tough, for at times the wind gusted so fiercely that I was obliged to stop to await a lull. It was the first headwind I'd encountered since entering the Western Sahara, and a sure sign that I had reached the southern limit of the dessicating trade wind. In the humidity (the wind blew from the Atlantic), the heat rained down on my head like leaden cannonballs. I was uncomfortably surprised at quite how much my physical shape had deteriorated in the desert, despite the several days' rest in Nouakchott. I found that I had little energy, and even less willpower, to combat the hindering wind. My bicycle seemed to have put on weight, in spite of the fact that I was no longer obliged to carry seven, eight or nine litres of water. In other words, things were soon going to have to come to an end.

Life in the first village was already well underway when I arrived. It was every inch a scene from the Africa of Kipling or Livingstone: a few palm trees, a lot of dust, and about three dozen sturdy mud huts topped with parasols of grey rush thatch. In the granaries, fenced off to thwart the thieving goats, stacks of millet heads awaited conversion into semolina or couscous. Yet now – early June, with the harvest still four, long months away – the stocks were almost exhausted, and the hungry season loomed near.

In a clearing, shaded by a muddy date palm and a gnarled and barren mango tree, a gang of barefoot children with shorn scalps were busy chasing chickens around a well. On seeing me, they rushed up yelling and screaming, to touch my arms and my legs as well as the bicycle, giggling and grinning wide, ivory-toothed smiles. Anything I said or did elicited great merriment. When I pretended to be a gorilla, one little boy laughed so much that he curled up helplessly on the ground and hollered louder still. In all the commotion, mothers and sisters appeared, standing politely on the periphery in a colourful blaze of *faneau* wrappers, holding their hands over their mouths as they pointed. Beside them sat an old man, bald and very dark-skinned, who chuckled as he observed the spectacle. He wore a simple brown smock with cut-away sleeves, and leaned on a long, black staff. At one point, he motioned that I come over to him, and as I did so, he got up and walked into the village. I followed him past another small clearing, which housed the charred remains of a small fire, a pile of tree roots, an old truck tyre, and a sack of rice or flour. Another clearing resounded to the rhythm of half a dozen women pounding millet with six-foot wooden pestles, while a few others panned the flour into brightly coloured plastic bowls. I followed the man to the low entrance of a small reed hut, from which he reappeared holding a dish of cold water and a couple of mangos. He handed them to me in a gruff, fatherly sort of way.

'*Jere jef*,' I said, in a maiden attempt at Wolof: thank you. He led me back to the well where I was mobbed by the children. They, of course, wanted their photographs taken.

As I cycled away, with the steady thumping of the pestles resounding in my ears, the vegetation suddenly disappeared. In its place stretched an awfully familiar plain, arid and grey. It was dotted with scant few tamarisks, acacias, and the telegraph poles that ran beside the road. Further on, amidst spiky clumps of *khram-khram* grass, lay the skeleton of a hump-necked zebu bull. I was also shocked to notice, far away to the east, sand dunes looming over the horizon. Further on, planted amidst a great wash of sand, a tin plaque prohibited the laying of fires in the forest. As far as I could see, there remained nothing of the kind. Although I knew that I was temporarily leaving the irrigated lands of the Senegal valley, that the land here should be so barren came as a depressing revelation. Since 1950, the Sahel has lost over half its trees.

As I paused in reflection and tiredness, tall bobbing figures emerged from the heat haze to my left. As they approached, I could make out the lithe forms of four women, who carried baskets of firewood on their heads. The sweat glistened on their skins. At first, the two teenage girls skipped and laughed, but on seeing me fell quiet. Their mothers only glanced once, then never looked again. It is not uncommon for women to have to walk over five hours to collect enough firewood to last barely two days. It is one of the many perversities of the Sahel that it is often cheaper and easier to fill a cauldron with food, than it is to obtain the fuel to heat it. Much as the Sahara was once a land quite different to what it is today, so West Africa and the Sahel were also much more verdant in times past. Archaeologists have discovered that the nomadic tribes who first settled here around 800BC were attracted by a profusion of jungle vegetation and prey. Polybius, writing in 146BC, described the region as vast tracts of dense forest, jungle and bush, and even at the turn of the century the land was in parts so thickly grown that it was impossible to cross.

As the road continued along the stark succession of telegraph poles, the soil grew paler and dustier. In places, even the tarmac disappeared under the sand. I passed more signs announcing nonexistent forests, and more skeletons. The gradual dessication of northern Senegal, despite being relatively well protected from Mauritania's marching dunes by the river, is a story that threatens to become as tragic as that of its Moorish neighbour. Personally, I found that seeing the process of desertification only half-complete was infinitely more depressing than to see the final outcome. To see the condemned is always more heart-rending than to see the already dead.

The day wore on and the road seemed endless.

As I neared Saint-Louis, a few small settlements and a little fresher foliage began to return. They were followed by healthier palm groves, larger villages, and before long the road was twisting around and past small but welcome lakes. I passed marshes and banked irrigation ditches spread like cobwebs, splicing the land into a patchwork of colour as the road once more neared the sluggish waters of the river. I would have liked to have swum in one of the creeks, populated by small but resplendent malekite kingfishers, and haunted by the howls of sandcats and jackals. But on arriving in the leafy seclusion of one grassy cove, sheltered by sedges and rushes and water hyacinth, I saw two bare-breasted old women, who had already spotted me, scrubbing their washing in the drab bayou waters. They smiled and waved, but I must have stared gormlessly, because they then pointed to their breasts as though to say: 'Poor little boy, have you really never seen a pair of these before?'

* * *

Saint-Louis is one of those magical places that can safely be placed in the same league as Havana and Venice, Fès and old Alexandria. At first glance no more than a low-down huddle of palm trees and terracotta tiled rooves sheltering helplessly on a digital sandy island at the mouth of the Senegal, Saint-Louis seems almost to have arrived at the coast by having floated downstream from some mysterious inland kingdom. Here, the hot and murky waters of the Senegal – sluggish at the end of their languorous journey – merge with the cool blue of the Atlantic and its rolling peasoup fogs. Saint-Louis is a haven for world-weary spirits, a marvellously decrepit old relic where the heavy-eyed traveller can slouch around aimlessly and carelessly, his bones soaking up an intoxicating atmosphere of decay.

The town was founded early in the 17th century by France's flamboyant 'sun king', Louis XIV, and was named in honour of his 13th century namesake, the fabled leader of the Sixth Crusade. It was the Portuguese, however, who (as usual) had been the first Europeans to set foot here, when in the 1440s the caravels of Lancarote disembarked at the sand-barred mouth of the river. But it was the French who, attracted by a fine natural harbour and easily defended position, had the foresight to settle, when the *Compagnie Normande*, under the instigation of Cardinal Richelieu, established a small slaving post on the island in the year 1638. 'If you give me six lines written by the most honest man,' boasted the Cardinal, 'I will find something in them to hang him.'

Situated at the junction of desert and tropics, river and ocean, Saint-Louis was an ideal place from which to begin the colonisation of West Africa. Perhaps more than the French had ever dared imagine, the site afforded a position of immeasurable strategic import, especially over the commercial intercourse with the hinterland. For over two millennia prior to their arrival, a thriving network of trading routes had existed within Senegambia, where cloth, amber, salt, gaudy trinkets, and later European guns and hardware, were exchanged for gum arabic, ivory, Phoenician glass beads, ostrich feathers, guinea pepper, gold dust and, most notoriously but profitably, slaves. Taking advantage of these trade routes, the French were quick to assert dominance over the burgeoning trade in 'black ivory', which necessitated the foundation of Saint-Louis herself in 1658. From then on – under the guidance of Saint-Louis – the expansion of French West Africa was prodigious, and by the turn of this century encompassed an astonishing 1.8 million square miles.

The dubious perfume of the French conquest lingers still. French is the language of commerce, the currency (CFA) is linked to the franc, and bicycles jostle with battered Citroën and Peugeot jalopies in narrow and angular streets. Many still carry the names of eminent Frenchmen: rue Nicolas Carnot, quai Henri Jay, rue André Lebon, place Faidherbe, rue Blanchot... But most striking of all is the charming, almost quaint, hybrid architecture, whose bewitching old-time aura owes as much to French architects as to the town's largely Muslim inhabitants, to whose wishes the French graciously deferred by forbidding any construction taller than the Grand Mosque. As a result, very few buildings rise above three storeys, so giving the town its uniquely down-beat style. Typical are the beige-painted townhouses of the Louis Phillippe period, with their sienna-tiled rooves, cool interior patios, verandas, galleries, and charming wooden balconies that crumble slowly into the steamy Atlantic mists. Others have balconies of intricate iron fretwork, with wooden shutters placed over once-elegant arcades, the walls of which are plastered a dusky pink. There are battered wooden doors painted river-green or blue, with brick arches over which hang old brass lanterns. There's an inescapable atmosphere of warm, decaying, but above all, aristocratic grandeur.

Saint-Louis' *belle époque* is personified by its older womenfolk, invariably dressed as though every day were a Sunday. With their pince-nez spectacles, silk scarves and cloche hats, they look as though they could all have been Josephine Baker in Paris' Roaring Twenties. These refined ladies were children at the tail end of the *signare* epoch, a legacy of the Europeans that will last forever. The *signares* [from the Portuguese *senhora*] were the 'Children of Senegal' from whom so many of Saint-Louis' latter-day inhabitants descend. They were a wealthy and privileged élite of half-castes, fathered by Portuguese or French merchants who had married, against the wishes of their superiors, à *la mode du pays*. Of course, the interbreeding created ties between motherland and colony – desirable or otherwise – that came over and above the more usual relationship of conqueror and conquered. In the wake of Europe's summer of revolution of 1848, imperial Saint-Louis was even granted limited self-government, and was allowed to send a deputy to the National Assembly in Paris. Another spin-off of the *signares* was the increasingly lavish attention that French merchants showered on the town (including great shipments of brandy, it is said), making of Saint-Louis quite the most pleasant place in all West Africa. The town was a welcome haven for beleaguered and foot-weary soldiers to escape to on leave from the uncomfortable and disease-ridden interior. As Jean Baptiste Durand, a visitor late in the 18th century, remarked:

> the Isle of St. Louis contains a civilized, humane, gentle, and economical people, who are consequently happy... The women [have] an invincible inclination for love and voluptuousness... and they may be said to combine all the perfections of beauty.

It seems to me that Saint-Louis is a town that makes a point of being seen to enjoy its life.

I was stopped at a police roadblock just outside town, on a wide boulevard flanked with a few 19th century buildings, scented palm groves, orchards, and imposing clay walls crowned with hibiscus, bougainvillea and coils of barbed wire. Opposite the roadblock was a girl's secondary school, which pleased the two officers no end, mainly because they were drunk. They greeted me warmly (like all drunkards), making it a condition of my passing that I drank with them. On the table outside their hut were two opaque plastic bottles filled with 'toddy-wine': the unfiltered, fermented sap of palm trees. Three other bottles, empty, rolled about drunkenly on the pavement, tended to by swarms of wasps.

The officers guessed immediately that I was British (who else would care to cycle across the Sahara?), and when I mentioned Manchester, they proceeded to interrogate me about George Best, Bobby Charlton, and Diego Maradona. As to their booze: 'Welcome to Africa Guinness,' they announced, before, in unison, as though a spell had been cast, they fell asleep!

Almost without exception, every traveller to West Africa has remarked on palm wine. Herodotus, typically, was the first, albeit in the context of its being a vital ingredient in Ancient Egypt's most perfected embalming procedures – it was used to cleanse the abdomen (*plus ça change...*) The 17th century English explorer Richard Jobson seemed to like the stuff, for he judged it to be 'toothsome' in taste, and 'wholesome' in operation. In 1804, a certain Mr. Martyn travelling with Mungo Park's second (and ill-fated) expedition to the river Niger, was kind enough to elaborate on its effects: 'Whitbread's beer is nothing to what we get at this place, as I feel by my head this morning, having been drinking all night with a Moor, and ended by giving him an excellent thrashing.'

My evening was spent in the agreeable company of a cheerful Catholic clergyman from Charleston, South Carolina, who was known to the kids loitering outside the cathedral compound as Papa. Papa was ordained in 1952, at the time when the American Civil Rights movement was still in its infancy, and when Senegal was still a French colony. Papa saw many parallels between African and Black American history and, although mild-mannered and perhaps overly polite, he did not shy away from expressing his sometimes outspoken views (for example, he thought it necessary to *fight* one's oppressors, rather than absorb their pressure in the hope of eventually flinging them off like an elastic band. Tibetan culture, Papa believed, was doomed to extinction by the Tibetan's refusal to fight). His attitude had brought him three spells in South Carolina State Penitentiary.

We discussed politics at great length in the somewhat incongruous stately luxury of the mission's drawing room. It was panelled from floor to ceiling with carved mahogany, and was cluttered with sombre, over-polished late 19th century furniture. The room smelt of floor polish and varnish, and was adorned with cruxifixes, various icons, and even a few animist masks. The portraits of fathers-past were hung in strict chrono-logical sequence around the walls. To complete my culture shock, we were served icy strawberry cordials in crystal glasses by a pretty maid dressed all in black but for her pinafore, and later some After Eight mints from a silver platter decorated with lace doyleys. 'Well then, bottoms up!' said Papa.

Papa's task, in a country where over 80% of the population are Muslim, and where the French had often shown themselves to be more than a little intolerant of the religion, seemed to me to be futile. How, I asked, could he still harbour hope for what was still officially his mission? Papa explained that even in these post-colonial times, the Catholic minority was respected and tolerated by the Muslims, a truism that compared favourably with my personal experiences in Morocco and Mauritania. In any case, Islam Senegalese-style is much less rigid than elsewhere (as regards the drinking of alcohol, for example). To underline his point, Papa called upon Léopold Sédar Senghor, Senegal's widely admired first president who was himself Catholic. Religion, said Papa, is a personal matter in Senegal. Herein lies a lesson for those of us too blinkered by dogma to live the tolerance preached by both Islam and Christianity.

I left Papa at dusk, with vague directions for the home of a Dutch-American family who lived in Sor: the newer, and therefore classier, continental part of town (it is less afflicted by mosquitoes). A few hours later, having become hopelessly lost despite the directions, I pressed the intercom-button on a metal gate, and waited. The gate was battle-ship grey, and was partly covered with a drape of arterial bougainvillea. A sign advised: 'Beware of the Dog'. The cartoon rottweiler made to snarl; gone are the days of white supremacy.

Over a meal of imported fish fingers, canned potatoes and processed peas, I discovered that the husband worked for an irrigation project on the river Senegal. He'd been working abroad for some ten years now, and, like Albert and the others in Nouakchott, was woefully depressed about his work. The lack of urgency betrayed by the government and its officials frustrated him greatly, and as a result he sorely missed the calm efficiency of Holland. I also sensed that my uninvited intrusion – even if only for the night – was awkward, and so the dinner ended in silence, save for the snuffling of the corgi (so much for the rottweiler), and the family's grey parrot which kept squawking: '*Bonjourah, signorah!*'

We were waited upon by Bass, the butler, who had only two weeks before moved up from the Casamance with his sister (the Casamance is a region of animists and Catholics, and therefore preferable for a family of Calvanist sensibilities). Bass was thin, but slow and lumbering in his movements. His sister, who had been enlisted as the family nanny, bore him no resemblance whatsoever. She had a gigantic backside and a broad, toothy grin, and was quick and supple in her movements. As seems to be fashionable among the Malinké of the south, her lips, gums, and brow were tattooed blue, which was surprisingly fetching. And given her stature, she was the sort of woman to put the fear of God into anyone if she really wanted to, which was why the family had hired her. I could see that she had a hell of a job. The five-year-old monster would stick pens into the Habitat furniture, pick up glasses only to drop them on the tiled floor, tie doll's limbs into my now knotted rastafarian hair, and seemed particularly fond of hurling his Matchbox car collection at my face, and then punching or biting me if I dared tell him to behave.

The morning fog rolling in from the Atlantic smelt salty, and merged easily with my sweat. I set off with Bass, who was to be my guide around Saint-Louis, although it soon turned out that he was as ignorant of the place as I. It was a case of the blind leading the blind.

To get from Sor to the island district of Ndar (Saint-Louis' Wolof name, and the town's oldest quarter), one has to cross an iron cantilever bridge which, incredibly, spanned the Danube until 1897. The bridge is named after General Louis Faidherbe, governor of Senegal in the latter half of the 19th century. His rule saw the great expansion of the colony's frontiers, something which secured the continued prosperity of Saint-Louis' traders. It is an irony that Faidherbe, alongside his old Muslim adversaries who fought him vainly for independence, is nowadays considered to be a father of Senegal, for it was his conquests that finally defined the country's latter-day borders.

Under the bridge, fishing *pirogues* made of hollowed-out trees glided out towards the open sea. They were invariably gaily painted, and many were named after celebrated saints and *marabouts*. The fishermen were dressed in tatty shorts and shirts stained by the ocean breeze, and unveiled great strands of gossamer nets into the river to catch the high tide. A little way up the levee, a group of men were busy dragging billy goats by their tails into the river. They were being washed for the Muslim feast of Aïd el-Kebir, which was drawing near.

Across the bridge, our pockets were assailed by a host of hawkers and beggars, and our noses by the heady aroma of garlic, donkey shit, woodsmoke, freshly baked bread, drying fish and diesel fumes, that drifted like a bag lady's perfume through the narrow streets of Ndar. Other pedlars sat patiently beside piles of grotesquely contorted ginger roots, small bales of mint and precarious pyramids of sweet muskmelons. The equivalent of ten pence bought a delicious grilled mullet. Fifty bought a handful of kola nuts, which I gave Bass as a token of my thanks and friendship.

Ndar is an area thick with ancient tumbledown offices and shopfronts, and dark alleyways that at night might be reminiscent of Paris' XIV^{em}, if only it wasn't for the sand. Tattered old signs read 'Menuserie', 'Boulangerie Laporte' and 'Boucherie'. Narrow dank sidestreets with mysterious doors reveal even more mysterious plaques: 'Fernand Abdallah, Chiropodiste' at number 12; 'René Herrault, Advocat Commerciale' in faded gold leaf at numbers four and five. A fat old woman in a flashy gold and white gown turned and grinned at me as I walked past. Her hands held a string of brown prayer beads. *'Eeeh... Tubabo!'* she cackled, and then pointed. *Toubab* is mildly abusive Wolof slang for an American or European, a word whose origins mean 'to convert'. The term is a legacy of over-zealous French and Portuguese missionaries. Nowdays, the white man is much more likely to encounter zealous Muslims attempting to convert the infidel. It is rôle reversals like this that give many Senegalese their pride.

Rue Blaise Diagne, named after the first Senegalese deputy to the Paris Assembly (an early example of rôle reversal), is home to a flurry of small-time merchants and beggars. Its gutters overflow with rotten vegetables and rancid meat, sewage and plastic. We walked past haberdashers full of neatly stacked rolls of colourful *faneaus*. Their counters were inlaid with brass rules and guides, and small knots of women ummed and aahed, unable to decide as they admired both themselves and the fabric in stainless Sheffield mirrors. Elsewhere, a battered Michelin man watched over the portal of a garage, where several elderly gentlemen in navy blue overalls and skullcaps were sat smoking amidst all the bits and pieces of an engine belonging to a navy blue 2CV. Through a small alleyway I could see large boats and the masts of ocean-going freighters nestling on the blue horizon.

Two bridges – Servatius and Mangin – link the island city of Ndar to the peninsular Barbary Tongue: a 25 kilometre long sand spit, with breeding grounds for endangered Atlantic sea turtle and tortoise at its southern end, and the desert wastes of Mauritania to the north. Only the central section of the Barbary Tongue – immediately facing Ndar – is built-up. Avenue Dodds is the main thoroughfare, a wide street lined with telegraph poles and tall palm trees. It leads north to Saint-Louis' busiest market, the hub of northern Senegal's small-trade. There were women everywhere, shouting, yelling, bartering, haggling, and even squawking if prices were deemed too high. A large woman in an orange Bruce Lee T-shirt waddled by, puckering her purple lips. On her head rocked a bowl containing one fat, slippery fish. Other women balanced baskets containing sheaves of millet or wheat, clothes and even a television. Kids were dragged along behind them, picking their noses or burping.

Fierce market madames – not to be trifled with – bawled out their presence to all and sundry from behind plastic sheets draped with bloody fish steaks. More permanent stalls sold red and green chillis, dried *gejieu* fish, and their owners yelled this or that many CFA. It is always the women who do the selling of home-made produce to make ends meet at the end of the week. It is always the women who do the cooking, the fetching and the carrying, the chopping of wood, the dying and spinning of cotton, the laundry, and the child-rearing. And yet, to my mind, the women also seemed brash, self-confident, and basically happier than their male counterparts. This was in spite of their greatly unequal share of the burden of work, and the fact that the law allows men to take two wives, if they can afford it. The women seemed to appear more relaxed, more at ease, and better sorted out than their male counterparts. Perhaps this is due in part to the old standards of upbringing (submissiveness, docility and modesty) now being cast aside with a fevour that frightened Bass! Wolof and Fulani women are alone among West Africans for not having to undergo the customary clitoridectomy as initiation into womanhood, and perhaps as a result, the rather prim 1950s traveller Elspeth Huxley noted that: 'Husbands are picked, enjoyed, exploited and exchanged with a most un-African laxity'.

By any standards, Wolof women are uncommonly beautiful, and a lot of care is taken about appearances. The *marché* brags an incredible selection of immaculate hairdos: crimped, tied-back, braided, smeared with rancid butter like the Tibetans, Medusa-style snakes, spiky... Many are in styles uncannily similar to those depicted in 5,000 year-old Saharan cave paintings. There is jewellery and adornment to be admired everywhere: red and yellow coconut shell earrings, red-painted finger-nails, gold, silver, and copper bracelets and bangles, hair brooches in every colour, mascara, maroon lipstick and silver rings. Yet nothing is excessive, and very few women appear gaudily dressed or overly made up. Nonetheless, the market, perhaps more so than any other I had seen or was to see, was simply a deluge of colour. Much of it came from the expensive *faneaus* and headcloths that the women wear, a suffusion of whorls, stars, stylised leaves and flowers in dripping shades of venetian red, earthy brown, leafy green, gold and purple. My eyes were spinning through so much colour. Almost all the women still wear the traditional off-the-shoulder dresses, a little like Indian saris – tight around their long legs and loose about the top, accentuating their bottoms, broad backs and long necks. The way they walked (and the men too) was especially beautiful: an impressively graceful, seemingly effortless swaying gait, a world apart from the heavy-legged strut of the *Toubab*. Elspeth Huxley remarked of the Wolof women: 'they glide along dusty streets... like flowers on the move.' Such beauty, especially after the desert and the hidden, constricted aesthetics of the Arab world, was simply soothing. In fact, just like Saint-Louis.

* * *

I left Saint-Louis in the afternoon. The sky was a muggy grey – faded but luminous – under which everything had a bleached or washed-out appearance. This kind of sky is common to all the tropics in the eerie 'hungry season' that greets the onset of the monsoon rains.

To my consternation, the bicycle gears wouldn't engage properly but instead ground disconcertingly as my legs span around in vain. Both the gears and the pedals, it turned out, had been irreparably damaged by sand, and would have to be replaced in Dakar. My only saving thought was that this hadn't happened in the desert. The noise of the gears, of course, attracted attention, and although the crowd that followed me was generally good natured, one man kept grasping my arm very tightly as I tried to cycle away, and hissed: '*Mon ami, mon ami, un cadeau, des* CFA, *donne moi un cadeau, des* CFA, *un cadeau...*'

Enough presents, I thought angrily as my furious pedal strokes finally reconnected with the gears and I was off again, with my 'friend' in hot pursuit. But then, again I came to a halt, this time in deep sand.

'Ah, my friend! My friend, a present for me.'

For the next few hours, I learnt gradually to cope with the gear problems, if not the hustler. He followed me by moped for a whole hour, repeating his demands incessantly, until, finally, I gave in and gave him some money.

The road was mostly sandy, flanked in the outskirts of Saint-Louis with a hotchpotch of open-fronted garages, shops, and a dilapidated suburb of shacks. A short while on the sea mist receded, and hot desert air took its place to smother a landscape of tree-topped hillocks. On looking closer, they turned out not to be hillocks at all, but 'stabilised' sand dunes, scattered with larger mounds of loamy clay and small shrubs. There were only few trees – mostly gum acacia – and plenty of red dust and clay that in the rainy season becomes a slurry through which no vehicle can hope to pass. This land, I found out later, is the western reach of the Ferlo desert.

Now that the initial elation at having crossed the Sahara began to subside, the dry monotony of the land became more depressing. As I cycled, it unfurled only as vast waves of a great undulating greyness, dotted with depressing shades of green and beige. The soil was poor, being entirely dependent on the munificence of the rains that have been coming later and leaving earlier these last few years. The contrast with the irrigated river lands was glaring. Northern Senegal has become the bride of the desert, to be toasted with confetti of yellow sand, and to followed by a bridal train of irreversible desertification. I passed more roadside signs announced no longer existent forests, stubble-beard at most, live dunes at worst.

The road joined the tracks of the 165-mile Saint-Louis to Dakar railway, lined with white picket fencing to keep donkeys and goats at bay. Just past the market town of Louga, a column of vultures turned a tight circle over the horizon, like the spout of a tornado. A few miles closer I counted fifty or sixty of the ugly things – lappet-faced vultures – wheeling up, then swooping down and across the road at breakneck speed. Closer still, I came to the apex of their spinning cloud. There was a donkey carcass lying to one side of the blood-stained road, around which were perhaps another twenty of the birds, squabbling amongst themselves. They were busily devouring what little remained of the donkey, ripping it apart with violent beaks and claws.

It was still windy, and cycling was tiring. The gear problems annoyed me. The humidity was oppressive, and made the heat feel worse than it really was. I realised just how tired I was when I had to dismount and push the bicycle up a gentle incline that would have been child's play a few months earlier. I began for the first time – at least that I can remember – to think fondly of home, and of all the comforts that it could provide. I'd even made a list of all the luxuries I'd craved in the desert, such as marzipan, cold milk, chocolate, beer, and (perversely) *hot* baths. Cycling was now too exhausting and too slow a means of transport, and I had neither the money nor the inclination to travel much further. Tentative plans hatched in Nouakchott of cycling across West Africa to Ghana or Timbuctoo evaporated. I had had my fill of excitement for the time being, and now just needed to rest. It was somewhere around here that I finally decided to put an end to my trip, and to finish in Dakar.

After Louga the landscape became more pleasant, albeit dustier too. There were a few villages, and circles of acacia, tamarinds, spiny jujubes and oily soump trees. The villages consisted of about twenty or thirty huts, built around clearings that often contained a solitary palaver tree. In the past, the huts had been circular and made of straw thatch, but many had now progressed to angular tin and zinc, which to my eyes replaced a homely charm with a somewhat slummy appearance. Nevertheless, at every village, I picked up chains of inquisitive children, all wanting me to stop, and who were pleased as punch when I took their photographs and gave them 'presents' of my name and address, even though they were far too young to read or write. Women in brightly coloured *faneaus* worked small fields of cassava and cotton, fenced with straw palisades, mimosas intertwined with drooping cascades of creepers, and motley barriers of posts and rails. Many women sang as they worked, and waved and shouted as I sped by. I would have loved to have spent some time with them, to discover exactly what it was that made their world, to discover what they thought... but I wanted to go home.

As I neared Thiès - seventy kilometres from Dakar - incredible forests of baobab began to colonise the land. The baobab (*Adansonia digitata*) is a tree as awesome as the Californian redwood or the banyan of Asia. It is the world's thickest tree, with girths of upto 180 feet. It is the mighty emblem of Senegal, and not only because of its great size. The baobab is a most useful tree. Its bark, in texture like cork, contains anti-malarial quinine, and its fibres can be made into rope or wigs. Its leaves contain ascorbic acid, and are reputed to cure asthma, rheumatism, anaemia and inflammations. The seeds are used for soaps and fertilizer, and the fruit (monkey bread) is good against circulatory diseases and dysentery. Like the cactus, the baobab can also store water in its hollow trunk - apparently upto a thousand litres - a succour for thirsty travellers. As a result of its varied uses, as well as its grotesque appearance, the baobab has become fabled in tribal societies. Its branches, which resemble a tree's roots, have spawned the belief that the devil himself uprooted the baobab only to plunge it back into the earth upside down. In certain communities, itinerant *griot* minstrels were (and perhaps still are) interred in hollow baobab trunks, a practice that has only served to increase the wonder of this strange tree. In the evening, as I cycled through these nightmarish forests, I felt as though I had trespassed onto the land of some fearsome giant, and I had the constant and worrying impression of being stared at.

The large market town of Thiès is one of Senegal's most ancient cities, and the erstwhile capital of the powerful kingdom of Kayor. It sits, like a spider, at the country's most important crossroads, the conjunction of highways connecting the trading centres of Saint-Louis and Louga, with Dakar, Djourbel ('the groundnut capital of Senegal') and Kaolack (a major exporting centre for groundnuts and salt). Thiès itself grew wealthy from the 14th century onwards, mainly because its *damels* made their fortunes selling slaves at first to the Moors, and then to Portuguese and French traders – often, it must be said, at the expense of their own peasantry.

Not surprisingly, the French soon gained a healthy interest in Thiès and Kayor, but it took them until the mid 19th century even to be able to begin the conquest and for Kayor to be 'pacified' (as anodyne a euphemism as 'surgical strike' or 'ethnic cleansing'). Yet even this 'achievement' proved to be premature, for, following the humiliating and expensive defeat at the hands of Prussia in 1871, the French were unable to resist the remarkably successful rebellion of one Lat Diop, who single-handedly ousted the French from Kayor and installed himself as *damel*. Only when Lat Diop died, in 1896, was Kayor re-annexed. This time, the French conquest (under the shrewd leadership of General Faidherbe) was rendered easier by the railroad, which had been constructed eight years earlier. From then on, until independence was regained in 1960, Thiès became the commercial nucleus of the expanded colony, far outstripping the importance of Saint-Louis.

Yet, for many Senegalese today, by far the most important legacy of Thiès' speckled past is not temporal but spiritual, because the years at the height of the slave trade (in the 18th and 19th centuries) coincided with the birth of Senegal's largest and most influential Islamic brotherhoods: the Tidjiana, and the Mouride. Tivaouane, a village twelve miles north of Thiès, is the seat of the former. They were founded in 19th century Morocco by Sheikh Ahmed al-Tidjiani, a *marabout* who had studied at both Cairo's al-Azhar, and in Medina (his Moroccan birth is nowadays reflected in the predilection among older dignitaries for wearing the fez). Through his doctrine, Islam spread rapidly among merchants, theologians, and bureaucrats, and as a result his order was carried across the Sahara by the caravans. Islam, incidentally, had first been brought to West Africa by the Almoravids, but the following centuries had succeeded in diluting much of its substance. Once in West Africa, al-Tidjiani's doctrine was popularised by al-Hajj Umar Tall: Senegalese nationalist, scourge of the infidel French, and Senegal's first pilgrim to Mecca, who in consequence became a *marabout* credited with the ability to perform miracles.

In contrast to the Moroccan *marabouts* – who now exist only as corpses in their mausolea – the West African variant are still very much alive, presiding as regional heads over their own brotherhoods. As among the Berber Sufis, the Senegalese *marabout* combines more orthodix Islam with earlier animist traditions, and effectively performs the rôles of priest, sage, soothsayer and mystic – in a society where little was written, an ability to read Arabic, and therefore knowledge of the Qur'an, verged on the magical. Through their supposed ability to predict and so alter the future, many *marabouts* have become immensely powerful, and are rumoured to have played an influential part in the political shenanigans of the late 20th century. By way of example, the presidential elections that were held shortly before my arrival, brought the following decrees: Sheikh Abdul Ahad M'backé, chief of the Mourides, urged his followers to vote for the incumbent president, because: 'In not doing so, you will have betrayed the commitment which links you to Amadou Bamba [founder of the Mourides].' Similarly, the nephew of the Tidjiana leader wished that 'God give to his compatriots the will to re-elect Abdou Diouf in February 1988.' Diouf was duly re-elected, with a landslide majority.

In the last century, it was the slave trade that was the cause célèbre of the brotherhoods, inspiring them not only in resisting the French occupation, but also to concentrate their wrathful attentions on the slavers of Kayor. Out of these militant protests grew perhaps the greatest and most vociferous of the brotherhoods, the Mouride [the name means 'aspirant']. They were founded in 1887 by Sheikh Amadou Bamba. Central to his belief was the saying: 'Work is part of religion', an ethic that bears resemblance to the Calvinistic work ethic. As a result, one of the few remarkable things I found about Thiès – given its all-stifling heat and humidity – was the energy and zeal with which I was harassed by the Baye Fall. These are gaily-clothed and often dreadlocked Mouride disciples, armed with wooden clubs and begging bowls for the benefit of their *marabouts*. Ibra Fall, so the legend goes, was one of Bamba's earliest disciples who, although personally devoted to the *marabout*, was a poor Qur'anic student. So, it is said, Bamba gave him an axe and told him to work for God with that. 'If you work for me I shall pray for you,' Bamba said, upon which Ibra Fall went on to found the slavishly fanatical Baye Fall movement, whose devotees are exempt from study and even from the fast of Ramadan, and whose love of palm wine is tolerated in recompense for their uncommon religious fervour. Even more than Bamba himself, the Baye Fall made a virtue of labour. 'Hard work is the key to paradise,' they say, and because begging for alms is seen as hard work, there are now over a dozen Senegalese *marabouts* who are multi-millionaires in whichever currency one may care to choose.

Despite its chequered past, Thiès is a ramshackle sort of place, sprawled across acres of red sandstone. The soil and vegetation is surprisingly Mediterranean, and together with the town's plentiful horse and mule drawn traps, evokes a sense of rural Portugal. That is, if one ignores the oppressive humidity and consequent lethargy of the place, for the town is situated in a large, bowl-like depression that allows for little wind. There are escarpments to the south, and opencast phosphate mines to the north and west. Its compact clay roads and avenues are shaded by trees with whitewashed trunks, under one of which, every day, a blue-scaled lizard did its push-ups as little children ran circles to try and catch its tail!

I spent several days in Thiès, simply too hot and too tired to bother cycling to Dakar. I was also bored, and apart from the stench of sweat that hung everywhere, I have few memories of the town. One that does stick in mind was when, on first arriving in Thiès, I saw a blind beggar crouched beside the entrance of an import-supermarket. He listened intently to people approaching, and then stumbled towards them with his right hand formed into a cup. Samba the hustler, whose wrists were stiff with bracelets and bangles to sell to tourists and French schoolgirls on educational holidays, disapproved vehemently when I gave the man a few coins. So much so that he violently forced the beggar to return the money I had given him. 'It's not good,' he said. 'Can't you see?' and then chased away the children who had also been asking for money. Samba – whose brother was a devotee of Baye Fall – then offered me a choice of gold, silver, bronze or ivory jewellery, at fat, extortionate prices.

On finally wrenching myself away from Thiès, it occured to me that, as a traveller, it would be almost impossible to fully share the life of Senegal. I always had the impression that I was merely passing through, at best looking in from above. I was beginning once more, as in Fès, to feel very much an outsider. In Mauritania, on the other hand, I think it is fair to say that I got a pretty good feel of the country, because its very soul lies in travelling. I had found the heart of Mauritania not by travelling to its geographical or cultural epicentre, but by the simple fact of my having travelled there. In Senegal, on the other hand, my reactions and feelings as a traveller were necessarily superficial in a land of settled people. The villages and towns were no longer islands or oases in a hostile desert sea, places to be aimed at and to be considered as sanctuary. Rather, they were places to escape from, as I was to find out in Dakar.

CHAPTER TWELVE

DAKAR

And pray what is Cape Verde? A stinking place?

attributed to King Charles II (1630-85)

At the westernmost extremity of the African continent there is a long peninsula of volcanic rock that juts out into the Atlantic like an inquisitive finger. Nearer Brazil than it is to Europe, Cap Vert is the first green land that Portuguese mariners saw after having passed Cap Blanc and the wasted Saharan coastline. On it is Dakar, burgeoning capital of the Republic of Senegal. A couple of miles to the leeward, and barely visible through the smog that hangs like a pall over the Bay of Saint Bernard, is the isle of Gorée.

In many ways, Gorée is the spiritual heartland for the millions of blacks around the world who are descended from West African slaves. For over three centuries, control of the island was fiercely disputed by the Europeans, for it came to be the world's most important slaving *entrepôt*, where 'black ivory' captured all over the region was taken before being shipped away to a new half-life in the sugar cane plantations of the New World. Although it is true that slavery was nothing new when the Europeans arrived on the scene, it is they who elevated the trade to previously unprecedented levels. Under the Europeans, there was a regular demand for cheap labour, and every level of the trade, from the hunts to the transportation and selling of slaves, was more highly organized than ever before. Shortly after the breakthough of Gil Eannes' rounding of Cap Bojador, Portuguese caravels captured a caravan of Sanhaja nomads, who were brought back to Lisbon for inspection. A few years later, an entire cargo of slaves was shipped back, and very quickly the Europeans acquired their taste for slavery, and for the easy money to be made from it. The Dutch, who came after the Portuguese, called the island *Goede Reede*, the Good Harbour, which in time became Gorée. Finally, in the year 1677, both Gorée and the isle of Arguin (near Nouâdhibou) were captured by the French, which signalled the start of a long period of rivalry with England.

By the close of the 15th century, one thousand slaves were being transported each year from Arguin alone, and throughout the following centuries, a steady flow of between 2,000 and 3,500 slaves was exported annually. Altogether – from the first transatlantic slave cargo of 1513, to the trade's demise in the 19th century – some 24 million people were forcibly taken from their homes, to be sold or bartered like little more than sacks of flour. It has been estimated that of these, almost 20% perished on the cramped 'floating coffins' that were the slave cargoes, before even setting foot on the American continent. They suffered variously from disease, shortages of fresh foodstuffs and water, and the frequent lashings that the traders sardonically called 'exercise'. The coffins continue to be washed up on the beaches of history: racism, inner-city riots in Europe and America, bigotry in West Africa, extreme black militancy, the Ku Klux Klan... Almost all of today's white on black, or black on white, racism can be traced back to the violence of the West African slave trade.

So much for Gorée. Dakar, meanwhile, remained a small and tranquil Lébou fishing village until 1857, when the French decided that it would make the perfect site for a new port to serve their rapidly expanding colony. From its 19th century population of 2,000, by 1926, having taken over from Saint-Louis as the capital of French West Africa, it had exploded to over forty thousand. Ten years later it had almost reached six figures, and by the time of Senegal's independence, Dakar had almost a third of million inhabitants. It is now estimated that of its one and a half to two million inhabitants, over half are under twenty years of age. The great majority live in squalid and overcrowded slums on the outskirts of town. Alluring tales in the vein of Dick Whittington – of great wealth, luxury and gold (like Timbuctoo's ancient legend) – have attracted migrants in their thousands to this great neocolonial whirlpool: intense, dynamic, sophisticated, but above all, wretched. There are so many mouths to feed and so little food. Or money. Dakar has a reputation fast approaching that of Lagos, the Nigerian capital. It is dangerous, dirty, and stage for the enactment of a thousand travellers' tales of woe and despair. Like all big West African cities, Dakar has become something of a jungle, the false idol of Western wealth and prosperity. Most of all, it is a city of dregs, like Nouâdhibou a dead end peninsula, only larger and more primitive in its solutions.

From its humble beginnings, Dakar has matured to be one of Africa's most westernised cities. It boasts wide leafy boulevards that would scarcely be out of place in Paris, lined with whitewashed apartment blocks like those of pre-war Beirut or Damascus, and modest skyscrapers that try but fail to reconcile the 20th century with traditional Africa. Like every other African city, there are half-built or abandoned structures everywhere, some with their facades fallen away. Dakar is a strange and powerful place, a monster by any standards – poised, lumbering, and tumorous – at once enigmatic and blatant. Although the combined history of Dakar and Gorée, like Saint-Louis, mirrors that of Senegal, the city itself is a world apart. Dakar, with its veritable army of grotesquely deformed beggars, lepers and cripples that weave their way through indifferent crowds, is certainly not the Senegal of smiles and graceful figures that I had come to expect. Dakar is a land of scowls and limps, while Senegal is a land of honesty and kindness. In Dakar, often ill-gotten wealth lives alongside dehumanising poverty. Dakar – not surprisingly given its cataclysmic growth – is a monstrous anomaly, and in all honesty deserves to have an entire book allotted to it rather than the few fleeting impressions I can offer here. The city is every inch a capitalist's capital, the product of post-industrial dreamings, devoid of any veneer to wash over the system's failures. The markets are full of computers, air ionizers, and even electronic sunglasses. The streets are choked with diesel fumes, smog, pollution and ramshackle cars. In the sky, there are vultures as well as doves.

* * *

It was evening when I arrived in Dakar, and the airline offices around the Place de l'Indépendance had already pulled down their iron shutters. My hunt for cheap accomodation failed miserably. A room in even the cheapest of fleapits cost upwards of ten thousand CFA (£20), seven day's budgeting for me and one tenth of the annual per capita income. The hotels Provençal, de la Paix, Indépendance, and du Prince were all full. The Grasland, a celebrated old brothel at the intersection of Grasland and Raffenel, was also *complet*. Being seen to live in a hotel (or a brothel), or even attempting to find one, means that you've got more money than most, and even my fruitless search attracted the unwelcome attention of the usual motley band of hustlers, offering almost anything from friendship to weed and fake gold dust in return for my money (or my camera). Many others cannot be bothered with the patter, and just snatch and run before the poor bewildered tourist has even had time to realise what has befallen them. The patter was much the same as in Fès, only more threatening.

'Pssst, pssst... you on your own?' they ask gleefully.

'Hey, you want *yamba*? Good grass, *pas de probleme*. Good quality, follow me, follow me.' Once, when I didn't, he came back and I heard insults.

'*Toubab*,' he hissed. '*Toubab*, you are all the same. Lots money, no money. You are a bourgeois dog. Those who have no time are already dead.' Then, he spat at my feet. I couldn't even ask directions without having demands for CFA thrust at me. It is not the fact that Westerners are rich per se that angers Africans, I was told by Papa, but that their wealth is not shared. The Baye Fall alms-collectors were the worst, and on several occasions threatened me with their clubs, and even when I did cough up, still showered me with insults and curses. Dakar is not a place to flaunt one's wealth, with the exception only of well-guarded neo-colonial aristocrats, diplomats, and government ministers who glide around town in black, chauffeur-driven limousines. Neither is Dakar, to put it bluntly, a good place to be white in. Perhaps it is not surprising – given the past – that I experienced continuous racism. The era of the slave trade was in effect the true Dark Age for Africa, a time when Europeans of all nations convinced themselves that 'whites' were a superior kind of human being, and that it was their duty, therefore, to 'civilise' the Dark Continent. For too long, Africa has been the epitome of savagery, and the victim of unforgivable distortions wrought by imperial historians (who conveniently forgot the glorious empires of Ghana, Mali and the Songhai, which in their time were much more advanced than their European counterparts).

The once widely-read and respected 4th Earl of Chesterfield, who had taken it upon himself to educate his son in the marvels of the world, wrote to him in 1742: 'The Africans are the most ignorant and unpolished people in the world, little better than the lions, tigers, leopards, and other wild beasts...' Indeed, most colonists considered Negroes to be too retarded to have created their great empires on their own, and therefore believed that contact with the supposedly more intelligent Hamitic-speaking North Africans was undoubtedly the real cause. In fact, it was the Negroes who had always been more culturally advanced than the infiltrating desert nomads. The Neolithic revolution began well before the Arabs or Berbers had even heard of the place, and as the prehistoric rock art of the Sahara shows, the first cultivators of the then rich Sahel had been black.

The darkest thing about Africa, of course, has always been our ignorance of it. As the Nigerian poet Chinweizu puts it in *Colonizer's Logic*: 'These natives are unintelligent – We can't understand their language.'

The thing I found hardest to understand was why so many of Dakar's inhabitants seemed to consider anything European as being inherently superior to the products of their own culture. Every day, I would see men strutting about aimlessly, bedecked with personal stereos, which were invariably mere pretence for they always lacked the money to buy batteries. Perhaps I am unwittingly conforming to the petty tourist mentality of wanting to see 'elsewhere' as 'authentic' or 'unspoilt'. Perhaps my attitude betrays the vain hope that Western consumer culture isn't as strong as I fear, that it will not after all conquer the world. But on reflection, I find little ground for such optimism. It was distressing to see the extent to which so many Africans have discarded, and to some degree also forgotten, their indigenous cultures and values, and have looked instead to the so-called First World for their guiding principles. Almost anything that I cared to mention regarding England or Europe was treated by many Dakariens as Gospel. In fact, they seemed to expect nothing short of it. There was nothing I could say to dissuade them from believing that Europe, America, capitalism and even Margaret Thatcher were the best things to have happened to the world. In the main, the citizens of Dakar strive to dress like us, eat like us, smile like us and, ultimately, to *be* us. It is a vicious circle. Sembène Ousmane, a celebrated Senegalese writer and film director, made the point in *The Last of the Empire*:

> Look at the inhabitants of the towns, Saint-Louis, Dakar, Rufisque, Gorée … Because of their long period of contact with Europeans, they thought themselves more 'civilized' than the other bush Africans living in forest or savanna. Their arrogance grew when they alone were given the vote and considered French citizens… They began to parody [the Europeans], and acquired a pretentious mentality… These alienated, rootless people, enslaved from within… were unconsciously the most faithful and devoted servants of the then prevailing system of occupation.

Similarly, Ben Okri (author of the brilliant *Famished Road*) writes:

> The oppressed always live with death… And yet they often think of their victors as their standard of aspiration… They have not as a people learned as yet how to snatch historical confidence.[13]

To my mind, the developed world is in many ways the most primitive. Corporate giants continue to export condemned and otherwise illegal products to Africa: dangerous fertilizers and pesticides, tainted foodstuffs banned from sale in Europe, and medicines whose side-effects have long been proved to outweigh their benefits. While I was in Dakar, a political storm was only just breaking over a secretive and illegal shipment of high-level toxic waste from Europe to Nigeria. The Pentagon, Downing Street and the Kremlin have always been guilty of supporting inhuman dictators, and not just in Africa, and seemingly with no thought for the people that they help to condemn. One of the many reasons for this is the money that we make from Africa. For example, of the foreign aid 'donated' to Senegal each year, over thirty five percent is returned to service the interest due on debt repayments. It is a situation both sick and absurd, and yet Senegal is relatively well-off in these matters. Other nations have to return *twice* the amount that they receive in aid.

Still, I suppose that there is some hope in all of this. The Africans – if I may generalise just once – are an exceptionally optimistic people, even in the direst of dire straits. They have to be. *Ex Africa semper alquid novi* remarked Pliny: there is always something new from Africa. There is a Bantu proverb that compares the African race to a ball of India rubber. The harder you throw it to the ground, the higher it will rise.

* * *

I decided to try the Cathédrale du Souvenir Africain and its adjacent mission on the Boulevard de la République, in the hope that – like Papa in Saint-Louis – they might help my search for accommodation. Unfortunately – as I'd been warned – when my turn came to be seen by the relevant official, I was wearily told of the large number of similar requests that the mission received every day, of the lack of space, of underfunding, et cetera. At the time, my selfishness determined that I saw these quite valid reasons merely as excuses. My unreasonable reaction was an early omen of the problems that were to beset me later on... I did, however, have the good fortune to meet two young West African refugees, one from Ghana, the other a Liberian, who were so pleased at being able to converse in English with somebody else that they kindly offered to put me up for as long as I wished. Along with another young refugee, a Guinean who spoke only Fulfulde and rudimentary Portuguese, we walked back along the west coast of Cap Vert and into the Medina.

Taking its name from the Arabian refuge of the Prophet Muhammad, Dakar's Medina was hurriedly erected to house survivors of a disastrous plague that swept through much of the country between 1914 and 1915. Though temporary in nature, its population has – perhaps ironically – never ceased to increase. Its streets, set in a grid of right angles, have been assigned numbers rather than the dignity of names. Many alleyways are almost impassable because of sand and rubbish, and occasionally, dangerously sharp splinters of glass and metal catch the feet of the unwary. Elsewhere, there are flame-gutted husks of cars and vans, their tyres salvaged, along with broken bricks and lumps of mortar, to keep down rooves. Where there is tarmac, it is shattered and uneven, with murky puddles in its many potholes. The low compound-houses sandwiched in between the streets look as though they have been squashed flat by the heat and humidity. Many are spartan in the extreme, with canvas awnings or corroded sheets of metal for rooves, and crumbling unadorned walls that seem never to have been plastered or painted. Other walls bear oddly polite graffitied notices reading 'URINER INTERDIT S.V.P.', which were by and large ignored, as I could tell from the smell. Infrastructure and facilities are woefully inadequate. Parts of the Medina are shrouded under a jumbled mesh of telephone and electricity wires, even though few dwellings are actually connected. Many streets are unpaved, and in winter, the Medina tends to be flooded with a noxious mixture of rainwater, mosquito larvae and sewage. Everywhere, great ridges of waste lie festering along the lengths of the wider streets – sometimes still smouldering from fires – around which grubby children scramble and play. Even official publications refer to 'insalubrious and un-integrated quarters', yet the government is powerless to do anything about them – it has no money.

At the end of one alleyway, hidden amidst a clutter of cracked Evian spring water bottles and rusty cans and plastic bags, was a solitary cardboard box, under which lived a scabby ginger cat and her three remaining five-day-old kittens. The father, a one-eyed tom, prowled around at the entrance to the alleyway, kept at a distance by the claws of the mother who, I was told, had killed and probably eaten her three other offspring.

The refugees lived in a makeshift compound in the more squalid northern fringe of the Medina, a squatter camp that has for years been earmarked for demolition. It has only been 'saved' by a lack of resources for building a healthier alternative. We arrived as a chill wind blew in from the Atlantic. Dozens of women armed with tin buckets and plastic tubs milled around a standpipe beside a solitary flame-tree, suckling toddlers from large floppy breasts, and yacking amongst themselves. For the most part, I was to be pleasantly surprised by the cheerful resilience of the Medina's inhabitants, who would respond to a friendly greeting with graceful smiles and offers to sit and talk for a while. The cliché, 'blitz mentality', comes to mind.

For the refugees, however, life here was another story. Their compound was, by already low standards, one of the more rudimentary. The bathroom, especially, was repulsive in every sense of the word – a dark, slimy cubicle that I will only say was festering from top to bottom with maggots. Thin sheets of cardboard served as partitions between four largely unfurnished rooms, with four or five people to each. Whereas in Nouakchott, even the poorest had managed to adorn their walls with pictures and images culled from magazines and old newspapers, these rooms were utterly bare but for a coating of mould. The contrast, I think, served only to further entrench the refugees' isolation from the world outside. The floor was covered with equally mouldy PVC, ripped and shredded, exposing crumbling cement foundations that were infested with cockroaches and woodlice. The only window in the room was broken, which let in the stench of a stagnant well, in addition to nocturnal swarms of mosquitoes. My hosts could not even afford smoke coils, although that was the least of their worries. None of them had eaten properly for five whole days, and as a result, they suffered from frequent headaches, sudden foul tempers, stomach aches, bad skin, bad eyes, and alternate spells of light- and heavy-headedness. The Guinean actually threw up the first meal I bought him, because his stomach wasn't used to food. Needless to say there was no electricity either, and candles were too expensive, so that when they had been studying at Dakar university they had worked in the dark.

I say that my hosts *had* been studying, for all three had recently been expelled, and their grants from the United Nations had been suspended. Slowly and painfully, over several days and usually over lukewarm bowls of *mafé* meat stew that I bought them, they explained the events that had brought about their presently hopeless situation. I listened to their stories with increasing disbelief. They painted sad and gloomy pictures that made me more miserable than I had felt for a very long time. What follows is the little I remember or can reconstruct of these tales, for I was later, in rather unfortunate circumstances myself, to lose my diary and all the notes that I had taken. Above all, the three stories – whether true or otherwise – serve to illustrate, even symbolise, the tragic fates that have overtaken many West African countries in the pioneering period that has followed independence which, as I write, is barely thirty years old.

I begin with the Guinean, whose Fulfulde was translated for me by Tokpah Kennedy, the Liberian. Guinea stumbled rather prematurely into the international limelight in 1958, with Ahmed Sekou Touré's celebrated snub to the visiting Charles de Gaulle: 'We, for our part, have a first and indispensible need, that of our dignity. Now, there is no dignity without freedom... We prefer freedom in poverty to riches in slavery.' It was a sentiment much applauded by other Africans at the time (with the exception of Francophiles such as Léopold Senghor, and the Ivory Coast's Houphouët-Boigny). As a result, the French, piqued at being humiliated by such a small and insignificant country, abandoned Guinea in much the same way that a swarm of locusts would leave a once green pasture. Files and documents were burned, aid was cancelled, vehicles destroyed, and anything of value that wasn't nailed down was taken away, including by some accounts even the lightbulbs from government offices. The country and its economy was left in ruins, isolated, suspicious, and with precisely six university graduates to its name. Yet, aided at first by Stalin and the Eastern Bloc, and then from 1962 by the Americans – who feared Guinea becoming another Soviet cold war satellite – the country painfully began to pick up the pieces of its shattered past.

Progress was slow, however, and perhaps as a result, Touré resorted to dictatorship, in its time one of the harshest and most draconian regimes in all Africa. The Fulfulde-speakers of the Fouta Djalon, especially, were prime targets for Touré's paranoia and the fear of the 'Permanent Plot', and were subjected to much the same treatment as the Jews and dissidents of the USSR. In 1966, inspired by the Chinese example, Touré led his country into a miserable 'cultural revolution', which was essentially a wholesale purge against degenerate intellectuals, bureaucrats, and other potential troublemakers. 'Enemies of the State' were discovered with alarming frequency, and terror became widespread: torture, mysterious disappearances, summary executions, and detentions without trial. The country was plunged into a dark and sinister twilight from which it has still not properly recovered. Even the refugee, who was still only in his twenties, remembered the terror, and called it 'a nightmare in sight of the sun'. Salvation for Guinea and the refugee's family should have come in 1984, upon the despot's long awaited death but, if anything, the situation since then has degenerated still further. The price of food basics – rice especially – soared, as did hunger, as the shroud of famine drew closer. Starving, the Guinean abandoned his family and fled Conakry, once hailed as the Paris of Africa, to seek a better life elsewhere.

The Ghanian was called Richard, a tall and amiable young man with the exquisite off-beat English accent that all cultivated Ghanians seem to possess. Ghana, the first African country to gain independence, has, in stark contrast to Guinea, long been able to pride itself on a broad reaching and high standard of education. Many Ghanian children are taught from an early age to speak several languages, which undoubtedly goes some way to reducing inter-tribal tension, something with which Ghana, like Senegal, is little affected. Richard, by his account, had been at the top of the class throughout his childhood, something that enabled him to study legal science at Accra. There was every prospect of his going on to becoming a successful businessman or even a politician.

So what had gone so horribly wrong, that I now found him half-starving, one and a half thousand miles adrift in the slums of Dakar, and with little hope of escape? He was, after all, from that tiny and privileged minority of Ghanians rich enough to afford servants and even a BMW. In supreme irony, it was his very intelligence that was his downfall. The problem was that he'd been recruited at university by the secret police – to become a spy, in other words – and initially this was more than he had ever dared dream. It meant plenty of money, and golden prospects of rapid ascent up the political ladder. Both his father and uncle were government functionaries, something that seemed to ensure a bright future. The young Richard was also an idealist, and admired greatly the style and politics of Flight-Lieutenant Jerry Rawlings, who had come to power at the second attempt in the coup of June 1979, and who had envisioned a 'moral revolution' based on socialist principles. The subsequent ideological purges, albeit small on an African scale, did not seem to worry the young student. After all, it was all for the good of the nation.

Richard's military training lasted two years, ending early in 1983. By then, however, something had changed. Rawlings had been in power for barely four years, during which time the continued stability of the country (which had once seemed inviolable) seemed rather less certain. Rawlings himself engineered a third coup on New Year's Eve, 1981, ostensibly to stamp out corruption, and several other attempts followed in short succession during 1982 and 1983. For Richard, there was to follow another year of more specialist training before he was to become a fully-fledged secret agent, yet suddenly he got cold feet. As he explained: 'What if there is to be another, but this time successful, coup? I would be seen as an enemy of the new state. My family would be compromised. My life would be threatened...' Furthermore, if he is to be believed, Richard began to dislike the prospect of spying and informing on his own people. This was not part of the caring socialist society that he had hoped for, but what could he do? He knew too much simply to refuse the career that awaited him. He had come too far. And so he ran, far away from Ghana, towards any place where Ghanian agents wouldn't be able to find him. And so it was that I found Richard in Dakar.

Tokpah Kennedy, lastly, was the Liberian, and in many ways his situation represented what Richard feared had he stayed on in Ghana. Like Richard, Tokpah's family had for a long time been involved in government. From what I can recall, Tokpah said that his father had been high up in the Ministry of Economics, possibly even the minister himself, and had been financially as well as politically powerful. The government at the time was that of William Tolbert, who presided over something of a family empire. But Liberia, as it has recently shown, is one of the least stable of all African countries, racked with tribal conflict (even outside the bloody confusion of its civil war). Every government since independence has, without exception, been of a tribal nature, and there seems to be little room for power-sharing or tolerance. In consequence, its frequent changes of government have all had a significant element of blood-feuding to them. There is a coup d'état, then a purge and endless reprisals, repression, atrocities, and even genocide. By the close of the 1970s, the economy was in a mess and the cost of rice, as in Guinea, had risen beyond of the reach of many.

April 1980 was one of many black months in Liberian history, for it saw the coup d'état that brought to power the tyrant Samuel Doe. Tolbert and most of his supporters were murdered, along with Tokpah's family. His father, mother, brothers, sisters, uncles, all were killed. Their bodies were dumped alongside Tolbert's in shallow coastal graves, the same graves into which Doe himself would be thrown ten years later. Tokpah, the only member of his family to survive the massacre, fled initially to Sierra Leone. That country, however – like Liberia – is one ravaged by drought, and Tokpah found it hard to survive. So he decided to take a risk by smuggling a small quantity of diamonds (a commodity with which Sierra Leone is well-endowed) into Senegal. Tokpah was lucky, and found himself with enough money to live on for a whole year. The second time he tried the ruse, however, a couple of years later, he was discovered at the border and thrown in jail. His passport and papers were confiscated. Finally, last year, he escaped to Dakar, stowed-away in an onion lorry.

Like Richard and the Guinean, Tokpah had found help at the door of the United Nations High Commission for Refugees. Their stories, however, do not end with their flight to Senegal. Until a few months prior to my meeting them, they had been studying at Cheikh Anta Diop university – half a mile from the compound – and their fees and living expenses were footed by the UN.

February 28, 1988 – the day of my departure from Manchester – was also the date of the Senegalese presidential and legislative elections, in which the incumbent Abdou Diouf, Senghor's successor, was duly returned for another term in office. The ballot, however, did not pass entirely without incident. In the tense atmosphere that preceded the elections, students and pupils all over Senegal went on strike to protest about a disciplinary measure taken against a student in Thiès. To the dismay of Diouf, the protests quickly took on a political slant, and soon embraced a score of other grievances. They protested at the lack of teachers, at the lack of basic equipment, and then at the declining state of the economy. They protested about the spiralling cost of food and then, spurred on by a rash of similar protests that had broken out throughout North and West Africa, they protested against the government. I saw graffiti in Dakar proclaiming 'Death to Diouf' and 'Wade for President', and everywhere the letters S-O-P-I [the opposition alliance] scrawled beside big Vs.

The government responded to the protests with a number of heavy-handed police raids on the university campus. Then, when disappointed opposition supporters took to the streets after the first election results became known, more tear gas followed, in addition to looting and burning, the stationing of tanks on the streets of Dakar, three bomb attacks, the arrest of Wade for incitement (he claimed to have been defeated by a rigged poll), the declaration of a state of emergency, the imposition of a dusk to dawn curfew, and the suspension of the three refugees, who, rightly or wrongly, were suspected to be among the ringleaders of the violence.

The aftershocks of all this were still very much in evidence, despite the emergency decree having been lifted three weeks previously. Many of the Medina's inhabitants – not least the refugees – were loathe to venture out of their shacks at night, and when I once inadvertently mentioned Wade, I was urgently and anxiously told to shut up for fear of government spies and informers. As a result, and in desperation, Richard had started entertaining ideas of fleeing to Libya, where he had heard he would be able to train as a terrorist commando, with all the benefits of good pay and a Libyan passport, and even the possibility of reaching Europe. Although I'd heard similar stories in Morocco, in Dakar there seemed to be more substance to the rumoured Libyan connection. Jerry Rawlings himself was well known for his friendly rapport with Ghaddafi, and in Senegal, the leader of a militant Tidjiana sect, Ahmet Khalif Niassa, had been exiled to Libya at the end of the

308

1970s for allegedly plotting an Islamic revolution. In 1987, Libyan bombers were arrested in Senegal in possession of detonators of the same type that were used to down Pan Am 103 over Lockerbie, and in the Gambia, three coup attempts (1980, early 1988, and 1992) also had alleged Libyan links. The problem for Richard was how to get there. Even if he had the money, his refugee papers restricted his movements to Senegal.

Tokpah was more pessimistic about the future, and placed what little remained of his faith in fate and religion. 'My dear brother Jens,' he wrote later: 'We are starving here. We are hungry. Brother Gaye, you are my loyal brother, I wish I was not here. I wish that you could help me. I pray in the name of our Lord Jesus Christ to deliver us from our present situation.' For the most part, I did not how to react, now that I was actually face-to-face with a 'starving African'. What could I do? Give money? I could afford a little, but my hosts preferred that I bought them meals with it. I once even considered giving them all my money, but then I'd be as stuck as they were, and there were so many other people in the same position. I suggested buying them a charcoal burner, since most of their money disappeared into eathouses, but they said that they wouldn't be able to afford the fuel. In any case, they wanted to get out of Dakar. For them, acquiring a stove only represented their inability to flee.

'This place is truly evil,' said Tokpah. 'It is the Devil's Paradise.' Even their university friends had, without exception, disowned them. Dakar really is a city that sucks in people so that they can never escape. There was also an irony in my own situation, for I had discovered that I could not afford any of the flights back to Europe, and would therefore have to cycle on to Banjul (capital of the Gambia) where, I had been told, flights were much cheaper. Having intended to stay only a few hours in Dakar, I had ended up staying almost two weeks.

On the morning of Friday, 17 June, Richard and Tokpah had reached breaking point. They resolved to visit the office of the UNHCR, and to remain there until they were either granted an audience with Abdou Diouf himself, or given transportation out of Senegal. The Guinean tried to dissuade them (they had previously been ejected with a warning not to come back), but Tokpah and Richard just pushed him aside and strode purposefully away. What happened next, when they reached the office, is unclear, for I never saw them again. When I went to the police station the next day, I was brusquely bundled away by two officers who said that it was none of my business. At the UN, I was refused entry and was told that the refugees had smashed up the office, ripping out telephone and electricity cables, and that they had been fighting with the guards. Tokpah himself wrote me, half a year later via the Red Cross, that he and Richard had been imprisoned for two months, that they had been beaten up by the jailers, and that they had both fallen ill, although he didn't say from what. I replied to the letter, but heard no more.

The Guinean came back to the shack in the evening, so scared that his cheeks had bleached to a pale yellow-brown. His skin was covered with a film of oily, grey sweat. I'd never seen a man so scared. He said that there was nothing that I could do, and that I should leave the next day. Never in my life had I felt so helpless.

CHAPTER THIRTEEN

THE GAMBIA AND BANJUL

The White Man's Grave.

Popular epithet for West Africa

I was relieved to be rid of Dakar and underway once more, if only as far as Banjul. I felt a strange, subdued elation as I cycled away, back up through Cap Vert, past the belching chimneys of an oil refinery, and past the chalky factories of Rufisque the old slaving post. As the stains of industry and overpopulation grew lighter, I found myself happily bemused as to how I'd managed to survive Dakar so totally unscathed, especially given the preconceptions I'd had, and the mess in which the three refugees had found themselves. As Dakar receded in reality, so it receded in my memory.

At a small unmarked village, some 50km along the road, a handful of garrulous women were gathered in the shade of an old palaver tree. They whispered as I passed, clicking their tongues and tutting. At this village, I turned south along a corrugated dirt track, which wound listlessly over stony ochre hills and across dusty parched valleys, intertwined like a hundred writhing snakes. The land shimmered, and the air trembled. Amber-brown termite needles, from afar resembling decapitated tree trunks, pricked the land. Some were as tall as men. Others had been reduced to mounds of snake-infested rubble.

The road dipped down towards the sea and the so-called Little Coast, which at the height of the slave trade was dotted with innumerable forts and trading posts. There were forests of baobab, kapok and coconut palms, dwarfing the handful of settlements scattered in between. An eagle soared high above, another in the far distance. Mbour, the busiest port of the Little Coast, with a population of around four thousand, is a fishing village shrouded in woodsmoke and the stench of drying fish. The people hereabouts are the dark-skinned Serer and Lébou, pushed

311

southwards in the 19th century by the French conquest of Kayor and Cap Vert. The Serer are Senegal's second largest ethnic group (the Wolof are the biggest), counting among their number the former president, Léopold Senghor. Many Serer still hold traditional animistic beliefs, or else are Roman Catholic like the former president, a legacy of the Portuguese and French occupation. Dusk in Africa and dawn in America – for millions, the Little Coast was the last they were ever to see of their homeland, a misty jumble of trees shrinking away into the ocean breeze.

After the Little Coast, the road swung inland for a long, featureless, largely lifeless, and seemingly endless ride to the village of Fatick, where I decided to take a short cut by crossing the marshlands of Sine-Saloum that lie between here and the river Gambia. Unfortunately, the wind was blowing strongly from the south, which too often made walking both easier and faster than cycling. Past the last few dwellings of Fatick stretched a large salt lake, the first of the Sine floodlands, in which children danced and cavorted after school. One little kid walked up to me and quite unabashedly demanded five hundred CFA. When I grinned back, shaking my head, he began to barter for the sum that I should give him! 500, 400, 300... We eventually settled at sharing my five remaining mangoes with him and a few of his friends.

Sine-Saloum. To me, even the name evokes the land, a magical aqueous kingdom of wide and snaking *bolong* estuaries and thick mangrove swamps, of fresh water marshes, and Atlantic salt flats, whose oyster creeks are a veritable paradise for birds. The marshes rise at most to a dozen feet above sea level, with an infinite horizon broken only by the odd clump of coconut palms or a miniscule hamlet. There is little to be heard besides the flapping of palm fronds and the rustling of grasses and reeds. Some settlements have even been built in the waterways themselves, floating webs of reed houses anchored on great rafts of split tree trunks. Sine-Saloum is a land of great seers and diviners, and of Voodoo black magic. It is a land teeming with *djinn* spirits, some of them evil, scheming and devilish, others kindly and beneficial. This is a land conducive to meditation, especially when coming directly from the crazy confusion of Dakar: swampy, dreamy, calm, almost too calm.

The road itself tiptoed over narrow ribbons of land reclaimed from the marshes, and cycling was at times like swooping low over a lake, much like the herons who lived here. The sight of so much water made me want to swim, and as the wind showed no sign of abating – indeed it stiffened as I advanced – I called it a day and rolled the bike into the shelter of a clump of palm trees on the fringes of a long, white beach of silvery sand. Beyond, a wide and placid lake sparkled in the sunshine. The evening sun was a perfect disc, like yellow cardboard stuck onto a hazy, cottonbank sky. I stripped off, and then laughing, a little self-consciously I admit, walked away across the sand. Sploosh! My feet disappeared into a steaming, fine, hot and glutinous swamp, and I soon found that paddling was much easier than wading towards deeper water. The only problem was that, having paddled for ten minutes, the water was still only about a foot deep, and then got shallower as I neared the opposite bank. By the time I'd given up swimming, I was covered from head to toe in a slimy jet black silt, dripping from my armpits and groin like treacle.

I fell asleep at the foot of a palm tree, worried that a coconut might fall on my head, and awoke early, with the psychotic thumping of raindrops pummelling my eardrums. I packed quickly and left. The land grew grassier here, and in the rain looked as though it had been painted in oils. Before long, I reached a small riverbank settlement, built entirely of reed and wicker. The huts here were larger than those of the Senegal valley, were round rather than square, and had tightly thatched rooves. The problem was that the ferry that my map indicated had sunk the year before, and its replacement was still being awaited.

'Is there no way across?' I asked the fishermen on the crumbling jetty, as the grey silhouette of a shipwreck about a mile upriver caught my eye.

'Impossible.' All four shook their heads in unison. 'You will have to drive back to Fatick, and then to Kaolack, and then...'

'But I haven't got a car,' I explained, 'I'm cycling.'

To my relief, there were a handful of *pirogues* that still made the crossing – aged double-prowed dugouts made from tree trunks lashed together with hibiscus fibres. We sat for an hour on the north bank of the sludgy waters, to await a few more passengers, and were then ferried across to the village of Foundiougne Venetian-style by a shorn-headed Serer youth, in a fashion that might have been most relaxing had I not noticed my bicycle rocking so perilously over the water that on several occasions I became convinced that my journey would end right here in the murky depths of the Saloum.

Sokone – some 50 kilometres further on – is a great little village: a petrol stop for Banjul-bound traffic, where old men chewing kola nuts and puffing on short pipes sit around playing draughts, dominoes and backgammon. I found an eathouse there, a smoky little shack with two tables and a chair, where I was served a wicked pimento ragout that all but blew my head off. Later, in the shaded calm of afternoon, I was beckoned over by a group of grandfathers who wanted to teach me their version of draughts, which despite all their patient explanations, I never came close to understanding. All around us were irrigated fields of vegetables, and groves of mango and apple wreathed with Tarzan-style vines. It was late afternoon, and it was hot and humid. A few vultures sat hunched in the treetops, sweating. Red and green parrots squawked loudly from the pepper trees. The vultures coughed uneasily.

* * *

'You must not be so jolly,' scolded the stern-faced officer at Amdalai borderpost, so I helped him instead with his geography O level paper that he was moonlighting on, and as a result obtained extended stay of residence in the Gambia. Not so fortunate was a would-be textile smuggler, one of many participants in the so-called 'traditional trade' between Senegal and Gambia, who had been caught with a pick-up truck full of brightly coloured *faneaus* bound for Dakar and Thiès. He was bundled away to hoots of derision from a small group of mucky children, and in the confusion I noticed a couple of *faneaus* disappear over grinning shoulders.

I was greeted on the other side of no-man's-land by the now familiar throng of pedlars and traders. My first impression of the Gambia was of an almost comical nature, an incongruous place where people speak a funny broken English, where food is still weighed in pounds and ounces, and where street signs and pelican crossings in the middle of the bush pretend that they are in 1950s England. It was an impression that altogether reminded me of Gibraltar.

'Excuse pleace, meester, you is well my Sir?'

'Yes, thank you, and you?'

'Yes, I understand. Sir! Wonderful!' I asked him how far it was to Banjul.

'Yes, yes! Banjul! Wonderful!' he replied.

The Gambia is Africa's smallest country, and one of the world's poorest; a tiny sliver of land that has burrowed into Senegal like a grub in an apple. The Gambia is a bleakly flat country, at only 13.5° north of the Equator, a steamy river basin that at times seems to suffocate in its own humidity. Here, there are oil and coconut palms, small rice paddies, coastal salt marshes, lagoons and mangrove swamps. Further inland there are snaking waterways and *bolong* creeks accessible only by dugout. It is the river Gambia, not the Senegal, that forms the true geographical watershed between the dry Sahelian scrublands of the north and the tropics further south. But like the Senegal, the river that forms the spine of this anomalous country was for centuries believed to be a mouth of the Niger, an easy route – or so the Europeans thought – to the riches of Timbuctoo. In fact the river, like the Senegal, rises in the Fouta Djalon highlands of Guinea, home to an ever dwindling population of elephant, lion, giraffe and other big African game.

The Gambia in its present form is a creation of the British, a curious legacy of the days when Britain and France vied for colonial ascendancy. It measures precisely 193 miles from east to west, but no more than thirty at its widest, because it was agreed that the colony's borders were to be determined by the distance that a cannon ball could be shot from a frigate in the river – apparently, it seems, just over ten miles. It began life early in the 19th century, as a naval base from which to launch anti-slaving operations against the predominantly French traders. As was the case all along the Atlantic coast, the Portuguese were the first Europeans to reach the river. They were also the first to stay, attracted by an ample wealth of cotton, rice, exotic animals and golden jewellery. As a result, they called the river *Cambio* ['trade' or 'exchange']. In 1455, shortly after the Portuguese landfall, the Italian explorer Cà da Mosto received slaves, as well as gold, from a local chief, a commodity that was to shape over three and a half centuries of West African history.

British involvement dates from Elizabethan times, when, in 1587, two English vessels returned from the river laden with cargoes of hides and ivory, an expedition which resulted in a charter being awarded to the Company of Adventurers, enabling them to trade in rice, beeswax, hides, ivory and gold, and later, slaves. The British received lasting control as part of the spoils of the Napoleonic Wars, and declared it a protectorate in the 1820s during the height of the Timbuctoo gold rush. For the most part, however, the British experience in the Gambia was not a happy one. In fact, so disastrous was it that it now seems almost absurd, for the misfortunes of the would-be colonisers were caused not only by bad luck (and a lot of it at that), but by a remarkably sustained tendency to gross ignorance, arrogance and stupidity that almost defies belief. In the year 1618, for example, a British-led gold-searching expedition got 250 miles upriver (in the quixotic hope of sailing to Timbuctoo) before being massacred by hostile tribes. A second foray, also in the 17th century, was led by 'Richard Jobson, Gentleman' under the similar illusion that the Senegal and Gambia rivers conjoined, but nothing much came of the venture except for a hopelessly optimistic description of the region entitled *The Golden Trade* (in which Jobson spoke of 'a great Towne... the houses whereof are covered onely with gold').

After these initial disappointments, the following century or so saw little more in the way of further exploration, the Europeans being by now far more interested in plundering the wealth of India and the Far East. Then, in 1790, an Irish major named Houghton left the river Gambia for Timbuctoo. Alas, his last communication read: 'Major Houghton's compliments – Is in good health on his way to Timbuctoo, [but] robbed of all his goods.' He was never heard of again. Five years later saw the arrival of Mungo Park, the first explorer since Leo Africanus to make any substantial inroads into the interior, and one of the few Britons not to make a fool of himself. In 1805, however, he returned to the Gambia for the second time, and 'set sail to the east with the fixed resolution to discover the termination of the Niger or perish in the attempt.' Park's last despatch, in similar vein to Houghton's, read: 'I am sorry to say... that of the forty-four Europeans who left the Gambia in perfect health, five only are at present alive...' Weeks later, some 400 miles from the Bight of Benin, Park and his remaining entourage were murdered by vengeful Tuareg warriors, for it appears that wherever he went, Park's rifle had wreaked a trail of havoc. Still the expeditions continued. In 1816, a sixteen-year-old René Caillié narrowly escaped death by being refused permission to join a disastrous expedition under a certain Major William Gray. Death and disaster were commonplace. Of a contingent of 199 soldiers who arrived in Bathurst (Banjul) in May 1825, 160 had died from disease by Christmas. The next year, 101 of a further 200 soldiers had died. In an 1830s expedition sponsored by the Birkenhead merchant and shipbuilder Macgregor Laird (the sponsor of the first steam-powered Atlantic crossing), 38 of its 48 members perished. A decade later, on a government expedition, 48 of the 145 Europeans were lost within two months of leaving Bathurst. It has been estimated that of any group of Europeans newly arrived on the coast in the 18th century, between twenty-five and seventy-five percent died within their first year. It is with good reason that West Africa became known as the White Man's Grave.

Sir Richard Francis Burton, in inimitable jocular fashion, remarked: 'There is no place where a wife is so much wanted as in the Tropics; but then comes the rub – how to keep the wife alive.' Similarly, Mary Kingsley, one particularly remarkable woman who did survive West Africa (1897), was advised before her departure:

> When you have made up your mind to go to West Africa (the Deadliest spot on earth) the very best thing you can do is to get it unmade again and go to Scotland instead; but if your intelligence is not strong enough to do so... get some introductions to the

Wesleyans; they are the only people on the Coast who have got a hearse with feathers.

* * *

From Sokone to Barra – on the north bank of the Gambia estuary – lies the ancient kingdom of Niumi-Banta (literally 'upward of the coast'). In the 16th century, many wars were fought over this fertile land, between the people of the Saloum and the Niuminka, wars that are fabled to have ended with an epic fight against a huge dragon-snake. The land of Niumi-Banta is a largely level plain, with a soil of sand and clay that absorbs the autumn rains like a sponge. There is an abundance of grasses and trees, mainly short and scrubby, with the exception of a few kapoks and lonesome baobabs. Passing Amdalai, the soil becomes clayish, dotted with bushes and termite nests stood to attention like sentries.

There was dust everywhere, though the colour of the soil – a deep Venetian red – was quite startling in the evening sunlight. The termitaria though, were empty and crumbling, their ruins inhabited only by the deadly-poisonous Gaboon viper or python. The cry of a faraway goat resonated about my ears, gouging streaks across the deserted airscape. Screams, echoes, silence. The rustle of highway leaves and the wind, not quite strong enough to whistle, just sighed. Further on, a village rounded the savannah road, all brown and buff, with low, squat buildings and low, squat walls. They were picture book buildings, with thatched coronet rooves and straw ochre hues. Some had tiny missionary churches made of wooden planks, with quaint pointed rooves painted white, green and blue. Circular granaries stood on stilts, containing heads of Guinea corn, millet, rice, and pumpkins when in season. I passed several hand-dug wells – funded by international charities – their existence blazing forth from large painted signs that were posted outside fenced enclosures. From inside them, scraggy kids yelled and gesticulated at me as they hauled up rubber-tyre buckets splashing water, and then placed them dripping on the dusty ground. The odd lark circled around the luscious green canopies of Scotch bonnet pepper trees, cawing with a couple of lovebirds and the odd grey parrot.

Gnarled old men and trees stood motionless beside the road. In one clearing, beside a dusty mango tree, children were busily collecting the first windfalls into piles of orange and green, which were then packed into the wicker baskets that I saw everywhere along the road, accompanied by cries of 'Hey, meester, man-go man-go, fresh, goood!' and competing 'Hey, here *very* goood!' I stopped to buy some. They were cheap but hard, tasted acidic and made me nauseous. A few miles on, though, beside great porcupine clumps of bamboo interwoven with pink and orange bougainvillea, the fruit was larger and more tender, and tasted much better. Many people told me that I would soon be able to live on mangos, but whether through choice or compulsion, they did not say.

In the evening, the northern horizon whence I had come clouded over and the wind stiffened. Storm birds in crimson, peacock-blue and saffron circled high above, but then fell silent as the wind died to suffocate the trees. The sky became mottled in greys and browns.

The lightning metamorphosed the trees into split-second alabaster statues. A dog yelped in the silence. A couple of unconcerned zebu cattle walked slowly over a nearby hillock, silhouetted against a sombre patina of myrtle, jade and pepper green. Then came the deluge.

I had been asleep only for an hour or so, when I was awoken by a rustling beneath me. I removed my kipmat to reveal a couple of snake holes, which on reflection probably belonged to a puff adder. Unthinkingly, I stuffed them shut with twigs and leaves, then replaced the mat and fell asleep. I woke up a few hours later, dreaming of welcome faces and hot baths and beer. I was looking forward to getting back to Manchester. It was still raining – the second rain of the season – and I was soaked despite my Gore-tex shroud. I shivered and felt hungry, and the wind was cold and blustery. I packed up by belongings, and set off towards Banjul in a miserable grey dawn, the going decidedly slow and cumbersome over the muddy quagmire that the red laterite road had become. At least the rains of that year were to be the best for almost a decade, and wherever I went, people were already talking excitedly about the prospects of a good harvest. After what seemed like an age, the road swung sharply to the left beside the riverine hulk of Fort Bullen, built by the British on Barra Point in 1826 to defend Banjul against French slavers. The road dropped gently down to the shore of the Gambia itself and the ugly settlement of Barra, once the capital of a powerful Mandingo kingdom. Behind Barra and its ferry quay stretched true forest, in parts almost rainforest. I was pleased to think that I had cycled this far south.

As I arrived – as frozen and miserable as the sky – the heavens seemed to redouble their efforts to flood the country. Lumpy sewage overflowed their gutters, spewing shit and greenish brown gristle into murky potholes in which lived empty bottles and plastic bags. People were huddled in the shelter of dripping tin rooves, and greeted the arrival of the bedraggled *Toubab* with a kind of bewildered amusement. While waiting for the ferry, I observed a man who, I was frequently assured, was quite definitely *the* worst fisherman in all the Gambia. I watched him for a while, with his wrinkled mouth and cloth flatcap, eternal emblems of patience. He had a circular net, weighted at its fringes, which he spun into the the river like a mop. Then, when he caught a score of heavy fish, he quietly packed up his belongings and made his way back home. My confidants were speechless.

I caught the eleven o'clock boat for the forty minute crossing to Banjul. Peddlars sold tricorned Cornish fish pasties, fresh fish, and ice from shoulder-slung plastic crates. Fat, sweating men hawked biscuits and fishcakes, and grubby kids strutted about with bags of flavoured ice: plain, ginger, orange essence, and red *bissap*, made from hibiscus flowers. A few ocean-going freighters were moored in the estuary, alongside small Portuguese-style wooden cutters with their sails arranged like butterfly wings. Between them phutted motorised canoes, carrying salt in palm leaf baskets from the coast. The salt trade would shortly be closing down because of the rains. Eventually, through the mist, appeared the low skyline of Banjul, its few palms tickling the clouds like enormous feather dusters. It was a most welcome sight, because Banjul was the end of my journey.

* * *

I stepped off the Barra ferry to the sound of thunderclaps echoing dully from a murky brown cloud base that hung low over the town. For a while, I grew cold and miserable again as I cycled around in search of accomodation, drenched not only from above but by great dollops of rancid mud thrown up by passing cars. Once-bright shopfronts and neatly whitewashed offices, too, were coated in mud. Beside them, poorer people crouched under the cardboard packaging that probably served as their nocturnal shelters as well.

Banjul began life in the 19th century, upon the request of Sir Charles Macarthy[14], then Governor of Sierra Leone, for a garrison to control violators of the Abolition of Slavery Act which had been passed by Parliament in 1807. Then, in 1816, the settlement of Bathurst (named after the Secretary for War) was founded on Saint Mary's Island, intended as a haven for liberated Africans. Saint Mary's Island, however, is a forlorn place, flanked for the most part with steaming mangrove swamps. 'Like all European settlements of that date,' remarked Burton of Bathurst, 'that site is execrable and the buildings excellent.'

To be fair to Banjul, I thought at first that the town had something of an eclectic atmosphere to it. In fact, it was just the kind of place I had come to expect from an old English colony. It is flat, misty, sweaty, and sometimes quite serene. I considered the place to have a certain charm, a kind of laid-back dilapidation not dissimilar to that of Saint-Louis. Banjul, as the town was renamed in 1973, is the crumbling capital of the Gambia, a strange place still lingering with the old ghosts of the British Empire. Collapsing colonial town houses line streets called Oxford, Wellington and Stanley. The signs at the taxi ranks read 'For Hackney Carriages Only' whilst others, long since corroded, still proclaim the health-giving properties of Ireland's most famous brew. There are Kenyan-style safari jeeps adorned like zebras for bush-hatted tourists to see crocodiles, and there is even an English-style fish and chip shop. Other immediate impressions included London-style letter boxes, Morris Minors, the odd Bedford lorry, adverts for 'Tizer the Appetizer', and ancient wooden chests that were stamped 'HORLICKS MALTED MILK'. On Buckle Street there were tailors who still crouched over Imperial sewing machines supplied by the Crown Agents, and there was even an old truck from Leeds, unceremoniously buried under a fallen tree. Beside it, pinstriped businessmen sauntered past carrying briefcases under their arms. Banjul is an odd place. As Richard West put it in 1965: 'Gambia is more English than England, more English even than India.'

The town that was created by the British now survives only amidst their rotten legacy (latter-day British visitors are treated with a curious mixture of hate and respect). Infrastructure was woefully neglected, even during the halcyon days of the Empire, and in the years since independence (1965), investment has been, with the exception of the coastal package-tour hotels, virtually nonexistent. Like so many cities on the West African coast, Banjul has become a dead end, a stagnant place exuding little in the way of hope or optimistic bravura for the future. The corrugated rooves of once pristine sandstone houses are now rusted and corroded, their paint discoloured and leprous. The streets are full of murky potholes, mud-slurry and piles of rubbish. Rotting fruit, vegetables and fish offal lie everywhere, adding another layer to the often choking stench of open sewers that have nowhere to flow to. Once covered with iron grates or concrete slabs, most of these have long since been lost or stolen, though in places planks have been thrown over the rocking flagstones as an alternative to having to leap across the stinking ditches. In places there are dogs in the gutter, dead and bloated, and everywhere children can be seen playing in the mud or trying to catch rats. Clouds of flies and mosquitoes gather above the more rancid patches, and the stench is often indescribable. In consequence, one of the strongest impressions I have of Banjul is of a city drowning in itself. Add to this the hot and cloying climate of the tropical verges, and it becomes easy to see why ministers and officials deign no longer to live in the capital. Banjul, like Dakar, is a place where diplomatic limousines with smoked windows cruise along in silence past ragged beggars and pitiful hawkers, the latter almost pleading for your custom.

Wellington Street brought me to the iron railings of Macarthy Square, a grassy enclosure that doubles as a cricket field. On one side, it is flanked by the State House, a small bandstand and a memorial to both World Wars (in which both Gambian and Senegalese soldiers lost their lives). On the other side of the square is Gloucester Street, lined with aged casuarina trees and the tiny Anglican Cathedral of Saint Mary. Here, the more established street pedlars sell cigarettes and Chinese-built portable stereos. Other pedlars surreptitiously pass me bootleg Bob Marley and Michael Jackson cassettes as though they were heroin. Others push the real thing, invariably more openly. The less fortunate sell underpants and socks of behalf of rich importers and smugglers. The legal status of the hawkers is uncertain, and consequently their relationship with the police is something of a cat-and-mouse affair. The police, though no better and no worse than other West African forces, spend much of their time bullying and extorting extra wages from those hawkers too slow to pack up and disappear into the crowds. Once, when a telegraph pole beside the guarded entrance of the ministries caught fire, sparking like a crazy Catherine wheel, the police reacted by rushing into the laughing crowd with leather-bound truncheons.

Past the hawkers is the waterfront Albert Market, a lively place despite having been gutted by fire a few months previously. Fat women with bulging backsides sold bundles of thatch for roofing, and mangos of every description and size. Some displayed as few as half a dozen on plastic sheets laid out on the ground. Others, in contrast, were sat on top of hessian sacks full of the things. I saw great piles of red and green chillis, peppercorns, and chickens and limes for making 'Chicken Yassa'. Elsewhere, men were busy working leather into handbags, belts and wallets. The punter with money can choose from crocodile, python, giraffe, and many other endangered species. Other stalls sold carved wooden figurines, and sometimes ivory, despite the ban.

In one corner, a little old man dressed in a black and white polka dot robe, sat fiddling with a chain of worry beads. Like an emperor, he lorded over his barrowful of kola nuts. The man had a slim, wizened face, with a goatee and shorn hair. He also had a digital watch, which he made a point of frequently looking at. His hands were much the same colour

321

as half of his kolas, a burnished orange-brown. The others were a creamy white[15].

Past the last few blackened husks of the fire-gutted stores was the shore, where fishermen serviced and repaired their dugouts and nets, or else crouched beside smouldering blankets of ashes, over which fish were placed for smoking. Nearby rose odorous piles of discarded oyster shells, harvested from the mangrove swamps around the black, shark-infested waters of Oyster Creek (where else?). Once, on my way back through the market, I came across a jeering crowd, in the centre of which a fight was in progress. A couple of policemen prowled around on the periphery, waiting to see whether the fight would resolve itself naturally and so save them the paperwork. By the time the officers eventually decided to intervene – a good twenty minutes later – the two men had already been separated by a group of children. Five minutes later, when the police had gone, the shouting and fighting began all over again, the crowd having decided that the fight was about a woman. Accusations flew, alongside insults, feet and fists. At times the two combatants assumed karate-style postures, but their composure quickly became submerged by more kicking, pulling and punching. The crowd eventually called an end to the fight with one bloody nose, a cut arm, two ripped shirts, a bleeding eye, and humiliation to both, crowned by the loud smirks and jeers of the children.

Another fight I saw was between a woman and a man, and seemed to be much more of a family affair. Although she was much thinner than he, she was a much better fighter, and hoots of delight arose from the assembled throng as her assailant/ex-lover/accuser was clobbered mercilessly around the head with a bag of groceries.

The Ministry of Tourism, consisting of a man, a desk and a cupboard, furnished me with the addresses of Banjul's cheaper establishments, meaning a tenner a night for a damp windowless room in a bordello, service *not* included. I faced the same problem as on arriving in Dakar and Saint-Louis, namely, that I needed almost all my remaining money for the flight back to Europe. The City Traveller's Lodge on Dobson Street was first on the list, a dingy whorehouse with no locks on the doors, and too expensive all the same. Little better, but unfortunately full, was the Duma Guest House on Hope Street. Also full was the Teranga on Hill Street. Empty, but far too expensive, was the Numa, just past Sam Jack Terrace. Probably the best of a particularly bad bunch was Uncle Joe's on Cameron Street, cosy in a damp mahogany kind of way, but certainly not worth the $20 asking price. In any case, I managed to offend old Joe himself, by not replying to him when he called me over. I'd been told that he was senile, although obviously not enough to let my rudeness go unchecked.

Put off by my lack of success, I made my way to the shack-like Anglican cathedral, in the hope that they might direct me to somewhere cheaper, or even have lodgings themselves. There, I had a stroke of luck. The gardener, a short youth with spindly, stubbled legs, offered to put me up. He was from Sierra Leone, and claimed to be Christian despite being called Abdul. He spoke Krio, a strange mixture of African dialects, English, French and Portuguese that sounds very like Afrikaans. Abdul was in much the same kind of mess as the refugees I'd met in Dakar, and like Tokpah Kennedy, had been discovered trying to smuggle diamonds into Senegal. In consequence, his only form of identification was a blotched photocopy of a letter from the Red Cross, stating only that he had been to them for help. He had found temporary lodging in an Aku compound (the Aku are English-speaking descendants of former Sierra Leonean slaves).

I was led to an ancient brick building on Clarkson Street, named after one of the initiators of the 18th century anti-slavery movement. Its walls were now gangrenous with a decaying film of mildew. Only two of the three floors were inhabited, because the uppermost had rotten floorboards and no roof. Most of the windows had long been broken, their frames used for firewood, and a mesh of unconnected wires hung limply from the top of the building, at times used to hang washing. Tall walls topped with shards of glass enclosed a muddy courtyard spiked with more broken glass and bits of wood brandishing rusted nails. The overall appearance was of a bomb-damaged Ulster police station. In the far corner, opposite the main building, was a smaller shack, its oxidised roof held down with bricks and shredded tyres. It doubled as a restaurant, although as far as I could see, it had no customers other than the Akus who lived here. The toilet shed, beside the restaurant, was utterly stomach-turning (the slop bucket had never been emptied, and was infested with maggots).

Abdul's room smelt strongly of sandalwood, excrement and blood – the smell of squashed mosquitoes. He shared the room with his brother, who sold silky lingerie beside the railings of Macarthy Square: bras, stockings and briefs emblazoned with irreverent slogans like 'Men at Work', and a sideline in cheap cologne aftershave and bead necklaces. Inside the room, the holes in the floor were covered with plastic sheeting, and like the refugees' compound in Dakar, the walls were bare but for the mould stains and a few fist-sized holes. Excepting a small table, on which another guy made Cornish pasties every evening, there was no furniture, not even a bed to sleep on. At night, the room was plagued by mosquitoes, and the heavy air gave rise to frequent headaches. Outside, the balcony was too rotten to stand on, but if you dared anyway, the ledge would crumble away under your hands as you leant on it, adding yet more rubble to the pile that had begun to block up the passageway below. Still, it was home and a roof, better at any rate than sleeping in the street.

* * *

Things began to go awry after I discovered that I could not afford a flight out of Banjul either. I spent most of my days traipsing increasingly heavy-footed from airline office to travel agency to embassy to consulate, all without much luck. I became a frequent visitor to the docks in the hope of finding a freighter that might take me back to Europe, but without much success either, although I realised that short of somehow stowing myself aboard an aircraft, the port was my only hope. With this in mind, I made friends with the guards at the gates, buying them cigarettes and offering them meals if they wanted. I also met Doudou, a young Senegalese from Rufisque who worked at the port whenever he could (which wasn't all that often). The port has only two berths, and even they lie empty for most of the time, there being at most four or five ships a week, mostly southbound. The gates outside were more or less permanently besieged with men, hopeful for the chance of precious little work.

In the absence of freighters, Doudou sometimes helped with the unloading of small fishing boats, but would only be paid with a few fish. He lived in a room quite literally made of cardboard at the southernmost reaches of Hagan and Buckle Street, the thin partition walls held together with makeshift rivets of nails and bottle-tops. At times, his expression would be almost childlike, with a wide mouth and big, questioning eyes; but when he got stoned at lunchbreak with a few other workers, his countenance changed markedly. He sucked on the joints with an urgency that betrayed his smoking *yamba* as a necessity and relief, rather than for pleasure. Together, the group had the same sad, gaunt faces and flaring, bloodshot eyes as had the workers at the iron ore terminal at Nouâdhibou.

One lunchtime, Doudou slunk off to buy half a bottle of *cana*, a near-lethal spirit illegally distilled from palm wine. It tasted like paint-stripper, so I left it alone. Africa Gin, as it's known here, is sold by word of mouth only. Most of all, it is fear of the corrupt police force that keeps Africa Gin in the underground shebeens of Banjul.

One night it rained as never before, raindrops punching through the trees like water-filled balloons to bombard Banjul's tin rooves like some dreadful apocalypse. At the same time, or perhaps because of this, there was a power failure, accompanied by much shouting and screaming. Once again the roads were churned into a bubbling fury of mud and sewage, and after the rainstorm had subsided, the stench if anything was worse than it had been before. That night, I decided to pay a visit to the Ritz Cinema, which was showing some trashy American desert-romp in T-shirts and beach-buggies. The support feature, however, was what most people had paid their two dalasis to see: a scratchy film of Youssou N'dour and his band Super Etoiles de Dakar, to which the entire audience, despite the dire sound quality, got up from their seats and started dancing wildly, shouting, clapping, singing along, waving their arms, and even old ladies swirling their dresses! The place stank of sweat. Half way through the second film I threw up. I ran outside, took one lungful of the sewers, and to my embarrassment threw up again, to the disgust of passers-by.

'Ah, Banjul belly,' laughed Abdul's brother, who suddenly stopped laughing when I threw up over the floor and his tape player. I felt worse when, on looking through the bicycle panniers, I discovered that two hundred French francs had mysteriously disappeared, and that my camera had been tampered with. The brother suggested that I talk to Abdul.

The poor guy was so scared when I eventually confronted him that he immediately admitted taking the money, saying that he had only 'borrowed' it. I offered to take a walk with him, which he couldn't really refuse, and then over roasted butterfish threatened him with the police if my money did not reappear. With hindsight, this was the worst thing that I could have done. Good humour and a long leash, I learned much later, is the best way to deal with *tifing*. Or better still, amnesia. Abdul pleaded with me to let him have the money as a gift, but I didn't relent, so eventually he said he'd give it me back midday tomorrow. No hard feelings, I said. I had committed my first mistake.

Midday. The door was locked. Abdul was late. One o'clock. Two o'clock. Still no sign of Abdul. I went to find his brother in Macarthy Square, but he said that he hadn't seen him all day. He gave me the key to the room. Confused, I walked back to the compound and unlocked the door. Inside, I found my bike, only minus my camera, my cagool, my harmonica, a bunch of clothes, and all my money. It took a few minutes for the reality of things to sink in, and then I was mortified. I checked and rechecked my bags in a panic, wailing. How on earth would I get back to England? Then I noticed that my diary too was missing. I slumped on the floor, half-sobbing and half-shouting that the fucker couldn't even read.

I was left with 22 pence, fifty dalasis (£5) and my passport that had been in my pocket. I had no credit cards, no cheques and no means. I went to the police station, but they refused to issue an insurance declaration because I had no money to pay for it. In any case, I wasn't even insured. God knows why, I just hadn't thought it necessary. 'Sorry, rules are rules,' they said. A woman officer smiled weakly, and seemed to pity me, but she couldn't help either. '*Boné, boné,*' she said, bad luck.

The next day the gut feeling set in. I broke down in the evening when the captain of a Spanish tanker refused point-blank to listen to my pleas. Rules are rules, he said. I sat by the bow mooring ropes, sobbing quietly as I watched a large barracuda splashing in the murky water, free of cares, or so it seemed. Later I met a Dutch couple who had the first white hair I'd seen in ages, sat at a cafe on Wellington Street with bottles of coke, Guinness, Julbrew, and eggs and sausages that I could no longer afford. They were surrounded by hustlers, and much to my chagrin, they seemed to be enjoying the attention.

'Oh, you've been robbed,' they said. 'Akh, that's bad news. Um, aah… Well, we've had a great time,' they said, not really knowing what else to say.

'Good for you,' I muttered, feeling even more depressed.

'Why didn't you stay at Uncle Joe's?' they asked. Christ, why didn't I bloody stay at Uncle Joe's? Because I needed the money for the flight, that was why, and now it was gone all the same.

The day after – July 1st – I was more angry than anything else. The situation was that although Abdul had obviously taken all my stuff and run off somewhere, his elder 'brother' had been taken in by the police as a suspect. There, it turned out that he wasn't Abdul's brother at all, and he said that he didn't even know him. I went again to the police station to see how they'd got on, and immediately noticed a change of mood. The inspector in charge of the case became angry with me because I'd said 'Hello' instead of 'Good afternoon, Sir,' and he obviously wasn't prepared to take me seriously. After half an hour of futile arguing I left red-faced, confused, and depressed. I had also found out that the 'brother' had been released on bail, which made me angrier still because I knew that he was involved (he had the only key to the room). I tried to stay cool, though I must have seemed to be steaming with rage as I went back to the Aku compound to pick up my bicycle. Upon checking the panniers to see if anything else was missing, I found to my consternation that five hundred francs had been returned, I suppose to give me something to live on whilst I sorted out my predicament. I still can't understand what was intended by the gesture, if anything at all. Perhaps it was meant to stop me going to the police, or maybe Abdul or his 'brother' had been forced to repay at least part of the sum by the other members of the compound. Perhaps, even, Abdul was feeling guilty or remorseful. I shall never know, although I discounted the latter as I was now convinced that Abdul was the most evil man that I had ever had the misfortune to meet.

I put it to several people in and around the compound that I knew that Abdul was still in Banjul, and indeed that they'd seen him, and that they knew where he was. To my relief and yet irritation, nobody denied this. Maybe... As I carried on my hot-headed accusations, in marched two policemen and the inspector I'd argued with earlier. Before I knew what was happening, a pair of cold handcuffs snapped around my wrists. Facts didn't seem to matter as I, along with my bicycle, was bundled out of the compound and into a jeep where another two officers waited. Abdul's 'brother' stayed behind, staring blankly at me as I was driven away.

'What have I done? Where are we going?'

'Keep your mouth shut, *Toubab*, you have caused enough trouble already.'

'Trouble? What trouble? I didn't decide to be robbed of...'

'You have been causing trouble,' he interrupted. 'You have been hitting people, and trespassing,' he added. By now I didn't know what to think. I was confused and very frightened.

'What have I done?' I asked again. 'It's Abdul you should arrest, not me.'

'Abdul?' the inspector asked, as though he had quite forgotten.

'You have no right to accuse people *willy-nilly*, *Toubab*. Now keep your mouth *shut*.'

Slowly, the realisation dawned that the police had been paid off with my money.

'HATE! Sickening frustration, dead-hearted. Heavy legged. Want to get out, escape. I hate this... I'm going to find Abdul and beat his brains out!' I wrote while I spent the rest of the day in jail. It scared me as I wrote it, because I'd never felt so much rage before. In a way I felt proud that I'd at last managed to think of such a thing, for I was convinced that I would never have hurt a soul before this affair. I also decided that if I wanted to get myself out of this mess, I would have to fight. With hindsight, this was not only misguided, but sounds like all too much exaggerated bravura, but that's quite simply the way I then felt. The problem was that there was no one to fight. Abdul had disappeared, and if I approached his 'brother' or the police again, I would be re-arrested. The feelings of pride and invincibility that I'd gained from having crossed the Sahara quickly withered away, and for a long time after meant nothing any more. The difference was that the Sahara had been my choice, and to a large extent its problems, and my success or failure, had depended on my own efforts, whereas in Banjul I suddenly found myself in a situation that I had neither planned for, nor wanted. It felt like some perverse punishment for having succeeded so far.

Alas, I only now realise that I had forgotten the most important lesson of those crazy days between Atâr and Akjoujt, namely that I was largely responsible for whatever happened to me, good or bad. And not only was I responsible for my own well-being, but it should have been my duty as a foreigner *not* to conform to the hateful stereotype of the rich and arrogant *Toubab*, whom, regardless, I played to a tee. Not once, for instance, had I thanked Abdul for putting me up, nor had I seriously considered offering to pay for his troubles.

I did not understand the society that I was in, but more damning, I did not much feel the need to. As I mentioned in an earlier chapter, the reason for this was partly the anticlimax I felt after leaving the beautiful extremity of the desert. The desert had left in me a desire for extremes, and as a result, my way of regarding people and events had become more polarised, and I only saw things (ironically) in terms of black and white. Abdul, that night when I had confronted him about the 200F, had tried to reach a compromise, but instead I had menaced him and had caused him fear. By threatening him with the police, I killed his hope, and at the same time gave him no other way out of his predicament (I knew that he had spent the money). By my stubbornness, I merely showed Abdul that I did not understand him, that I saw him only as a thief. And since I saw him only as a thief, then he had nothing to lose by acting like one. Not once did I try to put myself in his position, to understand his helpless poverty, the squalor of life as a refugee, to comprehend his temptation. So, by pushing Abdul over the brink, I pushed myself over too. I was *made* to understand Abdul's poverty by being reduced to the same penury and misery. It was as though Abdul was saying: 'You, you who are so rich, if you still will not understand us, then we'll impoverish you so that you will. You will become one of us.'

That night, as I wheeled my bike down Buckle Street towards Doudou's, with whom I was now staying, a skinny youth, about twenty, latched onto me and tried to start a conversation.

'Hello my friend, what are you doing?'

'I don't want to talk to you,' I replied, paranoid.

'I want to be your friend,' he said.

'I don't,' I said.

'But, but I like...'

'I don't! Get lost – LEAVE ME ALONE!' I was close to tears. Then another guy appeared and started following me. When he tried to take the bicycle pump that was attached to my now half-empty rear panniers, I stopped, turned around and simply punched him as hard as I could in his face. I knocked him out. Christ, I knocked him out! His friend withdrew to a safer distance, then ran away. I picked up the pump and walked on. It was the first time that I'd ever hit someone without them hitting me first. I was scared out of my wits.

I went for a midnight swim beside the port to calm my nerves, but I kept touching seaweed and floating planks which in my paranoia became corpses and dismembered bodies. Doudou said he'd stake out Clarkson Street for me to await any sign of Abdul's reappearance, but the next morning, I found that both Doudou and the rest of my money (the five hundred francs) were missing. I can't remember how I reacted. Probably cold, dull shock: *déjà vu*. Then despair. My last friend in the world, or so it seemed, had turned out to be even more two-faced than Abdul.

Doudou's friend came back about midday. He admitted that he knew Doudou had taken the money, but that he hadn't realised what I had already been through, and whether through guilt at not stopping Doudou or pity for me, the *Toubab*, he even showed signs of sympathy. He took me to his house – without exaggeration a mound of rubble – then took me to an eatery for a meal, all the time waiting for Doudou. We went to the port, but the guards said that Doudou hadn't turned up for work that day, which they thought was odd. At dusk, in a cloying hot breeze, I went to see a woman at the Teranga hotel who had known Doudou, and who had had a large butane gas cylinder stolen from her by him. She told of a couple of other *Toubabs* who had been similarly treated in the past, and she advised I try the City Traveller's Lodge, the brothel I'd visited on my futile hotel-search on first arriving in Banjul.

'Hello, little boy!' they purred mockingly, fat legs and short skirts splayed out on tables lining the hallway. The only light came from a couple of dim, orange bulbs.

'Oh, you're a friend of Doudou's,' they said, I guess a little disappointed that I was not a customer. They told me that he'd gone home for a while to get changed. So, Doudou was spending *my* money in a *whorehouse*. I was so angry that I decided that I would kill him, or at least slash him a few times. I was mad with rage, irrational, but above all pathetic.

We spotted Doudou at the far edge of a large gravelly square, lined with low eathouses and stores. I took large strides, I don't think deliberately. I took out my penknife, and pulled out its laughable two-inch blade. Suddenly, not looking, I fell into a sewage ditch. Doudou's friend took away my knife. I staggered out of the pit, my legs cut and bleeding, and my whole body trembling. My anger dissipated in the shock. Doudou looked on, fresh-faced and smirking, and muttered something about having been up all night but still no sign of Abdul.

'Where's my money?' I demanded.

'What money?' he replied glibly, still trying to look innocent.

'I'm going to kill you,' I hissed, but without much conviction – the peak of my rage had deserted me. 'I'm going to kill you!' He laughed and sneered, and a little of my anger returned. He unbuttoned his shirt and let it fall to the ground.

'If I am your thief,' he said, 'then fight me. Hit me, come on, hit me.' His sneer was gone as he braced himself. God, how I hated him, but still my legs trembled and reminded me of my sudden fall, and to my deepest humiliation, I decided that I would gain nothing by fighting him. So instead, I just stared at him, trying to leave a mental scar by letting him know that at least I hated him more than anyone else in the world, even Abdul. I stared and he sneered. He won and I lost. So much for having to fight my way out of things.

* * *

I walked back alone to Doudou's to collect my bike. I considered burning down his hut, but then came to the conclusion that it wasn't even worth the money he'd stolen (it shows something about the state of mind I was in that this was the only reason why I didn't commit arson). It was almost midnight. I was sat at the roadside by a reeking sewage ditch. Two prostitutes tried to talk to me, giggling, but I was so depressed and uncommunicative that they soon left me alone, which made feel even worse. A woman with her little daughter walked past, but the little girl screamed and ran behind her mother's legs wailing '*Toubaaab! Mama, mama!*'

I went to the police station to ask for a night in the cells, but the officer refused. So I said that seeing as they'd already jailed me once before for nothing, would they please do so now. No. I begged. No. Then did I have to attack someone, or steal, I asked. Yes, the officer replied.

Though I was blind to the irony, my situation now exactly mirrored that of Abdul. He, too, had needed to steal in order to have a roof above his head.

To my eternal gratitude, on leaving I met a policeman who turned out to be one of the few honest and kind people I was to meet in this damned place, and spent the night in the police barracks on the western periphery of town. The officer on the gate, though, suspected that I was a spy, and so I was kicked out the next day, against the wishes of my host, who was probably hauled up in front of his superiors for his kindness.

I tried the embassies again. The British said no-go because of my German passport. The German consul was suspicious because of my faltering German, and in any case she said that regulations meant that I could have no money unless it was wired from Europe. And yet, having money wired from my parents was anathema for me, even though it would long ago have solved my problems. I finally tried to sell my bicycle, the only thing of value that I had left, but the few offers I did get were nowhere near enough to pay for a ticket.

One morning I sunk so low as to try begging alongside the hawkers of Macarthy Square. I must have squatted there for about three hours, without once getting myself to ask for money. I felt so humiliated. Then, one guy selling homemade biscuits asked *me* for money. When I asked him why, he said it was because I was rich and he was so poor. So I yelled obscenities at him, and asked if I was so fucking rich, then what the hell was I doing here squatting against these bloody railings without so much as a penny in my pocket? He just laughed, perhaps because he didn't believe me, or perhaps because the sight of a *Toubab* begging on the streets of Banjul was just so funny. Either way, I didn't have the energy or willpower to carry on. I went to the Catholic Cathedral of Our Lady of the Assumption to beg for help, and a safe roof to sleep under while I waited for the nonexistent ship to take me away from all this, but on the way I was attacked for no reason. He had a look of absolute hatred in his eyes, looking for a fight like I had been. I restrained my tears, and to my shame but equal relief was rescued by a band of children who had been playing in the cathedral grounds. A wedding procession was leaving as I arrived, delicately hopping over the open sewers. It was a strange sight: gauze veils, cloche hats, white chamois gloves, monocles, and fat little feet squeezed into little Sunday best shoes. The men wore dinner jackets, black bow ties, silks and cravats, and their wives hung on their husbandly elbows, crooning about the happy couple. In any other circumstances, I might have laughed at them. As it was, I just tasted bile burning up my throat.

The Irish priest gave me a ten dalasi note, and told me not to bother him any more because he already had too many things to worry about. Where was I going to sleep? I wanted to sleep so much, but I didn't even trust the bush outside of Banjul anymore, and there were several unused rooms here, that were used only once a week for bible studies or some such thing. The priest said that it was impossible. I broke down on a pew, which was especially shattering for me as an atheist. I felt as though there was no place left to which I could turn. My nightmares had come true, nightmares that children have when they are trapped but cannot move, where they scream but no one hears, and they want to run but their feet are stuck fast to the ground like in a swamp and they are terrified. I vividly recalled my depression the previous autumn on all my plans for a world cycle ride falling through, when I'd never in my life felt worse. Then I'd imagined, horrifically, being locked up inside a bare pale blue padded cell inside an asylum – long walls echoing silently, distant cries, anguished, forgotten ghosts, endless walls. On asking for at least a pen and some paper so that I could write something, I was handed a huge joke pencil made of rubber because I was considered a suicide risk. Through my sobbing tears I remembered my mind's reaction: smashing my head against the padding on the walls, so much so that I visualised my battered head gaping open, spattered with brain and mangled bone. And I remembered breaking down in consequence, for the first time in my life. And now, one year on, I was thinking these same thoughts all over again...

Children gazed in through gaps in the stained glass at the feet of the saints, shouting insults, until they saw my tears and walked in silently, staring and no doubt bewildered at this apparent manifestation of the power of a religion alien to most Africans.

* * *

A month later I found myself back in Europe, back home, having managed, to my unspeakable relief, to hitch a lift on a German groundnut oil tanker, whose captain had only taken me aboard on account of my German passport. It felt odd being back home, escapee from Banjul, swamped with very indeterminate and confused feelings, the exception being the great joy on having first sighted the grim, misty, grey and overcast Humberside coastline, and on seeing my mother and sister surprise me at the port. Beyond that, I can't recall thinking much about my journey at all, whether it was the Sahara and the exhaltation at having crossed it, or the depths to which I had fallen in Banjul. My mind was, for a month at least, merely dazed, ticking over from day to day, exhausted, digesting, and unthinking. After a month, however, I found myself beset with nightmares, vengeful things that kept me awake at night. Bloody nightmares, gut-strewn daydreams, murderous fantasies. Every night, over and over again, I visualised killing both Abdul and Doudou. But not just killing – that would be too clinical a word – but joyously, deliriously, and hypnotically murdering in cold blood.

For a month I had these nightmares. It frightened me to see within. I found that I could not sleep, and when I did, I would wake a few hours later sweating and sometimes screaming, shocked and scared at the perverse innards of my twisted mind. The joke is that I never escaped at all. I merely accepted. I merely found solace in enacting revenge. Finally, I decided to write down these terrible fantasies, in the hope that I would then cope with them, and eventually, having barely slept and my nerves in tatters, my nightmares slipped away, and I had my first untroubled dream:

The desert. The burning sun. The burning sand. Upon which a man crawls. Dehydrated, semi-conscious. A lizard's tail flickers, far away. Crawling. Crawling towards a stone. The stone is a bird. Gold and black. Tiny, delicate, beak closed. 'Brother,' the man says, 'can you tell me how to find water? I don't suppose that you can tell me? I don't suppose that you can hear me?' The beak opens a fraction, but there is no reply. It seems that I can hear a whisper, a breath... Feathers ruffle gently in the breeze. Black grains of sand. The bird is dead. Its beak has become a mouth. 'Eat me.' Says the mouth. Says the little boy. The little boy is me.

Throughout my journey, I had thought only of me. It is not always a bad thing – if it hadn't been for my selfishness, my stubbornness, the belief in myself, I would never have managed to cross the solitary desert. And yet, in Banjul too I had thought only of me. I had thought only of me. If a grain of sand were to say, I am but a grain of sand, then there would be no Sahara. If a drop of water says that it is but a lone drop of water, then there is no rain. There is no music without notes to make it, without a heart there is no life. Man without man is nothing.

As the Moorish proverb says: it is man, not the desert, who eats you.

NOTES

1 Quoted in E.W Bovill.

2 Born in 1483 in Muslim Granada. In 1518, the young Hasan ibn Muhammad al-Wazzan al-Fasi was captured from an Arab galley by Christian corsairs (at the time, piracy was endemic in the Mediterranean). Because he had travelled widely, despite being only in his thirties, he was spared slavery and taken instead for an audience with Pope Leo X, who had acquired a commendable reputation for welcoming fresh intellectual talent into his Renaissance court (though he was later to excommunicate Luther). Leo X baptised the young Moor as Giovanni Leone, who was then given the freedom to complete his astonishing *History and Description of Africa and Notable Things therein contained*, published in Italian in 1526. It is still considered to be one of the most competent and indeed enduringly fascinating works on the continent's history.

3 Until the arrival of the French in 1912, Moroccan Jews were obliged to remove their shoes in Moorish quarters, and when passing mosques or the houses of sherifs. They were expected to yield right of way to Muslims in the street, and were forbidden to wear fine clothes or to ride horses. In addition, Jews had to pay the *jizya* poll tax to the Sultan for the privilege of living in the Mellah, the relatively secure ghetto within Fès Jdid's solid walls. The Moroccan Jews were also given what Arabs considered the more menial jobs; the name *mellah* is Arabic for salt, and was used to describe the Jewish quarters because they were given the task of salting the severed heads of criminals before they were put on public display.

4 *Pleurez vieux paresseux des temps incohérants*
Vos prétentions nous feront rire
Nous avons fait notre ciment
De la poussière du désert.

My translation. In a collection of etchings on display at the Musée National Fernand Léger, Biot, France.

5 *Parmis tous les vêtements, que Dieu confonde le voile!*
   tant que nous vivrons, ce sera un fleau pour les jeunes.
   Il nous cache les belles, sans que nous puissons les voir,
   camoufle les villaines pour nous induire en erreur.

My translation. In René Khawam's *La Poésie arabe, des origines à nos jours*, (Paris, Marabout Université, 1960).

6 This stanza (V.6) is taken from an anonymous translation in Cloudsley-Thompson's *Sahara Desert*, (Oxford, Pergamon, 1984). The original 17th translation is by Sir Richard Fanshawe: The Lusiads. Ed. and intro. by Geoffrey Bullough. London, Centaur Press, 1963.

The epic poem 'breathes all the zeal and aspiration of the Renaissance in its physical and social aspects and may be truly regarded as the first great modern heroic poem in the classical flower.' (Bullough).

7 Amnesty International has frequently expressed concern at the flouting of human rights in Morocco and the occupied Western Sahara:

> since 1976 when the Moroccan army became engaged in the Western Sahara, detention camps have been established, not only for prisoners of war, but also for members of the civilian population suspected of sympathising with the Polisario guerillas... Fear of such treatment has caused many thousands to flee from southern Morocco and Western Sahara into Algeria.

Amnesty International Briefing Paper, No. 13, 1977.

A 1979 report details 're-education' programmes in several jails, including Layoune's 'Calabozo' prison. *The Report of an Amnesty International Mission to the Kingdom of Morocco [in 1981]* (1982), reported illegal practices which: 'have led to serious human rights violations involving the "disappearance" of large numbers of people and the deaths in custody of others...' The disappearances, torture, and detentions are detailed, alongside evidence of napalm and phosphorous bombing of Saharawi civilians, in *Al-Mukhtufin (the disappeared): a report on disappearances in Western Sahara*, by Teresa K. Smith, in Lawless and Monahan's book *War and Refugees – The Western Sahara conflict* (London, Pinter, 1987). Smith concludes: 'Testimony from former disappeared persons, who subsequently escaped or were released, suggests that the Saharawis abducted are routinely subjected to imprisonment, torture and death.'

The disappearances are nothing new. In October 1965, Ben Barka, a Moroccan nationalist leader and politician, and co-founder of Istiqlal party, disappeared without trace in Paris, presumed dead. The affair was linked to the Moroccan Minister of the Interior, and it is assumed that Barka was assassinated on orders from Rabat. More recently, international media attention was focused on Morocco's semi-secret penal colonies. In December 1991, the three Bourequat brothers – long presumed dead – were released after nineteen years of internment without trial (they had been implicated in the 1971 and 1972 coup plots against King Hassan). For eleven of these years, they were kept in solitary confinement in lightless cells at Tazmamart (a military base not far from Rich) (see *Middle East Economic Digest* – Maghreb, issue 2, May 1991. See also Caroline Moorehead's article, *The Shame of King Hassan*, in *The Independent Magazine*, 22 February 1992).

See also: Tony Hodges *The Western Saharans*; John Damis *Conflict in Northwest Africa* (which describes the flight of Saharawi refugees to Tindouf); John Gretton *Western Sahara: The Fight for Self-Determination*.

For a pro-Moroccan view of the Western Sahara and the conflict, see Attilio Gaudio's *Le Dossier du Sahara Occidental*. Paris, Nouvelles Editions Latines, 1978.

8   In Sir Ernest A. Wallis Budge's *The Alexander Book in Ethiopia*, Oxford, 1933.

9   *on y remasse de l'or en paillettes. Il fait savoir que la plus grande partie des gens qui habitent la contrée sont occupés à ramasser de l'or dans ce fleuve qui, large d'une lieue, est assez profound pour les plus grands navires du monde*.

My translation, from the text of the secret archives of Genoa, in G. Gravier (1874). Quoted by R. Hallet (*The Penetration of Africa: European enerprise and exploration principally in Northern and Western African up to 1830*, London, Routledge, 1965).

10   My translation of a poem in *Il était une fois... en Mauritanie*. by Touré and others (Paris, Ligel, 1968). Included is a similar version of Tarkhit's story of the woman and the son.

11 Atâr itself was graced with the aura of a certain Captain Bonnafous (or Bonafos). In the 1920s, a decade after the French conquest of the Adrar, Bonnafous was given charge of the Atâr Camel Corps, an unenviable task given that the surrounding desert was then still swarming with unfriendly Moors determined to retake Atâr from the French. Clothed in traditional Moorish dress, Captain Bonnafous managed for almost ten years to hold out against the attempts of innumerable Moorish razzias to recapture the town. As the years passed by and his resistance remained as impassive as ever, a legend began to grow about him. Antoine de Saint-Exupéry, in *Wind, Sand and Stars*, describes him thus:

> he stands there like a guerdon to be won, and such is his magnetism that the tribes are obliged to march towards his sword... There is something magnificent in the possession of an enemy of Bonnafous' mettle. Where he turns up, the nearby tribes fold their tents, collect their camels and fly, trembling to think that they might have found themselves face to face with him... Even as men who desire a woman of her indifferent footfall, toss and turn in the night, scorched and wounded by the indifference of that stroll she takes through their dream, so the distant progress of Bonnafous torments these warriors.

See Capit. V. Bonafos, *Vestiges humains dans le Sahara occidental*. Rev. Milit. de l'A.O.F., No. 18 (15-7-1933).

12 Quoted by Sir Richard Francis Burton (1821-90) in *Abeokuta and the Camaroons...* (London, Tinsley Bros., 1863). "'Man,' says the Arab proverb, "eats you; the desert does not.'" (p112, vol.II).

Burton, incidentally, is the man who first translated the Kama Sutra of Vatsyayana, as well as the Arabian Nights.

13 Ben Okri, *Redreaming the World – An Essay for Chinua Achebe* in *The Guardian Review*, 9 August 1990.

14 Charles Macarthy. He met an untimely and gruesome death in 1823 (recounts Burton) through an unfortunate mistake. When under attack by Ashantis, his ordnance-keeper brought Macarthy some biscuits and macaroni instead of ammunition. As a result, they were beheaded! Macarthy's body was subsequently roasted, his fat was boiled into a lump, and his heart was eaten. His brains were removed, and his skull was sewn into his uniform and then

filled with gold, to become a fetish which was worshipped until (at the earliest) the 1860s.

15 Both varieties of kola nut are extremely bitter, for they contain both caffeine and theobromine, the latter a mild narcotic used both to relax one's mind and apparently also to increase one's virility if eaten often. In Gambia, a man who cannot eat his kola nuts is only half a man, or so the guide in his flashy pants and Italian brogues will tell you. Kolas have been used in the western Sudan since the very earliest times; its twin interlocking kernels are regarded by many as a symbol of peace and friendship, used as a gift much as henna is given to Berber housewives. The older generation swear oaths over the kola. More practically, farmers eat them in the lean 'hungry season' to assuage hunger and thirst, and in the past, Fulani and Mandingo men used them to gain courage when undergoing 'Soro' (a trial of manhood by flagellation). Heinrich Barth, an explorer in the mould of Caillè, called them 'one of the greatest luxuries of Negroland'. So valuable were kolas, that Richard Jobson mentioned the fact that only fifty of them were required to buy a wife from a king. The original medicinal Coca-Cola, made from both kola nuts and coca leaves, must have been quite some drink.

GLOSSARY

Abbreviations used:

A	Arabic (current throughout northwest Africa);
F	French;
H	Hassiniyah (Mauritanian);
M	Moroccan dialect (usually Berber);
P	Portuguese;
S	Saharan;
WA	West African;
WS	Western Saharan.

Abid (sing. abd)	A	Slaves/servants (of); Negro slave caste in Moorish society
Aïd el-Kebir	A	Festival held 50 days after Ramadan in commemoration of Abraham's willingness to sacrifice his son Isaac for the love of God
Aït	A	Lit. 'children of', hence tribe
Alhamdulillah/-i	A/H	'Praise be to Allah' (spoken at end of meal)
Ali		Cousin and son-in-law of Muhammad. 4th Caliph of Islam (656-61AD), but considered the first by the Shiites
'Ameria	M	Covered carriage for the bride on her wedding day
Amzil	A	Blacksmith
Aoud	A	11-stringed lute
Ashashin	M	Opium poppy; juice thereof (often confused with *hacheichi* or *hashish*)
Ash halak	H	'How are you?'
Bab	A	Gate; door; entrance
Baboush	A	Pointed leather slipper

Baisa	M	Ful soup of Chefchaouen and Rif
Balise	F	Desert road marker
Baraka	A	Divine blessing
Barkhan	S	Fast moving crescentic sand dunes
Barrage	F	Roadblock
Bayoud	S	Palm tree disease
Bazaar	A	Shop where a range of artisan goods is sold
Beni Hassan		One of several Yemeni tribes who emigrated to northwest Africa and the Western Sahara in the Middle Ages
Bidan	H	Upper noble caste of Moors, comprising *hassanes* and *marabouts*
Bidonville	F	Lit. 'tin-town', hence slums
Bismillah	A	'In the Name of Allah' (spoken as grace before meals). Full version: Bismillah al-Rahman al-Rahim, 'In the Name of Allah, the Beneficent, the Merciful'
Bled el-Bidan	M	'Lands of the Bidan' (Mauritania)
Bled el-Makhzen	M	'Lands of the Treasury' (ie governed by sultans)
Bled es-Siba	M	'Lands of Dissidence' (until 1930s, Berber – [Buber-dominated] dominated Rif, Atlas and Sahara)
Bled es-Sudan	M	'Lands of the Blacks' (the Sudan; Black Africa)
Bolong	WA	Creek; waterway
Bonava	WA	Meat and potato stew
Boné	WA	(Mandingo) bad luck
Bou	M	Father of (= Arabic *abou*)
Boubou	H	Light flowing Moorish robe
Brakna	H	Moors of southern Mauritania
Brochette	F	Meat roasted or grilled on a skewer (kebab)
B'slama	A	Goodbye
B'stilla	M	*Millefeuille* pigeon pie

Bukhakes	M	Sort of flying darkling beetle
Caliph	A	Title of the successors of Muhammad as rulers of the Islamic world
Cana	WA	Distilled palm wine
Chagi	S	Desert wind
Cheche	S	Face-muffler; turban
Couscous	A	steamed semolina, often served with meat or fish, and vegetables. National dish of Morocco
Damel	WA	(Wolof) king
Desert rose		Crystallised sandstone in form of flowers
Dhab	S	Large lizard. Its name means 'sound of running fast'
Djebel	M	Mountain; mountain range (from Arabic *jabal*)
Djinn (sing. djinni)	A	Supernatural spirits
Doum	A	Species of palm tree, often with several trunks
Ebliss	A	Dust-devil; the devil of carnal desires; the charms of a young woman
Erg	S	Range of sand dunes
Evil Eye		Curse; hex
Factoria	P	Slaving entrepôt
Fana	A/M	The Day of Judgement, when the universe will cease to exist – annihilation. Used by Moroccan Sufis to describe ecstatic communion with Allah/Paradise
Faneau	WA	Cotton fabric; body wrap
Fassi	M	Pertaining to Fès; citizen of Fès
Fatima		Daughter of Muhammad and wife of Ali
Fondouq	A	Courtyard (usually with a purpose)
Foul	A	Fava or lima beans. National dish of Egypt
Foum	M	Narrow river gorge

Fouta	A	Towel
Friq	S	Nomad encampment (upto about a dozen tents)
Ganga	M/WA	Drums played by Negro griots
Garro	M	Cigarette vendor (from *cigarro*)
Gnawa (sing. gnawi)	M	Clan of Negro griots originally from Guinea
Griot	WA	Itinerant musician, praise-singer and genealogist
Guedra	WS	Saharawi fertility dance; name of drum to which it is performed
Guelta	S	Water pool, usually formed in rock
Guerba	S	Animal skin water bag
Guetna	H	Date harvest; date-picking festival
Hacheichi	A	Lit. 'hashish-eater'; dope-fiend
Haejuj	M	3-stringed bass lute
Haik	A	Arab woman's outer garment for the head and body
Hajj	A	The pilgrimage to Mecca (one of the five Pillars of Islam) that every Muslim is required to make at least once in his life
Hammada	S	Flat, stone-strewn desert plain
Hammam	A	Moorish/Turkish bath
Hand of Fatima	A	Protective charm in form of hand and eye
Haratin	H	Moorish caste of mulattos whose slave status was often unclear. Often used to mean slave or, nowadays, ex-slave
Harira	M	Soup including chick peas, noodles, and tomato
Harissa	M	Red chilli and garlic sauce
Harmattan	S	Dry dusty wind from Sahara that blows towards the West African coast
Hashish	A	Cannabis resin
Hassane	H	Moorish caste of warriors. They claim

		direct descent from the Yemeni Beni Hassan tribe
Hassiniyah	H	Dialect of classical Arabic spoken in Mauritania. From Beni Hassan, a tribe of Yemeni nomads
Hejira	A	The flight of Muhammad from Mecca to Medina in 622AD; beginning of the Muslim era
Hijab	A	Lit. 'protection'. Woman's veil; magical charm (amulet)
Hivernage	F	Rainy season
Imam	A	Leader of a Muslim community; leader in prayer
Imazighen	M/S	'Noble ones' (Berbers or Saharans free of the control of sultans, kings, etc)
Insha Allah	A	'If Allah is Willing'
Jellaba	M	Loose woollen cloak with hood, worn by men
Jizya	A	Poll tax (paid by non-Muslim subjects as a form of protection)
Jrad	A	Locust
Juju	WA	Talisman/charm
Ka'bah		Sacred pilgrim shrine of Islam, contains the Black Stone believed to have been given Abraham by the archangel Gabriel
Kaftan	A	Long coatlike garment; in Morocco, a looser woman's version with wide sleeves
Kasbah	A	Castle or citadel of north African cities
Kefta	A	Spicy mincemeat, meatballs, meatloaf.
Khram-khram	S	Spiny prickly-seed grass of Sahel which marks the southern limit of hyper-arid desert
Kif	M	Marijuana mixed with black tobacco. From Arabic *kaif*, pleasure
Kif-kif	M	Quits, 50-50 (Lit. 'pleasure-pleasure'

Koubba	A	Mausoleum of saint (marabout)
Ksar (pl. ksour)	A	Fortified (desert) village made of mud
Labass	M/H	'No evil?' (greeting)
Litham	S	Cotton face-muffler
Madrasa	A	Qur'anic school
Mafé	WA	Meat stew, usually eaten with rice
Mansouria	A	Woman's gown, worn under the kaftan
Marabout	M	Saint; religious sage
Marhaba w'sahala	A	'Be welcome and feel at ease'
Medina	A/M	Old quarter of city (from Medina in Saudi Arabia, the Prophet Muhammad's refuge in 622AD)
Méréyé	S	Low waves of dunes in parallel ridges set a few hundred yards apart
Merguez		Tunisian-style sausages
Moqqadam	A	Village headman; official
Moussem	M	Commercial and religious gathering about the shrine of a marabout
Muezzin	A	Man who sings calls to prayer from mosque minaret
Muhammad		(c.570-632AD) Prophet and founder of Islam, born in Mecca on the Arabian peninsula. The Qur'an was revealed to him by God. Fled from persecution to Medina in 622AD. Last in the line of prophets including Adam, Moses, Abraham and Jesus
M'zaza	M	Mad, insane
M'zien	M	Good
Narghili	A	Water pipe (hookah)
N'srani	A/M	Nazarine (derog. for European/white man)
N'zala	A	'Setting-down place', caravan encampment
Ornières	F	Tyre ruts in sand
Oued	A	River

Oulad (sing. ould)	A	Sons (of)
Pillars of Islam		Five obligations of Muslims: recitation of the creed; worship five times daily facing holy city of Mecca; almsgiving; fasting sunrise to sunset during Ramadan; pilgrimage to Mecca (= the Hajj)
Pirogue	F	Double-prowed canoe
Pisé	F	Form of adobe: sun-dried mud packed with straw, palm fronds or spliced tree trunk, used for building
Piste	F	Track, trail
Polisario Front		Saharawi guerilla organisation founded 1973. Acronym for: *Frente Popular para la Liberacíon de Saguia el-Hamra y Río de Oro*
Qa'ida	A	Code of conduct/manners for gentlemen
Qur'an	A	Lit. 'the recitation' or 'reading', the Word of God as conveyed via Muhammad in the year 610AD
Ramadan		One of the five Pillars of Islam: 30 days in 9th month of Hejiran calendar, during which strict fasting is observed between sunrise and sunset
Razzia	S	Nomad attack/raid on village or caravan
Reguibat	WS	Powerful tribe of Western Sahara, to which Sidi Mohamed Ma el-Aïnin belonged. Founded by Sidi Ahmad al-Rgibi
Rhaita	M	Droning oboe/flute; fluted flowers of datura tree.
Saharawi	WS	Collective name for Western Saharan nomads, including Reguibat, Oulad Delim, Tekna, and Chnagla
Salaam Alaikum	A	'Peace be on you'. Reply is Alaikum Salaam
Sebkha	M/WS	Salt lake/pan (dry)

Sebkhet	H/WS	Salt lake/pan (dry)
Shaitan	A	Satan
Sherif	A	A descendant of Muhammad through Fatima; honorific title accorded to any Muslim ruler
Sibsi	M	Long pipe for smoking kif
Sidi	M/WS	Honorific title like 'Sir', always used to prefix saints
Signares	WA	Half-caste élite of West African coastal cities
Souk	A	Open-air marketplace
Sura	A	One of 114 sections of the Qur'an
Tajakant	H	Moors of northern Mauritania
Tajine	M	Earthernware dish; stew cooked in it
Tarboush	A	fez (felten cap)
Tawarik	S	Tuareg (sing. Targui)
Tayammum	A	Religious ablutions using sand when no water is available
Tié-bou-dienne	WA	Lit. 'rice-with-fish'
Toq-toqa	M	Disreputable Riffian dance for young boys
Toubab	WA	(Wolof) Lit. 'to convert'; white man/ foreigner (derog.)
Trarza	H	Moors of southern Mauritania
Wadi	S	(dry) river bed
Yallah	A	Exclamation: 'come on!' 'hurry up!'
Yamba	WA	Marijuana
Zaouia	A	Religious retreat
Zebu		Domesticated ox with humped back and long horns.
Zenaga	H	Middle caste of Moors including semi-nomadic herdsmen, cultivators and artisans
Zrig	H	Mixture of water, sugar, sour milk culture and milk